New Zealand/Aotearoa

Scale
0   50   100   150 miles
0   50   100   150   200   250 kilometres

Cities and towns:
- ▣ over 500,000 inhabitants
- ◼ 100,000 – 500,000 inhabitants
- ● 40,000 – 100,000 inhabitants
- ○ under 40,000 inhabitants

<u>Wellington</u>   National capital

- ━━ Railway
- ━━ Mayor highway
- ━━ Other roads
- ▨ National park
- ┅┅ Regional border

Land heights:
- 2000 m
- 1000 m
- 500 m
- 250 m
- 0 m

North Island

Three Kings Islands
Cape Reinga
North Cape
Great Exhibition Bay
Kaitaia
Kerikeri
Kaikohe
Paihia
Bay of Islands
Opononi
Northland
Waipoua Forest ★
Whangarei
Dargaville
Great Barrier Island
Wellsford
Kaipara Harbour
North Shore
Hau-raki Gulf
Coromandel Peninsula
Coromandel
Auckland
Auckland
Whitianga
Manurewa
Thames
Bay of Plenty
White Island
Hicks Bay
Raglan
Hamilton
Tauranga
Whakatane
Bay of Plenty
East Cape
Waikato
Otorohanga
Rotorua
Opotiki
Tokomaru Bay
Waitomo Caves ★
Te Kuiti
Lake Taupo
Taupo
Lake Waikaremoana
Tolaga Bay
North Taranaki Bight
Taumarunui
Turangi
Gisborne
Gisborne
New Plymouth
Taranaki
Whan-ganui NP
Whaka-papa
Tongariro NP
Mt. Ruapehu 2797 m
Wairoa
Mahia Peninsula
Mt. Taranaki 2518 m   Stratford
Ohakune
Mana-
Napier
Hawke Bay
Hawke's Bay
Hawera
Wanganui
-watu
Hastings
South Taranaki Bight
Wanganui
Waipukurau
Wanganui
Palmerston North
Levin
Masterton
Lower Hutt
Wellington
Wellington
Wellington
Cape Palliser

South Island

Tasman Sea
Cape Farewell
Golden Bay
Abel Tasman NP
Tasman Bay
Nelson
Kahurangi NP
Motueka
Karamea
Nelson
Picton
Karamea Bight
Richmond
Blenheim
Cook Strait
Westport
Tasman
Marlborough
Nelson Lakes NP
Mt. Travers 2338 m
Greymouth
Lewis Pass
Kaikoura
Hokitika
Hanmer Springs ★
West Coast
Arthur's Pass NP
Canterbury
Franz Josef Glacier Village
Fox Glacier Village
Christchurch
Westland NP
Mt. Cook NP
Banks Peninsula
Haast
Mt. Cook 3764 m
Akaroa
Mt. Cook Village
Lake Tekapo
Ashburton
Mt. Aspiring NP
Lake Pukaki
Timaru
Canterbury Bight
Darren Mountains
Wanaka
Omarama
Waimate
Milford Sound
South Island
Fiordland NP
Queenstown
Oamaru
Te Anau
Alexandra
Resolution Island
Otago
Lumsden
Southland
Otago Peninsula
West Cape
Gore
Dunedin
Cape Providence
Invercargill
Milton
Kaitangata
Foveaux Strait
Bluff
Oban
Stewart Island (Rakiura)
Southwest Cape

Tasman Sea

South Pacific Ocean

HIGHLIGHT 9

Mittelschule Bayern

für R-Klassen

Cornelsen

HIGH**LIGHT**

Mittelschule Bayern, Band 9
für R-Klassen

Konzepterarbeitung von
Susan Abbey, Nenagh, Irland
Wolfgang Biederstädt, Köln
Frank Donoghue, Nenagh, Irland

Erarbeitet von
Sydney Thorne, York
Susan Abbey, Nenagh, Irland
Frank Donoghue, Nenagh, Irland

in Zusammenarbeit mit der Englischredaktion
Klaus Unger (Projektleitung);
Silvia Wiedemann (koordinierende Redakteurin);
Karin Wedepohl

Vokabelanhang
Ingrid und Georg Raspe, Düsseldorf

Lizenzmanagement
Britta Bensmann, Silke Kirchhoff

Beratende Mitwirkung
Matthias Fischer, Aschaffenburg
Barbara Gehlhaar, München
Alexandra Mader, Eibelstadt
Sabine Schaffer, Würzburg
Christian Staniczek, Waging am See
Dr. Christoph Vatter, Donaustauf

Umschlaggestaltung
Cornelsen Verlag GmbH, Berlin, unter Verwendung
der Entwürfe von Klein & Halm Grafikdesign, Berlin

Layoutkonzept
finedesign – Büro für Text & Gestaltung, Berlin;
designcollective, Team für Mediengestaltung,
Berlin

Layout + technische Umsetzung
Yvonne Thron, designcollective, Team für
Mediengestaltung, Berlin

www.cornelsen.de

1. Auflage, 2. Druck 2021

Alle Drucke dieser Auflage sind inhaltlich unverändert
und können im Unterricht nebeneinander verwendet
werden.

© 2021 Cornelsen Verlag GmbH, Berlin

Druck und Bindung: Livonia Print, Riga

ISBN 978-3-06-033411-7 (Schülerbuch)
ISBN 978-3-06-033834-4 (E-Book)

PEFC zertifiziert
Dieses Produkt stammt aus nachhaltig
bewirtschafteten Wäldern und kontrollierten
Quellen.

www.pefc.de

PEFC/12-31-006

Dein Englischbuch enthält folgende Teile:

Unit 1 bis 4	Die vier Kapitel des Buches
Diff-Bank	Weitere Aufgaben – unterschiedlich schwer
Exam training	Vorbereitung auf die Abschlussprüfung
TF Text file	Weitere Lesetexte, passend zu den Units
SF Skills file	Beschreibung wichtiger Lern- und Arbeitstechniken
LF Language file	Zusammenfassung wichtiger Sprachregeln
Wordbank	Zusätzliche Wörter zu bestimmten Themen
Vocabulary	Wörterverzeichnis zum Lernen der neuen Wörter
Dictionary	Alphabetisches Wörterverzeichnis zum Nachschlagen (*English-German*)

Die Units bestehen aus diesen Teilen:

Lead-in	Einstieg in die neue Unit
Theme	Neue Themen mit vielen Aktivitäten und Übungen
Text	Eine Geschichte zum Lesen
Focus on language	Texte und Aufgaben zum Entdecken von Regeln und Üben wichtiger Strukturen
Skills training	Hören / Listening (L) – Lesen / Reading (R) – Sprechen / Speaking (S) – Schreiben / Writing (W) – Sprachmittlung / Mediation (M) – Hörsehverstehen / Viewing (V)

In den Units findest du diese Symbole:

🎧	Hörtexte / Buchtexte auf CD
▶	Filme auf der DVD
⊙	Leichtere Übungen
●	Schwierigere Übungen
Parallel exercise → *p.80*	Bei dieser Aufgabe gibt es eine leichtere oder schwierigere Variante in der Diff-Bank.
More help → *p.83*	Hilfen zu einer Aufgabe in der Diff-Bank
More practice 1 → *p.76*	Weitere Übungen in der Diff-Bank

Für deine Arbeit mit den Units ist außerdem wichtig:

- Am Anfang jeder Unit findest du eine Liste der angestrebten Kompetenzen. So weißt du, was du nach dieser Unit auf Englisch kannst.
- Unten auf den Unit-Seiten findest du Sätze mit einem grünen Häkchen (✔). Sie zeigen dir, was du nach der Erarbeitung dieser Seite kannst.

Do you speak English?

1 **Around the world**

a ⊙ Look at the four photos and the map.
Where are the four young people from?

b 👥 Look at the map with a partner.
Why are some countries in green, blue and yellow?
In the countries
in green ...

Aarav:
Enzokuhle:
Olivia:
Marama:

c Copy the list on
the right:

🎧 Then listen and take notes.
1.01 Match each person with A, B or C:

A speaks English at home
B speaks English at school
C learns English as a second language at school
You'll need two letters twice.

2 👥 **AND YOU?** **English and you**
Answer these questions with a partner:

1 What languages do you speak? Look online or
in a dictionary and find out the English names
for your languages.

2 What do you think: Is English an important
language in Germany? Why (not)? Have you ever
used English outside the classroom?
Where? When?
I read English words in ...
I listen to English when ...
I speak English when ...
There are many English words in ...
I often use English when I play ...

3 How do you think English can be
useful to you in the future?
If I work in ...
When I meet people who ...
When I want to ...

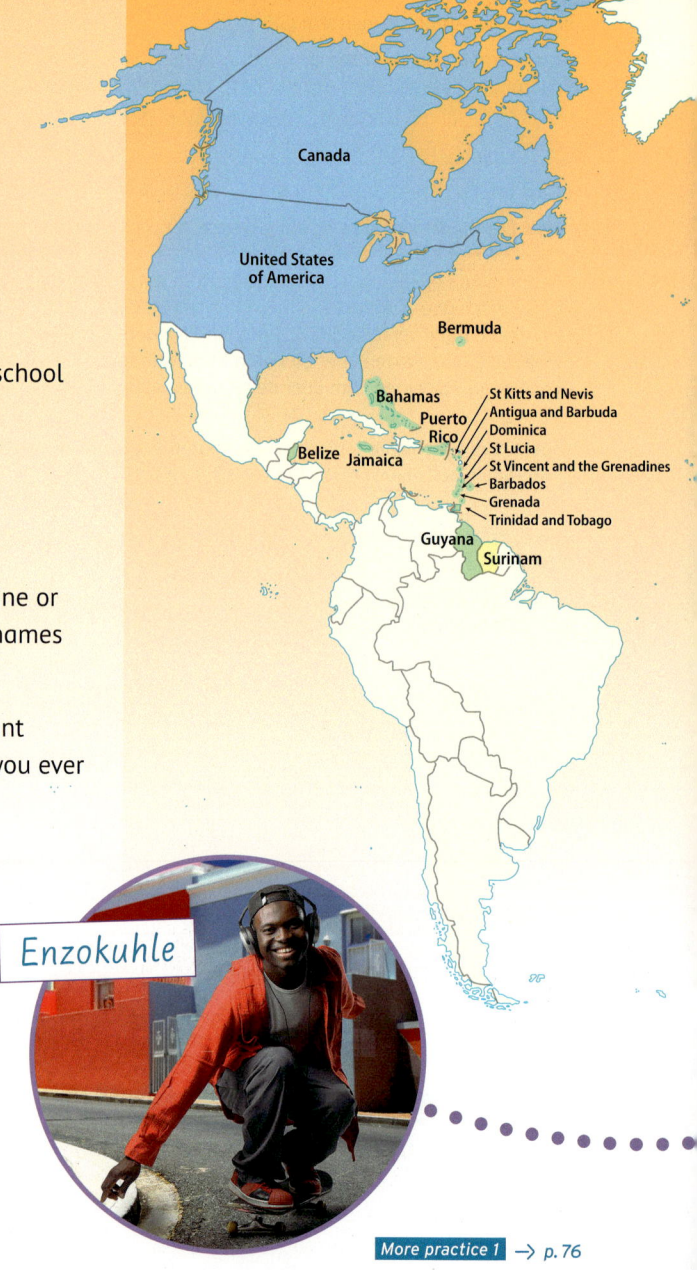

Enzokuhle

Canada

United States
of America

Bermuda

Bahamas
Puerto
Rico
Belize
Jamaica

St Kitts and Nevis
Antigua and Barbuda
Dominica
St Lucia
St Vincent and the Grenadines
Barbados
Grenada
Trinidad and Tobago

Guyana
Surinam

More practice 1 → p. 76

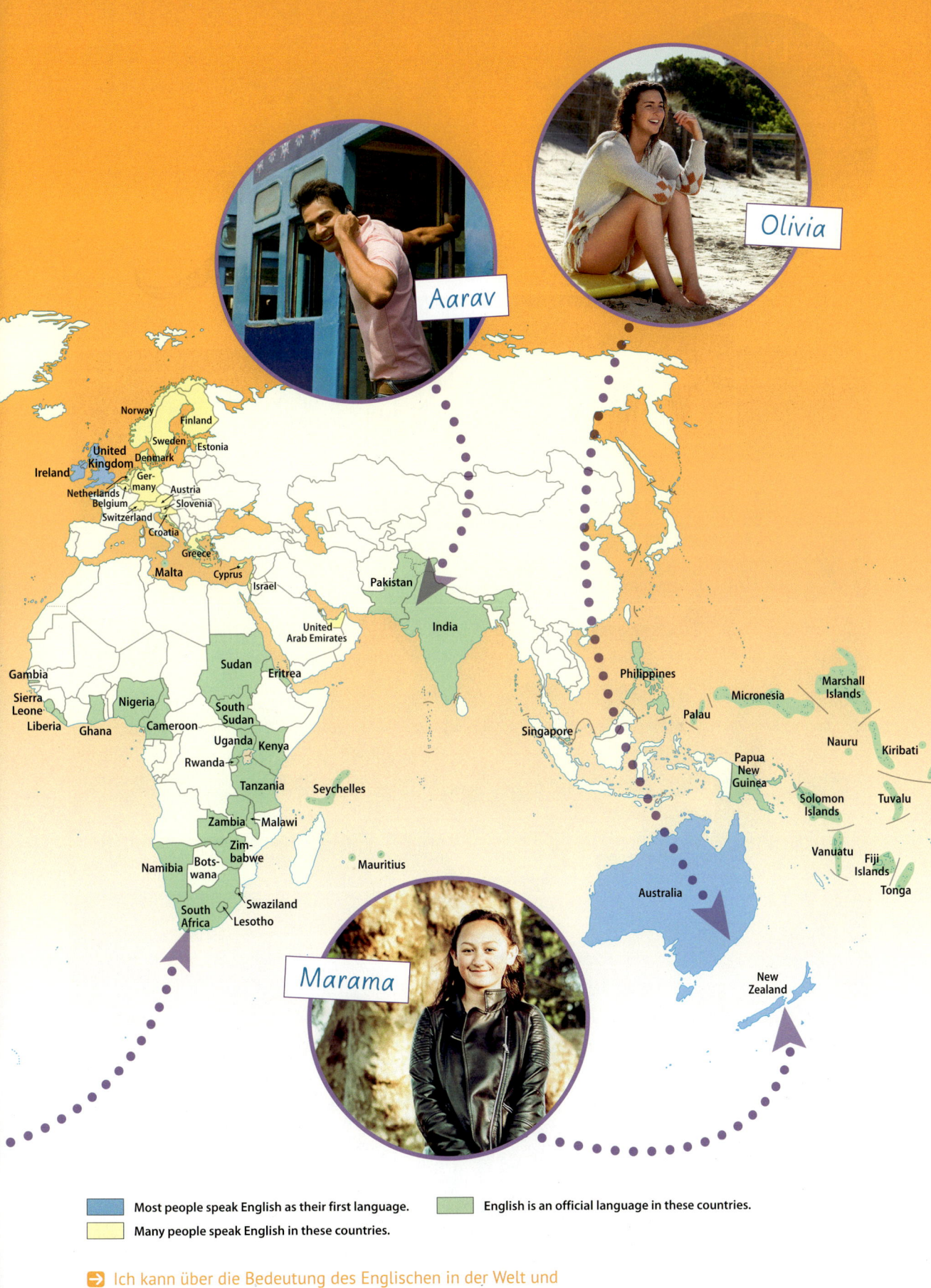

Aarav

Olivia

Norway
Finland
Sweden
Estonia
United
Kingdom
Denmark
Ireland
Ger-
many
Netherlands
Austria
Belgium
Slovenia
Switzerland
Croatia
Greece
Malta
Cyprus
Israel
Pakistan
India
United
Arab Emirates
Gambia
Sudan
Eritrea
Sierra
Leone
Nigeria
Liberia
Ghana
Cameroon
South
Sudan
Uganda
Kenya
Rwanda
Tanzania
Seychelles
Zambia
Malawi
Zim-
babwe
Namibia
Bots-
wana
Mauritius
South
Africa
Swaziland
Lesotho

Philippines
Micronesia
Marshall
Islands
Palau
Nauru
Singapore
Kiribati
Papua
New
Guinea
Solomon
Islands
Tuvalu
Vanuatu
Fiji
Islands
Australia
Tonga
New
Zealand

Marama

| | Most people speak English as their first language. | | English is an official language in these countries. |
| | Many people speak English in these countries. | | |

➡ Ich kann über die Bedeutung des Englischen in der Welt und
in meinem Leben sprechen. ✔

Unit 1

G'day from Australia

B Uluru – a very special place for indigenous Australians

C Australia is the only country where kangaroos live as wild animals.

Sydney is Australia's biggest city. Australia's capital city, Canberra, is much smaller.

D Diving at the Great Barrier Reef

E Christmas on the beach

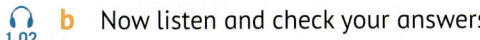

F DRIVE ON LEFT IN AUSTRALIA

A road through the
Australian outback

G

In dieser Unit lernst du …
- Faktenwissen zu Australien zu erarbeiten,
- über Gefahren zu sprechen,
- über Handlungen zu sprechen, die in der Vergangenheit im Gange waren,
- dich beim Arzt zu verständigen,
- Vorschriften zu verstehen.

1 Photos of Australia

a Look at the photos and texts and try to answer these questions:
1 What's the climate in the centre of Australia?
2 Is Uluru **A** a town? **B** a river? **C** a mountain?
3 On which side of the road do cars drive in Australia?
4 What's the flag in the corner of the Australian flag? Why is it there?
5 What sports can you do at the Great Barrier Reef?
6 When it's winter in Europe, what season is it in Australia?
7 What's the capital of Australia?
8 Which animal can you only see in Australia (except in a zoo!)? Do you know any others?

b Now listen and check your answers.
1.02

2 VIEWING An Australian road trip

a Before you watch: Answer these questions with a partner.
What do you think you'll see in the film (animals, places, activities, …) Wordbank 1 → p.140

b While you watch: Which of these animals and places do you see?

> a waterfall • a wood • kangaroos • a harbour • a track •
> the coast • cows • the sky at night • sheep • koalas

More practice 2 → p.76   More practice 3 → p.77   Workbook 1 → p.3

→ Ich kann Faktenwissen zu Australien erarbeiten. ✓

Help!

1 **People in trouble**

 a ⊙ You're on a beach in Australia and you hear three conversations. Listen and match conversations 1, 2, 3 with signs A, B, C, D. You won't need one sign.

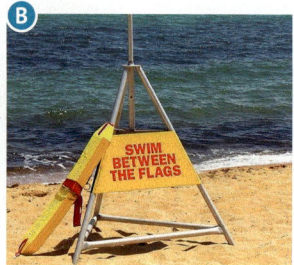

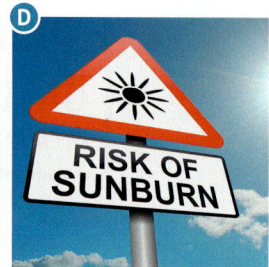

b What are the missing words?

> hurt • think • put on • shouldn't •
> safer • stay

1 "You … swim here. Swim between the flags. It's … over there."
2 "Your skin is very red here. Does it …? I … it's a jellyfish sting."
3 "I think you have sunburn. … in the shade and … suncream."

 c Now listen again and check your answers.

d **WORDS** Find the words for these pictures in exercise **1b**.

2 👥 **On the beach**

a **Partner B** Go to page 74.
Partner A First, describe your picture to your partner.

The picture shows a beach scene.
A boy is lying in the sun and a girl …
A sign on the right tells people that …
In the foreground there's …
I think the boy has a problem with …
A lifeguard …
I think that the lifeguard will …

Then ask your partner: What's the problem in my picture?
Can he/she answer your question?

b Now your partner will describe a different picture. Listen – and take notes or draw the picture. Then answer his/her question.

More practice 4 → p. 77   Skills file 7 → p. 123

→ Ich kann verstehen, wie ich mich vor Gefahren schütze. ✔

3 The *Flying Doctors*

a Look at the photo and answer the questions.
1 What do you think the *Royal Flying Doctor Service* (RFDS) does?
2 Why is this service important in Australia?

b 1.04 In which parts of Australia do the *Flying Doctors* work? Listen and take notes.

c 1.04 Read the sentences. Then listen again and answer the questions.
1 When did the RFDS begin?
2 Which Australian banknotes have a picture of the RFDS?
3 How many planes does the RFDS have?
4 The RFDS helps people in the outback. What else does the service do?
5 In the clip there was a man who was saved by the RFDS. Where did he work?

4 Staying safe in the outback

a Read the text. What problems can people have in the outback?

Staying safe in the outback

- Always take lots of water with you, enough for one litre per person per hour.
- If your car breaks down, don't leave it. Use your car for shade.
- If you are lost, climb a hill and make a small fire.
  At night, use a torch or a whistle.
  Don't rely on your phone – it might not work in the outback.
- If you feel very hot, sick and thirsty: go into the shade and drink lots of water, put wet towels over your face, call a doctor.

b Find the words in the text.
1 the cool place under a tree
2 go up something
3 you can see in the dark with it (2x)
4 when a car stops working
5 go away from
6 you dry yourself with this
7 the part of your head with your eyes, nose and mouth

c ● 👥 ROLE-PLAY
Partner A works for the RFDS. **Partner B** has a problem and phones the RFDS.
Act out short dialogues. Then swap roles.
– *Oh hi. I have a problem. I'm in the outback and …*
– *OK. You should … Now, where are you?*
– *I'm …*

More practice 5 → p. 78   Workbook 2–4 → pp. 4–5

→ Ich kann mich in Gefahrensituationen verständigen. ✓

Proud of my people

1 The first Australians

a 👥 Look at the pictures and headings. What is this article about?

A History and culture

Indigenous Australians have lived in Australia for about 50,000 years. They knew how to live in a hot, dry land and had respect for their environment. Indigenous Australians had no written language, so they told their stories in songs and paintings. Other examples of indigenous culture are boomerangs and didgeridoos. Boomerangs were used to hunt all kinds of animals. The didgeridoo is an instrument that makes a fantastic deep sound.

5

B Arrival of the Europeans

10

When the British began colonizing Australia in 1788, they brought new diseases – like flu – which killed the indigenous people. They took the best land for their farms and towns and they tried to destroy indigenous Australian culture. Many indigenous people were killed and others were put in prison.

C Indigenous Australians today

15

Today about 850,000 indigenous Australians live in Australia – about 3.3% of the country's population of 25.6 million. There are some radio and TV stations in indigenous languages and Australian indigenous art is famous. But racism, unemployment and bad living conditions make life difficult for many indigenous Australians.

b Which paragraph (A, B or C) tells you ...
1 how many people live in Australia?
2 why many indigenous Australians became sick and died?
3 about problems of indigenous Australians today?
4 about a musical instrument?
5 how many indigenous people live in Australia today?
6 that indigenous Australians lived in harmony with nature?

c Some words have different meanings. Which of the meanings is used in the text?

hot *(line 3)*	kind *(line 8)*	like *(line 11)*	station *(line 17)*
Ⓐ heiß *(Adj)*	Ⓐ Art, Sorte *(N)*	Ⓐ mögen, gern haben *(V)*	Ⓐ Bahnhof *(N)*
Ⓑ scharf (Essen) *(Adj)*	Ⓑ ziemlich *(Adv)*	Ⓑ wollen *(V)*	Ⓑ Sender, Sendestation *(N)*
Ⓒ beliebt *(Adj)*	Ⓒ nett *(Adj)*	Ⓒ wie *(Präp)*	Ⓒ Position, Platz *(N)*
Ⓓ hitzig, erregt *(Adj)*	Ⓓ freundlich *(Adj)*	Ⓓ Neigung, Vorliebe *(N)*	Ⓓ postieren, aufstellen *(V)*

Workbook 5 → *p. 6*

Skills file 2 → *p. 114*   **More practice 6** → *p. 79*

➡ Ich kann Sachinformationen erfassen. ✓

2 **VIEWING** **The Burdekin Crew**

These young indigenous Australians live in a town on the Burdekin River. They made a video about who they are.

a Watch the video. What do you think about it?
I like / I don't like ...

> the dancing • the lyrics • the beat •
> the energy • the singers • ...

b Watch the film again. Which examples of Aboriginal culture do you see in it?

body painting

traditional dance steps

a didgeridoo

the colours of the Aboriginal flag

c Now watch the video again – and do the steps with the Burdekin Crew! **More practice 7** → p. 79

d Discuss in class: The Burdekin Crew are proud of their culture. What things are you proud of?

> my country • my culture • my family •
> my football team • my school • ...

3 **Reasons for going to Australia**

a Jasmin, a student in Germany, has written a post about Australia. Read the post. Why doesn't Jasmin want to go to Australia?

Jasmin
Germany

One reason why I don't want to go to Australia is that you have to fly there and flying isn't good for the environment. What's more, the journey there is very expensive. And finally, the outback is hot and dry and I don't really like very hot weather.

b Now copy the three phrases that Jasmin uses to introduce her three reasons.

*1 One reason why I don't want to go
to Australia is that ...   2 ...   3 ...*

c Now write three reasons why you would like to visit Australia, e.g. sun, sports, ...
One reason why I would like to go to Australia is that the country has a fantastic coast and I love the sea! What's more, ... And finally, ...

TIP

Use the sentences from Jasmin's post. Use information about Australia on pages 10–13 or your own ideas.

Skills file 5 → p. 119f.   **Workbook 6** → p. 6

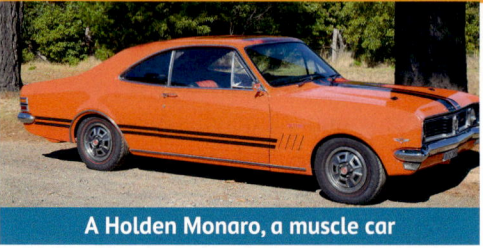

A Holden Monaro, a muscle car

1 Before you read

Scan the text and find out:

1 What are the names of the three characters?

2 Where did the trip start and finish?

Skills file 3 → p. 115

SWERVE

adapted from the book by Phillip Gwynne

1.05
1 *Sydney School*

An old guy with a ponytail was at the school gate one afternoon.

5

"Hugh," he said as I walked past.

"I want to talk to you. I'm your grand-father."

"No, you're not!"

10 Stranger danger, I thought. My mum's real father is dead.

"You were born on the seventeenth of February," he said. He knew lots of stuff about me and my mum. And he looked like us, the

15 same nose and chin.

That night I told mum that her father had come to the school.

"My father is dead!" she shouted.

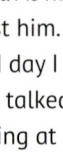

20 "He's dead to me!" Every day he came to the school. At first I walked past him. But the third day I

25 stopped and talked to him. Looking at him was like looking in a funny mirror. He was my grandfather – my 'Poppy'!

1.06
2 *Plans*

30 One day Poppy phoned me at school. He said he wanted to go to the Big Rock – Uluru.

So I visited Poppy at his flat.

He had a map of Australia open on the table.

"We're here in Sydney," he said.

35 "And Uluru is here, two thousand eight hundred kilometres away."

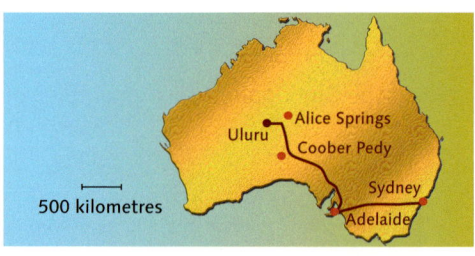

He looked at me. "Let's drive there together."

"But why?" I asked.

"Because I've always wanted to go there and now is the time to do it. But I can't drive."

40 Then he said. "I'd like to show you something."

We went into an old garage behind the building. There was a car in the garage – but it wasn't just any car. It was a muscle car, a Holden Monaro – a fantastic muscle car

45 with a big engine. It looked amazing. I love cars – especially muscle cars.

"Is it yours?" I asked. It was his.

I thought about my school, my music exam next week, my parents, my future …

50 Then I thought about 2800 kilometres to Uluru in a Holden.

"OK," I said. "I'll do it."

1.07
3 *The* **Million Star Motel**

55 We were on the highway going west. In the mirror Sydney got smaller and smaller and I got more and more excited. I smiled at Poppy and he smiled back at me.

It was getting dark so we left the highway
60 and drove on a track. Poppy had some advice:
"If you see a roo on the road don't swerve.
It's better to hit the roo than lose your life,"
he said.

We stopped next to a river – the Darling.
65 Poppy had cooking equipment, camping chairs
and two swags – our beds. He made a fire and
some tea. Poppy pointed at the sky.
"They call this the *Million Star Motel*," he said.

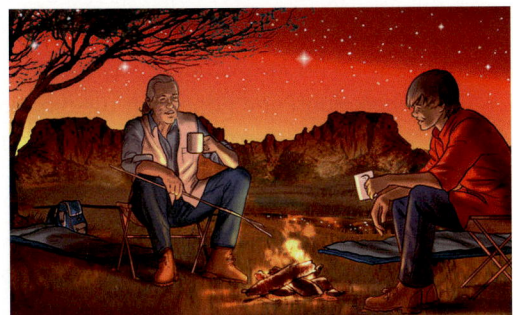

4 *South Australia*
70 We were driving through the desert. It was
1700 kilometres to Uluru. There were lots of
big trucks on the highway. And there were lots
of animals too – sheep, kangaroos and emus.
Then I saw a hitchhiker and I stopped.
75 He was small and he was wearing a hoodie.
He said he was Jimmy from Broken Hill.

After about half an hour a big black car went
past us very fast – it was a Typhoon.

Later we stopped for fuel and for something
80 to eat, but the hitchhiker stayed in the car.

5 *Bella*
I ordered a sandwich. Poppy went to the toilet.
Then a man and a woman came in.
The man was short, but big – like a body-
85 builder. The woman was glamorous.

"We're looking for our daughter," the woman
said, and showed a photo of a girl about
my age.
Back in the car I looked at the hitchhiker and
saw that his fingernails were pink.   90
"Your parents are looking for you," I said.
"They aren't my parents," she answered.
"Please don't say anything. Those people are
really dangerous," she said.
Then the bodybuilder and the woman came   95
out and they left the car park in their black
Typhoon – very fast.
"They've left," I said.
She pulled her hood
back. Short messy hair.   100
Big eyes. Nose stud …
She said her name
was Bella and she
was seventeen.

6 *At Yulara, near Uluru*   105
*Hugh, Poppy and Bella drive to Coober Pedy
together. Hugh really likes Bella and he
thinks that she likes him.*
*But at Coober Pedy Bella meets another guy.
She decides to travel to Uluru with him.*   110
*Hugh is disappointed. Hugh and Poppy go on
without Bella and they arrive at a campsite
in Yulara, a small town near the* Big Rock –
Uluru.
I heard my phone. It was Bella.   115
"Hello," I said. But there was no answer, only
the sound of a big car engine and voices.
Then I heard Bella.
"Help! We just passed *The Brain*. Please help!"
Then the phone went dead.   120
I knew that the bodybuilder and the woman
had found Bella.
"Bella's in trouble," I said to Poppy. I got into
the car.
"I'm coming," he said, and jumped out of his   125
swag.
"Where's *The Brain*?" I asked Poppy.
"It's near the *Big Rock*," he said.
We drove fast along the road to Uluru.

2 The different parts of the story

a Look at part **1**. Pick the right option.

1 When Hugh first saw Poppy he was **A** excited. **B** careful. **C** bored. **D** sad.
2 Hugh's mum is Poppy's **A** daughter. **B** sister. **C** mother. **D** half-sister.
3 Hugh thought Poppy looked **A** young. **B** like him. **C** different from him. **D** funny.
4 When Hugh's mum heard about Poppy she felt **A** happy. **B** nervous. **C** angry. **D** confident.

b Look at part **2**. In which lines do you get the information about …
1 in what sort of place Poppy lived?
2 why Poppy needs help to get to Uluru?
3 the owner of the Holden?
4 what Hugh has to do the following week?

c Look at part **3**. Answer the questions. Short answers are possible.
1 How did Hugh feel when he left Sydney?
2 How do we know that Poppy felt happy?
3 How do we know that it was evening when Hugh and Poppy left the big road?
4 What does the *Million Star Motel* mean?

d Part **4**. Copy and complete the sentences.
1 On the road Hugh and Poppy saw …
2 Hugh couldn't see Jimmy's face clearly because …
3 Hugh saw the black Typhoon car when it …
4 They stopped for a break because they needed …

e Look at part **5**. Find and correct a mistake in each sentence.
1 The man and woman showed a photo of their big black Typhoon car.
2 Hugh saw that Jimmy was really a boy.
3 Jimmy liked the people in the black car.
4 Jimmy and Bella were two different people.

f Look at part **6**. Finish the sentences.
1 Hugh knew that Bella was in trouble because …
2 Hugh was a good friend to Bella because …

3 The end of the story

a Listen to the end of the story. Why did Hugh and Bella drive to Alice Springs?
b Look at the two pictures and listen again. Note TWO things that are WRONG in each picture.

c How was the ending: exciting / realistic / violent / boring / just what you expected / stupid? Why? Compare your ideas in class.

Workbook 7–8 → p. 7

More practice 8 → p. 80

→ Ich kann einen authentischen Jugendroman verstehen. ✓

1 **A visit to Sydney**

Huong from Vietnam has just arrived in Sydney, where she's going
to visit her friends Mara and Lee.

a Read Huong's post in her travel blog. Why was she lucky on her first evening?

Huong

Sydney,
Australia

The sun was shining when I landed in
Sydney and I had a beautiful ride into Sydney
city centre. The sun was going down when
I got out of my taxi. I saw some people who
were taking photos of Sydney Harbour
Bridge. I took a photo of the bridge just when
the last light of the sun was falling on it and
two boats were passing under it.

b Copy the table and add the verbs from Huong's post.

1 The sun	was	shining.	
2 The sun			down.
3 Some people	were		photos.
4 The last light of the sun			on Harbour Bridge.
5 Two boats			under the bridge.

c Now look again at Huong's post above. Copy three sentences from the post. Decide:
   1 What's going on in the background? Colour this part of the sentence in red.
   2 Which is the new action? Colour this part of the sentence in blue.
   Example: The sun was shining when I landed in Sydney.

d Now complete the FOCUS-box.

FOCUS

Das *past progressive*
Das *past progressive* bildest du mit … oder … und der *ing*-Form des Verbs. Du sagst damit, was in
der Vergangenheit gerade im Gange war. Wenn eine neue Handlung dazu kommt, steht diese im …

The sun was shining
when Huong's plane
landed in Sydney.

Huong arrived at her
friends house.
while they were
tidying the house.

Language file 4 → p. 129

2 A beach barbecue

Huong and her friends went to the beach.
What was already going on when they arrived?

a ⊙ Fill in *was* or *were*.
1 The sun … shining.
2 Lots of people … enjoying themselves.
3 A few people … playing volleyball.

b ⊙ What's the correct form of the verb?
1 Somebody was … (talk) on the phone.
2 A woman was … (make) a fire.
3 A man and a woman were … (chat).

c Write the verbs in blue in the past progressive.
1 Some people … (swim) in the sea.
2 A man … (read).
3 Some young people … (eat) ice cream.
4 Some people … already … (leave).

3 Huong's morning with Mara and Lee

Write the verbs in blue in the past progressive.
1 When I came into the kitchen, Mara and Lee … (have) breakfast.
2 Their dog Fluffy … (sit) on my chair, but he jumped off when he saw me.
3 Mara's phone rang just as we … (leave).
4 It … (rain) when we walked to the station.
5 A train … (wait) at the station, so we got on.
6 The train was full. Some people … (stand), but luckily we found seats.

4 At Sydney Harbour Bridge

Read Huong's post, and choose the right option.

The sun shone / was shining (1) when we arrived / were arriving (2) in Sydney city centre. A band played / was playing (3) music in the street, and we stopped / were stopping (4) to listen to them. Lee, Mara and I watched / were watching (5) a group of tourists who climbed / were climbing (6) over the bridge – amazing! We had a great day, and the sun went / was going (7) down when we got / were getting (8) on the train home.

5 Manly Beach

Lee and Mara took Huong to their favourite beach in Sydney – Manly Beach.
Read the sentences in Huong's post. With a partner decide which part (A or B) should be in the *past progressive* and which part in the *simple past*. There is an example at the beginning. Then find the correct verb forms and write the sentences.

A
1 Lots of people … (have) a good time
   past progressive: were having
2 We … (see) lots of people
3 Two guys … (do) exercises in an outdoor gym
4 We … (watch) a woman
5 A man … (sell) tickets for a whale-watching trip,
6 We … (go) on the trip and we … (see) whales

B
when we … (arrive) at Manly Beach.
   simple past: arrived
who … (swim) in the sea.
and … (ask) us to take photos of them.
who … (swim) very well.
so we … (buy) three tickets.
which … (swim) near a small island.

Workbook 9–14 → pp. 8–10

➡ Ich kann sagen, was in der Vergangenheit gerade im Gange war.

6 *The Rocks*

Read Huong's post about her visit to *The Rocks,* a part of Sydney. Find a word in the box for each
gap 1–8. There is an example (0) at the beginning.

> about • because • but • has • living •
> of • since • ~~which~~ • who

Today we went to a part of Sydney which (0) is called
The Rocks. It's one of the oldest parts of Sydney – when
the British arrived in this part of Sydney Harbour in 1788,
they found that indigenous people were already ... (1)
here. For many years this was a very poor part of the city,
... (2) now it ... (3) become very popular. It is full ... (4)
cafes, restaurants and interesting little shops. I really liked it ... (5) I like old buildings and there are
lots of them here! One of the old houses – called Susannah Place – has been a museum ... (6) 1987.
I learned lots of interesting things ... (7) the people ... (8) once lived there.

7 **An email from Sydney** `Parallel exercise` → p. 80

Read Huong's email to her friend Theo. Write the right options 1–7.
There is an example (0) at the beginning.

Hi Theo!

How ~~is~~ / are (0) are you? I hope you're OK. I am / was (1) writing to you from Sydney, Australia!
I arrived here a few days ago and I stay / am staying (2) with good friends of mine, Lee and Mara.
Sydney is a great city! There is / are (3) lots of beaches which are great for surfing and you can get
to them with / by (4) bus.

Yesterday Lee and Mara took me to the Australian Museum, where / who (5) I learned a lot about
the culture of indigenous Australians. Now I want to see Uluru, who / which (6) is a very special
place for indigenous Australians. But Australia is so big and Uluru is nearly 3000 kilometres
along / away (7) from Sydney!

Please say hi to your parents!
Huong

8 The legend of the *Three Sisters*

Read the text from a tourist brochure. The words in bold are WRONG. Write the correct word(s). There is an example (0) at the beginning.

The Blue Mountains of Australia ~~has~~ *have* (0) been on the list of *Unesco World Heritage Sites* **for** (1) the year 2000. *The Three Sisters* are a special rock formation in **this** (2) mountains, and the indigenous people **which** (3) live in this area have a legend about how the rocks were made.

5   In the legend, there were once three beautiful sisters. They were **calling** (4) Meehni, Wimlah and Gunnedoo. The three sisters fell in love with three young men from a different part of the country. But women **was** (5)
10   only allowed to marry men from their own part of the country. So the three young men decided to fight for the sisters, and they attacked the **sister's** (6) family.

When the men **begin** (7) to fight, the three sisters were in great danger, so an old man
15   turned them into stone during the fighting. He wanted to turn them back into young women after the fighting, but he was killed – and that's why the three sisters are still rocks.

There **is** (8) legends like this in cultures all over the world.

9 An advert for a special trip

Read the advert. Change the words given in the brackets to make them fit the sentences. There is an example at the beginning (0).

Sydney Harbour is one of the most beautiful harbours in the world. And the BEST (0 GOOD) way to see it is a kayak tour.
Our boats and all our ... (1 EQUIP) is top quality and our kayaks are safe and ... (2 COMFORT). At the start of the tour we'll give you a short ... (3 INTRODUCE). We are sure that you will have a great time and really enjoy ... (4 SELF). Most of our ... (5 VISIT) tell us that this is the best activity that they have ever ... (6 DO) in Sydney. The tours are for adults and ... (7 CHILD) over 16 only.

TIPP

Mache Listen von:
a Wortfamilien, z.B.

VERB	NOUN
to visit	*a visit, a ...*
to introduce	*...*
to equip	*...*

b unregelmäßigen Steigerungsformen:
good – better – ...
c unregelmäßigen Verbformen:
do – did – ...
d unregelmäßigen Pluralformen:
man → men • child → ...
e Reflexivpronomen:
self → myself, yourself, ourselves, ...

   ➡ Ich kann Aufgabenformate der Abschlussprüfung bearbeiten. ✓

At the emergency services

1.12

1 **At the doctor's**

a Your Australian friend Jack isn't feeling well. He's at the emergency services. What should he do?

Doctor	G'day. What can I do for you?
Jack	I'm not feeling well. I have a headache and my arms and legs hurt.
Doctor	Do you have a sore throat? And a temperature?
Jack	Yes, I do. And I feel tired.
Doctor	I think you have the flu. You should rest. Sleep a lot and drink a lot. Take painkillers if the headache gets worse. And come back if you don't feel better in a week.
Jack	Thank you.

b ⊙ 👥 Read the dialogue with a partner. Read fluently. Not: *Yes/I/do,* but: *Yes‿I‿do.*

2 **So many things wrong with you!**

a Copy and complete the sentences.

> cut • should • skin • snake • sting • take

1 I've ... myself with a knife.
2 You ... have a good rest and sleep more.
3 I have a ... bite.
4 Your ... is very red. Put on some suncream.
5 If your headache gets worse, ... painkillers.
6 I have a bad insect ...

c ⊙ Who says sentences 1–6 – the patient or the doctor?

b ⊙ Match pictures A–D with sentences 1–6. You won't need all the sentences.

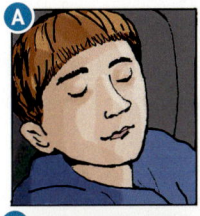
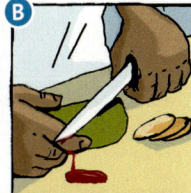

3 **MEDIATION**

An Austrian tourist who can't speak English asks you to come to the doctor's with her in Sydney. Interpret what they say.

Tourist	Eine Schlange hat mich gebissen. Es tut fürchterlich weh.
You	...
Doctor	I'm sorry. When did it happen?
You	...
Tourist	In der Nacht. Ich war im Zelt.
You	...
Doctor	Did you see the snake?
You	...
Tourist	Nein, ich habe geschlafen.

You	...
Doctor	Well, I'm glad to tell you that it's not a snake bite.
You	...
Tourist	Was ist es denn?
You	...
Doctor	Your skin is red, but you don't have a temperature. I'm sure it was an insect.
You	...

Skills file 9 → p. 125   Wordbank 2 → p. 141   More practice 9 → p. 81   Workbook 15–17 → pp. 11–12

➡ Ich kann mich beim Arzt verständigen. ✔

Anh Do: An amazing life

1 An introduction
Everybody in Australia knows Anh Do. He's one of the most popular TV stars and a man with lots of talents. Listen to a podcast about him.

1.13

a Listen to the introduction.

> 1 What are Anh Do's three professions?
> 2 What do we know about Anh Do's family?

1.13

b Now listen again and write the missing information.

> 1 Anh Do's travel show has been to Vietnam, Brazil, Italy and …
> 2 Anh Do was *Comedian of the Year* in Sydney in …
> 3 At the end of some of his TV shows he shows his guests a …
> 4 Anh Do's book is about the story of …
> 5 The book came out in …

> **TIPP**
>
> Lies vor dem Hören die Sätze und überlege, welche Informationen in die Lücken passen könnten.
> – In welchem Satz brauchst du den Namen eines Landes?
> – Und in welchen zwei Sätzen brauchst du Jahreszahlen?

Skills file 6 → p. 122

1.14

2 A dangerous journey
Now listen to more about Anh Do. What are the four TRUE statements A–G?

A Anh Do's father worked for the government.
B When Anh Do was a child, inhabitants of Vietnam were not allowed to leave the country.
C The boat was 19½ metres long.
D During the journey, pirates stole the boat's two engines.
E The refugees had no food or water on their boat.
F The refugees were at sea for less than a week.
G Anh Do came to Australia on a German ship.

1.15

3 Anh Do and his brother Khoa Do
Listen and write the missing details 1–7 about the Do brothers' experiences in Australia.

> Year of arrival in Australia: … (1)
> Good experience: people gave the family … (2)
> Bad experiences: Racism shown by … (3) and … (4)
> Title of Anh Do's book: *The* … (5) *Refugee*
> Khoa Do's prize won in 2005: … (6) *of the Year*
> Khoa Do's profession: … (7)

→ Ich kann einen Podcast über einen berühmten Australier verstehen. ✓

1

How to get your full driving licence
in the state of New South Wales in Australia

1 Learner licence
You must be at least 16 years old and take and pass the theoretical *Driver Knowledge Test*.
You may then drive under the following conditions: The car must have L-plates on the front
and back, and a driver with a full Australian licence must always sit in the front passenger
seat. L-platers must observe a maximum speed limit of 90 kph.

2 Provisional licence stage 1 (P1)
If you are at least 17 years old, have a minimum of 120 driving hours and have held
a learner licence for 12 months, you may take your practical driving test and a special
computerized test *(Hazard Perception Test (HPT))*. If you pass, you may drive with a
P1 licence. You must still keep to the speed limit of 90 kph and your car must have
P-plates (red P on white background) on the front and back.

3 Provisional licence stage 2 (P2)
You must have held a P1 licence for 12 months. The car must have P plates (green P on
white background) on the front and back and there is a speed limit of 100 kph.

4 Full licence
You must have held a P2 licence for a minimum period of 24 months and take a last
computerized test, the *Driver Qualification Test*.

a Read the rules and answer the questions using information from the text.
 1 How old do you have to be to get a learner licence?
 2 Is there a speed limit for drivers with a learner licence?

b Is the information true, false or not in the text above?
 1 The car driven by a learner driver must have two L-plates.
 2 Learner drivers may not use phones while driving.
 3 There is no speed limit for drivers with a P1 licence.
 4 You must take tests for each licence.
 5 Drivers with a P2 licence mustn't drive faster than 100 kph.
 6 Even with a full licence drivers may not drink any alcohol at all.
 7 You can get a full licence at the age of 18.

c MEDIATION
Stefan möchte wissen, wie man in New South Wales den
Führerschein machen kann. Beantworte seine Fragen
auf Deutsch.
 1 Ab welchem Alter darf man frühestens Auto fahren
 und unter welchen Bedingungen?
 2 Ich habe gehört, man muss bestimmte Schilder am Auto
 befestigen – kannst du mir dazu Genaueres sagen?

Skills file 9 → p. 125   More practice 10 → p. 81   Workbook → p. 13

→ Ich kann formelle Texte und Vorschriften verstehen. ✓

Kia ora from New Zealand

B The Māori people came to New Zealand 300 years before the Europeans.

A New Zealand has an amazing coast and beautiful lakes and mountains – great for rafting, bungee jumping and canyoning. New Zealand also has awesome geysers.

C New Zealand's head of state is the King or Queen of England.

D New Zealand is over 2000 kilometres from Australia.

1 **A first look at New Zealand**

a Look at the photos and read the texts. What's true about New Zealand?
1   It has a big population.
2   It has a president.
3   It isn't far from Australia.
4   It has great countryside.
5   Europeans were the first inhabitants.
6   Cars drive on the left.

b Lina from Erlangen has a video chat with her friend Hunter in New Zealand. Listen. What do you think: Will Lina go to New Zealand?
1.16

c Listen again and complete the sentences.
1.16
1   The Pohutu Geyser is up to … metres high.
2   *Kia ora* is Māori for …
3   A flight from Auckland to Sydney takes … hours.
4   Wellington is New Zealand's … city.
5   Most immigrants to Zealand today come from …
6   The population of New Zealand is about one … of the number of people who live in Bavaria.

More practice 1 → p. 82

E

G The first Europeans who landed and stayed in New Zealand were the British. That's why some things are like in Britain.

F Only five million people live in New Zealand.

In dieser Unit lernst du ...
- Faktenwissen zu Neuseeland zu erarbeiten,
- über Diskriminierung zu sprechen,
- zu sagen, was unter bestimmten Bedingungen passiert,
- über die Arbeits- und Berufswelt zu sprechen,
- die Vor- und Nachteile eines Themas zu erörtern.

2 VIEWING Run Rabbit

a Watch the film. Which of the following do you see in the film? People who are ...
- having a meal
- killing animals
- working on a farm
- having fun in the water
- climbing a tower

b Why is it difficult for Tarek to live in New Zealand? Pick phrases from the list and give your own reasons too.
- some people aren't nice to him
- the food is different
- nobody loves him
- it's often too cold
- he remembers terrible things from the past

It's difficult for Tarek because ...

c 👥 Compare your answers with a partner. Do you agree?

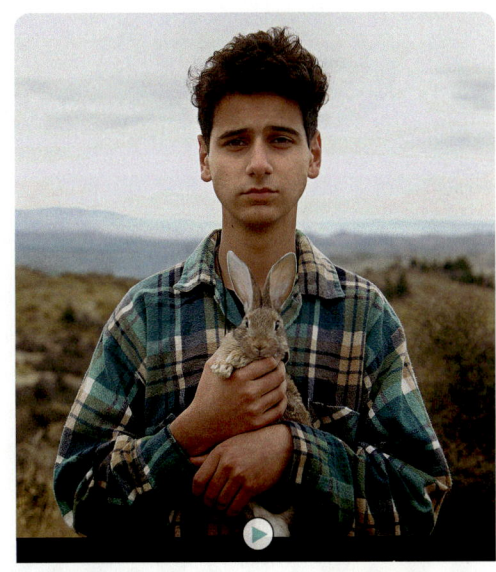

More practice 2 → p. 82   Workbook 1 → p. 14

→ Ich kann Faktenwissen zu Neuseeland erarbeiten. ✓

First visit to New Zealand

1 Lina's photos

a Lina has come to New Zealand and has posted these photos on her social media account. Which photos would you give a *like*? Write a comment for each photo. Examples:
A: Love the view!   B: Great shot!   C: Looks ...

b 👥 Choose one of Lina's pictures: Describe it to your partner. What can you see? Are there any people? What are they doing? How are they feeling?   More help → *p. 83*

Skills file 7 → *p. 123*

➡ Ich kann Fotos kommentieren und beschreiben. ✓

2 **Texts for Lina's photos**

a Lina wrote texts for her photos. Match each text 1–4 with one or two photos A–F on page 28.

1 Hi, travel-friends! I'm now a volunteer at Don and Anna's organic farm on South Island and I'm learning lots of great new skills. Tomorrow I'm going to work with the animals, so watch out guys: when I'm home I'll show you how to milk a cow!

2 *Kia ora* everybody! Today I went on a tour of Auckland with Tai, a Māori guide. Tai told me that tattoos are important for the Māori people because they tell you about a person's identity. It was a great tour. I always enjoy meeting local people when I travel. Tomorrow Tai is going to take me to Whangarei. If we're lucky, I might see kiwi birds there – cool, eh?

3 Hey guys, here I am in New Zealand after my 6-hour flight from Munich to Dubai and my 17-hour flight from Dubai to Auckland! I knew that Auckland is New Zealand's biggest city, but I didn't know that it has great beaches and about 50 volcanoes! I'm going to climb one of them tomorrow! And I might try the outside walk 192 metres up on Auckland's highest building. It looks awesome. You can even do a *SkyJump* from the tower. But I won't do that.

4 Hello guys, I took this photo today. It's a crazy sport if you ask me, but very popular here. I mean, with a population of only 5 million, New Zealand is one of the top countries in the world at rugby – how crazy is that?

b Read the texts again. Then answer the questions.

1 How long was Lina's journey to Auckland?
2 Why are tattoos important in Māori culture?
3 Which skill has Lina learned on the farm?
4 What are three things that Lina says about Auckland?
5 Why is it surprising that New Zealand is so successful in an international sport?
6 What can you see in the photo below?

 c ● Lina has a video chat with her friend Dan in Britain. What new information does she give? Listen and take notes. Skills file 6 → p. 122

d 👥 **Partner check** Compare your answers with a partner. Did you write the same?

3 **AND YOU?**

Look on the internet and find one or two photos of places in New Zealand. Imagine that they're photos that you posted on your holiday. Write a few sentences for a post (at least 60 words).
Hi from New Zealand! I'm still feeling a bit tired after my long flight! I'm staying in ... Yesterday I ... I thought it was amazing because ... In the next few days I'd like to ...

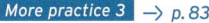 More practice 3 → p. 83   Workbook 2 → p. 15

Discrimination

1 **Talking about discrimination**

1.18

a A friend took Lina to a meeting about discrimination in Auckland. Listen to four speakers and match each speaker with sentence ending A–F. Use each ending only once.
You don't need all the endings.

1 Manaia		**A** make racist comments.
2 Amy		**B** look and point at her/him.
3 Ben	says that people	**C** think she/he doesn't have her/his own thoughts.
4 Wei		**D** put her/him in a category.
		E don't understand her/his mental health problem.
		F say that she/he should eat less cake.

b Now listen to the four speakers again and pick the correct option.

1 Manaia talks about …
- Ⓐ Māori food.
- Ⓑ which languages he uses.
- Ⓒ his favourite teacher.
- Ⓓ the job he wants when he's older.

2 Amy talks about what happened …
- Ⓐ when a friend was in a wheelchair.
- Ⓑ when she fell ill.
- Ⓒ after an accident.
- Ⓓ a year ago.

3 Ben talks about …
- Ⓐ his family.
- Ⓑ his depression.
- Ⓒ going swimming on Orewa beach.
- Ⓓ going to the doctor.

4 Wei says that …
- Ⓐ her family has a hard life.
- Ⓑ somebody attacked her.
- Ⓒ she is hurt by what people say.
- Ⓓ she never invites people to her house.

2 **Discrimination is when …**

a ⊙ Complete the sentences with the words in the box.

Discrimination is when …
1 people make … comments.
2 women earn less than men for the … work.
3 you're in a … and can't get into some buildings.
4 you have mental health …, but other people say that you're just lazy.

> problems • racist • same • wheelchair

b ⊙ 👥 Work with a partner. Copy and complete the sentences with your own ideas.
Discrimination is when …
– girls are scared to go out at night because …
– people laugh at you because …

3 **That has made my day**

a Sarah, who uses a wheelchair, wrote this post for an internet group.
A man made her happy. What did he do? Why did it make her happy?

> It was the end of a long day. My back hurt, so I was slow, and my sister and I were late when we
> arrived at our village hall this evening to see a show.
> Because we were late, there were no chairs for us.
> But a man saw us. "Wait there just a moment," he said, and he went out of the hall and came back
> with two chairs. Then suddenly he stopped, looked at me and said, "Oh, silly me! You don't need a chair,
> of course. I'm really sorry. I didn't think."
> But I started to laugh, and my sister and the man laughed too. And I said, "Don't apologize!
> I feel so happy. For a moment you thought of me as a person – not a wheelchair user.
> And that has made my day!"
> *Sarah*

b **MEDIATION**

Tell a German friend about Sarah's article. You don't have to translate word for word.
Sarah, die im Rollstuhl sitzt, und ihre Schwester ...

4 **VIEWING** *What you say matters* by Brothablack

a ⊙ Watch the video. Is the song against
A bad language? **B** drugs? **C** discrimination?

b Read the three speech bubbles with sentences from the video.

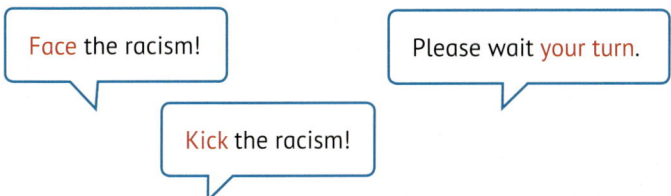

Face the racism!

Please wait your turn.

Kick the racism!

Then watch the video again and listen for the sentences in the speech bubbles.
What's the meaning for each red word?

face	kick	turn
A Gesicht *(N)*	**A** Tritt, Stoß *(N)*	**A** Drehung *(N)*
B gegenüberstehen *(V)*	**B** Schuss, Kick *(N)*	**B** *It's my turn.* Ich bin
C (einer Sache)	**C** treten, kicken *(V)*	dran. *(N)*
entgegentreten *(V)*	**D** (Idee, Gewohnheit) aufgeben,	**C** Biegung, Kurve *(N)*
D vor etwas stehen *(V)*	sich davon befreien *(V)*	**D** drehen, verwandeln *(V)*

c 👥 Discuss in groups: What's the message of the film?
And what do you think of the music?
The song is about racism / discrimination against ...   It tells us to say "no" to ...
I think the music is great because ... / I don't like the music because ...

Skills file 2 → p. 114   Workbook 3–4 → pp. 16–17

→ Ich kann über Diskriminierung sprechen. ✓

1 ⊙ **Skimming**

Look at the pictures and paragraph titles.
a How many people are telling this story?
b Are the main characters boys or girls?
c What are their names?

Skills file 3 → p. 115

The new girl

Sameena

I really like our class. We're a real mix. And
we all have different strengths and
weaknesses. But we all get on. Well, we fall
5 out with each other from time to time, but
then we get on again.

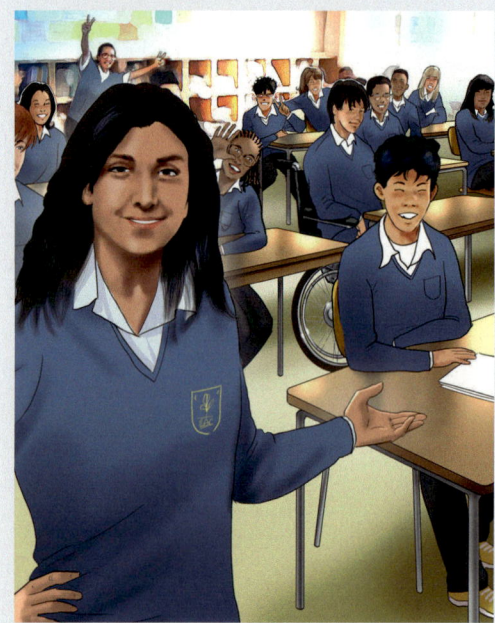

And then a new girl joined our class. Alison.
And she is different.

We really tried. We smiled, but Alison never
10 smiled back. We chatted with her at lunch,
but Alison didn't say much. When we ask her
to come bowling with us, she always says
"no". We all meet in town as often as we can.
But Alison? She never joins us. Even her
15 body language says "no".

Does she feel she is above us?

Alison

The girls chatted with me when I joined
the class. They were all really friendly – the
guys too. 20

But that only made things worse. What can
I say when they ask me about my family?
When they asked me to go bowling with
them, I wanted to say "yes"! But I had to
say "no". Why? Because I can't leave mum 25
alone and I have no money for going out.
I feel ashamed of my family. And that's a
terrible feeling.

Sameena

Alison wasn't in school today, so I told 30
Mrs Khan, our art teacher, that I could take
Alison's art folder home for her. To be
honest, I was a bit curious about Alison.
I wanted to see where she lives. In a great
big house, maybe? 35

I was surprised to find that Alison lives in a
small flat over an all-night cafe.

When Alison opened the door, she thanked
me for the art folder. She almost closed the
door again, but then she gave me a quick 40
smile and asked me to come in.

We went into a very small room. It was dark
and very full. Alison picked some books off
the sofa. I sat down – and almost jumped
up again with surprise. 45

We weren't alone in the room. A woman was sitting in an armchair on the other side of the room. She looked at me with empty eyes.

50 "My mother isn't well," Alison said. "I can't come to school when I have to look after her." "Your mother...?" I began. "But ...?"

"Come with me," Alison said, and we went outside. We sat on a wall outside the cafe.

55 For a moment nobody spoke. Then Alison talked, without looking at me.

"Mum has depression," she said.
"When she feels bad, she can't do anything. She doesn't want to get up in the morning. 60 Sometimes she doesn't want to live.

Nobody really understands what it's like to live with somebody with depression.

When it started, dad began to drink. Then he lost his job and we had to sell our house.

65 Now dad has a new job but he's on minimum wage. I have no money for going out."

I didn't know what to say. For the first time I noticed that Alison was really thin.

"I try to do what I can for mum," Alison said. 70 "But I often worry about her when I'm at school."

At that moment Alison's mother called her. "I have to go," Alison said.

She looked at me for the first time. 75 "Thanks for bringing my folder," she said, and went back inside.

But I sat on that wall for a long time.

Alison 🎧
1.22
When Sameena stood at the door, I was so 80 embarrassed. Mum was very bad and our flat was messy. I had just yelled at mum and told her that she should see a doctor. But she said that she didn't want to do that.

I didn't want to tell the students in my class 85 about my life at home. I was too ashamed.

But now Sameena knows ...

And I'm thinking: what will they say when I go back to school?

2 Tell the story

Put pictures A–F in the right order.

More practice 4 → p. 84

3 Alison and Sameena

Pick the right option.

1 The kids in Sameena's class …

    A always get on. **B** all have the same problems and backgrounds.

    C are all very different. **D** never wanted Alison to join them in town.

2 Sameena took Alison's folder because …

    A she wanted to help Alison. **B** Mrs Khan asked her to do it.

    C Alison asked her to bring it. **D** she wanted to find out more about Alison.

3 When Alison opened the door …

    A she was really happy to see Sameena. **B** she felt ashamed about how her home looked.

    C she didn't want to take the folder. **D** she shouted at her mother.

4 Alison has not played a full part in her class because …

    A she didn't like the other kids. **B** her mum has a serious mental health problem.

    C her dad is in prison. **D** the other kids never invited her.

5 At the end of the story …

    A Sameena understands Alison better. **B** Alison feels confident about the kids in her class.

    C Alison asks Sameena to come again. **D** Sameena decides to tell her friends about Alison.

More practice 5 → p. 84

4 Thinking about the text

a Read the story again and then write what you think about sentences 1–4.

    1 Is Sameena's class a class with no discrimination? *Yes / No, because …*

    2 Why does Alison feel ashamed? *Because …*

    3 Do you think Sameena has more respect for Alison at the end of the story?
    Yes / No, because …

    4 Do you think Alison will have a hard time when she goes back to school? *Yes / No, because …*

b 👥 Compare your answers with a partner and then in class. Do you all agree?

Workbook 5–7 → p. 18

➡ Ich kann Stimmungen und Gefühle in einer Geschichte interpretieren. ✔

1 **Lina's first day on the farm**

It's Lina's first morning on Don and Anna's organic farm. Read the sentences.
Write FOUR things that Lina wants to do today.

> I don't have many warm clothes. I'll be in trouble if it's cold today.

> I love animals. I'll feed the sheep today if I'm lucky.

> I'll feel happier if I'm not the only new volunteer.

> But I'll have to clean the cow sheds if I'm unlucky. Yuck!

> I won't be thirsty if I take my bottle of water with me.

> I must be quick. It won't look good if I'm late for work on my first day.

> I'll learn about New Zealand if I join the family in their activities.

2 **If ...**

a Read the FOCUS-box.

b Write the four conditional sentences from exercise **1**. Begin with the *if*-clause.
Example: *If I'm not the only volunteer, ...*

Language file 10 → p. 133

FOCUS

Bedingungssätze (Teil 1)

Bedingungssätze *(conditional sentences)* geben an, unter welchen Voraussetzungen etwas geschieht.
I'll be in trouble if it's cold today.
Der Satz besteht aus zwei Teilen:

Hauptsatz mit *will* / *'ll* oder *won't*	+	Nebensatz mit *if* im *simple present*
I'll be in trouble		*if it's cold today.*

Der Nebensatz mit *if* kann vorne oder hinten stehen:

If it's cold today,   *I'll be in trouble.*

---

3 **Going to work in Auckland**

Lina's friend Hunter works in Auckland. Copy and complete his sentences.

1 If it's sunny tomorrow, I ... (cycle) to work.

2 But if it rains, I ... (go) by bus.

3 If I get up early, I ... (not miss) the bus.

More practice 6 → p. 85

4 But if the bus ... (be) late, I'll scream!

5 If I ... (have) time, I'll make myself sandwiches for lunch.

6 If I ... (not have) time, I'll buy myself a burger.

4 ● **What will happen if …?**

a Look at the picture. Then write as many sentences about the picture as you can.

If the cat jumps, the baby will be surprised.
If the baby is surprised, the ice cream will fall.
If the ice cream …, the dog …
If the dog …

b 👥 Compare your sentences with a partner.

c Read your sentences in class.

5 **Applying for work on a farm**

a Read the FOCUS-box.

> **FOCUS**
>
> **Bedingungssätze (Teil 2)**
> – Der Hauptsatz kann statt *will* auch *can* oder einen Imperativ (Befehl) enthalten:
>   *If you want free food, you can work on a farm.*
>   *If you have work experience, put it in your CV.*
> – Bei allgemein gültigen Wahrheiten steht sowohl im *if*-Satz als auch im Hauptsatz das
>   simple present. *If* bedeutet dann so viel wie „immer wenn":
>   *If you have a bad boss, life is hard. Life is easier if you smile.* | Language file 10 | → *p. 133*

b Now match the beginnings 1–6 with the right endings A–F.

1 If you apply early,	**A** you work hard, but you have a great time.
2 If you want to have a choice of jobs,	**B** milking can be good fun.
3 If you read the reviews of the farms,	**C** apply to lots of different farms.
4 If you have a health problem,	**D** you can see where other volunteers have been happy.
5 If you work on a farm,	**E** tell the farmer in advance.
6 And if the cows and sheep are happy,	**F** you have a better chance of getting a place.

Workbook 8–10 → *pp. 19–20*

➡ Ich kann sagen, was unter bestimmten Bedingungen passiert.

6 **Plans for a short holiday**

a First read the FOCUS-box.

> **FOCUS**
>
> ### *Going to*-future
> Verwende das *going to*-future, um über Absichten zu sprechen: *I'm going to start a new hobby.*
> Das *going to*-future besteht aus drei Teilen:
>
> | Formen des Verbs *be (am, are, is)* | + | *going to* | + | *action verb* |
> |---|---|---|---|---|
> | What *is* Sam | | *going to* | | *do?* |
> | He *is* | | *going to* | | *spend* a day with his dad. |
> | But we *are* | | *going to* | | *go* bowling. |
>
> Language file 7 → p. 131

b Lina and the other volunteers on the farm are going to spend two days in Queenstown.
What are they going to do there? Write sentences 1–6 with the *going to*-future. Use colour
coding like in the FOCUS-box.

1 Vihaan and Faiza / go bungee jumping.

2 Simona / visit a Māori village.

3 Leo and Harper / go rafting on the Kawarau River.

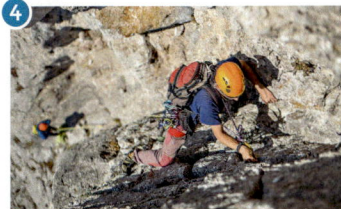

4 Harry / go rock climbing.

5 "What / you / do, Dan and Lizzy?" "We / explore the *Te Anau Caves*."

6 "And what / you / do, Lina?" "I / try the 800-metre luge track."

7 **AND YOU?**

a ☉ Imagine: You're on South Island, New
Zealand, and you have a choice of three of
the activities on the right.

Which do you choose? Write three
sentences: *I'm going to ...*

> See the **penguins** on the beach at Oamaru!
> Go **bungee jumping** at Hanmer Spring!
> **Swim** with the dolphins in Akaroa Harbour!
> Go **mountain climbing** near Queenstown!
> Go **sea kayaking** in New Zealand's Fiordland!
> Ride a **jetboat** on the Kawarau River!

b 👥 Walk around the class. Say your
sentences and make a group with students who have the same three sentences as you.
Which three activities are the most popular in your class?

More practice 7 → p. 85   Workbook 11–13 → pp. 20–21

→ Ich kann über Pläne und Absichten sprechen. ✓

8 **Filming in New Zealand**

Read this text from a film studio brochure. Find a word for each gap 1–8.
There is an example (0) at the beginning.

A large number of (0) films are made in New Zealand because the country ... (1) a number of advantages. The countryside is so amazing ... (2) it is perfect for action and fantasy films. And companies can film in December and January when it's often ... (3) dark for filming in Europe and North America. There ... (4) teams of experts ... (5) have many years of filming experience and there are lots of film studios with good equipment. ... (6) of these studios is the Weta Workshop Studio in Wellington where

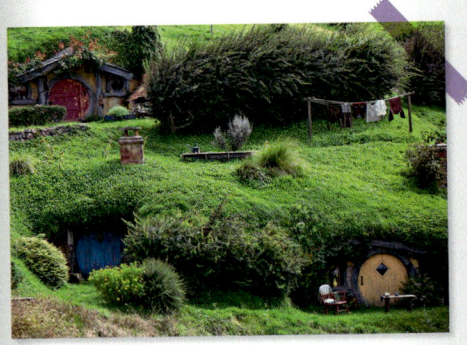

tourists can learn ... (7) we make special effects for films ... (8) *Lord of the Rings*.

9 **A very special area**

Read the post. Change the words in brackets to make them fit the sentences. There is an example at the beginning (0).

Wai-O-Tapu is an amazing (0 AMAZE) area! It's ... (1 BIG) than I was ... (2 EXPECT) and you can see geysers and very ... (3 COLOUR) pools of water. The Lady Knox Geyser is one of the most ... (4 RELY) ones: You can see it every morning at 10.15 and it can be over 10 metres ... (5 HEIGHT). There's a great ... (6 VISIT) centre and the car park was full of cars when I ... (7 BE) there. I was ... (8 SURPRISE) that the whole area is cashless – you can only pay by card.

10 **Penguins on the beach**

A tourist is asking her hostess about going to see penguins. Find eight mistakes and write the corrections in your exercise book. Write one word only per answer. There is an example (0).

- *When is the best season to seeing the penguins?*   0 *see*
- *Now is a good season, before they lay there eggs.*   1 *...*
- *And what's the best time of the day?*
- *They usually come to the beach at the evening.*   2 *...*
  You'll more often see the birds before the sun
  goes down as during the day.   3 *...*
- *That's a good tip. Is it OK near the birds to go?*   4 *...*
- *No, you shouldn't go too close to her because they*   5 *...*
  easy get frightened. And don't take flash photos   6 *...*
  because penguins doesn't like lights.   7 *...*
- *Thanks. I try to see the penguins if I can!*   8 *...*

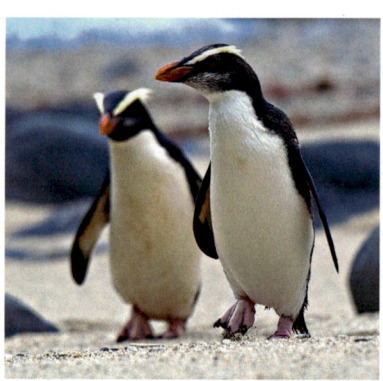

➜ Ich kann einen Text überprüfen und korrigieren. ✓

Talking about jobs

1.23

1 **Maya's job**

a Lina is talking to Maya, a Spanish volunteer on the farm.
Read or listen to the dialogue. What's Maya's job back in Spain?

Lina What's your job back in Spain, Maya?

Maya I'm doing an apprenticeship in a nursing home.

Lina In a nursing home! Is that hard?

Maya Yes, it's hard work, but the people are nice and my
manager is OK. There's a good atmosphere.

Lina And what about the pay? Is it OK?

Maya I get the minimum wage. But I can sometimes get extra pay if I work longer hours.

Lina That's handy. Do you want to stay there long-term?

Maya Yes, I do. I'll be happy if I can work there long-term. It's a good job.

1.24

b Listen again and repeat. Speak fluently. Not: *Is/it/OK?*, but: *Is⌣it⌣OK?*

c Copy and complete the sentences.
1 Maya's job is good because … 2 But the disadvantages are that …

2 **Talking about work**

a Work with a partner. Copy and complete the wordweb with as many words as you can.

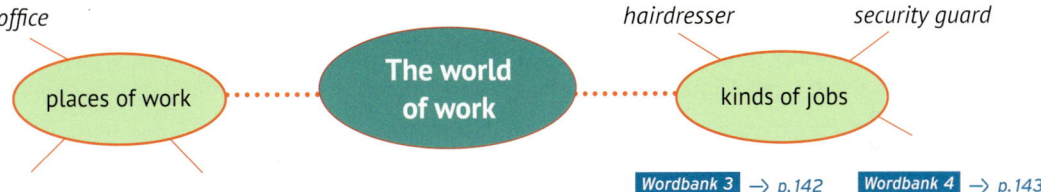

office

places of work ······ **The world of work** ······ **kinds of jobs**

hairdresser   *security guard*

Wordbank 3 → p.142   Wordbank 4 → p.143

b Give a short talk about having a job while you're still at school. Choose three
aspects in the wordweb. Take notes on a few things that you can say about them.
Partner A Talk for at least one minute about your three aspects.
Partner B Time your partner's talk. Then swap roles.

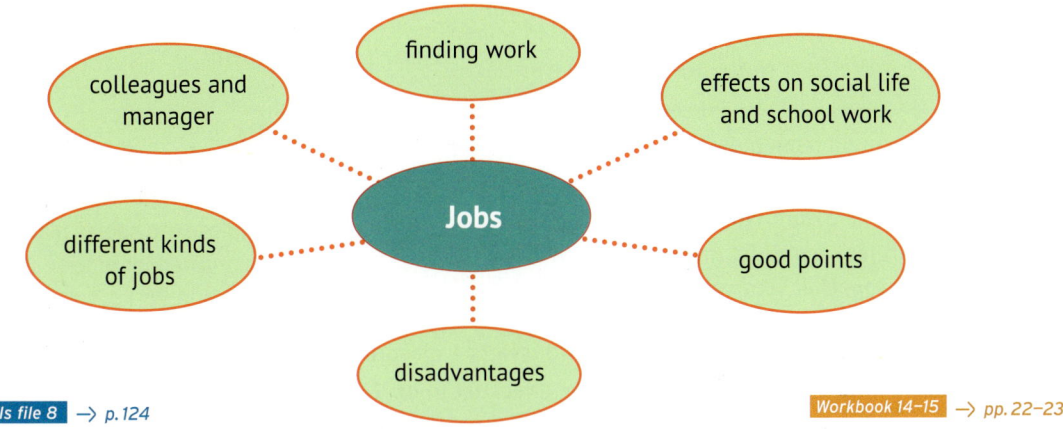

colleagues and manager

finding work

effects on social life and school work

Jobs

different kinds of jobs

good points

disadvantages

Skills file 8 → p.124

Workbook 14–15 → pp. 22–23

➡ Ich kann über die Arbeits- und Berufswelt sprechen. ✓

Doing well in a job interview

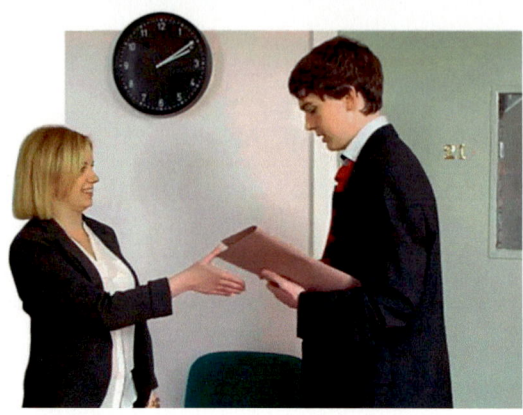

▶ 1 VIEWING **Interview stress**
Your English friend Mike is practising for a job interview.

a Read and copy the manager's checklist for the interview.
The candidate ...
1 looks smart.
2 smiles.
3 has good body language.
4 talks about strengths.
5 talks about weaknesses.
6 gives well-prepared answers.

b Watch part 1 of the film. Give Mike a tick or cross for 1–6 on the checklist.

c 👥 **Partner check** Did you give the same ticks and crosses?

d Now watch part 2 of the film. What does Mike do better this time? Make notes for categories 1–6 on your form.

e Watch part 2 again. What's true?
1 Mike says that ...
Ⓐ his strengths are important.
Ⓑ he has six strengths.

2 Mike says ...
Ⓐ his weaknesses aren't important.
Ⓑ how he is working on his weaknesses.

More practice 8 → p. 86

2 AND YOU? **Your job interview**
a Read these three typical interview questions. Write your answers – as much as you can.

> How would you describe yourself?

Well, I'm honest and reliable. And I ...

TIP
Use positive adjectives.

> What are your strengths and weaknesses?

*I react well to criticism. For example when I ...
My weaknesses? Well, I wasn't punctual at school, but now I make sure that I always arrive early.*

TIP
Turn your weaknesses into strengths – say that you know about them and are working on them.

> Are you a good team player?

*Yes, I am. I like group work at school. Last month we did a project about ... and I worked with ...
We worked together and we were very successful.*

TIP
Always say "yes"! And give an example, e.g. a sports team, a band or a school project.

b 👥 **Partner check** Partner A says his/her answers – as confidently as he/she can. Partner B gives feedback in English or in German (use the checklist in ex. **1a**). Then swap roles.

Workbook 16 → pp. 24–25   Wordbank 5 → p. 143   More practice 9 → p. 87

Reasons for and against

1 **Would you like to leave Germany and live in a different country?**
Write a short text with reasons for and against.

STEP 1 Collect ideas. Think of one more idea for each side.

Yes	No
– sunny weather (Australia)	– family is in Germany
– exciting places (New Zealand)	– language problems
– ...	– ...

STEP 2 Decide: Yes or no?

STEP 3 Write your text.
Use the structure and phrases from the example text on the right, but give your own reasons.

a Start with a short introduction.

b Then write three sentences and give arguments *for*. Use phrases from the example text:
One reason why ...
What's more, ...
And I also think that ...

c Now write three sentences with arguments *against*. Use phrases from the example text:
On the other hand, ...
I'm also ...
And above all, ...

d At the end give your opinion.
So all in all, I think ...

STEP 4 Check and correct your text.

Lots of people say it's good for young people to leave Germany and live in a different country for some time.

One reason why I'd like to do that is that I like sunny countries like Australia. What's more, I think it's exciting to live in a country like New Zealand, with its geysers and amazing mountains. And I also think that you can learn a lot from people who have a different culture and lifestyle.

On the other hand, all my parents, brothers and sisters live in Germany and they are really important in my life. I'm also a bit nervous about speaking English. And above all, I don't want to fly because planes are bad for the environment.

So all in all, I think I'll stay in Germany.

2 **AND YOU?**
Would you like to travel for one year before you get a job?

a Write a short text with introduction, three reasons for, three reasons against and your personal opinion. Follow steps 1–4 above.

b 👥 **Partner check** Can you find any mistakes in your partner's text?
And can you tell your partner what could be better?

Skills file 5 → p. 119f.   Workbook → p. 26

Sawubona from South Africa

Languages and cultures

WELKOM IN DIE WES-KAAP
WAMKELEKILE
ENTSHONA KOLONI
WELCOME TO THE WESTERN CAPE

South Africa has eleven official languages. Zulu is the most widely spoken language. Fewer than 10% of South Africans speak English as a first language, but English is often used by people who have different languages as their first language.

Find out: *Sawubona is a Zulu word. What does it mean?*

The world in one country

South Africa has dramatic mountains, a long coast, desert and fields with fruit and vegetables. But many parts of the country don't get enough rain and people don't have clean water.

Find out: *What South African products can you buy in your town or village?*

The *Big* Five

Africa's *Big Five* are five of the most famous and most dangerous animals: elephants, rhinos, leopards, lions and buffaloes. Most of them live in big national parks.

Find out: *Which five other wild animals can you see in South Africa?*

Cities and and sports

About half of the 59.1 million South Africans live in big cities like Johannesburg, Cape Town and Durban. Johannesburg is the biggest city and its Soccer City Stadium is the biggest in Africa.

Find out: *Which are the three most popular sports in South Africa?*

The children of apartheid

Before 1994 there was terrible discrimination against non-white people (over 80% of the population). They weren't allowed to live near white people. They weren't allowed in the same schools, hospitals, parks or toilets and weren't allowed to vote. This racist system, called apartheid, came to an end in 1994, but inequality is still a problem in South Africa today.

Find out: *What's the name of South Africa's first black president?*

In dieser Unit lernst du …
- Aspekte des Lebens in Südafrika kennen,
- eine Biografie zu verstehen,
- die korrekte Satzstellung anzuwenden,
- über Bilder zu sprechen,
- einen verlorenen Gegenstand bei der Polizei anzuzeigen,
- eine formelle E-Mail zu verfassen.

1 All about South Africa

a Read the texts and make notes on THREE things that surprised you about South Africa.

b Answer the *Find out*-questions at the end of the texts. Look on the internet.

c 👥 **Partner check** Compare your answers with a partner and then in class. **More practice 1** → *p. 87*

 2 A visit to South Africa

a Listen to a conversation with a German tourist who has been to South Africa. Note the order of the topics.

> animals • apartheid • food •
> languages • seasons

b Listen again and note …
  1 what was surprising about the restaurants.
  2 the time in South Africa when it's 6 pm in Germany.
  3 where black people weren't allowed to live under apartheid.
  4 how fast the fastest snakes can move.
  5 what was amazing about the people there.

Skills file 6 → *p. 122*

3 VIEWING Soccer in Soweto

Soccer is another word for football, and Soweto is a part of Johannesburg.

a Watch the film. Do you think the title is right for the film? Why (not)?

b Read the sentences below. Then watch the film again and say if they are true or false.
  1 Cars drive on the right.
  2 The stadium was built for the 2010 World Cup.
  3 People wear very colourful clothes.
  4 A vuvuzela is a sort of drum.
  5 In *Freestyle Football* one person, alone, is doing amazing things with a football.
  6 Soweto houses look like German houses.
  7 *Freestyle Football* in South Africa mixes sport and dance.

Workbook 1–2 → *p. 27*

Holidays in South Africa

1 👥 **South African adventures**

Describe one of the photos to a partner. Say as much as you can. When you have finished, can your partner say more about the photo? Repeat with another photo.

Useful phrases

This is a photo of … • On the left there is a … • Between the … and the … there is … • In the foreground I can see • In the background there are some … • The weather is … • Some of the people are … • I think the people are feeling a bit … and maybe also … • It looks exciting, but also a bit … • I would/wouldn't like to do this because …

Visit a national park	Go shark diving

Go on a safari and see some of the world's most amazing wild animals.	Go down in a cage and the sharks come and look at you!

Discover South African music and dance	Go paragliding over Cape Town

Cape Town's young musicians play a mix of hip hop, reggae, rock and R & B. Or listen to the Afrobeat of Tzaneen rappers.	Get the best views of the city on a 20-minute flight, then land on the beach next to the ocean. Great fun!

Skills file 7 → *p. 123*

➡ Ich kann über Bilder sprechen. ✓

2 **Ideas for a visit**

a Scan this internet forum. Make a list of at least six things that you can do. Skills file 3 → p. 115

> **Baz: Looking for ideas for a two-week trip to SA?**
> I'm from Australia and my family is planning a two-week trip to South Africa. We would like to know what other travellers think are must-dos. Thanks in advance for your help.
>
> **Replies:**
>
> *AP:* You must go on a safari in Kruger National Park. You can't leave South Africa without seeing a lion or an elephant!
>
> *Capetowngirl:* Enjoy a drink in a cafe in Cape Town with a view of the famous Table Mountain. Then go to Boulders Beach and see the penguins or go whale watching in Hermanus. Or go shark diving. It's very exciting – and it's safe.
>
> *Vulu:* Visit Robben Island, where Nelson Mandela spent 18 years in prison for fighting against apartheid. In 1994 he became our first black president. The prison is now a museum.
>
> *Stef:* Want to see the real South Africa? Then go on a tour of a township. On the best township tours you meet local people. They earn some money and you get an idea of life for many people in South Africa.

b 2.02 Now listen to four visitors to South Africa. Are the sentences true or false?
   1 She saw lions.   **2** He didn't take any photos.   **3** She saw Mandela's cell.
   4 He wasn't scared when he saw the sharks.

c 2.02 Listen again. Note one thing about each visit that wasn't good. More practice 2 → p. 88

3  **You choose** Do **a** or **b**

a Prepare a presentation on South Africa for your class.
Step 1: Choose a topic (famous sights, national parks, activities, history, …)
Step 2: Collect information and make notes. Think of photos or videos too.
Step 3: Plan your talk and think of a good structure (beginning – middle – end).
Step 4: Practise your presentation. Speak clearly and freely. Don't read your text, but it can be useful to have keywords on a piece of paper.
Step 5: Now give your presentation.
Be prepared to answer questions.

b Imagine you had a holiday in South Africa and you did some of the activities on these two pages. Write about your visit for your school magazine. Write at least 100 words.

> **TIP**
> Use the simple past:
> *Go to Boulders Beach and see the penguins.*
> → *We went to Boulders Beach and saw …*

Last year I had a short holiday in South Africa. On the first day we …
It was …   because …
The best thing/The only problem was …

Skills file 8 → p. 124   Skills file 5 → p. 119f.   Workbook 3–5 → pp. 28–29

 Ich kann Gespräche über einen Urlaub in Südafrika verstehen. ✓

Young in South Africa

1 **Issues for young South Africans**
An online magazine asked young South Africans to write about the big issues for them.
Read the texts. What are the biggest issues for these four young people? Write them down.

What are the most important issues for you today?

About 35.7% of South Africans are between 15 and 34 years old. What issues are important for these young people? We asked four of them.

Kagiso: I live in a township in Cape Town, where many black people had to live before 1994, during the years of apartheid. These areas had small houses, little clean water and few toilets. Life is still hard in townships today, and when people are poor it's women who suffer most – for example, the sanitary products that we need cost too much. That's one of the most important issues for me while I'm studying to become a teacher.

Bandile: I'm one of the few students from my village who is at college. Here at college I do a vlog about the hard life of black kids in my village, and I'm now one of the most important influencers in the east of the country. Many influencers do marketing for big companies, who pay them for this work, but I don't do this. You see, most of my viewers live in cities and don't know much about life in the villages. So I tell them honestly about kids in villages like mine, who have little clean water and a long way to school. I tell my viewers about projects that are helping these kids to get to college and I ask them to support these projects.

Adem: More than half of all young South Africans are unemployed. I know it's much worse for black people than it is for me, but it is hard for me too. Many companies want you to have work experience before you can work for them – but how can you get experience if you can't work? That's a bigger issue for me than crime – which is the issue that most people talk about.

Lulama: I'm crazy about football! I play for our national under-17 team, and I'd love to play for one of the teams in the European Cup. But it's hard for many of us to practise our sports because there aren't enough sports clubs, football fields or stadiums near where we live. Many young people in our big cities don't even have space to kick a ball. I really hope things will get better soon.

5

10

15

20

25

30

2 **Working with the text**

a Match the titles (1–6) with the four people in the texts. Write the correct number for each name.
Use each number only once. There are two extra titles.

1 Why young people find it hard to train as much as they would like to
2 Hard to get a job
3 Life in the townships in the past and today
4 Disadvantages for teachers
5 Problems with crime
6 Information for young people in towns

b Are the following sentences true (T), false (F) or not in the text (N)?

1 Sanitary products are too expensive for many women.
2 Bandile's village is a long way from the nearest town.
3 Bandile uses his vlog to help young people who live in villages.
4 Adem says that companies prefer to give jobs to people who have already had a job before.
5 Adem has found a job.
6 Lulama plays for a football team in the European Cup.

c **MEDIATION** Erkläre auf Deutsch …

1 was bei den Wohnverhältnissen in Townships schlecht war.
2 wie sich Bandile von anderen Influencern unterscheidet.
3 warum es für junge Menschen schwierig ist, eine Arbeitsstelle zu bekommen.

3 **AND YOU?** **What are the biggest issues for you?** More help → p. 88

a 👥 What are the issues in your town? Work with a partner. Copy and complete the table
with as many ideas as you can. Then compare your ideas in a class discussion.

Issues	Good points	Bad points
transport	buses are cheap and reliable	very few night buses, …
sport	a good …	not enough …
environment		too many …, dangerous for …
things to do		… too expensive
jobs, flats, etc.		

b Now write …

– three things that make life in your town
good for young people.
One thing that is good in our town is that …
What's more, …
And I also think that …

– three problems for young people in your town.
On the other hand, …
It's also true that …
And the worst thing of all is that …

– your own opinion about life for young people in your town.
So all in all, I think that …

c **READING CIRCLE**
Put your text on the noticeboard.
Read your classmates' texts and
draw a smiley on the three texts
that you like best.

Skills file 5 → p. 119f.   Workbook 6–7 → p. 30

➡ Ich kann einen Artikel in einem Onlinemagazin verstehen. ✓

1 Before you read

👥 Compare with a partner: What do you already know about Nelson Mandela?

The life of Nelson Mandela

🎧 2.03

A When Mandela was born in 1918, his parents, who spoke Xhosa, called him Rolihlahla.
But the schools were organized by the
5 white minority and they often gave black children European names. Rolihlahla's school teacher gave him the name Nelson.

10 He did well at school and after university he went to Johannesburg where he became a lawyer.

🎧 2.04

B It was a hard time for black South
15 Africans. Under apartheid white people had their own schools, hospitals and churches. Black people, 80% of all South Africans, were not allowed to vote. They had to use different beaches, toilets and ambulances.

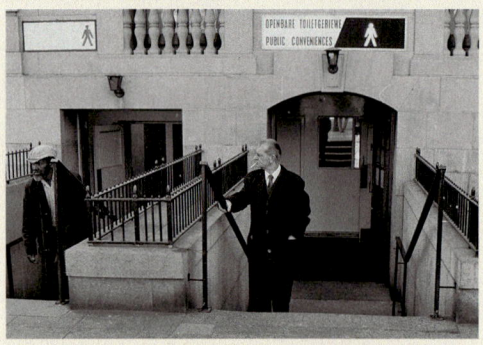

20 It was a crime for black people to marry or have sex with white people. And because they weren't allowed to live near white people, 3.5 million black South Africans had to leave their homes and move into
25 townships where houses were bad and life was hard.

Mandela's law firm was the first black law firm in the country, so he knew how bad life was for black people.

And it isn't surprising that he joined the 30 African National Congress (ANC), which organized peaceful protests against apartheid.

🎧 2.05

C Then, on a terrible day in March 1960, white police officers in Sharpeville shot 35 and killed 69 people who were protesting peacefully. About 180 people were hurt.

After that the ANC decided that peaceful protest was not enough, and Mandela took part in acts of violence against the state. 40 Two and a half years later the police arrested him. Together with other members of the ANC, Nelson Mandela was sent to prison for life on Robben Island, seven kilometres off the coast near Cape Town. 45

🎧 2.06

D In prison Mandela's cell was four square metres.

He had two plates, a spoon, a small wardrobe and a thin sleeping mat on the floor. He had no books and had to use a bucket as a toilet. The light was on day and night. His wife was only allowed to visit him twice a year, and when his mother and, later, one of his sons died, he was not allowed to go to their funerals.

But amazingly this hard prison life did not break him. Every day, while the prisoners did hard work outside, they taught each other English, Afrikaans, history and politics. Mandela also made friends with kind warders.

As a result, life slowly became better for the prisoners – they were allowed to wear trousers, not shorts, and they were allowed to read books.

E South Africa's racist government hoped that the world might forget Mandela – but the opposite happened. He became more famous.

The ANC organized a *Free Nelson Mandela* campaign at home and abroad. White South African rugby and cricket teams met loud protests when they played abroad, and South Africa wasn't allowed to take part in the Olympic Games.

People in countries all over the world stopped buying South African fruit and wine. And all the time there were more protests on the streets in South Africa.

By the 1980s South Africa was in serious trouble – and the white president, F.W. de Klerk, decided that only one man could help: the prisoner Nelson Mandela.

So Mandela was moved to a different prison and there were secret talks between Mandela and de Klerk. And finally, in 1990, Mandela was allowed to leave prison.

Nelson Mandela and his wife Winnie leave the Victor Verster prison, South Africa, 11th Feb. 1990.

F What would Mandela do now? He had spent 27 years in prison, 18 of them on Robben Island. Many white South Africans were scared that the people who they had treated so badly would now use violence against them.

But Mandela wanted peace for all South Africans. When he became South Africa's first black president in May 1994, he passed laws against all racist discrimination and tried to end inequality.

Nelson Mandela takes the oath of office in Pretoria, 10th May 1994.

When he died in 2013, he was a hero not only for black South Africans, but for most white South Africans too.

2 The story of Nelson Mandela

Look at the sentences and note the missing words.
Be careful: Sometimes you have to write more than one word.

1 Mandela's ... called him Rolihlahla.
2 Mandela joined the ANC, which organized ... against apartheid.
3 The police arrested Mandela after he took part in ... after Sharpeville.
4 Mandela spent 18 years in ... on Robben Island.
5 But in the 1980s, ... had secret talks with Mandela.
6 In 1994 Mandela became president and made laws against ... in South Africa.

3 People in the story

1 Who spoke Xhosa at home?
2 Who gave Mandela the name Nelson?
3 Who weren't allowed to vote under apartheid?
4 Who worked in the country's first black law firm?
5 Who organized peaceful protests against apartheid?
6 Who killed 69 black people in Sharpeville in 1960?
7 Who had to do hard work on Robben Island?
8 Who met protests against apartheid when they played in other countries?
9 Who allowed Mandela to leave prison?
10 Who thought that Mandela was a great leader in the
last years of his life?

More practice 3 → p. 89

4 👥 AND YOU?

Discuss with a partner, and then in class.
Do you think Nelson Mandela is a role model for young people? Why (not)?

Yes, I think he is a role model because he fought all his life ...
Even after 18 years in prison he ...
No, I don't think Nelson Mandela is a role model. He lived a long time ago and now ...

5 Words in the text

Some words have different meanings.
Which of the meanings A – D is used in the text?

call *(line 2)*	firm *(line 27)*	spend *(line 96)*	pass *(line 103)*
A rufen *(V)*	A Firma *(N)*	A ausgeben *(V)*	A vorbeigehen *(V)*
B anrufen *(V)*	B stabil *(Adj)*	B verbringen *(V)*	B vergehen *(V)*
C nennen *(V)*	C fest *(Adj)*	C aufbrauchen *(V)*	C bestehen *(V)*
D Aufforderung *(N)*	D unnachgiebig *(Adj)*	D Ausgabe *(N)*	D *(Gesetz)* verabschieden *(V)*

Workbook 8–9 → p. 31 Skills file 2 → p. 114 More practice 4 → p. 90

➡ Ich kann eine Biografie verstehen. ✓

1 Lerato's role model

A South-African website asked its readers:
Nelson Mandela was the role model for many of your parents.
But who is your role model today?

a Read Lerato's text. Why is Demi-Leigh Nel-Peters her role model?

> Demi-Leigh Nel-Peters became my role model when four men attacked her in Johannesburg because they wanted to steal her car. The men ran away when Demi used self-defence against them. And I decided that I should learn self-defence too.
> In November 2017 Demi travelled to Las Vegas where she became Miss Universe. *Lerato*

Demi-Leigh Nel-Peters,
11th February 2019,
in Hollywood California

b Look at the text again and finish the sentences. Use colours for Subject–Verb–Object.
1 She became my role model when four men attacked her in Johannesburg
  because … wanted to steal … .
2 The men … when Demi … … .
3 In November 2017 … where she … .

c Now copy and complete the FOCUS-box.

> ### FOCUS
>
> **Wortstellung**
> In Haupt- und Nebensätzen ist die Wortstellung im Englischen: … – … – … .
> Achtung! Im Deutschen ist es anders:
>
> | | V | … | … | | S | … | | … |
> |---|---|---|---|---|---|---|---|---|
> | *Im November 2017* | *reiste* | *Demi* | *nach Las Vegas,* | *wo* | *sie* | *Miss Universum* | *wurde.* | |

Language file 9 → p. 132

2 Walid's role model

Read Walid's text for the website. Copy the sentences.
Choose the right place for the verb in red.

1 (came) Hashim Amla is from a Muslim family that ▮ to South Africa from India ▮.
2 (was) He began to play cricket when he ▮ at school ▮.
3 (was) Soon ▮ he ▮ playing for the South African national team.
4 (stopped) Unfortunately ▮ he ▮ playing international cricket in 2019.
5 (was) He is famous because he ▮ one of the top South African cricket players ▮.
6 (is) But he is my role model because he ▮ very calm on the field ▮, and because he ▮ a great sportsperson ▮.

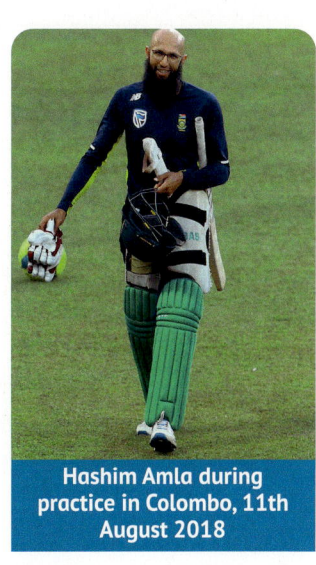

Hashim Amla during
practice in Colombo, 11th
August 2018

Workbook 10 → p. 32

→ Ich kann sprachliche Regelmäßigkeiten erkennen. ✓

3 ⊙ **Three role models?**

What's the right order of the boxes?

1 Meghan Markle became the first woman of colour in the British Royal family when she married Prince Harry (in Windsor Castle) (in 2018).

2 Harry and Meghan visited (in 2019) (South Africa).

3 They spent time with South African women (on the first day) (in a women's and children centre).

4 They met Archbishop Desmond Tutu (in Cape Town) (on the third day of their tour).

5 Tutu fought against apartheid (before 1994) (in his country).

6 Prince Harry visited projects (for the environment in Botswana) (a few days later).

TIPP

Weißt du noch?
Ortsangaben folgen nach dem Verb und Objekt.
Zeitangaben stehen ganz am Anfang oder ganz am Ende.

More practice 5 → p. 90

4 **MEDIATION**

You meet some German and South African students at the Africa Festival in Würzburg. Mediate for Julian, who's a bit shy and doesn't want to speak English.

1 Letztes Jahr habe ich eine südafrikanische Band bei einem Konzert in München gehört. Sie war großartig.

> Last year I heard …

2 Und ein paar Monate später bin ich zu diesem Festival hier in Würzburg gekommen.

> And a few months later I came …

3 Jetzt komme ich jedes Jahr hierher.

> …

4 Man hört immer etwas Neues. Ich habe zum Beispiel am Freitag hier eine tolle Band aus Cape Town gehört.

> …

5 Ich möchte gern nächstes Jahr meine Ferien in Südafrika verbringen. Dann könnte ich viel mehr afrikanische Bands hören.

> …

Skills file 9 → p. 125   Workbook 11–12 → p. 33

→ Ich kann in einer Alltagssituation dolmetschen. ✔

5 ⊙ **English in South Africa**

Copy and complete the sentences. Write the verbs in brackets in the present progressive.

> **TIP**
>
> Remember: You use the present progressive to say what's happening at the moment and when you're describing pictures:
> *The boy is wearing …*

Speech bubbles: "Turn left at the next robot!" · "Excuse me, we're looking for the Lion Park."

1 In this cartoon a boy … (ask) the way.
   His parents … (wait) in the car.
2 I think the boy is from Britain because he … (wear) a T-shirt with the British flag on it.
3 The tourists … (look for) the Lion Park.
4 They don't understand what the man … (say).
5 They don't know that in South Africa traffic lights are called robots. So the man … (say): "Turn left at the next traffic lights."

Language file 2 → p. 127

6 👥 **English as a world language**

A student has written a nice text about the English language, but the underlined words have mistakes. With a partner, read the comments on the right and write a correct version of the text.

> **English – a world language**
>
> Most people in the USA, the UK, Canada, Australia, Ireland and New Zealand are speaking English. There are also many other countries where English an important second language is.
> More people speak English in India, for example, than in any other country in the world.
>
> These days more and more people in Europe learn English. 80% of people in Sweden say that they can speak English well. In Germany say 50% of people the same. So it is true to say that English is a world language.

→ They speak English **every day** → simple present!

→ The word order is wrong here. S–V–O!

→ They are doing it **now** → present progressive!

→ The word order is wrong here. S–V–O!

More practice 6 → p. 91

→ Ich kann einen Text überprüfen und korrigieren. ✓

7 **Johannesburg**

Read the text about Johannesburg. Pick the correct words from the box. You won't need all the words in the box. There is an example (0) at the beginning.

> against • along • although • because • become • come • few • for •
> from • give • here • little • much • on • some • spend • there • these • this •
> what • when • ~~where~~ • who • with

Black African people lived in the area *where* (0) Johannesburg now stands before the first white people arrived. The new people were Dutch farmers ... (1) lived far from each other. ... (2) was no big town here then.

Everything changed ... (3) a farmer found gold on his land in 1884. When people heard about it, thousands came from all over the world to find gold and ... (4) rich. Most people didn't find anything, but a ... (5) people became very rich. Soon there were shops and bars where they could ... (6) their money. By 1896 the city had a population of one hundred thousand people.

From about 1900 the government brought workers ... (7) India and China. ... (8) Asian people were not treated well. One of the people who fought for their rights was an Indian lawyer called Gandhi – who would later become famous ... (9) his campaign against the British in India.

... (10) over four million inhabitants, Johannesburg is now South Africa's biggest city. It still produces gold, ... (11) there are fewer gold mines than before. ... (12) of the gold mines are now 4 km deep.

5

10

15

8 **A Chinese festival in Johannesburg**

Read the sentences. Change the words given in the brackets to make them fit the sentences. There is an example at the beginning (0).

0 *Chinese New Year* is a festival for adults and ... (CHILD). *children*

1 There are special events in Johannesburg at the ... (BEGIN) of the *Chinese New Year*.

2 The Chinese inhabitants of Johannesburg ... (CELEBRATION) together.

3 People shout and sing ... (NOISY) in the streets.

4 Many people wear ... (TRADITION) Chinese clothes.

5 The parades in the streets are colourful and ... (EXCITE).

6 There are markets with ... (AMAZE) food and drinks for sale.

Workbook 13–14 → p. 34

More practice 7 → p. 91

→ Ich kann Aufgabenformate der Abschlussprüfung meistern. ✓

Preparation for the speaking exam

1 👥 **Picture-based interview: Meeting friends**
Look at the picture for 30 seconds. Then talk about it with your partner.

Picture description
- Describe where the young people are.
- Describe what they are wearing and carrying.
- What can you see in the background?
- What's the weather like?

Talking about the picture
- What could the people be talking about?
- How are they feeling?
- Where and when do you go out with your friends?
- What do you do when you meet friends in town? *Skills file 7* → p. 123

Meeting friends

2 **Topic-based talk: My mobile**
a Choose three aspects in the wordweb and make notes for a short talk.

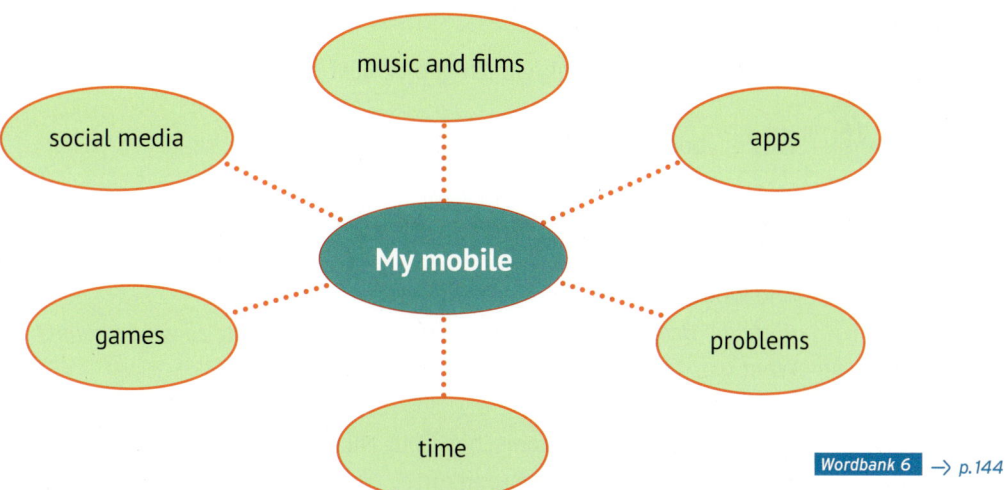

music and films

social media

apps

My mobile

games

problems

time *Wordbank 6* → p. 144

b 👥 Now talk to your partner.
Try to talk for 30 seconds about each of your three aspects. Then swap roles.

Skills file 8 → p. 124

Useful phrases
- I'm going to talk about …
- The reason why I think … is important is that …
- My favourite app allows me to …
  I can't imagine life without my phone because …

→ Ich kann über ein Bild und ein vorgegebenes Thema sprechen. ✔

At a police station

If you lose money or something of value when you're on holiday, many insurance companies want a certificate from a local police station.

a wallet

1 👥 **Describe your phone or wallet**
Work with a partner. Copy and complete the wordweb with as many words as possible.

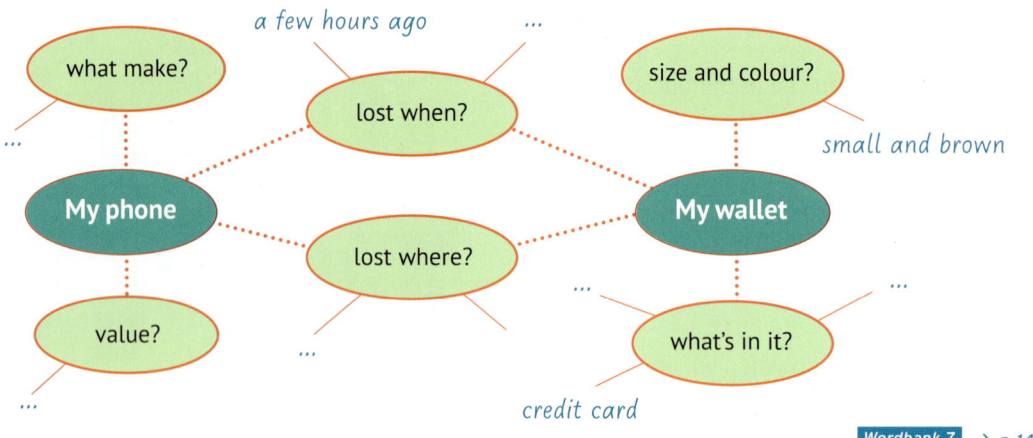

a few hours ago ...

what make?

lost when?

size and colour?

...

small and brown

My phone

My wallet

value?

lost where?

what's in it?

...

...

...

credit card

Wordbank 7 → p. 145

2 MEDIATION **A lost wallet**
You're on holiday in South Africa. Mediate for a German tourist who has lost her wallet.

Police officer	Where did you lose your wallet?
You	...
Tourist	Im Park. Bei einer Bank, wo ich gepicknickt habe.
You	...
Police officer	Was anybody with you?
You	...
Tourist	Zwei Freunde. Ich kann Ihnen die Namen geben.
You	...
Police officer	And what was in the wallet? Anything of value?
You	*(Bitte die Beamtin, langsamer zu sprechen und den Satz zu wiederholen.)*
Police officer	What was in the wallet? Any money or credit cards?
You	...
Tourist	Deutsches und südafrikanisches Geld. Nicht viel. Aber auch mein Führerschein und meine Kreditkarte.
You	...

Skills file 9 → p. 125

3 MEDIATION **A lost phone**
Mediate for a German tourist who has lost his phone.

🎧 **a** Listen carefully. Mediate for each speaker in the pause after each sentence.
2.09   The police officer begins.

🎧 **b** Now listen to the dialogue. Is the mediation like yours?
2.10
Workbook 16–17 → p. 36

➡ Ich kann den Verlust eines Gegenstands bei der Polizei anzeigen. ✓

A letter and a picture

1 **An email to a hotel in South Africa**

a Read the email. What are the missing words? Pick the right words from the box.

> ask • can • does • forward • from • questions • same • sincerely • single • stay

---

Dear Sir/Madam

I am writing to … (1) if I can change a booking in your hotel.

We have booked a double and a … (2) room (both with air conditioning) … (3) 27th December to 2nd January. The booking reference is JQR/492.

We would now like to … (4) one more night, until 3rd January. Is this possible?

And can we stay in the … (5) rooms please?

Also, I have two more … (6) please: Your website says that you have a sauna.

… (7) children use it too? And … (8) your restaurant have vegan food?

Many thanks for your help. We are looking … (9) to our stay in your hotel.

Yours … (10)

---

b AND YOU?

Schreibe eine Mail von mindestens 100 Wörtern an ein Hotel.

– Ändere eine Buchung: Du möchtest einen Tag später ankommen und abreisen.
– Gib die Buchungsnummer und die alten und die neuen Termine an.
– Frage, ob ihr zu eurer späten Ankunftszeit noch im Hotel oder in der Nähe essen könnt.
– Bedanke dich und sage, dass du dich auf den Aufenthalt freust.

2 **Tell the story** More help → p. 91

Schreibe die Geschichte in ca. 100 Wörtern: *Last year my dad found an ad for a hotel in …*

Skills file 5 → p. 119f.

Workbook 15 → p. 35   Workbook → p. 37

→ Ich kann ein formelles Schreiben verfassen. ✓

Unit 4

Namaste from India

Namaste means *Hello* in India.

A mega country

India is about nine times bigger than Germany and will soon have the world's biggest population. There are 30 languages in India that are spoken by more than one million people. Hindi is the most widely-spoken language and English is important in government, business and education.

Big changes

The number of poor people in India is high, but falling fast because more people are now working in modern industries. India's IT industry is growing fast, and the country has more smartphone users than the USA. It will also soon make more cars than Germany.

Solar energy

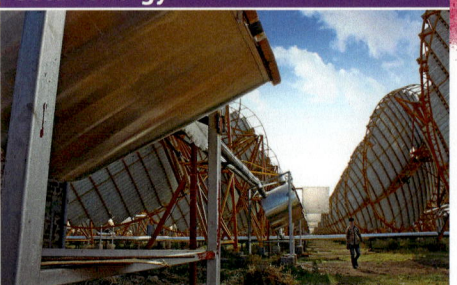

India is one of the countries that produces most solar energy. India produced 20,000 megawatts in 2018 – four years earlier than planned!

Holi festival of colours

This Hindu festival celebrates life and love at the beginning of spring. People go out into the streets and throw colours over each other. This festival began in India, but is now popular in many other countries, like Germany for example.

1 **India today** More help → p. 92

a What do **you** think of when you hear the name India? Think of people, food, sports, animals, cities, festivals, films, languages, …

b 👥 Now read the texts on page 58. Note at least two things that surprised you about India. Then compare your ideas with a partner and in class. More practice 1 → p. 92

In dieser Unit lernst du …
- die Vielfalt Indiens zu verstehen,
- über Klimawandel zu sprechen,
- zu sagen, was du schon einmal getan hast,
- über einen Unfall zu berichten.

🎧 2.11

2 **India, a land of surprises**

a 🔘 Priya is Indian, Brian is from Australia. They talk about India in a hostel. In what order do they talk about A–C? Listen and take notes.

A

B

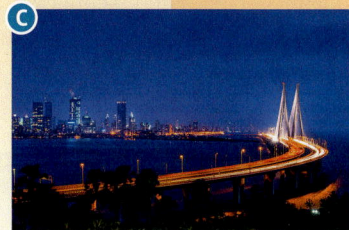
C

Skills file 6 → p. 122

b Listen again. Are the sentences true or false?
1 The amazing beaches were a real surprise for Brian.
2 The big bridge over the sea in Mumbai is like a bridge in Australia.
3 Brian says that he felt a bit scared when he rode in a tuk-tuk.
4 A computer engineer from India and his team invented USB technology.
5 India first used rulers about two thousand years ago.
6 Brian thinks that India is more modern than he expected.

3 **VIEWING** **Transport in New Delhi**

a Watch two short films about travelling in New Delhi. Answer the questions.
Cycle rickshaw:
1 How hot is it in the streets of Delhi?
2 Would you like to ride on a cycle rickshaw? Why (not)?
Delhi Metro:
3 Why is the station in the film especially important?
4 What's the same as going by underground in Germany? What's different?

b 👥 Compare your answers with a partner.

c 👥👥 Form groups of four students. Each group chooses one topic. You can use a dictionary.

1 Different sorts of transport   2 Clothes for women   3 Clothes for men
4 How people carry things   5 Animals

Then watch the first film and make notes about your topic. Note as many things as you can. Compare your ideas in your group, then report back to the class. Workbook 1 → p. 38

➡️ Ich kann Texte und Gespräche über Indien verfolgen. ✓

2.12

A bit of history

1 Five thousand years ago …

there were only three places in the world where people lived in cities – in Egypt, in Mesopotamia and in north-west India. Some of the cities in India had a population of over 30,000 people. However, life in these cities came to an end between 1700 and 1900 BCE. Why? Many experts think that the weather
5 became hotter and drier and people died when the rivers became dry.

2 From the 4th to the 6th century …

there was peace in India and people made great progress in maths, science and technology. Indian scientists found that the earth is round and they invented the zero. The
10 game of chess was invented too.

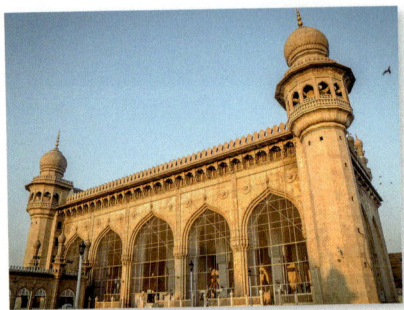

3 In the 16th century …

India's industries produced 25% of all the world's man-made products. Modern farms produced enough food for everybody and big ships brought Indian products to other countries. India was one of the richest countries in the world and had
15 some of the world's most beautiful buildings, like the Taj Mahal or the Mecca Masjid.

4 From the 1750s …

India became a British colony. Products from India now made
20 Britain one of the richest countries in the world, but many Indians lived in extreme poverty. Experts say that 60 million people died of hunger during the time that India was a British colony. Indians wanted their country to be free again. One of the leaders in the campaign for independence was Mahatma
25 Gandhi.

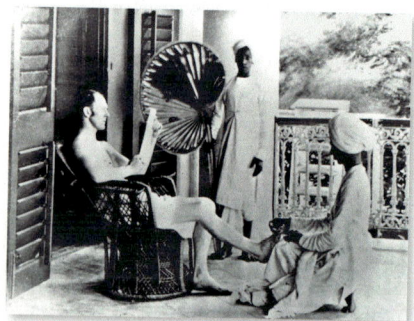

5 On 15th August 1947 …

India became free from the British. However, after 200 years as a British colony, there were problems between Hindus and Muslims which ended in terrible violence. About one million
30 people were killed and there were more than 15 million refugees. In the end, a part of the country in the west became Pakistan and a part in the east later became Bangladesh. At independence, India was one of the poorest countries in the world. It now has the fourth biggest economy in the world.

1 A quick look at Indian history

a Read the text on page 60. Match titles A–G with parts 1–5 in the text.
You won't need two titles.

- **A** Independence
- **B** Nowhere richer
- **C** Hard times
- **D** Important new ideas
- **E** Trouble in the north
- **F** Early city life
- **G** A rich queen

b Read the text again and give an example of …
1 what was special in north-west India five thousand years ago.
2 progress in India in the 4th to 6th centuries.
3 how India became so rich in the 16th century.
4 how life was unfair for many Indians while India was a British colony.
5 a problem in India in 1947.

2.13

2 India's most famous son

a Listen to a podcast about Mahatma Gandhi.
What's the right order of A–F?

- **A** Campaign against the unfair salt tax laws
- **B** Indian independence
- **C** Work in South Africa
- **D** The end of Gandhi's life
- **E** First visit to England
- **F** Talks in London about independence

b Listen again and write the missing details
in your exercise book.

Mahatma Gandhi

Early life
Gandhi was born in the year … (1).
He worked as a lawyer in … (2).
He came back to India in … (3).

Campaign against the British
Back in India, he told people to stop buying British … (4).
He believed that protests against the British shouldn't
use … (5). Gandhi was killed in … (6).

Today
Many Indians think of Gandhi as their country's … (7).
Gandhi's face is on most Indian… (8).

Skills file 6 → p. 122

Workbook 2–3 → p. 39

 Ich kann Details in einem Podcast verstehen. ✔

A land of big differences

On Independence Day, 15th August, an Indian TV programme asked people: "What's most important to you about India?" Here are some answers.

2.14

I love the beauty of our countryside – our rivers, our beaches and our mountains. I think it's amazing that we have rhinos and elephants, and
5 did you know that we're the only country that has lions and tigers? I think it's great that we have sent a spacecraft to the moon, that we make more films than any other country and that our new airports are some of the most modern in the world.
Mandeep

Indian civilization is one of the oldest in the world. How cool is that? 10
And our earliest languages have given birth to many European languages. India invented the zero symbol, the game of chess, yoga, shampoo – and probably henna too. And I'm not the only person who believes that the Taj Mahal is the most beautiful building in the world. 15
Imran

What's important to me is that we have so many different traditions, languages, cultures and lifestyles. Hinduism and Buddhism began here, but we also have lots of Christians, Sikhs and the world's third biggest population of Muslims. That's why
20 we have so many great festivals. We also have something that brings us all together, and that's cricket. As my mum always says: "We have many religions – but we all love cricket".
Geeta

It's important to me that we're a democracy – the biggest democracy in the world. And our newspapers and online media are allowed to say 25
what they want. That's why I love living in this country. But of course we have more to do. There's still much too much poverty in India and we must do more to save the environment.
Farida

30 What do I love about India? It's our food, man! It's awesome! Our fruit, vegetables and spices are colourful and tasty, and we have lots of different cooking traditions from the north to the south and from the east to the west. Our tradition of vegetarian and vegan meals is hundreds of years old, and now the rest of the world is taking our idea!
35 I live in Britain now – but when I think of food, I wish I were in India!
Karan

1 WORDS

a ⊙ Find the words for the following pictures:

b Copy and complete the table with words from the texts.

noun	adjective
beauty	
Europe	
difference	
colour	
	poor
	spicy

2 Questions on the texts

a Who talks about the following topics?

> animals • food • history • woods/fields/rivers •
> politics • problems • religion • sport • technology • things that began in India

b Which sentences in the texts tell you the same as statements 1–6 below?
1 India is the country that produces most films.
2 English, German and other languages in Europe have their origins in old Indian languages.
3 India is the country where two great religions were born.
4 We celebrate in different ways and on different days.
5 Our country still has challenges.
6 Many of us have been making meals without meat for a very long time.

🎧 2.15 3 👥 Misunderstandings

Listen to a podcast with tips for visitors to India.
Partner A Look at picture A and tell your partner about the tourist's misunderstanding.
Partner B Do the same for picture B.

She has a bindi, so she must be married.

I'll give you 4000 rupees for it.

The tourist thinks that … because she has a … | The tourist wants to … and tries to …
But this is a misunderstanding because … | But this is a misunderstanding because …

More practice 2 → p. 92

Workbook 4–5 → pp. 40–41

➔ Ich kann mich in Begegnungssituationen angemessen verhalten. ✓

India and climate change

India's future is looking better for the 65% of Indians who are under 35. They have more and better schools and hospitals than their parents had. 690 million people in India use the internet. India's economy is growing fast and before 2030 it will be bigger than the USA's. And the country is using new technologies. Some rich farmers, for example, now use drones to get information about where their fields are too dry or too wet.

But there are problems. One of the big problems in India is poverty. Although the number of people in extreme poverty is falling by about 44 people every minute, there are still large numbers of poor people in India.

Another big problem is climate change. If average temperatures rise, the heatwaves that killed thousands of people in 2015 will happen more often. India has a very long coast and many of its people live near the sea. They could be in danger if sea levels rise as a result of climate change.

But maybe the greatest danger of all is drought. Many cities have too little water. In June 2019, for example, the city of Chennai (population: over nine million) had no more clean water. Many thousands of people had to buy water in bottles or use dirty water. Schools, farms and factories closed. People were unemployed and the number of health problems grew.

Another problem is pollution. India has 21 of the world's 30 cities with the worst air pollution. The government decided in 2019 that all motorbikes, mopeds, etc. will have to be electric by 2026 and at least 30% of cars by 2030. This is progress – but will it come too late?

Carbon dioxide
Climate change is caused by greenhouse gases like carbon dioxide. India produces the most carbon dioxide after China and the USA.

Total production of carbon dioxide in billion tonnes per year

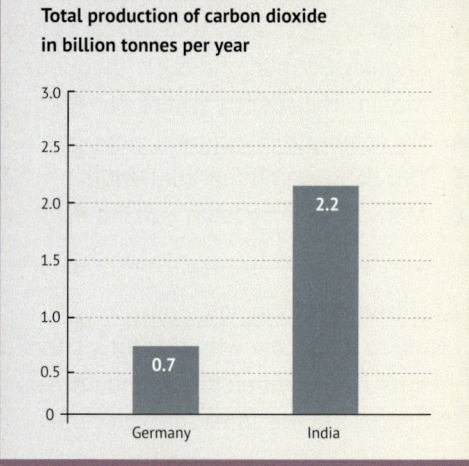

Germany 0.7
India 2.2

Production of carbon dioxide in tonnes per person per year

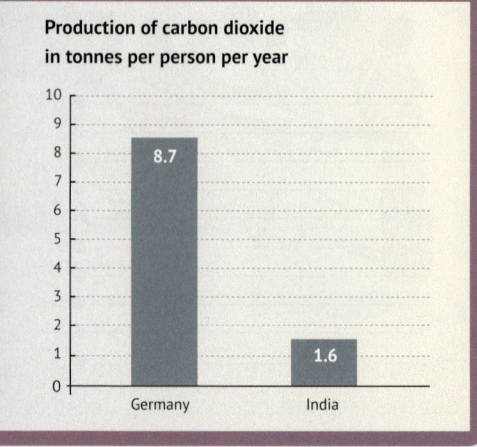

Germany 8.7
India 1.6

IEA Fuel Combustion 2019 Highlights

1 **India and climate change**

Read the text. In which lines do you get the following information?

1 Most people in India are under forty years old.
2 India's factories are producing more each year.
3 Today there's less poverty in India than some years ago.
4 Perhaps the most serious problem is that there isn't enough rain.
5 People in many big towns don't have enough to drink.

More practice 3 → p. 92

2 **Carbon dioxide and India**

Do people in India produce more carbon dioxide than people in Germany?

Look at the two bar charts on page 64 and make notes. The answer isn't just "yes" or "no"!

👥 **Partner check** Did you both give the same answers?

2.16

3 🔵 **Climate change in the world**

a A student is giving a short talk about problems in our environment. Listen and match topics 1–4 in the talk with pictures A–F.
You won't need two pictures.

b Listen again. Write the missing information (one or two words) at the end of each sentence 1–6.

1 If the world gets 1.5°C warmer, 20% or more of animals … …
2 And if the world gets warmer, there will be more forest …
3 Ice melts as temperatures … …
4 Millions of people need the water in rivers from the Himalayas for their … …
5 The countries which are most in danger are the small island countries in the … …
6 In the Philippines people found 40 kilos of plastic bags inside a dead …

More practice 4 → p. 93

4 **PLACEMAT** 👥 **What can you do?**

What other things could you do to protect the environment? Work in groups of four.
Draw a placemat like this on a big piece of paper.
Everybody thinks about three things and writes them in one part of the placemat.
Then agree on the three best ideas that you will try to do in the next month and write them in the middle of the placemat.
Tell the class.

use less
streaming services

buy less
new clothes

Charge mobile
with solar energy

turn down
the heating

…
…

…
…

More practice 5 → p. 93   Wordbank 8 → p. 146   Wordbank 9 → p. 147   Workbook 6 → p. 41

→ Ich kann über Umweltschutz sprechen. ✓

1 **Before you read**

This story is told by Aditi. Look at the pictures and skim the text.
Who do you think she works for?

Skills file 3 → p. 115

A mission to the moon

2.17

6th September 2019 – 15 minutes to moon landing …

Staff members working at a control room for the landing of Chandrayaan-2, BANGALORE,
6th September, 2019

The atmosphere here in the Satish Dhawan
Space Centre is amazing. We are all watching
pictures of the *Vikram* space module on our
5 screens. Will the mission be successful? We're so
excited. The next few minutes will decide …

The launch of our *Chandrayaan-2* spacecraft on
22nd July 2019 went perfectly. The spacecraft
went to the moon and then began to go around
10 it. When it was just 35 kilometres from the
moon, the smaller *Vikram* space module left the
Chandrayaan-2. The module is the part that
will land on the moon – in just 15 minutes from
now!
15 We have come far since the launch of India's first
rocket in 1961. Back then our scientists moved

around the space centre on bikes and even
carried parts of the rocket on their bikes! But the
launch in 1961 was a success. Will *Vikram* be as
successful today? 20

10 minutes to moon landing …

2.18

We're all nervous. Nobody is talking. The next few
minutes will be the most difficult in the whole
mission.

I started working here when I left university 25
in 1980 and I felt I was very proud. We were
working on a new communications satellite
called APPLE. For one of our tests, we put APPLE
on a cart and did our tests in the middle of
a field! 30

People laughed when they saw pictures of a satellite on a cart.

But nobody is laughing at us today. In 2008 we became the fourth nation in the world that sent a successful mission to the moon. And our Indian mission discovered that there is water on the moon. That was really important.

5 minutes to moon landing ...
2.19

We are all so nervous that everybody has stopped talking.

We have all worked for years to make this mission possible. We are all proud of our country's space programme. We know, of course, that some people ask why India spends money on a space programme when millions of Indians don't have enough to eat or clean water to drink.

But with satellites our country will have better communications, and we will understand our weather better. Then we'll be able to help the poorest people in our country because we'll know about floods and storms in advance and will be able to warn people.

And our space missions are cheap. For example, our spacecraft which travelled to Mars in 2014 only cost about 74 million US dollars, less than a third of just one of the *Star Wars* films.

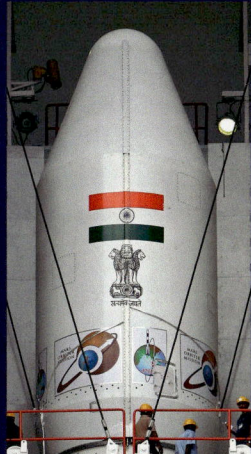

India's PSLV-C25, carrying the Mars orbiter, at Satish Dhawan Space Centre in Sriharikota.

What's more, our missions have carried nearly 200 satellites for 20 other countries, like Germany, Canada and the UK. And we earn money that way.

3 minutes to moon landing ...
2.20

Vikram is now just three kilometres from the moon, and ... Oh no! Suddenly, the screens go blank. We look at each other in horror. Then we look back at the empty screens. But the space module isn't there any more. We have lost contact. And it was just 2.1 kilometres from landing. We feel terrible, tired, and sad. My friend Pamir is crying. Aisha is holding her head in her hands. We know that the whole country has been watching this project, and everybody will be disappointed.

7th September 2019 ...
2.21

The next day our bosses, Ms Muthaya Vanitha and Ms Ritu Karidhal, talk to us. All is not lost, they tell us. Many parts of the project were successful.

We can learn from what went right and from what went wrong. So we feel more confident again. We will not lose hope. We'll go back to our offices and work on India's next big space project – to send the first Indian astronauts into space!

2 The *Chandrayaan-2* mission – in theory

This brochure from **before** the launch explained the *Chandrayaan-2* mission.
Write a sentence for each picture. Use the *will*-future.

 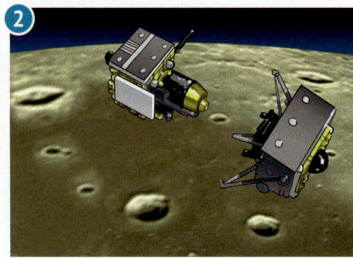 

What will happen?   What will happen?   What will happen?
When? From where?   Where?   When?

1 The Chandrayaan-2 spacecraft will ... from the ... on ...

3 Aditi's story

Answer the questions.

1 How were the scientists at the space centre following the *Chandrayaan-2* spacecraft?
2 What happened when the *Chandrayaan-2* spacecraft was 35 km from the moon?
3 Where did the Indian space scientists test the APPLE satellite?
4 How can satellites help poor people in India?
5 How does the Indian space mission earn money?
6 The 2019 Indian mission to the moon was and wasn't a success. Can you explain?

4 Aditi's feelings

How did Aditi feel ...

1 15 minutes before the moon landing?
2 10 minutes before the moon landing?
3 when she started work in 1980?
4 after the space centre lost contact with the *Vikram* space module?
5 after Ms Vanitha and Ms Karidhal spoke to the workers at the space centre?

5 When things happened

Match each date with a correct sentence.

1961	1980	2008	2014	22nd July 2019	6th September 2019	7th September 2019

1 India sent a spacecraft to Mars.
2 India sent its first successful mission to the moon.
3 India saw the launch of its first rocket.
4 Aditi's bosses talked about plans to send an Indian astronaut into space.
5 The perfect launch of the *Chandrayaan-2* spacecraft.
6 Aditi began working at the Satish Dhawan Space Centre.
7 The Satish Dhawan Space Centre lost contact with the *Vikram* module.

Workbook 7–8 → p. 42

1 **A questionnaire about things that you have done for the environment**

a ⊙ Read the questions. Pick the four questions that you think are most important. Write your four questions on a piece of paper.

Have you ever	walked or cycled to school?
	bought clothes from a second-hand shop?
	joined a local protest against climate change?
	given money to an environmental organization?
	planted a tree?
	worn a pullover instead of turning up the heating?
	said "no" to vegetables that are sold in plastic?

b Read the FOCUS-box. Complete the two verbs in the *present perfect*.

> ### FOCUS
>
> ***Present perfect***
> Mit dem *present perfect* sagst du, dass du etwas gerade, schon, schon einmal oder noch nie gemacht hast. Die Auswirkungen dauern noch an.
>
> Das Verb besteht aus zwei Teilen:
>
> | regelmäßige Verben: | *have / has* + Verb + *-ed* | z.B. *walk* → *I have ...* |
> | --- | --- | --- |
> | unregelmäßige Verben: | *have / has* + besondere Verbform | z.B. *give* → *I have ...* |

Language file 5 → p. 130

c 👥 **WALK AROUND**

Take your paper with your four questions from part **a**. Ask as many students as you can and note the answers. Answer your partners' questions.

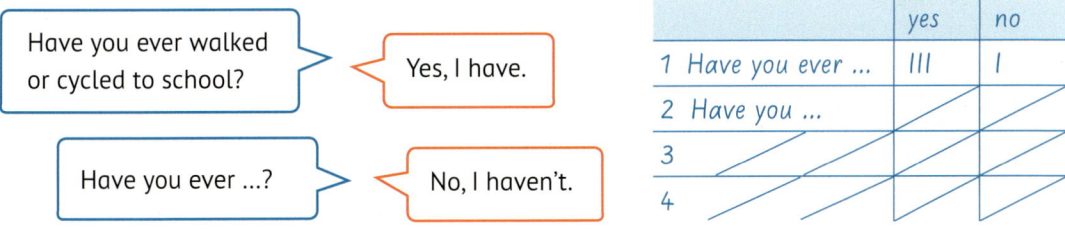

	yes	no
1 Have you ever ...	III	I
2 Have you ...		
3		
4		

d Now write a report.
I asked ten students about what they have done for the environment.
Six students have ...
No student has ...

2 ● **Your school** More help → p. 93

Discuss in class. What has your school already done for the environment? And what could it still do? Use your own ideas.
We have always sorted the rubbish / ...
We have begun to sell organic food / ...
But we could also ...

Workbook 9–10 → p. 43

3 **Air pollution in Delhi**

a Read the FOCUS-box.

> ### FOCUS
>
> ***Simple past und present perfect***
>
> Mit dem *present perfect* sagst du, dass du etwas schon einmal, manchmal, oft, oder noch nie gemacht hast. Signalwörter: *ever*, *never*, *often*, *up to now*, *since*, *for*.
>
> Mit dem *simple past* sagst du, was zu einem bestimmten Zeitpunkt in der Vergangenheit passiert ist. Die Handlung ist vorbei. Signalwörter: bestimmter Tag oder Datum, *yesterday*, *last week*, *a year ago*.

Language file 3 → p. 128   Language file 5 → p. 130

b Now read sentences 1–6.
Which are in the *present perfect*? Which are in the *simple past*? Look at the signal words.

1 Fifty years ago there were fewer people in Delhi and far fewer cars.
2 But Delhi has now had a problem with air pollution for at least 30 years.
3 In November 2017 the air was so bad that the city closed all its schools.
4 Some drivers couldn't see and crashed into the cars in front of them.
5 Since then the city says it has tried to cut the pollution in the air.
6 But up to now the results have been disappointing.

4 **A TV series that changed the world** Parallel exercise → p. 94
Pick the right tense: *present perfect* or *simple past*.

1 The BBC has shown / showed *Blue Planet II* in Europe, Asia and America in 2017.
2 And more than 80 million people in China have watched / watched *Blue Planet II* since 2017.
3 After watching the film millions of people have talked / talked about the problem of plastic on social media.
4 Since the series people have stopped / stopped using so much plastic.
5 Since 2017 people all over the world have begun / began to protest against plastic knives, spoons and straws.
6 In 2019 David Attenborough, who made the series, has won / won India's prize for peace.

5 👥 **Indian rhinos**
Decide if verbs 1–10 should be in the *present perfect* or *simple past* and find the correct form.

> Before 1905 thousands of rhinos ... (1 live) in India, Pakistan, Bangladesh and Nepal. Then British officers ... (2 begin) to hunt the animals and by 1905 only 75 rhinos ... (3 be) still alive in India and Nepal. But Kaziranga National Park ... (4 open) in 1905 and since then the number of rhinos ... (5 grow). In 2012 for example, the park ... (6 have) about 2700 Indian rhinos. Hunting rhinos ... (7 be) against the law since 1910. But the animals are still in danger. Hunters ... (8 kill) 102 rhinos illegally since 2008. In 2013 they ... (9 shoot) 41 rhinos and ... (10 sell) their horn to make money.

Workbook 11–14 → pp. 44–45

➡ Ich kann sprachliche Regelmäßigkeiten erkennen. ✔

Talking about an accident

2.22

1 **A traffic accident**

You saw an accident and now a police officer is asking you about it. What happened?

Police officer	Did you see the accident?
You	Yes, I did.
Police officer	Can you tell me what happened?
You	Yes. The cyclist was riding along this street. Then a lorry came out of that street over there, but it didn't stop and it knocked over the cyclist.
Police officer	Was the cyclist badly hurt?
You	Well, she got up, but her arm was bleeding, so I called an ambulance.
Police officer	And what happened to the lorry?
You	It drove away. But I wrote down its number. It's GJ 04 VW 7502.
Police officer	Ah, that's useful. Thank you.

2 **WORDS**

a   Match sentences 1–6 with pictures A–F.

1   The driver skidded.
2   I fell off my horse.
3   A car ran into a van.
4   He fell down the stairs.
5   She broke her arm.
6   It crashed into a tree.

b   Work with a partner. Complete the phrases with as many examples as you can.

1   The driver skidded on the oil / on the …
2   I fell off my horse / my … /…
3   A car / A … ran into us.
4   He fell down the stairs /…
5   She broke her arm /…
6   The van crashed into a tree /…

3 **Two accidents**

Partner B Go to page 75.

a   **Partner A** Look at the picture. Phone the police (your partner) and report what the problem is.

b   Your partner phones you (a police officer) about an accident. Find out:
1   What happened?
2   Is there anybody in the car?
3   Are people in danger?

More practice 6 → p. 94   Workbook 15–16 → p. 46

→ Ich kann von einem Unfall berichten. ✔

Life stories

1 Arunima Sinha

a Read the story of Arunima Sinha. Why is she famous in India?

Arunima was born in 1989. She began playing volleyball when she was five years old, and when she was 21, she played for the national team.

On 12 April 2011 she got into the train from Lucknow
5 to Delhi. During the journey some men tried to steal her bag, and when Arunima fought back, the men pushed her out of the train. Arunima fell onto the train track, and another train ran over her left leg.

The doctors had to cut off her leg below the knee, and Arunima had to learn to walk
10 with an artificial leg. But then she had a great idea. She decided to try to climb Mount Everest (8848 metres), the highest mountain in the world!

First Arunima trained on smaller mountains in the Himalayas. Then in 2013 she started climbing Everest. She walked for 52 days and arrived at the top on 21 May 2013. Arunima now works to help poor and disabled children to do more sport. She is a role
15 model for children who had a difficult start in life and still want to do great things.

b A life story can't tell you everything about a person. Does Arunima's life story tell you …

1 when she was born?
2 where she went to school?
3 about her family?
4 how tall she is?
5 about a terrible day in her life?

6 about Arunima's great plan?
7 what she did to train for her plan?
8 where she lives today?
9 what her work is today?
10 how people think of her?

More practice 7 → p. 94

2 An interview More help → p. 94

a Imagine you have the chance to interview Arunima. Write at least six questions for your interview. Example: *What sport did you do when you were young?*

b 👥 Now work with a partner. You are the interviewer, your partner plays Arunima.

You   What sport did you do when you were young?
Partner I played volleyball. I loved it!
You   And how …?

c Swap roles.   Workbook 17 → p. 47

Amar and you

1 👥 **Before you watch**

Imagine that a film-maker wants to make a 10-minute film about your daily routine. What do you think he or she will want to film? Work in a small group and make a list. Think of the following things: home, family, school, free time activities, friends, …

2 **VIEWING** **A film about Amar's day**

a Watch the film about an Indian boy called Amar. Make notes:

1 Does the film include all the points on your list in exercise 1?

2 What points on your list are missing in the film?

3 What parts of Amar's day **were not** in your list?

👥 Then compare your notes in your group.

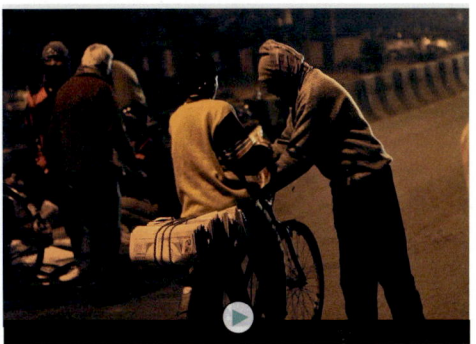

b Now choose one topic:

> home • job • school • town

Watch the film again and think about …

– your topic: What's different in Amar's life?

– your reaction: Were you surprised or shocked by what you saw?

👥 Then tell your group.

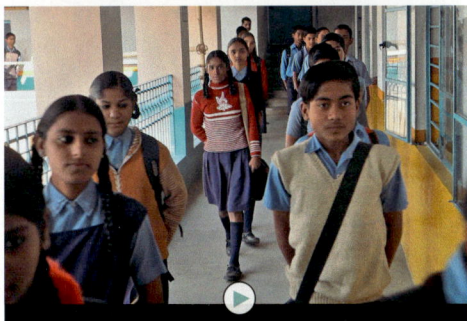

> Amar lives in a very small house. His brothers and sisters sleep on the floor. I was shocked.

> Amar cleans his shoes before he goes to school – so he must think school is very important. I was surprised.

3 **AND YOU?** **A project after your exams**

Make a film about your day for Amar and his classmates in India.

a Make a plan. Think of possible places and activities.

1 My bedroom – when I get up – our bathroom

2 breakfast – …

b Decide what you will say in the film. What will you need to explain?

I'll explain how I pay for the bus, what "Knödel" are, …

c Will you add music? If so, use music that is free of copyright.

d 👥 Work with a partner who can film you and make your film. Good luck!

Wordbank 10 → p.148   Workbook → p. 48

➡ Ich kann über meinen Alltag berichten. ✔

3 👥 On the beach

Partner B

Unit 1 | p.12

a Partner A will describe a scene.
Listen and take notes. Then answer your partner's question.

b Now look at the picture below.
Think about what you see, what's happening, how the people feel, etc.
Then describe the scene to **Partner A**.
When you have finished, ask your partner: Can you tell me four things
that are different in your picture and in my picture?

I can see There is There are	...	in the foreground. in the background. in the middle. next to... in front of ... behind ... on the right. on the left. between the ... and the ...

One person One woman	is isn't	sitting ... reading a ... standing in ...
The people The children	are aren't	sleeping ... wearing shorts ... enjoying ... playing ...

3 👥 **Two accidents**   Unit 4 | p.71

Partner B

a You're a police officer. Your partner phones you about a problem.
Find out:

1 What happened?
2 Do you need an ambulance?
3 Where are the animals now?

b Look at the picture. Then phone your partner (a police officer).
Tell him/her what happened.

Hello? Is that the police?
There's a problem here. ...

Lösung *More practice 2*   → S. 82

1 The first kiwi fruit came from China.
2 New Zealand has about 15,000 earthquakes a year.
3 New Zealand has lots of cows – more cows than people.
4 The first commercial bungee jump took place in 1988.
5 The town of Ushuaia in Argentina is the nearest town to Antarctica.
6 Women in New Zealand got the right to vote in 1893. In Germany
women only got the right to vote 25 years later in 1918.

DIFF BANK

Intro

1.01 | **More practice 1** | **Languages in India, South Africa, Australia and New Zealand** → Intro | p.8

Read the sentences below. Then listen again and pick **A** or **B**.

1 **A** India has two languages, Hindi and English.
   B India has lots of different languages.

2 **A** Hindi is the most important language in government, business and the media.
   B English is the most important language in government, business and the media.

3 **A** South Africa has four official languages.
   B South Africa has eleven official languages.

4 **A** The biggest language group in South Africa are the people who speak Zulu.
   B The biggest language group in South Africa are the people who speak Afrikaans.

5 **A** Australians have their own special accent.
   B Australian English is like American English.

6 **A** Many indigenous Australians speak their own languages.
   B Nobody speaks indigenous Australian languages any more.

7 **A** Most Māori people can't speak English.
   B All Māori people can speak English.

8 **A** The Māori language and New Zealand sign language are both official languages.
   B New Zealand sign language is an official language, but the Māori language isn't.

Unit 1

More practice 2 **Australia and Germany** → Unit 1 | p.11

a **Think** Think and make notes: How is Australia different from Germany?
Here are some ideas: size, climate, animals, cities, coast, …

 b Now watch the film again and take notes.
Pair 👥 Then work with a partner. You can complete the following sentences or use your own ideas.

> In Australia there are deserts. There are many parts where nobody lives.
> Many parts have no woods. The coast is very long.
> But in Germany there are … / there aren't any … / we don't have many …
> In Australia you drive on the … In Germany …
> In Australia you can go diving in the Great Barrier Reef and you can drive in the desert.
> You can work on a sheep farm. In Germany …
> In Germany winter is from December to … In Australia …

c **Share** Now compare your ideas from **a** and **b** in class.

More practice 3 👥 **Talk about the pictures** → Unit 1 | p.11

Pick a photo on page 10 or page 11. Describe what you can see to your partner.
Say as much as you can.

In the foreground In the background In the middle Behind the ... In front of the ... On the right On the left	there is	nobody. a sign. a diver. ...
	there are	some people. ...

		very big.
It's	very dry. very hot. amazing because ... a bit scary because ...

The people	are	swimming under water. celebrating Christmas. exploring the ...
The girl The diver	is	relaxing on the beach. ...

I'd like to I wouldn't like to	go to this place live here do this activity ...	because ...

1.03

More practice 4 🔘 **On the beach** → Unit 1 | p.12

Listen again to the three dialogues.
Pick the right options below.

Dialogue 1
1 The teenagers are/aren't between the lifeguard's flags.
2 The sea looks / doesn't look dangerous.
3 The teenagers know / don't know the beaches very well.

Dialogue 2
1 The boy has hurt / hasn't hurt his foot.
2 The boy has cut / hasn't cut his foot.
3 The problem was/wasn't a jellyfish.

Dialogue 3
1 The girl looks / doesn't look well.
2 Her temperature is/isn't high.
3 She wore / didn't wear a hat on the beach.

More practice 5 **What's the problem?**　　　　　　　　→ Unit 1 | p.13

a　Read what the four young Australians say.

> **Erin:** I was hiking in the outback and I was very hot and tired. So I found some shade under a tree and I sat down on some rocks. Then I felt a terrible pain in my hand. It hurt so much! And then I saw it. A long, thin black thing, slithering along the ground. It looked scary.

> **Danny:** We left the highway. It was getting dark and we wanted a place to camp. We drove along a track. Then there was a terrible noise and the car stopped. Something was wrong. We didn't know what to do and it was still hot …

> **Rob:** I love the sun … and I never have any problems when it's hot, really. Well, I was sitting in the garden, reading, and I guess I fell asleep. When I woke up, I felt quite funny – a bit sick. I didn't know what was wrong.

> **Laura:** We were walking through the outback. One track went left and another one went right. I checked on my phone and decided to go right. But after a little time I didn't know where we were. My phone didn't work and there were no other people around.

b　Now match each person with ONE of the problems A–H.

A　… got lost in the outback.
B　… drank too much water.
C　… had a snake bite.
D　… didn't have a mobile phone.
E　… was too long in the sun.
F　… had a problem with the car.
G　… didn't get to a doctor.
H　… had a jellyfish sting.

→ Unit 1 | p.14

More practice 6 **Indigenous Australians**

Pick the correct answer. Then check on p.14.

1 The indigenous Australians came to Australia …
- **A** after the Europeans.
- **B** at the same time as the Europeans.
- **C** just before the Europeans.
- **D** a long time before the Europeans.

2 Didgeridoos are …
- **A** things to eat.
- **B** musical instruments.
- **C** sorts of clothes.
- **D** things that you throw.

3 The indigenous Australians moved to the outback because …
- **A** they wanted to live in hot places.
- **B** that's where they had always lived.
- **C** Europeans took the best land.
- **D** they didn't like the coast.

4 The new diseases brought by the Europeans …
- **A** killed many indigenous Australians.
- **B** made the indigenous Australians healthier.
- **C** soon died out.
- **D** were no problem for the indigenous Australians.

5 Indigenous Australians are …
- **A** a huge part of the Australian population.
- **B** a quite big part of the Australian population.
- **C** about the same in number as Europeans.
- **D** a very small part of the Australian population.

6 The text says that indigenous Australians …
- **A** have lost their culture.
- **B** now have a European culture.
- **C** have their own special culture.
- **D** don't care about culture.

More practice 7 🔵 👥 **The Burdekin Song**

→ Unit 1 | p.15

a Pick one of the two verses from the song. What do you think it means?
Discuss this with your partner. Use a dictionary.

> **C**an you believe how far we've come?
> The journey is long, but it has just begun.
> Eyes wide open, walking into the sun.
> Pride in my people, roll as one.
>
> Remember where you come from, stay on track.
> Look to the future, don't look back.
> Stay positive, stand tall like my pop.
> Burdekin from the bottom all the way to the top.

b What do you think is the message of the song?

- **A** Life in a small town is boring.
- **B** It's great to be Australian.
- **C** Be proud of who you are.
- **D** Things are difficult for young people.

c Now compare your ideas from parts **a** and **b** in class.

More practice 8 **Tell the story** → Unit 1 | p.18

a Write the story. Use the ideas in the boxes.

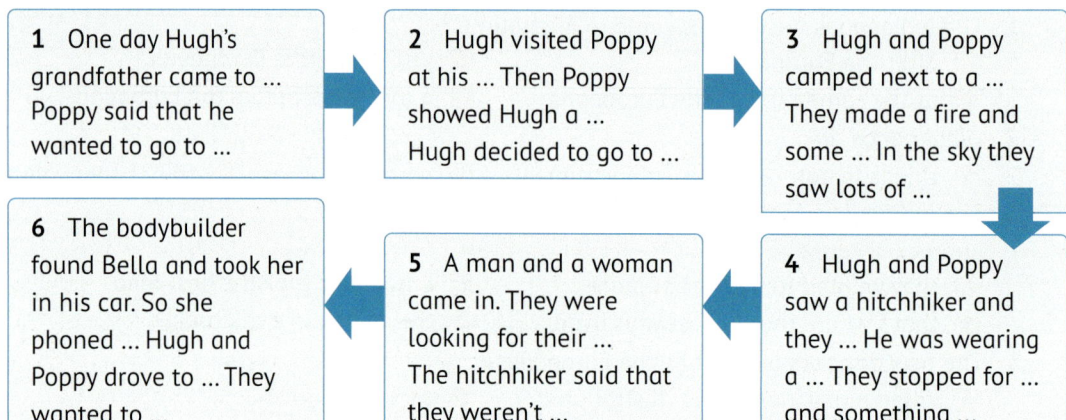

1 One day Hugh's grandfather came to … Poppy said that he wanted to go to …

2 Hugh visited Poppy at his … Then Poppy showed Hugh a … Hugh decided to go to …

3 Hugh and Poppy camped next to a … They made a fire and some … In the sky they saw lots of …

6 The bodybuilder found Bella and took her in his car. So she phoned … Hugh and Poppy drove to … They wanted to …

5 A man and a woman came in. They were looking for their … The hitchhiker said that they weren't …

4 Hugh and Poppy saw a hitchhiker and they … He was wearing a … They stopped for … and something …

b **Partner check** Now compare your text with a partner.

Parallel exercise **7** **An email from Sydney** → Unit 1 | p.21

Read Huong's email to her friend Theo. Seven sentences have ONE missing word.
Write the missing words 1–7. There is an example (0) at the beginning.

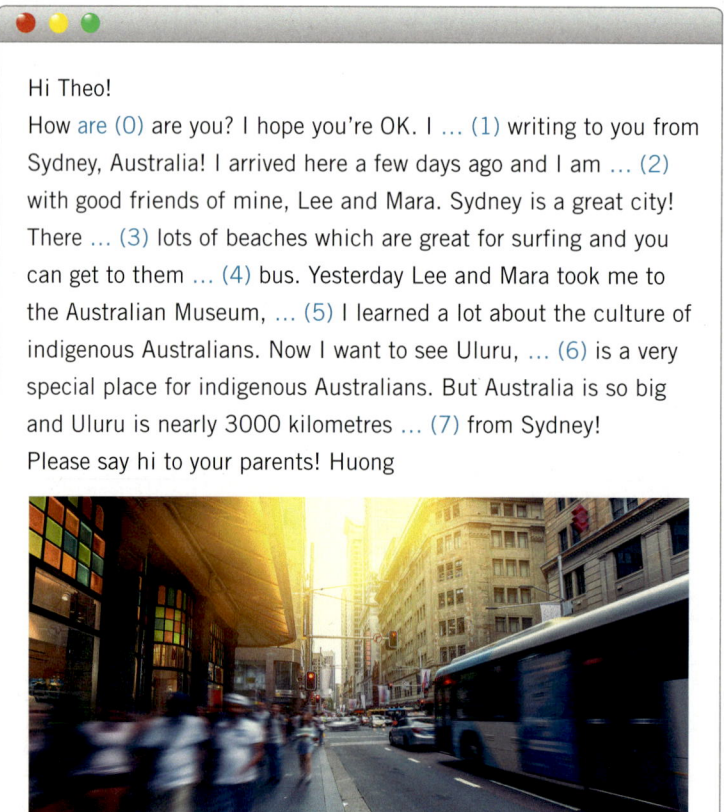

Hi Theo!
How are (0) are you? I hope you're OK. I … (1) writing to you from Sydney, Australia! I arrived here a few days ago and I am … (2) with good friends of mine, Lee and Mara. Sydney is a great city! There … (3) lots of beaches which are great for surfing and you can get to them … (4) bus. Yesterday Lee and Mara took me to the Australian Museum, … (5) I learned a lot about the culture of indigenous Australians. Now I want to see Uluru, … (6) is a very special place for indigenous Australians. But Australia is so big and Uluru is nearly 3000 kilometres … (7) from Sydney!
Please say hi to your parents! Huong

More practice 9 **WORDS** **At the doctor's**

a ● 👥 Work with a partner. Write the sentences. Write the words correctly.

1 I have a sore HOTART.
2 I think I have the LUF.
3 I have a EHCADAEH.
4 I feel DRETI.

5 My back THURS.
6 I have a snake TEBI.
7 I have a jellyfish GNIST.
8 I have a METEPARTERU.

b Find the sentences that go together. Match the sentences 1–6 with sentences A–F.

1 You should have a rest.
2 You should sleep more.
3 Put on some suncream.
4 Stay in the shade.
5 Take painkillers.
6 Put a wet towel over your face.

A Don't stand or sit in the sun.
B This is good for your skin if you have sunburn.
C Don't do too much work.
D Do this if it hurts a lot.
E This will keep your head cool.
F Stay in bed.

c 👥 Now work with a partner.
Copy and complete the wordweb. **Wordbank 2** → p.141

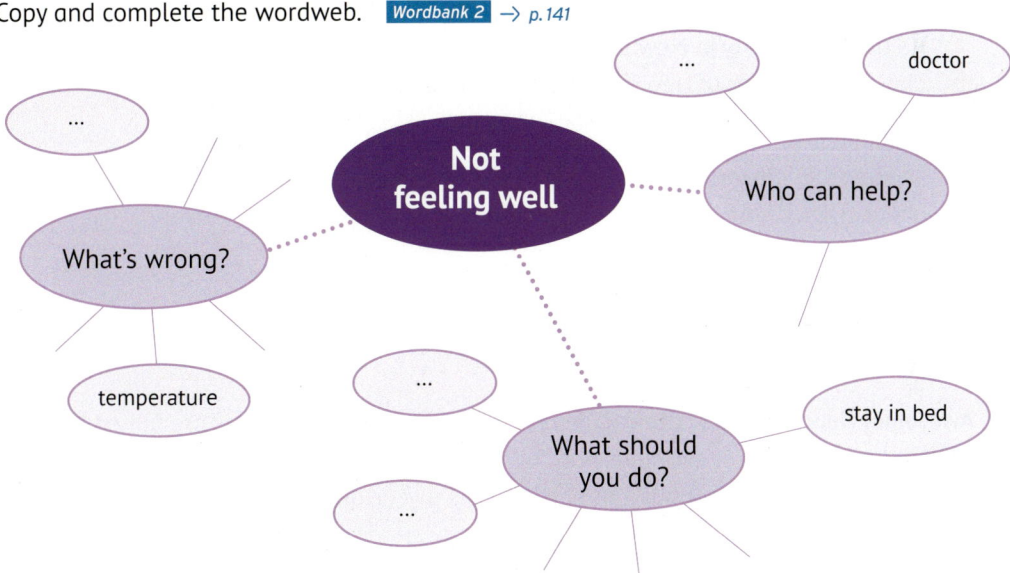

More practice 10 **Words in the text**

The following words have different meanings. Look at the text on page 25.
Which are the meanings of these words in the text?

full *(line 1)*	**state** *(line 2)*	**take** *(line 4)*	**plate** *(line 5)*
A voll, gefüllt *(Adj)*	A Zustand *(N)*	A bringen *(V)*	A Teller *(N)*
B satt *(Adj)*	B Staat, Land *(N)*	B nehmen, mitnehmen *(V)*	B Platte *(N)*
C ausverkauft *(Adj)*	C Bundesstaat *(N)*	C dauern *(Verb)*	C Schild,
D vollständig, voll gültig *(Adj)*	D behaupten *(V)*	D machen, ablegen (Prüfung) *(V)*	Plakette, *(N)*
			D Bildtafel *(N)*

DIFF BANK

Unit 2

1.16

More practice 1 **A first look at New Zealand** → Unit 2 | p.26

Read the options below.
Then listen again to Hunter and Lina and pick the right option Ⓐ – Ⓓ .

1 National parks cover ....
   Ⓐ one tenth of New Zealand.   Ⓑ one quarter of New Zealand.
   Ⓒ one third of New Zealand.   Ⓓ half of New Zealand.

2 The Māori are ...
   Ⓐ 6.5% of the population of New Zealand.
   Ⓑ 16.5% of the population of New Zealand.
   Ⓒ 26.5% of the population of New Zealand.
   Ⓓ 60.5% of the population of New Zealand.

3 Wellington is the capital of New Zealand because ...
   Ⓐ it's not too far from most parts of the country.
   Ⓑ it has the biggest airport.
   Ⓒ it's the biggest city in New Zealand.
   Ⓓ about one quarter of New Zealanders live there.

4 New Zealand is ...
   Ⓐ smaller than Bavaria.   Ⓑ about the same size as Bavaria.
   Ⓒ about twice as big as Bavaria.   Ⓓ about four times as big as Bavaria.

More practice 2 **Amazing New Zealand** → Unit 2 | p.27

a 👥 Read the fun facts. Then decide with a partner:
Which fact in each section is NOT true?

1 **Awesome!** New Zealand's countryside is so amazing that lots of films are filmed here –
   The Lord of the Rings, for example. And the first kiwi fruit came from New Zealand.
2 **Scary!** New Zealand has about 150 earthquakes a year, and people can feel about one
   hundred of them.
3 **Can you believe it?** New Zealand has no cows, but it has more sheep than people,
   a bird that can't fly (the kiwi) and an animal with three eyes (the tuatara).
4 **Action!** New Zealand is great for action sports like rafting, canyoning and bungee jumping.
   The world's first commercial bungee jump took place in New Zealand in 1888, when
   people paid 75 dollars to jump 43 metres off the Kawarau Bridge in Queenstown.
5 **Extreme!** Wellington is the most southern capital city in the world and Invercargill is
   the nearest town to Antarctica.
6 **Wow!** New Zealand was one of the first countries in the world to allow all adults, men
   and women, black and white, to vote in national elections – one year before Germany.

b Discuss your answers in class. Then check the correct facts on p.75.
Did most of the class guess right?

→ Unit 2 | p.28

More help **1b** 👥 **Lina's photos**

Choose one of Lina's pictures: Describe it to your partner. What can you see?
Are there any people? What are they doing? How are they feeling?

This is a picture of	a young woman who is … at a city. a couple with … a game of … a … a high …
In the foreground / background In the middle / Behind the … / In front of the … On the right / On the left	there is … there are … I can see …

The woman The person The men The couple The bird	is are	wearing … playing … sitting … standing … looking at …	I think	the woman is feeling relaxed the couple is … the players are feeling … the person jumping from the tower is …	because …
	has have	tattoos on …			

→ Unit 2 | p.29

More practice 3 **Here and there** **New Zealand and Germany**

a Copy the table with the information about New Zealand.
Then find the information for Germany on the internet.

	New Zealand	Germany
Size	268,021 km²	… km²
Population	5 million	… million
Population per km²	18 people per km²	… people per km²
Official languages	English, Māori, sign language	…
Popular sports	football, rugby, cricket	…
Head of state	UK King or Queen	…
Highest mountain	Mount Cook (3724 m)	…
Longest river	Waikato River (425 km)	…
Side of the road on which you drive	left	…

b Look at the information about New Zealand and Germany.
What information do you find the most surprising?

c Now write four sentences and compare New Zealand and Germany.
Example: *New Zealand has fewer people than Germany.*

More practice 4 **Write the story**   → Unit 2 | p.34

Write a sentence for each picture in exercise 2 on page 34.

D It's Alison's first day in ... and ...
B The students are inviting Alison ..., but Alison is saying ...
A Mrs Khan is giving Sameena ... and Sameena is taking ...
E Alison is opening ... and is ...
F Alison's mother is ...
C Alison is telling Sameena about ... and Sameena ...

More practice 5 **Questions about the story**   → Unit 2 | p.34

Read questions 1–6. Pick the right answers from the box.
Three questions can have more than one answer.

1 Is Sameena's class a good example of inclusion? Why (not)?
2 Why does Sameena take Alison's art folder?
3 What are the problems in Alison's family?
4 Why doesn't she talk to the kids about these problems?
5 How does Alison feel when she sees Sameena at her door?
6 How do you think Sameena feels when she listens to Alison?

A Her mother has bad depression and when her father lost his job they had to sell their house.

B She understands why Alison couldn't say "yes" when the kids invited her.

C Yes, because it is multicultural and includes students with disabilities.

D She knows that she was wrong to think that Alison wanted to be above the other kids – and she maybe feels bad about it.

E She's too ashamed.

F In many ways yes, but the class doesn't understand the reactions of a student who has problems.

G She doesn't really know how to react because she has mixed feelings. She knows that her flat is very messy and her mum is maybe angry because Alison has just shouted at her.

H Because she wants to find out more about her.

I Her father doesn't earn much in his new job.

More practice 6   **Your plans for the weekend**   → Unit 2 | p.35

What are your plans for next weekend? Copy and complete the sentences.
You'll need to put the verb in the right tense and add some extra words.

If the weather is nice,
I / ride / bike

But if the weather is bad,
I / stay / home

If I want to go out,
I / go / cinema

If I want to meet friends,
I / meet / them / in the park

If I'm alone at home,
I / play / new game

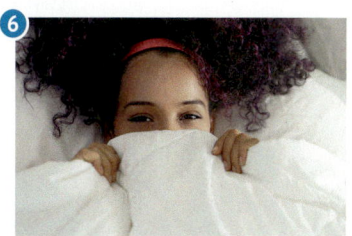

But if I'm really tired,
I / go / bed / early

More practice 7   **First day at work**   → Unit 2 | p.37

a   How are these teenagers going to prepare for their first day at work?
Write the sentences.

1   Alina and Luisa / have a good breakfast.
2   Ari / ask his neighbours to feed his cat.
3   Katie and Steve / buy some new clothes.
4   Ben / get up early.
5   Fatima and Omar / make sure their bikes are OK.
6   David / go to bed early the night before.

b   Now imagine that it's your first day at work in your
new job tomorrow. How are you going to prepare?
Write three sentences with *going to*.

More practice 8   **WORDS**   How would you describe yourself?   → Unit 2 | p.40

a Look at the adjectives in the wordweb. Then, with a partner, find an adjective for each sentence 1–11. You can check in a dictionary. There are three extra adjectives.

1 They don't get excited about things.
2 What they say is true.
3 They aren't messy.
4 They say "please" and "thank you".
5 They like to work alone.
6 They always arrive on time.

7 They do what they say they will do.
8 They are sure that they can do things well.
9 They are good at planning things.
10 They aren't loud or noisy.
11 They are full of energy.

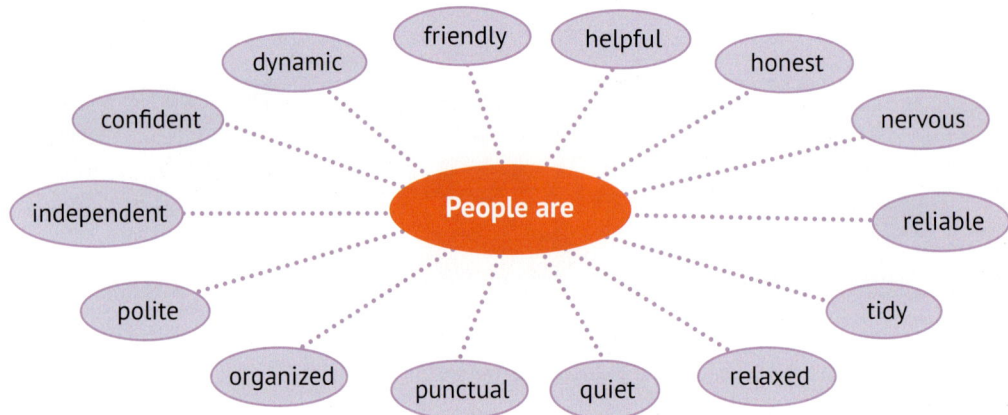

b Lina meets three people in a hostel. Read what they say, then copy the table and make notes about their strengths and weaknesses.

	strengths	weaknesses
Kara		
Kai		
Tom		

Kai: I'm usually confident and I know what I want to do. But I'm sometimes a bit bossy, and I don't react well when people criticize me.

Kara: I'm relaxed, and I react well when people criticize me. On the other hand, I'm not very organized and as a result I'm not very punctual. I know that I have to work at that.

Tom: I'm often a bit nervous in new situations and a bit scared to talk. But that's sometimes a strength because I listen to what other people say. That makes me a good team player.

a Read the CV that Lina wrote when she applied for work on Don and Anna's organic farm.

b Imagine that you also want to work on Don and Anna's organic farm. Write your CV.

Lina Schraml

Home address:	Fedora-Kelling-Str. 23, 93040 Pentling, Germany
Address in New Zealand:	The Friendly Hostel, 28 Cuba Walk, 1023 Auckland
Phone:	+64-295-557-83
Email:	Lina.Schraml@example.net

Personal statement
I am friendly and confident. I have work experience in a shop. I've never worked on farm before, but I'd like to learn new skills.

Key skills
– Punctual   – Good communication skills
– Good in a team   – I speak German and English

Education
I went to primary school and completed five years of secondary school in Regensburg, Germany.

Work experience
During my school holidays I worked in a computer shop in Regensburg.

Interests
I like travelling and meeting people from different cultures and backgrounds. I like games and I play the guitar in a band.

Unit 3

More practice 1 **Word families** → Unit 3 | p.43

Copy the table. Then complete it with adjectives in the text that are in the same word family.

Noun		Adjective in the text	
0 Africa	*Afrika*	African	*afrikanisch*
1 office	*Amt*		*amtlich, offiziell*
2 nation	*Nation*		*national*
3 racism	*Rassismus*		*rassistisch*
4 drama	*Drama*		*dramatisch*
5 danger	*Gefahr*		*gefährlich*
6 fame	*Ruhm, Berühmtheit*		*berühmt*

More practice 2 **WORDS** → Unit 3 | p.45

a Which words go together? The pairs of words are all on pages 44–45.

earn	diving
must	dos
whale	animals
local	park
shark	people
wild	watching
national	money

b Write a sentence with at least two of the pairs of words – three if you can!

c Copy and complete the phrases with *go*.

1 go o**n** a s*afari*
2 go s▩▩▩ d▩▩▩▩
3 go p▩▩▩▩▩▩▩
4 go w▩▩▩ w▩▩▩▩▩
5 go o▩ a t▩▩▩ of a township

d Find the form of the words on pages 44–45.

nation	*national*
amaze	▩
rap	▩
fly	▩
travel	▩
fame	▩
excite	▩

More help **3** AND YOU? **What are the biggest issues for you?** → Unit 3 | p.47

Issues	Good points	Bad points
transport	good buses, trains, trams, metro, … clean and cheap bus drivers friendly	buses too expensive and often late not enough buses, especially at night and at the weekends
sport	swimming pool a great modern football stadium good sports clubs you can do lots of sports an exciting skate park	no swimming pool swimming pool too expensive old football stadium no places to do sports outside boring and dirty skate park
environment	good cycle tracks car sharing clean air no pollution	no cycle tracks roads too dangerous polluted air dirt and pollution
things to do	clubs, cinemas, shopping centres, sports clubs, youth centres, cafes, fast food restaurants, …	no clubs, no youth centre, not enough … only one good … clubs are too expensive no place to meet
jobs	good jobs lots of jobs	not enough jobs more and more factories are closing
flats	cheap flats and houses	flats too expensive not enough flats
internet	good Wi-Fi lots of hotspots	bad Wi-Fi, too slow no hotspots

More practice 3 **A great South African**

→ Unit 3 | p.50

Read the text on pages 48 and 49 again. Pick the right option Ⓐ – Ⓓ.

1 When Mandela first went to school …
   Ⓐ his primary school teacher was called Rolihlahla.
   Ⓑ there was a black government in South Africa.
   Ⓒ he met a boy called Nelson.
   Ⓓ he got a new name.

2 At Sharpeville in March 1960 …
   Ⓐ black people were hurt, but nobody died.
   Ⓑ nearly seventy people were killed.
   Ⓒ 69 black people and 180 white people died.
   Ⓓ black people were killed because they had guns.

3 On Robben Island, Mandela …
   Ⓐ had to stay in his cell all day.
   Ⓑ only saw his wife every six months.
   Ⓒ always had to wear shorts.
   Ⓓ had no contact with the warders.

4 While Mandela was on Robben Island …
   Ⓐ the protests against apartheid died out.
   Ⓑ people in South Africa forgot about him.
   Ⓒ people outside South Africa forgot about him.
   Ⓓ the political situation in South Africa got worse.

5 As president, Mandela …
   Ⓐ tried to be fair to all South Africans.
   Ⓑ was hard on the whites because they had put him in prison.
   Ⓒ was disliked by most white South Africans.
   Ⓓ wanted to pass laws against racist discrimination, but wasn't able to do it.

More practice 4 **Tell the story**

→ Unit 3 | p.50

Write the story in your own words. Write at least two sentences for each picture.

Before 1994 there was …
Under apartheid …

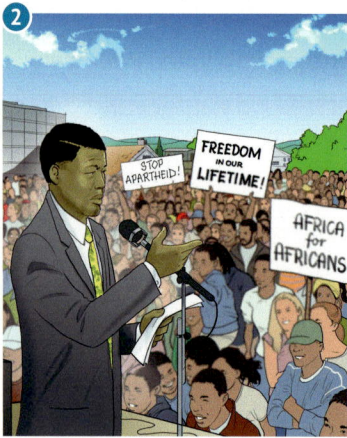

Nelson Mandela was born …
He became … and …

He took part in …
In 1962 the police arrested …

Mandela spent …
Life there …

In South Africa …
But in the 1990s …

In 1994 …
In 2013 …

More practice 5 **Timothy Berners-Lee**

→ Unit 3 | p.52

Read about Timothy Berners-Lee, the inventor of the world wide web.
Put the words of the sentences in the right order.

1 Timothy Berners-Lee / was born / in 1955 / in London
2 in 1984 / began to work / he / with an organization
   called CERN / in Geneva
3 soon / wanted / he / to improve / their communications
4 built / in 1990 / the first web browser / he
5 then / built / he / in August 1991 / the world's first
   website
6 by 2020 / more than four and a half billion people /
   the web / all over the world / were using

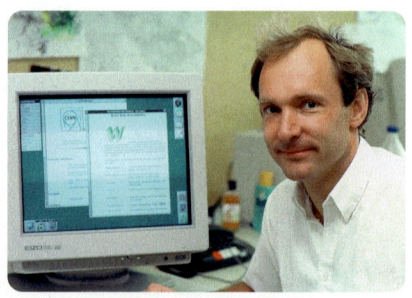

→ Unit 3 | p.53

More practice 6 **English in South Africa**

Read the text. Should the verbs in blue be in the simple present or the present progressive?

> Only 8.1% of South Africans … (1 have / are having) English as their first language, while
> more than 25% of South Africans … (2 speak / are speaking) Zulu.
> But these days more people … (3 learn / are learning) English, so the number of English
> speakers … (4 grows / is growing) fast.
> One reason why more and more young people … (5 choose / are choosing) to learn English
> today is that South Africans often … (6 use / are using) English in business, in government
> and on the internet.

More practice 7 **A tourist brochure**

→ Unit 3 | p.54

Read this text from a tourist brochure. Find a word for each gap 1–10.
There is an example (0) at the beginning.

The Drakensberg Mountains, *which* (0) are in the east of South Africa, are the highest mountains … (1) the country. Some of the mountains are over three thousand metres high. They are a popular tourist area as they are only a few hours … (2) from cities like Pietermaritzburg and Durban.

Many tourists come here to hike and enjoy the dramatic views of the mountains. You can have picnics next … (3) beautiful rivers and waterfalls and … (4) you're lucky you may see some wild animals too.

There … (5) great trails for mountain biking and other activities include abseiling, climbing and (… (6) November to March) rafting.

If you go out on the mountains, you should … (7) careful and always tell somebody where you're going. It can start raining or become foggy very suddenly, so … (8) easy to lose your way. … (9) winter there can also be snow. Luckily there are lots of cafes and restaurants … (10) will be happy to serve you hot food and drinks.

More help **2** **Tell the story**

→ Unit 3 | p.57

> Last year my dad found an ad for a great hotel in …
> The photos on the website looked great and …
> We booked …
> We were looking forward to …
> The flight was late so …
> When we arrived at the hotel, …
> It was raining and everybody felt …
> We tried to …
> Finally …

Unit 4

More help **1a** India today → Unit 4 | p.59

What do **you** think of when you hear the name India?
Use words in the box or your own ideas.

> beautiful old buildings • big population • colourful clothes • English-speaking •
> great festivals • mountains • poor people • science • spicy food • very big • very hot

More practice 1 Facts about India → Unit 4 | p.59

Read the texts on page 58 again.
Answer questions 1–8 below with information from the texts.
The questions are not in the order of the texts.

1 What's the name of India's spring festival?
2 What do people do at the festival?
3 Which language is the most widely-spoken in India?
4 Which country will make more cars in the future: India or Germany?
5 Why is the number of poor people in India falling?
6 When did India first produce 25,000 megawatts of solar energy?
7 In what parts of national life is English used in India?
8 Which country is the bigger market for smartphones: the USA or India?

More practice 2 AND YOU? Talking about India → Unit 4 | p.63

a Look back at pages 58–63. What have you found most interesting about India?
Choose these topics for a topic-based talk. Make notes.

b 👥 Then talk about the topic to a partner or the class.
Talk for at least 30 seconds about each topic.
I was surprised to learn that ... I thought that ..., but I found out that ...
And I also found out that ... This was a surprise because ...

More practice 3 India and climate change → Unit 4 | p.65

Read the statements 1–7. Are they true (T) or false (F) according
to the text on page 64?

1 The lives of most young people in India are getting easier and better.
2 Some farmers use drones to bring water to their fields.
3 Poverty is India's only big problem.
4 India could suffer more than other countries from the negative effects of climate change.
5 The high temperatures a few years ago were a problem, but luckily nobody died.
6 The city of Chennai ran out of clean water in 2019.
7 Most cars have to be electric in 2030.

More practice 4 👥 **Climate change in the world** → Unit 4 | p.65

Look at the blue, red and yellow box below. Copy the red and yellow box and complete them with your partner.
Use phrases on the right or your own ideas. Different solutions are possible.

> air pollution • drought • health problems • houses and animals burn • ~~more carbon dioxide~~ • floods at the coast • forest fires • not enough to drink • sea levels rise • ~~world hotter~~

	more carbon dioxide	world hotter
1 burn wood		
2 hotter weather	...	...
3 Arctic ice melts	...	...
4 use cars	...	...
5 climate change	...	...

More practice 5

What can we do to protect the environment and stop climate change? → Unit 4 | p.65
Make a presentation.

Step 1: Collect information and make notes. Look for photos or videos too.
Think of these aspects: travel, home, food, shopping, campaigns, work, ...
Step 2: Plan your talk and think of a good structure (beginning – middle – end).
Give reasons for your ideas.
Step 3: Practise your presentation. Speak clearly and freely. Don't read your text.
It can be useful to have keywords on a piece of paper.
Step 4: Now give your presentation. Be prepared to answer questions. Skills file 8 → p.124

More help 2 **Your school** → Unit 4 | p.69

Discuss in class. What has your school already done for the environment?
And what could it still do? Use some of the ideas below and your own ideas.

We have always	sorted the rubbish.
We have begun to	buy organic food. give money to an environmental organization.
Our school has asked us to	turn off the lights when we leave a room. use boxes (not plastic bags) for sandwiches or snacks. walk or cycle more often to school. open windows only for short airing in winter. say "no" to vegetables that are sold in plastic.
The school has begun to	turn down the heating. use solar energy.
But we could also	...

→ Unit 4 | p.70

Parallel exercise 4 ● **A TV series that changed the world**

Complete sentences 1–6 with the right verb form. Which tense do you need – present perfect or simple past?

1 The BBC ... (1 show) *Blue Planet II* in Europe, Asia and America in 2017.
2 And more than 80 million people in China ... (2 watch) *Blue Planet II* since 2017.
3 After watching the film millions of people ... (3 talk) about the problem of plastic on social media.
4 Since the series people ... (4 stop) using so much plastic.
5 Since 2017 people all over the world ... (5 begin) to protest against plastic knives, spoons and straws.
6 In 2019 David Attenborough, who made the series, ... (6 win) India's prize for peace.

More practice 6 **MEDIATION** **An accident**

→ Unit 4 | p.71

Mediate for a German tourist who saw a road accident in Chennai and an Indian police officer who is asking about the accident.

🎧 **a** Listen carefully. Mediate for each speaker in the pause after each sentence.
2.23   The police officer begins.

🎧 **b** Now listen to the dialogue with a mediator.
2.24   Is the mediation like yours?

More practice 7 **MEDIATION**

A special life story

→ Unit 4 | p.72

Du möchtest deinen Freunden von Arunima Sinha erzählen.
Notiere dir Informationen aus dem Text zu den folgenden Themen.
Schreibe Stichpunkte auf Deutsch.

1 *Kindheit: ...*
2 *Schreckliches Ereignis: ...*
3 *Folgen des Unfalls: ...*
4 *Ihre persönliche Leistung: ...*

More help **2** **An interview**

→ Unit 4 | p.72

What did you do ...?
When did you ...?
How long did it take ...?
How did you feel when ...?
Why did you want to ...?
Are you angry/proud/thankful/...?
Did the men who ... go to prison?
Can you tell me about ...?
Why did you choose ...?
What do children say when you tell them ...?

Anhänge

Exam training

Text File

Skills File

Language File

Wordbank

Vocabulary

Dictionary

Task 1

2.25

Tomorrow South Africa will play against England in the Rugby World Cup. Piet and Cebisa, who are friends and rugby fans, are talking about tomorrow's game. Listen and answer the questions. Write short answers. There is an example at the beginning (0).

0   How does Piet feel about the game against England tomorrow? *worried*
1   Against which country did South Africa play in the semi-finals?
2   How many points did South Africa get in the semi-finals?
3   When does the game against England begin?
4   Why doesn't Piet have to work tomorrow?
5   Where does Cebisa work?

Task 2

2.26

Look at the questions below. Then listen to a podcast about rugby, recorded by Sina, a rugby fan. While you listen, pick the right answers Ⓐ – Ⓓ. Write your answers in your exercise books. There is an example at the beginning (0).

0   The game of rugby …
   Ⓐ   is played with a round ball.
   Ⓑ   is a team game. *B is correct.*
   Ⓒ   is played with eggs.
   Ⓓ   is not played with a ball.

1   The game of rugby …
   Ⓐ   began in Ireland.
   Ⓑ   is more popular in the world than football.
   Ⓒ   got its name from a town in England.
   Ⓓ   began in New Zealand.

2   In the 2019 Rugby World Cup …
   Ⓐ   there were no teams from America.
   Ⓑ   the teams played in Japan.
   Ⓒ   the teams played in Italy.
   Ⓓ   31 teams took part.

3   Rugby players …
   Ⓐ   can hold, kick or run with the ball.
   Ⓑ   can hold the ball, but not run with it.
   Ⓒ   may pass the ball to a player in front of them.
   Ⓓ   may not take the ball in their hands.

4   In rugby, *tackling* means …
   Ⓐ   running with the ball.
   Ⓑ   scoring points for your team.
   Ⓒ   kicking the ball.
   Ⓓ   stopping a player in the other team.

5   In rugby you get points when you …
   Ⓐ   kick the ball
   Ⓑ   carry the ball
   Ⓒ   put the ball down on the ground
   Ⓓ   push a player in the other team
       … behind the white line at the end of the field.

6   Sina says that Samoa …
   Ⓐ   took part in the 2019 Rugby World Cup.
   Ⓑ   is a small country in the Atlantic Ocean.
   Ⓒ   has a population of about 500,000.
   Ⓓ   has football as a national sport.

Instructions in your exams → pp. 206–207

Task 3
2.27

Cebisa and Piet have just watched South Africa's Rugby World Cup final game against England. There is ONE mistake in each sentence below. Listen and write the correct information in your exercise book. There is an example (0) at the beginning.

> **TIPP**
>
> Lies die Sätze vor dem Hören und überlege, welche Informationen falsch sein könnten, z.B. in Satz 1:
> – die Zahl?
> – das Land?

0 People said that South Africa was the better team. *England*

1 South Africa won by twenty-two points to twelve against England.

2 South Africa was the winner of the World Cup in 1995, in 2007 and in 2013.

3 In 1995 the captain and all the players of the South African team were black.

The South African rugby team celebrates after winning the World Cup Final at Yokohama, 2nd November 2019

4 South Africa has won the Rugby World Cup more often than New Zealand.

5 The 2023 Rugby World Cup will be played in Wales.

6 There have been eight Women's Rugby World Cups and Australia has won five of them.

Task 4
2.28

The captain of South Africa's team at the 2018 Rugby World Cup was Siya Kolisi.
Listen to a radio report about him and note the missing details in your exercise book.
There is an example (0) at the beginning.

> **TIPP**
>
> Mache dir beim Hören nur kurze Notizen, damit du beim Schreiben nicht die Informationen für den nächsten Satz versäumst. Du kannst deine Notizen nach dem Hören noch ergänzen.

0 There were *60* white captains before Siya became South Africa's first black rugby captain in 2018.

1 Siya was born in June 1991 in a ... in South Africa.

2 His ... cared for him when he was a child.

3 He went to his first school because he could get a ... there.

4 He got a place at Grey High School because a teacher saw that he was a ...

Siya Kolisi at the Autumn Internationals, London, 3rd November 2018

5 When he grew tall the other students at school called him ...

6 We know that he played well against Scotland in 2013 because he was ...   *Skills file 6* → p.122

Workbook 1–3 → pp. 49–50

News stories from Australia

1 **No more climbers on Uluru**

Read the information about Uluru. There is ONE mistake in each line. Note the letter below the mistake. There is an example at the beginning (0).

0 Uluru is probably one of the places in Australia that tourists know good.
          A   B   C   D   → D

1 Over 250,000 tourists from all over the world travel to see them every year.
   A   B   C   D

2 Uluru, who is 348 metres high, rises dramatically above the flat land that lies all around it.
        A   B C   D

3 Most visitors want to see the rock at the evening when the sun goes down.
             A   B   C   D

4 There's a really specially atmosphere because Uluru becomes deep red.
      A   B   C   D

5 The indigenous Australians where gave the rock its name never wanted people to climb it.
               A   B   C   D

6 They said that people should show more respect, as the rock is a special place in there culture.
     A   B   C   D

7 But although they polite asked visitors not to climb the rock, many still walked up to the top.
          A   B   C   D

8 It was only in October 2019 that the government finally stopped tourists of climbing Uluru.
      A   B   C D

2 **Australia's dangerous wildlife**

Fill each gap with one word that suits the sentence.
There is an example at the beginning (0).

Say "dangerous animals" and many people think *of* (0) Africa. But in fact Australia is home to some of the ... (1) dangerous animals in the world.

Everybody knows that the country ... (2) snakes and spiders that can kill people. And every year we read ... (3) swimmers who are attacked by sharks somewhere on Australia's coasts. But other animals can be more dangerous ... (4) snakes, spiders and sharks.

Experts at the Australian Museum in Sydney have made a list of

dangerous animals, and snakes, spiders and sharks are not ... (5) the top of the list.

Even crocodiles ... (6) only number six on the list.

Number two are bees, because so ... (7) people are allergic to bee stings.

And top of the list are – jellyfish!

The sting of the box jellyfish, for example, ... (8) come into the waters off northern Australia in the warmer months, can kill a person in just ... (9) few minutes.

3 **Bush fires**

Read the text. Change the words in brackets, to make them fit the sentence. Write the correct words in your exercise books. There is an example at the beginning (0).

Bush fires are fires that move across big *areas* (0 area) of the country. They are very hard to put out, because they are big. They burn fields and trees and they move across the country very … (1 quick), especially when there's a strong wind.

The state of New South Wales, in the south-east of Australia, has had many bad years with fires, but the year 2019 was one of the very … (2 bad). The fires … (3 begin) in September and killed two people the following month. And on one day in November there … (4 be) more than 80 … (5 difference) bush fires across the state.

A thousand fire … (6 fight) tried to put out the fire on the ground and 70 planes and helicopters brought water to the areas where the fires were burning.

The fires are … (7 usual) in parts of the country where very few people live, so few people get hurt, but on 12th November one of the fires got to within 15 kilometres of Sydney city centre.

One of the problems is that many parts of Australia aren't … (8 get) enough rain, so the trees and … (9 bush) are very dry. Tuesday 17th December 2019 was the … (10 hot) month that Australia … (11 ever experience). And the outlook for the future is more hot summers to come.

4 **Camels in Australia**

Read the text. Pick words from the box for the gaps. Use only ONE word for each gap.
There is an example (0) at the beginning.

> about • along • at • because • between • ~~called~~ • few • for • from • if • little •
> many • much • on • that • to • was • were • when • where • who

When a ship *called* (0) *The Apoline* arrived in the harbour in Adelaide … (1) 12th October 1840, three brothers were waiting … (2) it. They were excited because the ship was bringing camels … (3) the brothers had ordered from the Canary Islands. However, … (4) the brothers went on board, they found that all the camels had died. All except one. And that camel, which the brothers called Harry, was the first camel in Australia. In the next … (5) years, many more camels arrived. People were exploring the outback and trying to cross the big Australian desert from the south to the north and they used camels for their expeditions. About 15,000 camels arrived … (6) 1870 and 1900. In the twentieth century, however, people began to use cars and lorries and the camels went wild.

Their numbers grew quickly and by 2019 there … (7) about a million camels in the outback. In the north camels are found in … (8) 40% of the land area. They are a problem for farmers because camels drink so … (9) water – and there isn't enough water in some parts of Australia. And experts found that the camels are making life harder for Australia's kangaroos.

Christchurch since its earthquake

A Christchurch, the largest city on New Zealand's South Island, has always been thought of as a quiet place where not much happens. Wellington, though smaller, has the buzz of a capital city, a busy ferry terminal and a centre of excellence in the international film industry. Auckland, with almost two fifths of its population born overseas, is one of the most diverse cities in the world. The country's business centre,
5 it is also within easy reach of the country's awesome geysers and steaming mud pools in Rotorua.

B But Christchurch? Its title of New Zealand's Garden City is hardly dramatic. While Auckland and Wellington are surrounded by volcanoes, Christchurch lies among the fields of the Canterbury Plain – great for farming, but low on the country's list of dramatic scenery. And while Queenstown, over on the west coast, offers jetboating, skydiving and an exciting luge track, Christchurch is famous for punting – a
10 sport in which you drop a long pole into the river, push against it and move a boat gently along the river. It is surely the quietest, slowest and least exciting water sport in the world.

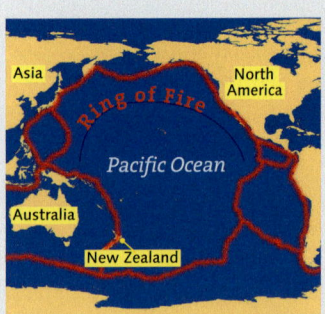

C But the city's hills and gardens don't tell the whole story. For Christchurch lies on the *Ring of Fire*, a line that goes up America's west coast, down the east coast of Asia, and then – missing Australia – swings across to New Zealand. Most of the world's
15 earthquakes take place along this line, and Christchurch, too, has a history of earthquakes. There were minor earthquakes in the nineteenth century, for example, and an earthquake in 2010 injured two people and destroyed a small number of buildings.

20 **D** All the same, nobody was prepared for the earthquake that shook the city at lunchtime on Tuesday 22nd February 2011. Though no stronger than an earthquake of the year before, its epicentre was more central and so it was more deadly. It was the country's second worst natural disaster after the Hawke's Bay earthquake. 185 people were killed, 130 of them in a six-storey office block that collapsed. Thousands more were injured. The Anglican cathedral lost half of its tower and some of its walls were
25 so weakened that they fell in further earthquakes later the same year. The city's second tallest building was so badly damaged that it had to be taken down later. Hundreds of family homes were damaged and almost 80 per cent of the buildings in the city's CBD (Central Business District) were destroyed.

E In most countries, land in a city's CBD is so expensive that it is rebuilt after a disaster. But in an under-populated country such as New Zealand, a number of businesses that had been hit by the
30 earthquake found space for their new offices on the outer edge of the city. This left a large area of unused land in the city centre and the city has tried to find a mix of creative uses for it. The new Riverside Market, for example, is a huge food hall where producers sell their fruit, vegetables, meat and seafood in market stalls, shops, cafes and restaurants. Together with a new library housed in an impressive new building, it is designed to attract the crowds back into the CBD.

F Some parts of the unused land are turning green. This is partly because when people took down [35] the damaged houses, they left the trees that had been growing in the gardens – and these trees have now multiplied. Many of them are fruit trees and residents of Christchurch are now encouraged to come and pick apples, pears, apricots and plums where houses and offices once stood. So you could say that city life in Christchurch has experienced a revolution. But a quiet one, of course.

1   Match the correct titles 1–8 with the paragraphs in the text. Use the letters only once.
    There are two extra titles. Write your answers in your exercise book or on paper.
    1   New attractions   5   The day after the disaster
    2   A dangerous zone   6   The catastrophe
    3   A tourist centre   7   Find your own food
    4   Three rival cities   8   A boring sort of place

2   Answer the questions. Short answers are possible.
    1   Why is Auckland a diverse multicultural city?
    2   Why does the author like Queenstown's sports more than punting?
    3   How is Australia luckier than New Zealand, as far as earthquakes are concerned?
    4   Why did the earthquake in February 2011 kill more people than the earthquake in 2010?
    5   Where did many of the businesses that had been hit by the earthquake move to?
    6   Why are some parts of the city's redevelopment zone turning green?

3   Pick the correct option according to the text.
    1   According to the author, Auckland …
        A   has lots of banks and big companies.
        B   is the centre of New Zealand's film industry.
        C   is situated a long way from Rotorua.
        D   has two fifths of the population of Christchurch.
    2   Christchurch is …
        A   a place with dramatic scenery.
        B   proud of its green spaces and flowers.
        C   famous for kayaking and sailing.
        D   not too far from New Zealand's geysers.
    3   The earthquake in February 2011 …
        A   was the country's worst disaster.
        B   killed 130 people and injured 185.
        C   totally destroyed the Anglican cathedral.
        D   destroyed most buildings in the CBD.
    4   As a result of the earthquake …
        A   lots of businesses have moved to other towns.
        B   land has become more expensive.
        C   there are new opportunities in the city centre.
        D   the city has no more libraries.

4   Which of the meanings below is the one used in the text?

busy *(line 2)*	plain *(line 7)*	track *(line 9)*	hit *(line 29)*	turn *(line 35)*
A beschäftigt *(Adj)*	A einfach, schlicht *(Adj)*	A Weg, Pfad *(N)*	A schlagen *(V)*	A drehen *(V)*
B arbeitsreich *(Adj)*	B klar *(Adj)*	B Gleis *(N)*	B treffen *(V)*	B abbiegen *(V)*
C belebt, geschäftig *(Adj)*	C halbbitter *(Adj)*	C Bahn, Renn-bahn *(N)*	C Schlag, Stoss, Treffer *(N)*	C werden *(V)*
D besetzt *(Adj)*	D Ebene *(N)*	D verfolgen *(V)*	D Erfolg, Hit *(N)*	D Kurve *(N)*

Workbook 1–2 → pp. 53–54

Skills file 1 → p. 112   Skills file 2 → p. 114

Working with elephants in India

Deine 35-jährige Nachbarin liebt Tiere und sie reist auch gern. Sie hat im Internet folgende Anzeige gefunden und fragt sich, ob dieses Programm eventuell etwas für sie wäre. Da sie nicht so gut Englisch kann, bittet sie dich, die wichtigsten Informationen für sie kurz auf Deutsch zu notieren (ca. 100 Wörter):

- Art der Tätigkeiten und Arbeitsbedingungen
- Unterkunft
- Freizeitmöglichkeiten
- mögliche Probleme

Volunteer work with elephants

Volunteers are required to help us to look after our elephants in our 30-hectare *Elephant Village* near Jaipur, Rajasthan, India.

Your working days will be three to four hours a day, five days a week, Monday to Friday, and your work will begin early (about 5 am). We provide accommodation in host families who will serve three vegetarian meals a day. Be aware that you might find it hard to adapt to the food and climate during the first few days and make sure you drink enough.

Our project coordinator will tell you all about the elephants and their mahouts (professional elephant trainers). You will spend your time bathing the elephants, feeding them, taking them for a walk and cleaning their housing areas. You will help to prepare the elephants' food and may even learn to massage them. Your host families will be happy to tell you about local festivals and interesting things to do in your spare time, for example to explore the exciting city of Jaipur. But you may of course book your own accommodation if you prefer.

Reviews

 I had so much fun during my time in *Elephant Village*! My host family was very kind and even invited me to some of their family festivals. I would recommend this programme to anyone who loves animals. *Michel van Damme, Belgium*

 Touching and looking after such huge animals is an experience I'll never forget. I was afraid that the elephants might be dangerous, but I always felt safe at work. Maybe I should add that most volunteers were around 20 years old – I am 40. And I felt very ill for the first few days. But after a few days in bed I felt a lot better, and I enjoyed the rest of my time. So although it was quite a hard time for me, it was a great experience. *Anna Warlow, UK*

Workbook 1–2 → pp. 55–56

1 An email to *Elephant Village*

Die Anzeige über das Elephant Village hat dich interessiert – nun möchtest du selber nach Indien fliegen und dort arbeiten.
Du hast ein paar Fragen an die Verwaltung des *Elephant Village* notiert:

- Arrive Sunday 10th June – OK?
- Stay for two weeks – OK?
- Stay in a host family: yes please!
- Cost for two weeks (including host family)?
- Weather in June?
- Bring special clothes – boots (rain?)

Schreibe eine E-Mail ans *Elephant Village* und stelle deine Fragen. Schreibe ca. 100 Wörter.

> **TIPP**
>
> Denk daran, die richtige Form für eine formelle E-Mail zu verwenden:
> – höfliche Anrede,
> – höfliche Frageformen,
> – höfliche Schlussformel.
> Mache auch deinen Enthusiasmus für das Programm deutlich:
> – *I am really looking forward to …*
> – *I would very much like to …*

2 An email to a friend

Schreibe eine E-Mail an Emma, deine Brieffreundin in England, über deinen Plan, im *Elephant Village* zu arbeiten. Nimm die notwendigen Informationen aus:
– dem Text im Mediation-Prüfungsteil,
– den Notizen oben in Aufgabe 1.

- Teile Emma deinen Plan mit.
- Fasse die Arbeit im *Elephant Village* kurz zusammen.
- Erkläre ihr, was dir am Programm besonders gefällt.
- Beschreibe deine Gefühle: wovor du Angst hast, worauf du dich freust.
- Frage Emma nach ihren Plänen – ob sie vielleicht sogar mitkommen möchte?

Schreibe ca. 100 Wörter.

> **TIPP**
>
> Denk daran, die richtige Form für eine informelle E-Mail zu verwenden:
> – freundliche Anrede,
> – frage, wie es Emma geht,
> – berichte Emma von deiner Aufregung, deinen Ängsten und deiner Vorfreude,
> – beende die E-Mail mit einer passenden Schlussformel.

Workbook 1 → p. 57

1 CORRESPONDENCE Email

Du hast dich auf einen Job in Neuseeland beworben. Adrian und Lisa Jones haben dir eine Stelle auf ihrem Biobauernhof angeboten. Schreibe an Adrian und Lisa Jones.

- Bedanke dich für ihr Angebot.
- Sage, in welchem Zeitraum du arbeiten möchtest.
- Erzähle von deinen Erfahrungen bei Praktika oder sonst in der Arbeitswelt.
- Beschreibe Eigenschaften von dir, die hilfreich für die Arbeit auf einem Bauernhof sein könnten.
- Frage, was du mitbringen solltest (z.B. Gummi-stiefel).
- Erkundige dich nach Freizeitaktivitäten in der Nähe.
- Sage, dass du dich sehr auf den Aufenthalt freust.

Verfasse eine E-Mail von 100 Wörtern.

TIPP

Die sieben Punkte links sagen dir genau, was du schreiben sollst. Lies diese Anweisungen sorgfältig und befolge sie.
Denke daran, wie du eine E-Mail be-ginnen und beenden musst.
Du verlierst Punkte, wenn deine E-Mail zu kurz ist – aber nicht, wenn sie zu lang ist.

2 CREATIVE WRITING Picture and prompts

Schreibe eine Geschichte auf Englisch, in der du das Bild und die Stichpunkte berücksichtigst. Schreibe ungefähr 100 Wörter.

Beginne wie folgt:
It was a beautiful sunny day and ...

TIPP

Ein Bild erzählt eine Geschichte.
Denke beim Erzählen an eine logische Reihenfolge der Ereignisse. Gib den Personen Namen und beschreibe ihre Gefühle.

Entspannung und Spaß

Regen

Wolke

Bienenstich

Fußverletzung

Picknick

3 **CREATIVE WRITING** **Picture and prompts**

Schreibe eine Geschichte auf Englisch,
in der du die Bilder berücksichtigst.

Beginne wie folgt:

On the first day of their holidays Ellie, Jess,
Hamza and Noah went …

TIPP

Schreibe zwei Sätze zu jedem Bild und
ergänze, was zwischen den Bildern passiert,
z.B. ruft das Mädchen zwischen Bild 4 und 5
den Krankenwagen. Verwende time phrases
wie *suddenly, an hour later, …*

Workbook 1–2 → p. 58

1 Picture-based interview: At the Taj Mahal, India

👥 Work with a partner. Look at the picture.
Then take turns to ask and answer questions about it.

Yes, we're in front of the famous Taj Mahal in India!

Picture description
Where are the people?
What are they doing?
What can you see in the background?
Describe the people's clothes.
What's the weather like?

Talking about the picture
How are the people feeling?
What do you think the people will do after they leave?
Do you like visiting famous buildings? Why (not)?
What activities do you like doing in the holidays?
Do you like travelling to other countries? Why (not)?

TIPP

Antworte möglichst ausführlich:
– *Where are the people?*
– *They're in India, at the Taj Mahal. It's one of the most famous places in India.*

Du musst nicht immer alles wissen und kannst Vermutungen äußern:
– *How are the people feeling?*
– *I'm not sure. Maybe they're really happy, but maybe they're hot and tired and a bit bored!*

Workbook 1 → pp. 59–60

Skills file 7 → p. 123

2 👥 **Topic-based talk: sport**

a **Partner A** Choose three aspects in the wordweb.
Think of a few things that you can say about each aspect and make notes.
Then talk about your aspect for two minutes.

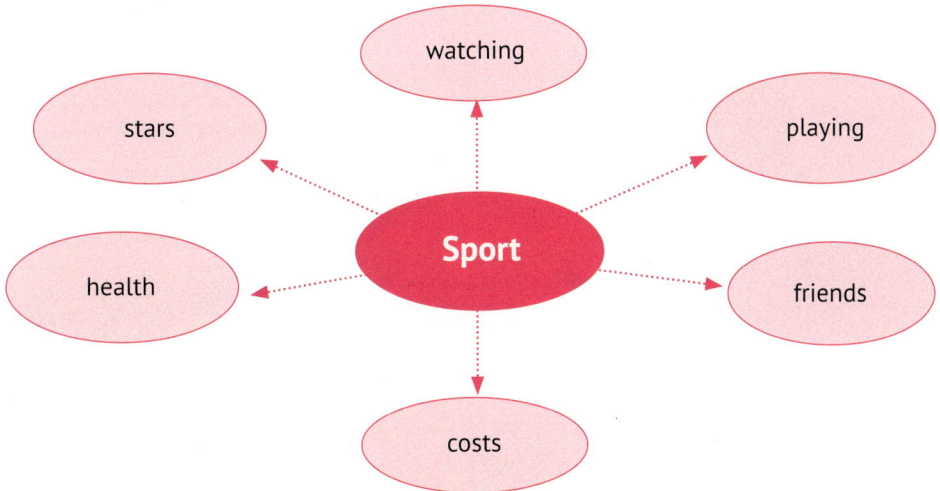

Partner B If Partner A stops talking, you can ask some of these questions:
Do you do a lot of sport? Why (not)?
Do you watch sports events live? Why (not)?
Have you ever been skiing/canyoning/bungee jumping? If yes – tell me about it.
If no: Would you like to try?
Which famous sports star would like to meet? What would you ask her/him?
Are there any good sport centres and swimming pools in your town?

b Now swap roles. Talk about three aspects, including at least two new aspects. `Skills file 8` → p. 124

2.29

3 **MEDIATION**

You're at the entrance kiosk at the Taj Mahal.
In front of you is a German family.
They want to buy tickets, but they can't speak English.
Listen carefully.
Listen to the German mother and mediate into
English for the Indian assistant.
Then listen to the Indian assistant and mediate into
German for the German mother.
The German mother begins.

TIPP

Lies die Einführung genau, damit
du weißt, worum es im Dialog
geht.
Hier sind die Touristen am
Eingang vom Taj Mahal – sie
werden also Eintrittskarten
kaufen. Welche Informationen
werden sie erfragen bzw. geben?

`Workbook 2` → pp. 59–60

`Skills file 9` → p. 125

TF 1 All about Australia

SIZE

7,700,000 km² (Australia is 21 times bigger than Germany: 357,000 km².)

POPULATION

25.6 million (Germany has three times more people: 83.1 million.)

CLIMATE

Most of the land is hot and dry: 70% of Australia gets less than 500 millilitres of rain every year. The north of Australia has a tropical climate with hot wet summers and warm dry winters, but the mountains in the south have snow and you can go skiing in the Australian winter – that's from June to September.

THE AUSTRALIAN FLAG

The British flag in the top left corner of the Australian flag represents Britain's role in the history of Australia. The Southern Cross, on the right, is a group of stars that can be seen from Australia, but not from Europe.

BUSH FIRES

Australian summers are hot, so fires can start easily and strong winds can make the fires grow quickly. The bush-fires in the summer 2019/2020 killed 34 people and more than a billion[2] animals. It destroyed almost 3,000 homes and burned an area bigger than Bavaria.

SPORTS

The most popular spectator[1] sports are *Australian Rules* football, horse racing and rugby. Cricket, tennis and golf are also very popular.

BIG CITIES

Sydney 4.9 million
Melbourne 4.9 million
(Compare to Germany: Berlin 3.8 million, Munich 1.5 million.)
86% of the population lives in towns or cities. 85% of the population lives near the coast. Australia's capital city is Canberra.

MEDIATION

Look at the infographic. Then explain the following numbers to your partner – in German.

	a)	b)	c)	d)
Partner A	25.6 million	500 ml	86%	34
Partner B	4.9 million	70%	85%	1 billion

[1]**spectator** [spekt'teɪtə] *Zuschauer/in*   [2]**a billion** ['bɪljən] *eine Milliarde (= tausend Millionen)*

Skills file 1 → pp. 112f.

Wildlife in Australia

Kangaroos are a symbol of Australia. They can be up to two metres tall and they hop on their strong back legs. They can run at up to 60 km an hour. The number of kangaroos in the wild is growing.

5   **K**oalas are smaller (only 60–85 cm long) and they live in trees in the east and south of Australia. Thousands of koalas were killed in the terrible 2019/2020 bushfires.

Camels were brought to Australia. Ostriches[3] were also brought to Australia from Africa, but Australia's second biggest birds, the emus, are native to[4] Australia. Emus can sprint up to 50 km an hour. They can also survive[5] a few days without drinking and a few weeks

10   without eating.

Australia has about 170 different sorts of snakes. Some of the world's most dangerous snakes live here, although not many could kill a person. And snake bites are very rare. When they happen, it's usually because people weren't careful.

"Sorry"

In 2008 Australian Prime Minister Kevin Rudd spoke to the indigenous Australians. And he said something special. He used a word that no Australian government had used for more than 200 years. He said "Sorry".

5   When the British arrived at the end of the 18th century, they said that the land was *terra nullius*, nobody's land. But that wasn't true. Indigenous Australians had lived there for 50,000 years. It was their land. "Sorry", said Kevin Rudd.

From 1910 to 1970 the government took 100,000 children away from their indigenous mothers and put them in white families or institutions. These children weren't allowed

10   to see their families or speak their own languages. That was wrong. Very wrong. "Sorry", said Prime Minister Rudd. Of course, saying "Sorry" is not enough.

There is more to do. Life is still harder for indigenous Australians than for white Australians. But saying "Sorry" is maybe a good start.

---

[3] **ostrich** [ˈɒstrɪtʃ] *Strauß*   [4] **native** (to) [ˈneɪtɪv] *einheimisch*   [5] (to) **survive** [səˈvaɪv] *überleben*

TF 2 Cleaner of the world's oceans

A The problem

Millions of tonnes of plastic rubbish – bags, bottles, helmets, etc – are floating[1] around the world's oceans.

After many years the sun breaks the plastic down into very small pieces less than five millimetres big. Seabirds, dolphins, fish and other sea life eat these small pieces of plastic. 5

When we eat fish or seafood, the plastic is a danger for us too. 10
Ocean currents[2] carry the plastic rubbish around the world. Most of it collects in big areas in the middle of the oceans.

One of the biggest areas of plastic rubbish is in the Pacific Ocean between Hawaii and California. It is an area of about 1.6 million square kilometres. 15

B One person's vision

Boyan Slat was still a teenager in Holland when he went diving during a summer holiday in Greece in 2011. He was shocked. "I saw more plastic than fish," he says. 20

Slat thought about the problem and soon had an idea: barriers that float on the sea and catch the plastic. 25

He collected 2.2 million dollars from 38,000 people in 160 countries. He then started an organization called *The Ocean Cleanup* with scientists and engineers to build and test his idea. 30

Boyan Slat and his team studied the ocean currents and found something important: The water 300 metres down in the ocean moves more slowly than the water at the top.

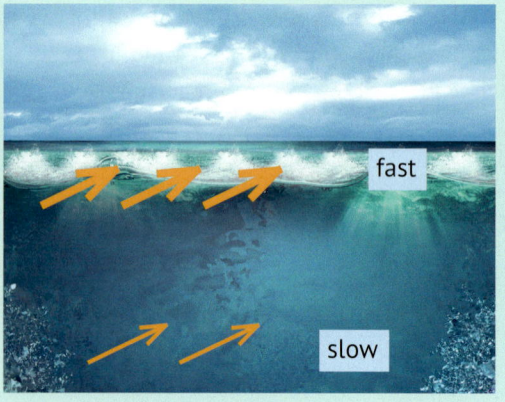

---

[1] **(to) float** [fləʊt] *schwimmen, treiben*   [2] **current** [ˈkʌrənt] *Strömung*   [3] **garbage patch** [ˈgɑːbɪdʒ pætʃ] *Müllstrudel*

C The system – in theory

Boyan Slat and his team designed the following system:

A floating barrier, in the form of a U, is fixed[4] to an anchor[5] that sinks 200–300 metres down into the ocean.

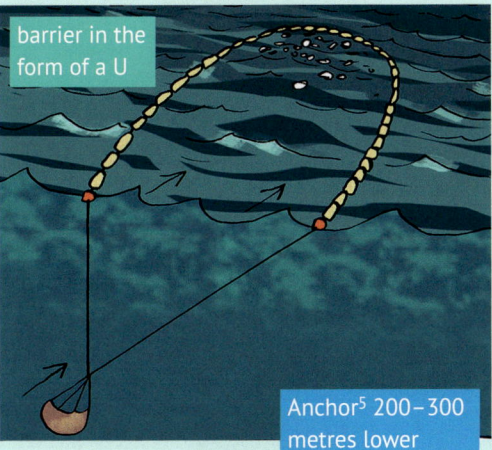

barrier in the form of a U

Anchor[5] 200–300 metres lower

How the system works:
The anchor moves slowly. The barrier is fixed to the anchor, so it also moves slowly.

But the plastic moves faster, so it moves into the U of the barrier.

When the barrier has collected lots of plastic, a boat comes to take the plastic back to land where it can be recycled.

Boyan Slat's plan is to make special objects with the ocean plastic. So he wants to recycle and sell the plastic again.

He will then be able to use the money to build more barriers.

D The system – in action

In autumn 2019 a boat pulled a test barrier called *System 001B* out of San Francisco and out into the Pacific Ocean.
And it worked! The barrier took the U-form, it didn't break, and most important of all, it collected lots of plastic – not only big pieces, but very small pieces as well.

A boat brought the plastic to Vancouver, in Canada, in December 2019.
You can see a video of System 001B in action on the website of *The Ocean Cleanup*.
It's still in the test phase. It needs more work before the team can build dozens of barriers (System 2) for use in the oceans.

And of course we have no guarantee that the system will work. Boyan Slat has his critics who say that the system might never work and that it's a lot of trouble for a minimum result and a waste of money.

But thanks to Boyan Slat we have the hope that one day we'll be able to attack the problem of plastic rubbish in the ocean.

MEDIATION
Read the text.
Partner A Explain parts A and B to your partner – in German.
Partner B Explain parts C and D to your partner – in German.

[4](to) **fix** [fɪks] *befestigen* [5]**anchor** [ˈæŋkə] *Anker*

SF 1 Unbekannte Wörter verstehen

→ Unit 1 | p.13   → Exam training | p.101f.   → Text file | p.108ff.

Du kannst englische Texte verstehen –
auch wenn du nicht alle Wörter kennst.

1 Schau dir die Bilder an.
Bilder zeigen dir oft Dinge aus dem Text. Was bedeutet
z.B. *crutches* in der Bildunterschrift rechts?

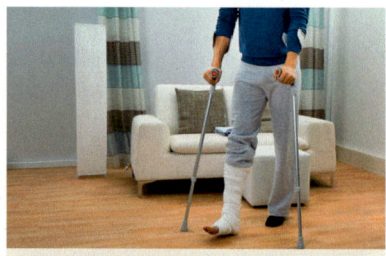

**He had an accident and broke his leg.
Now he has to walk on crutches.**

2 Denke an ähnliche Wörter im Deutschen.
Oft sind englische und deutsche Wörter sehr ähnlich:

- *concentrate* heißt auf Deutsch „sich konzentrieren",
- *conflict* bedeutet „Konflikt".

Was bedeuten die folgenden Wörter auf Deutsch?

> continent • cosmetics •
> decoration • miniskirt • muscle •
> politician • souvenir • spinach

Hmm, *continent*
sieht so ähnlich
aus wie das
deutsche Wort
„Kontinent".

3 Schau dir den ganzen Satz an.
Du kannst ein unbekanntes Wort auch erschließen.
Lies den ganzen Satz und überlege, welches Wort
Sinn macht. Was könnten z.B. *plaster* und *ingredients*
bedeuten?

1 *I've cut my finger. Do you have a plaster?*
2 *The ingredients for the cake? Just eggs, butter,
flour and sugar.*

4 Erkenne zusammengesetzte Wörter und Ausdrücke.
Oft kennst du die Einzelteile eines Worts bereits.
Wie heißen die folgenden Wörter auf Deutsch?

> baby car seat • cotton field •
> filmgoer • good-looking •
> one-way street • sailing boat

Baby car seat? Car seat ist
der „Autositz". Also könnte
es „Kindersitz" sein.

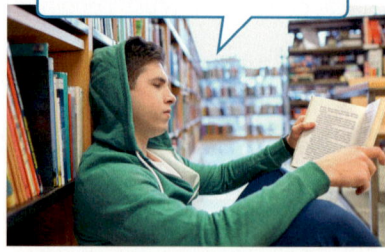

1 crutches Krücken **2** cosmetics Kosmetikartikel decoration Dekoration miniskirt Minirock muscle Muskel
politician Politiker/in souvenir Souvenir, Andenken spinach Spinat **3** plaster Pflaster ingredients Zutaten
4 cotton field Baumwollfeld filmgoer Kinogänger/in good-looking gutaussehend one-way street Einbahnstraße
sailing boat Segelboot

5 Erkenne Wortteile und Wortbildungsregeln.

Manchmal steckt in einem neuen Wort ein anderes Wort oder ein Wortteil, das du schon kennst.

a Suffixe (Nachsilben) bei Adjektiven und Substantiven

- Viele Adjektive im Englischen enden auf *-ful*, *-less*, *-ic*, *-al*, *-ous*, *-y* oder *-able*.
  Wenn du also das Substantiv oder das Verb kennst, verstehst du auch das Adjektiv:

  noise → *noisy*
  tradition → *traditional*

  In den Adjektiven im Kasten rechts steckt immer ein Wort, das du schon kennst. Kannst du die Bedeutung erschließen?

- Viele Substantive enden auf *-ance*, *-ant*, *-ence*, *-er*, *-ion*, *-ment* oder *-ness*.
  Wenn du also das Verb oder Adjektiv kennst, verstehst du auch das Substantiv:

  nervous → *nervousness*
  (to) explore → *exploration*

  Was bedeuten die Substantive im Kasten rechts?

b Präfixe (Vorsilben) bei Adjektiven und Verben

- Die Vorsilben *dis-*, *in-*, *im-* oder *un-* bedeuten meist das Gegenteil:
  dependence = Abhängigkeit
  independence = Unabhängigkeit

  Was bedeuten also die Wörter im Kasten rechts?

- Die Vorsilbe *re-* bedeutet etwas erneut oder nochmal machen:
  (to) use = benutzen, verwenden
  (to) reuse = wiederverwenden

  Was bedeuten also die Verben im Kasten rechts?

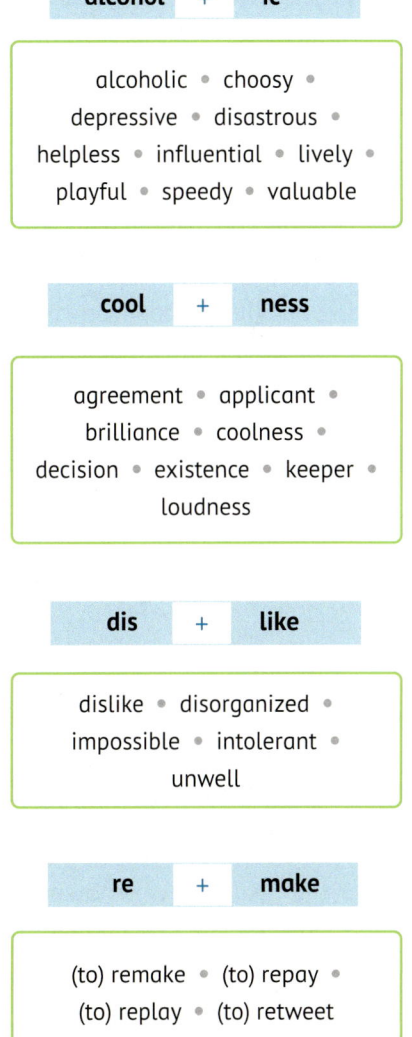

| alcohol | + | ic |

alcoholic • choosy • depressive • disastrous • helpless • influential • lively • playful • speedy • valuable

| cool | + | ness |

agreement • applicant • brilliance • coolness • decision • existence • keeper • loudness

| dis | + | like |

dislike • disorganized • impossible • intolerant • unwell

| re | + | make |

(to) remake • (to) repay • (to) replay • (to) retweet

---

a **alcoholic** alkoholisch **choosy** wählerisch **depressive** depressiv **disastrous** katastrophal **helpless** hilflos **influential** einflussreich **lively** lebendig, lebhaft **playful** verspielt **speedy** schnell **valuable** wertvoll **agreement** Vereinbarung, Zustimmung **applicant** Bewerber/in **brilliance** Genialität **coolness** Coolness **decision** Entscheidung **existence** Existenz **keeper** Torwart/in, Bewahrer/in, Halter/ in / **loudness** Lautstärke **b** **dislike** Abneigung **disorganized** unorganisiert **impossible** unmöglich **intolerant** intolerant **unwell** unwohl, krank **(to) remake** erneuern, neu machen **(to) repay** zurückzahlen **(to) replay** erneut spielen **(to) retweet** retweeten

SF 2 Im Wörterbuch nachschlagen

→ Unit 1 | p.14   → Unit 2 | p.31   → Unit 3 | p.50   → Exam training | p.101

1 **Beachte die alphabetische Reihenfolge.**

In elektronischen Wörterbüchern brauchst du nur die Suchrichtung (Englisch–Deutsch oder Deutsch–Englisch) einzustellen und das Wort einzutippen. In gedruckten Wörterbüchern ist alles alphabetisch aufgelistet:

- *U* kommt vor *V*
- *van* kommt vor *vegan*
- *vacation* kommt vor *van*

> **us** [ʌs], [əs] uns 5
> **use** [juːz] benutzen 5
> **usually** ['juːʒʊəli] meistens, normalerweise 5
>
> **V**
>
> °**vacation** [vəˈkeɪʃn] *(AE)* Urlaub, Ferien
> **van** [væn] Transporter, Lieferwagen 7
> **vegan** ['viːgən] vegan; Veganer/in 8: 2 (39)
> **vegetables** *(pl)* ['vedʒtəblz] Gemüse 5
> **vegetarian** *(infml auch* **veggie***)*

2 **Finde zusammengesetzte Ausdrücke.**

Der Haupteintrag (z.B. *noise*) steht farbig oder fett am Anfang. Daneben oder darunter findest du oft zusammengesetzte Wörter oder Redewendungen (z.B. *(to) make noises*).

> **noise** ▶ **(to) make noises** *(umg)* Andeutungen machen

3 **Beachte unterschiedliche Wortbedeutungen.**

Die Ziffern 1, 2 usw. zeigen, dass ein Wort mehrere Bedeutungen hat.

> Egal, ob du ein englisches oder deutsches Wort suchst: Lies immer den ganzen Eintrag und entscheide dann, welche Bedeutung die richtige ist.

a **Englisch-Deutsch**

Was heißt *arm* in diesen Sätzen?

1 *Can you repair this chair? The arm is broken.*
2 *They walked away arm in arm.*
3 *The soldiers were armed with new guns.*
4 *The arms of the T-shirt are too long.*

> **arm¹** *Substantiv*
>   1 *(Körperteil)* Arm
>   2 *(eines Kleidungsstücks)* Ärmel
>   3 *(eines Sessels)* Armlehne
>
> **arm²** *Verb* bewaffnen

b **Deutsch-Englisch**

Welches sind die richtigen englischen Wörter für *glatt* in diesen Sätzen?

1 *Er war glatt rasiert.*
2 *Das ist eine glatte Lüge.*
3 *Die Creme macht deine Haut weich und glatt.*
4 *Vorsicht – es ist glatt draußen.*
5 *Sie hat langes, glattes Haar.*

> **glatt** *Adjektiv*
>   1 *(allgemein)* smooth
>   2 *(Haar)* straight
>   3 *(rutschig, eisig)* slippery, icy
>   4 *(Betrug, Lüge)* downright
>   5 *(glatt rasiert)* clean-shaven

3a 1 Armlehne 2 Arm 3 bewaffnet 4 Ärmel **3b** 1 clean-shaven 2 downright 3 smooth 4 slippery 5 straight

→ Unit 1 | p.16   → Unit 2 | p.32   → Unit 4 | p.66

SF 3 Texte besser verstehen

1 Skimming

Mit dieser Technik kannst du dir schnell einen Überblick über einen Text verschaffen.
Dabei liest du nur schnell das Wichtigste und achtest besonders auf:

- Überschriften,
- Bilder, Bildunterschriften,
- fett gedruckte Wörter.

Du brauchst nicht jedes Detail zu verstehen.

2 Scanning

Mit dieser Technik kannst du einen Text nach ganz bestimmten Informationen durchsuchen.
Du sollst z.B. eine Frage zur Bevölkerung Australiens beantworten und suchst das Wort *population*.

- Suche nur nach Schlüsselwörtern (hier *population*) und lasse alles andere beiseite.

- Gehe dabei mit den Augen und dem Finger schnell über den Text. Das gesuchte Wort wird dir „ins Auge springen".

3 Understanding diagrams

- Schau auf den Titel.
  Welches Thema zeigt die Grafik rechts?

- Schau auf die Farben und Zahlen.
  Was zeigen z.B. die grünen Säulen und die Zahlen rechts?

- Sammle alle Informationen.
  Für welches Land gilt die Statistik?
  Wie aktuell ist sie?

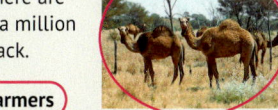

Camels in the outback

How they came to Australia

Camels were first imported to Australia in the 1800s and then they went wild. The number of camels has since exploded and there are now more than a million across the outback.

A problem for farmers

The camels are a big problem for farmers as they drink water (there isn't much of that in some parts of Australia) and they destroy fences.

Today there are about 670,000 Aboriginal Australians in Australia – less than 3% of Australia's **population** of 25.6 million. Most Aboriginal Australians today live in two cultures. Some of them live a good life, but many young Aboriginal Australians leave school early,

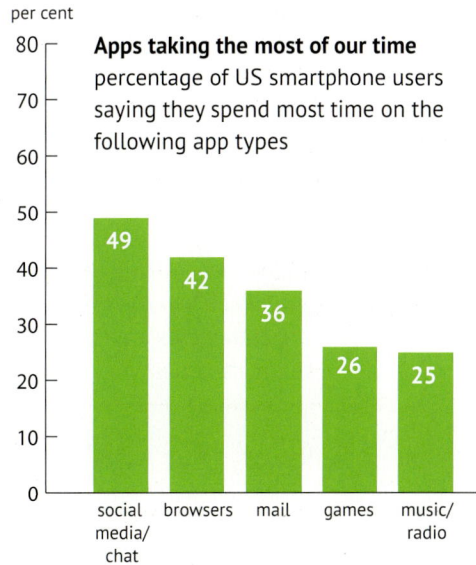

per cent

Apps taking the most of our time
percentage of US smartphone users saying they spend most time on the following app types

- social media/chat: 49
- browsers: 42
- mail: 36
- games: 26
- music/radio: 25

Source: *AudienceProject/Statista*, Nov 2019

3 Die Grafik zeigt, für welche Apps am meisten Zeit verwendet wird. Die grünen Säulen zeigen die einzelnen App-Typen und wieviel Zeit in Prozent dafür verwendet wird. Die Statistik bezieht sich auf die USA und stammt aus dem Jahr 2019.

SF 4   Proben und Abschlussprüfung

→ Exam training | pp.96–107

Bei Proben und Prüfungen sind die Arbeitsanweisungen ganz wichtig! Deshalb:
1 Lies zuerst **alle** Arbeitsanweisungen.
2 Lies die Arbeitsanweisungen **sehr genau** – auch zwei- oder dreimal!
   Sie geben dir wichtige Hinweise und Hilfen. Erinnere dich an das, was du gelernt hast.
3 Prüfe am Ende: Hast du alle Anweisungen befolgt? Kannst du alle Punkte abhaken?

1 READING

Hier ist ein Beispiel für eine Leseverstehensaufgabe.

> *First read the text. Then do tasks 1–9:*
> *Decide if the statements are true or false and tick the correct box.*
> *Then finish the sentences. You can quote from the text.*

Together with Sydney Harbour Bridge and the Great Barrier Reef, Uluru is probably the best-known tourist sight in Australia. 270,000 visitors travel there every year.
In the past it was allowed to climb the rock, but Aboriginal people weren't happy about that because for them Uluru is a sacred place. And it's dangerous too to climb the rock – 37 people died because the sun is so hot there.
So in October 2019 the National Park Board put a ban on climbing Uluru.

> 1 *Uluru is very popular with visitors.*
>   *This statement is* **a)** ☐ *true*   **b)** ☐ *false because the text says ...*
>
> 2 *It's no longer allowed to climb the rock.*
>   *This statement is* **a)** ☐ *true*   **b)** ☐ *false because the text says ...*
>
> 3 *...*

Lies zuerst die Arbeitsanweisung. Unterstreiche, was du tun sollst.
Hier ist ein Beispiel:

> *First read the text. Then do tasks 1–9.*
> *Decide if the statements are true or false and tick the correct box.*
> *Then finish the sentences. You can quote from the text.*

Musst du also bei dieser Aufgabe nur Kästchen abhaken?

Nein, du musst auch Sätze vervollständigen.

2 LISTENING

Lies auch bei Höraufgaben die Arbeitsanweisungen genau und unterstreiche das Wichtigste.

> *There is ONE mistake in each sentence.*
> *Listen and write the correct information on the line.*
> *There is an example (0) at the beginning.*

Wie viele Fehler gibt es in jedem Satz?

Soll man den Fehler durchstreichen?

Wohin soll man die korrekte Information schreiben? Gibt es ein Beispiel?

3 WRITING

Hier ist ein Beispiel für eine Schreibaufgabe.

1 Lies zuerst die Arbeitsanweisungen. Welche wichtigen Wörter würdest du unterstreichen?

2 Nun lies Annas Lösung der Aufgabe.

Sind der Anfang und das Ende des Textes wie bei einer E-Mail?

Enthält Annas E-Mail **alle** geforderten Punkte in der Arbeitsanweisung?

Hat sie 100 Wörter geschrieben?

> *Du warst mit deinen Eltern im "Bluetree Hotel" in London und hast dort deine Jacke vergessen. Schreibe eine E-Mail ans Hotel (ca. 100 Wörter).*
> – *Berichte, dass du vom 15–18 August im Hotel warst.*
> – *Sage, dass es euch dort gefallen hat.*
> – *Sage, dass du deine Jacke dort liegen gelassen hast.*
> – *Nenne eure Zimmernummer.*
> – *Beschreibe die Jacke.*
> – *Bitte darum, die Jacke nachzuschicken.*
> – *Nenne eure Adresse.*
> – *Sage, dass du für die Versandkosten aufkommen wirst.*
> – *Bitte um baldige Antwort.*

> Dear Sir / Madam
>
> I'm writing to you because we forgot a jacket in your hotel. We were at the Bluetree Hotel last week from 15.–18. August and enjoyed the stay very much. Unfortunately I forgot my jacket on the bed in room number 214. Could you please send the jacket to the following adress:
>
> Anna Schwarz
> Eichelhäherweg 4
> D-84028 Landshut
>
> I look forward to hearing from you soon.
>
> Best wishes
> Anna Schwarz

---

2 Es gibt einen Fehler in jedem Satz. Nein, man soll den Fehler nicht durchstreichen, sondern die korrekte Information auf der Linie eintragen. Ja, es gibt ein Beispiel.

3.2 Anna hat drei Punkte nicht berücksichtigt: Sie hat die Jacke nicht beschrieben und nicht gesagt, dass sie die Kosten für den Versand übernehmen wird. Außerdem hat sie keine 100 Wörter geschrieben.

SF 5 Eigene Texte schreiben und überarbeiten

→ Unit 1 | p.15   → Unit 2 | p.41   → Unit 3 | p.45, 47, 57   → Exam training | p.102f.

A Welche Art von Text willst du verfassen?

1 Persönlicher Brief oder E-Mail

- Beginne mit einer persönlichen Anrede, z.B.
  Dear Victoria oder *Hi Ege!*
- Frage, wie es deinem Freund oder deiner
  Freundin geht: *How are you?*
- Erzähle, wie es dir geht, und was bei dir
  gerade los ist:
  *I feel OK. I'm working hard for school at
  the moment because ...*
- Frage, was bei deinem Freund oder deiner
  Freundin passiert oder geplant ist:
  What did you do last ...?
  What are your plans for ...?
- Schreibe am Ende immer einen freundlichen
  Gruß, z.B. *Best wishes* oder *Lots of love*
  und deinen Namen.

2 Formeller Brief oder E-Mail

Bei formellen Briefen (z.B. eine Beschwerde
oder ein Bewerbungsschreiben) beachte
diese Gestaltungsmerkmale:

- Beginne mit *Dear Sir / Madam*
- Nenne dann den Grund deines
  Schreibens, z.B.:
  I am writing to ... because ...
- Verwende keine Kurzformen:

I'm	→	*I am*
I'd	→	*I would*
wasn't	→	*was not*
won't	→	*will not*

- Beende den Brief mit diesem Satz:
  *I look forward to hearing
  from you soon.*
- Dann schreibe:
  Yours sincerely
  und deinen Vor- und Nachnamen.

Dear Sir / Madam

I read your online advertisement for part-time
sales assistants at your store and I would like
to apply for this job.

I am a student and last year I had a Saturday
job in a department store for five months.
I worked at the cash desk in the shoe
department, so I think I would be very suitable
for the job.

I am dynamic and reliable, and I enjoy working
with people. I speak good English, it is my
favourite subject at school. I am doing my final
exams in May and am available from 1st June.

I attach my CV and I look forward to hearing
from you soon.

Yours sincerely

Max Mustermann

3 Story

- Finde einen guten Titel für deine Geschichte.
- Beschreibe am Beginn die Situation:
  - Wann spielt die Geschichte? *(When?)*
  - Wo ist es passiert? *(Where?)*
  - Welche Personen kommen vor *(Who?)*
  - Was tun die Personen? *(What?)*
- Erzähle dann im Hauptteil, was den Personen passiert.
- Finde ein interessantes Ende und schreibe einen guten Schlusssatz.

Deine Geschichte wird besser, wenn du …

- sagst, wie sich die Personen gefühlt haben,
- genaue Zeitangaben machst,
- deine Sätze mit *linking words* verbindest.

4 Post oder Blog

- Du schreibst über dich und sagst deine persönliche Meinung oder erzählst von deinen eigenen Erlebnissen:
  I think, in my opinion, my day, …
- Verbinde deine Sätze mit *linking words*.
- Bitte um Kommentare:
  What do you think? Please comment.

5 Argumentativer Text

In einem argumentativen Text sollst du das Pro und Kontra einer Fragestellung erörtern. Befolge diesen Aufbau:

- Beginne mit einem Einführungssatz und stelle das Thema vor.
- Dann trage Argumente vor, die für das Thema sprechen.
- Danach folgen die Kontra-Argumente.
- Am Ende sage deine Meinung.

Dein Text wird besser, wenn du …

- deine Sätze mit *linking words* verbindest,
- die Satzanfänge im Kasten rechts verwendest.

Time phrases for storytelling

yesterday	gestern
last week	letzte Woche
first	zuerst
then	dann
after	nach, nachdem
before	bevor, vorher
suddenly	plötzlich
while	während
when	als
two years ago	vor zwei Jahren

Linking words

and	und
because	da, weil
so	daher
but	aber
although	obwohl

Sentence starters

Many people say that …
    Viele Menschen sagen, dass …
On the one hand, …
    Einerseits …
On the other hand, …
    Andererseits …
One reason why …
    Ein Grund warum …
What's more, …
    Ferner …
I also think that …
    Außerdem finde ich, dass …
Above all, …
    Vor allem …
So all in all, …
    Alles in allem …
In my opinion …
    Meiner Meinung nach …

B Folge diesen vier Schritten beim Schreiben:

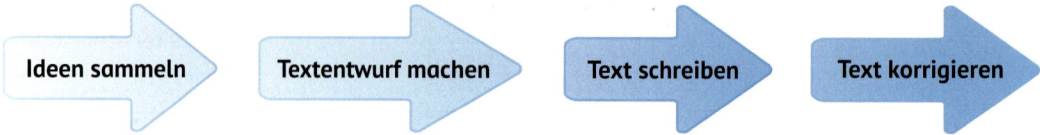

Ideen sammeln → Textentwurf machen → Text schreiben → Text korrigieren

1 Ideen sammeln

Sammle zuerst wichtige Ideen und Wörter, z.B. in einem *wordweb* oder einer Liste.

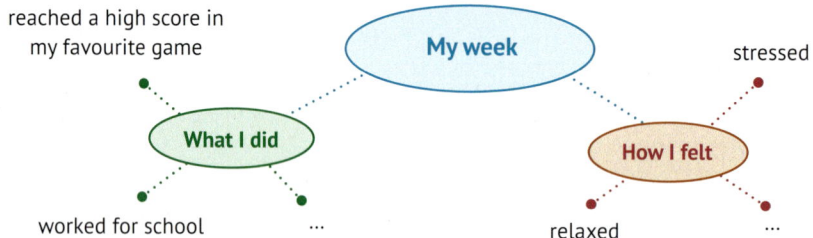

reached a high score in my favourite game

My week

stressed

What I did

How I felt

worked for school

...

relaxed

...

2 Textentwurf machen

- Mache einen ersten Entwurf auf einem Blatt Papier oder am Computer.
- Schreibst du eine E-Mail oder einen Blog? Beachte die Hinweise auf den beiden vorherigen Seiten.
- Überlege dir eine sinnvolle Reihenfolge und mache Absätze bei neuen Punkten.
- Texte aus dem Buch sind oft ein gutes Muster. Nimm sie als Basis, ändere sie und ergänze deine eigenen Ideen.

3 Text schreiben

- Verwende *time phrases* und *linking words*.
- Wenn du eine Geschichte schreibst: Sage, wie sich die Personen *fühlten (happy, disappointed, scared, tired, ...)*.

Vergleiche z.B. diese beiden Texte.
Welcher klingt besser?

> **A bad day**
> I got up late. I missed the school bus. The maths test didn't go well. My favourite football team lost.

> **A bad day**
> Last Monday was a terrible day. First my mobile didn't wake me and I got up too late. So I missed the bus and arrived late at school. I felt stupid. Then the maths test didn't go well and I was sad. Later in the evening my favourite football team lost an important game. I was so disappointed!

4 Text korrigieren

Ein Text ist noch nicht fertig, wenn du ihn zu Ende geschrieben hast! Lies ihn danach noch zweimal durch.

a Rechtschreibung
- Achte auf die richtige Groß- und Kleinschreibung.
- Bist du nicht sicher, wie man ein Wort schreibt? Dann schlage es im Wörterbuch nach.

b Grammatik
- Schreibst du über die Gegenwart?
  Oder über Dinge, die du regelmäßig machst?
  (Signalwörter: *today, often, always*)
  → Dann brauchst du das *simple present*:
    I *always go* to school by bike.

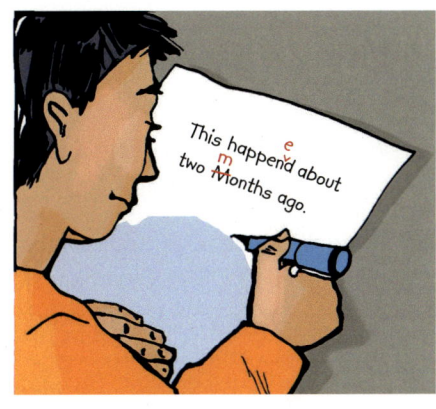

- Schreibst du über die Vergangenheit,
  also über Sachen, die schon passiert sind?
  (Signalwörter: *yesterday, last Friday*)
  → Dann brauchst du das *simple past*:
    Last summer we *went* to the seaside.

- Schreibst du über Dinge, die du vorhast oder
  für die Zukunft planst?
  (Signalwörter: *tomorrow, next Monday*)
  Dann brauchst du das *going to-future*:
  Tomorrow I'm *going to visit* my grandparents.

- Ist die Wortstellung korrekt? Achte besonders
  auf Nebensätze. Dort ist die Wortstellung
  im Englischen anders als im Deutschen.
  I'd like to be a zoo keeper because I *love* animals.
  Ich möchte Tierpfleger werden, weil ich Tiere liebe.

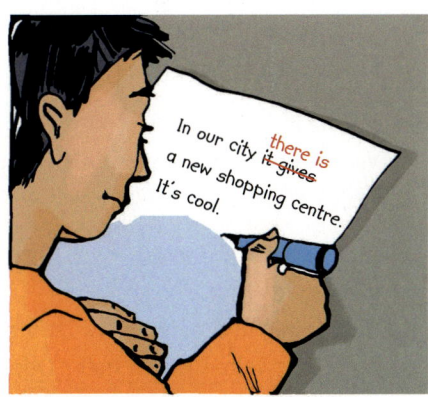

  Häufigkeitsadverbien wie *always, never, usually*
  etc. stehen im Englischen immer vor dem Verb:
  I *usually get up* at 6.30.
  Ich stehe normalerweise um halb sieben auf.

Partner check:
Falls möglich: Suche dir einen Partner/eine Partnerin und tauscht eure Texte aus. Versteht ihr den Text des/der anderen? Findet ihr noch Fehler?

SF 6   Hören und Notizen machen

→ Unit 1 | p.24   → Unit 2 | p.29   → Unit 3 | p.43   → Unit 4 | p.59, 61   → Exam training | p.97

1   Vor dem Hören

a   Lies immer zuerst die Aufgabe.
Lies sorgfältig. Schau dir Beispiel 1 an.
Sollst du ein oder mehrere Häkchen machen?
Wie oft wirst du den Text hören?

b   Stelle dir die Situation vor.
Worüber könnten Lynn und Anthony sprechen?
• Gemüse? Salat? Was noch?

c   Wenn du das richtige Bild abhaken sollst:
• Schau dir die Bilder vor dem Hören genau an.
• Welche englischen Wörter wirst du in Beispiel 2 wohl hören?

2   Beim Hören

a   Achte auf die Wörter in der Aufgabe.
• Achtung! Die Informationen könnten in einer anderen Reihenfolge auftauchen.
• Im Hörtext könnten andere Ausdrücke mit ähnlicher Bedeutung vorkommen.
In Beispiel 3 hörst du vielleicht *a small village* statt *country* oder *punctual* statt *on time*.

b   Mache dir Notizen.
Verwende Symbole oder Abkürzungen, z.B. „+" für *and*.

c   Gib nicht auf, wenn du etwas nicht verstanden hast.
Bleib ruhig und höre weiter zu. Vielleicht verstehst du beim zweiten Hören mehr. Oder vielleicht brauchst du diese Information gar nicht.

3   Nach dem Hören

a   Vervollständige deine Notizen sofort.

b   Konzentriere dich auf deine Lücken. Achte beim zweiten Hören auf das, was du beim ersten Hören nicht gut verstanden hast.

1
*You're going to hear a radio programme.
Lynn Baker and Anthony Sheldon are talking about healthy eating.
First read the tasks 1–6.
Then listen to the programme.
Tick the correct box. Tick only one box.
At the end you will hear the programme again.*

2
*What's Lynn's favourite food?
Tick* A, B *or* C.

A ☐   B ☐   C ☐

3
*Tim was away for the weekend.
Listen to his report. Tick* A, B *or* C.
You will hear the recording twice.

Tim was   A ☐ *in London.*
               B ☐ *in the country.*
               C ☐ *at his grandpa's house.*

He visited   A ☐ *his grandpa.*
               B ☐ *his friend Jo.*
               C ☐ *his sister Emma.*

Tim is   A ☐ *always on time.*
               B ☐ *often very late.*
               C ☐ *sometimes a bit late.*

1a   Man soll nur ein Häkchen machen. Man kann die Aufnahme zweimal hören.
1b   wenig Süßigkeiten, viel Obst, viel trinken, …
1c   cake, pasta, salad

SF 7 **Über Bilder sprechen**

→ Unit 1 | p.12   → Unit 2 | p.28   → Unit 3 | p.44, 55   → Exam training | p.106

Wenn du über ein Bild oder ein Foto sprechen sollst, dann merke dir die folgenden Schritte:

1 **Beginne allgemein.**

Sage zunächst in ein oder zwei Sätzen, was du auf dem Bild siehst. Welcher Ort ist zu sehen? Welche Menschen? Was tun sie?

In the picture I can see four young people. They're in a park. Three of them are walking along a path, one man is riding his bike.

2 **Sage, wo sich was befindet.**

Sage, was du im Vordergrund und im Hintergrund siehst und was links, in der Mitte und rechts auf dem Bild zu sehen ist.

In the foreground there are four young people, three men and a woman.

In the background you can see some trees and a small orange building.

3 **Ordne die Personen und Dinge einander zu.**
Verwende Präpositionen:
Two young men are on the left and the other man is on the right. The young woman is between the two men on the left and the man on the right.

4 **Beschreibe die Personen und sage, was sie gerade tun.**
Verwende das *present progressive* (siehe auch *Language file 2*, S.127):
Three young people are walking along a path, one man is riding his bike. It's a sunny afternoon in autumn or late summer. The young men and the woman are talking and smiling. They look sporty and fit and they are all wearing sports clothes – shorts and trainers. The man on the left is riding a blue BMX bike. He's wearing yellow trainers, a grey hoodie and a grey cap. The man next to him is wearing black trainers and a blue sports jacket. The woman is carrying a skateboard. She has long, blonde hair and is wearing a yellow hoodie and green trainers. The man on the right is wearing a white T-shirt and black shorts and trainers. He has an orange ball in his left hand.

5 **Formuliere Vermutungen über die Personen und begründe sie.**
I think the young people are friends and they often do sports together.
Perhaps they will go home now and spend the evening together.

SF 8 Einen Kurzvortrag halten

→ Unit 2 | p.39 → Unit 3 | p.45, 55 → Unit 4 | p.93 → Exam training | p.107

1 Erarbeitung

a Sammle Ideen und ordne sie.
- Was passt zum Thema und was nicht?
- Welche Reihenfolge ist am besten? Womit fängst du an? Womit hörst du auf?
- Wie kannst du das Interesse deiner Zuhörer/innen wecken? Mit einem ungewöhnlichen Anfang? Mit interessanten Bildern?

cities · the *Big Five* · **South Africa** · history · soccer · languages

b Besorge dir Informationen.
- Verwende mehrere Quellen. Informationen aus dem Internet sind nicht immer korrekt.
- Schreibe die Texte nicht wörtlich ab.
- Erkläre schwierige oder unbekannte Wörter für deine Zuhörer/innen.

c Erstelle einfache Computerfolien.
Wenn du eine Präsentation am Computer machst:
- Wähle ein einfaches Folienlayout und eine gut lesbare Schrift von mindestens 16 pt.
- Die Informationen auf den Folien sollten kurz und verständlich sein.

Places to see
- Johannesburg
- Cape Town
- Kruger National Park
- Robben Island

d Übe deinen Vortrag.
Übe die Präsentation mehrmals und achte auf die Zeit.

2 Durchführung

a Am Anfang des Vortrags
- Sage, worüber du sprechen möchtest.

b Während des Vortrags
- Sprich langsam und deutlich.
- Lies deine Computerfolien nicht ab.
- Schaue deine Zuhörer/innen an.
- Erkläre unbekannte Wörter.
- Weise auf Bilder hin.

c Am Ende des Vortrags
- Sage, wann dein Vortrag zu Ende ist.
- Bedanke dich fürs Zuhören und frage deine Mitschüler/innen, ob sie noch Fragen haben.

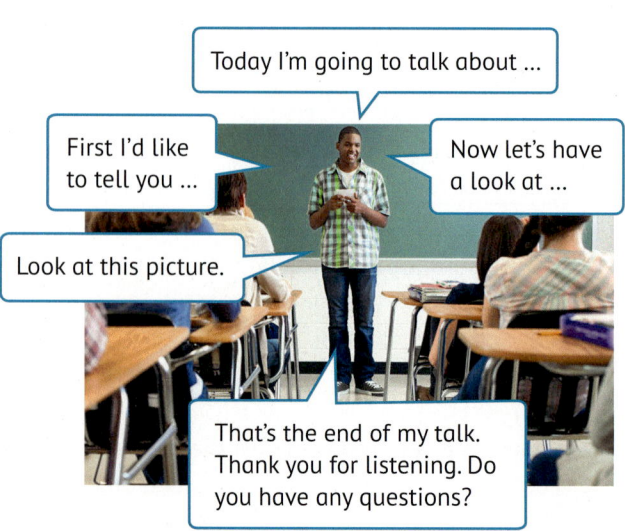

Today I'm going to talk about …

First I'd like to tell you …

Now let's have a look at …

Look at this picture.

That's the end of my talk. Thank you for listening. Do you have any questions?

SF 9 Mediation

→ Unit 1 | p. 23, 25   → Unit 3 | pp. 52, 56   → Exam training | pp. 104, 107

1 Worum geht es?

Mediation bedeutet, zwischen zwei Sprachen zu vermitteln, z. B.

- englische Informationen auf Deutsch weitergeben: Du bist z. B. mit deiner Familie im Auto unterwegs und dein Vater möchte wissen, was auf dem Schild rechts steht.

- deutsche Informationen auf Englisch wiedergeben: Vielleicht ist bei dir zu Hause ein Austauschschüler zu Gast, der kein Deutsch spricht.

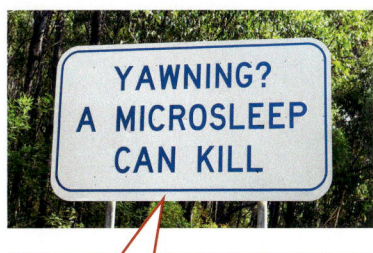

Da steht was von gefährlichem "Mikroschlaf" – also Sekundenschlaf. Man soll eine Pause machen, wenn man müde ist.

2 Worauf musst du achten?

- *Mediation* ist keine wörtliche Übersetzung.
  Deshalb gib nur das Wesentliche wieder und lasse unwichtige Informationen weg.
- Verwende kurze und einfache Sätze.
- Beachte die Wortstellung – sie ist im Englischen oft anders als im Deutschen.

You're here – in Clayton Road.
There's a cafe in Grove Street.
It's nice and cheap.
Just walk along Clayton Road,
then turn left into Grove Street.
The cafe is on your right.

Sie kennt ein Café in der Nähe. Wir sollen die nächste Straße links abbiegen.

- Wenn du ein Wort nicht kennst, sage es anders. Beispiele:

(Busanzeige) Betriebsfahrt	– *This is the wrong bus.*
Außer Betrieb	– *It doesn't work.*
Hunde sind an der Leine zu führen.	– *Dogs can't run free.*

- Wie könntest du Folgendes auf Englisch sagen?
  - *Bitte Schritt fahren.*
  - *Kein Winterdienst.*
  - *Für Garderobe wird nicht gehaftet.*
  - *Ferienwohnung belegt.*

There's no waiter.

---

2 Please drive very slowly.   Be careful in winter, it can be icy.
Look after your coat or jacket.   The holiday apartment is not free.

LF 1 *Simple present*

bejahte Sätze	Yes
I You We You They	start early.

| He
She
It | start**s** early. |

verneinte Sätze	No
I You We They	**don't** start early.

| He
She
It | **doesn't** start early. |

Fragen mit do/does	?
Do I Do you **Does** he/she/it Do we Do they	like crabs?

Fragen mit Fragewörtern	?
Where do I go now? Why do you do this? What **does** he/she/it do? When do we arrive? How do they run?

Mit dem *simple present* (einfache Gegenwart) sagst du, was oft oder jeden Tag passiert und auch was selten oder nie geschieht:
I often go to the sports club.
We never have lunch at school.

Mit *he/she/it* musst du immer ein -*s* an das Verb anhängen. **Achtung:** bei einigen Verben wird -*es* angehängt:

do	–	*do**es***
wash	–	*wash**es***
watch	–	*watch**es***

Wenn du sagen willst, dass etwas nicht passiert oder der Fall ist, setzt du *don't* vor das Verb. Mit *he/she/it* verwendest du *doesn't*.

He doesn't want to dive.

Fragen, auf die man mit *ja* oder *nein* antworten kann, beginnen mit *Do* oder *Does*.

Mit *I/you/we/they* verwendest du *Do*.
Mit *he/she/it* verwendest du *Does*.

Auch Fragen mit Fragewort *(What? When? Where? Who? Why?)* stellst du mit *do* bzw. *does*.

Du verwendest *do* bei *I/you/we/they* und *does* bei *he/she/it*.

Das Fragewort steht wie im Deutschen am Anfang.

LF 2 *Present progressive*

→ Unit 3 | p.53

I'm reading a comic.
Ich lese grade einen Comic.

Dad is cooking dinner.
Papa macht gerade das Abendessen.

What are you doing at the moment?
Was machst du jetzt gerade?

bejahte Sätze	Yes
I'm You're He's She's It's We're You're They're	helping.

verneinte Sätze	No
I'm not You aren't He isn't She isn't It isn't We aren't You aren't They aren't	helping.

Fragen	?
Am I Are you Is he Is she Is it Are we Are you Are they	helping?

Mit dem *present progressive* (*ing*-Form) sagst du, was jetzt gerade passiert.
Damit beschreibst du auch, was man auf Bildern tut.

Diese Zeitangaben findest du oft in Sätzen im *present progressive:*
now, at the moment, today.

Das *present progressive* besteht aus zwei Teilen:

'm oder *'re* oder *'s*	+	Verb + *-ing*

They're feeding the birds.

Achtung: Bei Verben, die auf *-e* enden, fällt das *e* bei der *ing*-Form weg:

come	–	coming
make	–	making
ride	–	riding

Bei einigen Verben wird der letzte Buchstabe verdoppelt:

plan	–	planning
stop	–	stopping
sit	–	sitting

LF 3   *Simple past*

→ Unit 4 | p.70

Yesterday evening I watched TV.
Gestern Abend habe ich ferngesehen/sah ich fern.

Last week I didn't go to football training.
Letzte Woche ging ich nicht zum Fußballtraining.

Did you watch the fireworks last night?
Hast du gestern abend das Feuerwerk gesehen?

bejahte Sätze	Yes
I/You He/She/It We/They	helped.

verneinte Sätze	No
I/You He/She/It We/They	didn't help.

Fragen mit did		?
Did	I/you he/she/it we/they	help?

Fragen mit Fragewörtern			?
What	did	she	watch?
When	did	it	finish?
Where	did	they	go?

What did she watch?
She watched the fireworks.

Kurzantworten	Yes	No
Yes, I/you did.		No, I/you didn't.
Yes, he/she/it did.		No, he/she/it didn't.
Yes, we/they did.		No, we/they didn't.

Mit dem *simple past* sprichst du über Dinge, die in der Vergangenheit geschehen sind. Du verwendest es oft mit Zeitangaben wie *yesterday, last week, last year, last summer, in 2019*. Die Vergangenheitsform ist für alle Personen gleich.

Bei regelmäßigen Verben hängst du *-ed* an das Verb: *walk – walked   look – looked* Bei Verben, die auf *-e* enden, wird nur *-d* angehängt: *arrive – arrived*

Unregelmäßige Formen musst du lernen: *buy – bought*, *go – went* Du kannst sie auf S.200–201 nachschlagen.

Wenn du sagen willst, was nicht geschah, setzt du *didn't* vor das Verb.
Achtung: Das Verb steht dann immer in der Grundform: *He didn't watch*.
! **nicht:** *He didn't watched*.

Fragen im *simple past* bildest du mit *did* und der Grundform des Verbs.
Achtung:
Das Verb bleibt immer in der Grundform: *Did he watch?*
! **nicht:** *Did he watched?*

Manche Fragen beginnen mit Fragewörtern. Auch hier verwendet man *did* bei allen Personen und das Verb in der Grundform: *How did it go?*
! **nicht:** *How did it went?*

Achtung: Bei den Antworten musst du das Verb in die Vergangenheitsform setzen.

Kurzantworten bildest du mit *did* oder *didn't*.

LF 4 *Past progressive*

→ Unit 1 | p.19

At two o'clock we were still wait**ing** for the bus.
Um zwei Uhr warteten wir noch immer auf den Bus.

Dad was cook**ing** dinner when I came into the kitchen.
Papa machte gerade das Abendessen als ich in die Küche kam.

bejahte Sätze	**Yes**
I was	
You were	
He was	
She was	eat**ing**.
It was	
We were	
You were	
They were	

verneinte Sätze	**No**
I wasn't	
You weren't	
He wasn't	
She wasn't	eat**ing**.
It wasn't	
We weren't	
You weren't	
They weren't	

Fragen	**?**
Was I	
Were you	
Was he	
Was she	eat**ing**?
Was it	
Were we	
Were you	
Were they	

Mit dem *past progressive* sagst du, was in der Vergangenheit gerade im Gange war.

Wenn eine neue Handlung dazu kommt, steht diese im *simple past*.

Das *past progressive* wird mit *was/were* und der *ing*-Form des Verbs gebildet.

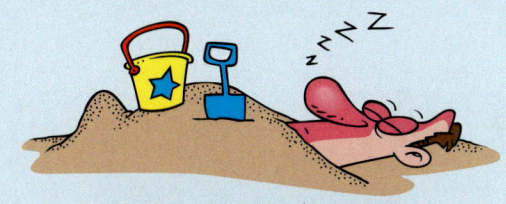

When I came to the beach he was sleeping.

He wasn't singing at the concert yesterday– he was rapping!

What were you doing when I phoned you? – I was cleaning the flat.

LF 5 *Present perfect*

→ Unit 4 | p. 69, 70

I have already done my homework.
Ich habe meine Hausaufgaben schon gemacht.

My little sister has never been on a plane.
Meine kleine Schwester ist noch nie geflogen.

Have you ever ridden a pony?
Bist du schon einmal geritten?

bejahte Sätze	Yes
I You We They	have started early. 've started early.
He She It	has started early.

verneinte Sätze	No
I You We They	haven't started early.
He She It	hasn't started early.

Fragen und Kurzantworten	?
Have you started?	– Yes, I have. – No, I haven't.
Has she started?	– Yes, she has. – No, she hasn't.

Since oder for?

We have lived in this flat since 2018.
She has been in our class for two months.

Mit dem *present perfect* sagst du
– dass du etwas schon oder eben gemacht hast. Signalwörter: *already, just.*
– dass du etwas schon einmal, öfter oder nie gemacht hast. Signalwörter: *ever, never, once, twice, lots of times.*

I've just done exercise.

Das *present perfect* besteht aus zwei Teilen: *have* oder *has* (Kurzformen: *'ve oder 's*) + *past participle* (eine besondere Verbform)

Wie bildest du das *past participle*?
Bei regelmäßigen Verben hängst du *-ed* an das Verb: *walk – walk*ed

Bei Verben, die auf *-e* enden, wird nur *-d* angehängt: *arrive – arrive*d

Unregelmäßige Formen musst du lernen:
be	*– been*	*find*	*– found*
go	*– gone*	*have*	*– had*
make	*– made*	*meet*	*– met*

Du findest sie in der dritten Spalte der Liste der unregelmäßigen Verben auf S. 200–201.

Mit dem *present perfect* sagst du auch, wie lange etwas schon andauert. Dann verwendest du *since* zur Angabe eines Zeitpunkts: *since 3 o'clock, since May.*

For brauchst du zur Angabe eines Zeitraums: *for ten weeks, for two days.*

LF 6   *Will-future*

I think you**'ll have** a great birthday party.

Ich glaube, du wirst eine tolle Geburtstagsparty haben.

Maybe we**'ll have** a barbecue in the garden.

Vielleicht grillen wir im Garten.

bejahte Sätze		**Yes**
It	will 'll	be sunny tomorrow.

verneinte Sätze		**No**
It	will not won't	be sunny tomorrow.

Fragen und Kurzantworten	**?**
Will it be sunny?	Yes, it will. / No, it won't.

Wenn du vermutest, was in der Zukunft geschehen könnte, verwendest du das *will-future*.

Die Sätze beginnen oft mit *I think, maybe, I'm sure*.

Du bildest das *will-future* mit *will* und mit dem Infinitiv eines Verbs.

Die Kurzform von *will* ist *'ll*.
Die Kurzform von *will not* ist *won't*.

I won't be able to go on the bike tour next Sunday.

LF 7   *Going to-future*

→ Unit 2 | p.37

We**'re going** to have a picnic on Sunday.

Wir haben vor, am Sonntag ein Picknick zu machen.

Oh no, he**'s going to** fall!

Oh nein, er fällt gleich herunter!

bejahte Sätze			**Yes**
It	's	going to	rain tomorrow.

verneinte Sätze			**No**
It	isn't	going to	rain tomorrow.

Fragen und Kurzantworten	**?**
Is it going to rain?	Yes, it is. / No, it isn't.

Mit *going to* … sagst du
- was du vorhast oder für die Zukunft geplant hast,
- was wahrscheinlich bald passieren wird.

Du bildest das *going to-future* mit *'m, 're, 's* + *going to* + Verb.

Achtung:
Das Verb bleibt immer in der Grundform:
I'm going to watch a video.
! **nicht:** *I'm going to watching a video.*

LF 8 *Simple present* mit Zukunftsbezug

Our bus leaves tomorrow at 8.30.
Unser Bus fährt morgen um 8.30 Uhr.

The concert takes place on 28 July.
Das Konzert findet am 28. Juli statt.

> Man verwendet das *simple present* für zukünftige Ereignisse, wenn diese durch einen Fahrplan, Kalender oder ein Programm festgelegt sind.
>
> Häufige Verben:
> *start, begin, end, arrive, leave, open, close*

LF 9 Wortstellung

→ Unit 3 | p.51

Hauptsätze

S	V	O
My mum	loves	old cars.

> In Aussagesätzen lautet die Reihenfolge wie im Deutschen: Subject – Verb – Objekt.

Nebensätze

	S	V	O
He cried when	he	left	his family.
I work because	I	need	the money.

> Dies gilt auch in Nebensätzen.
> Im Deutschen ist die Wortstellung anders:
> *He was happy when he got his present.*
> *Er war glücklich, als er sein Geschenk bekam.*

Zeitangaben

(When?)	S	V	O	(When?)
At 12.30	he	has	lunch.	
	He	has	lunch	at 12.30.

> Zeitangaben (*at 2 o'clock, in the morning, yesterday* etc.) stehen ganz am Anfang oder ganz am Ende des Satzes.

Ortsangaben

S	V	O	(Where?)
I	have	lunch	at school.

> Ortsangaben (*in town, at home, at school* etc.) stehen nach dem Verb und Objekt.

Orts- und Zeitangaben

S	V	O	(Where?)	(When?)
She	met	him	in Dublin	yesterday.
He	has	lunch	at home	at 12.30.

> Bei Orts- und Zeitangaben in einem Satz gilt im Englischen die Regel:
>
> Ort vor Zeit (wie im Alphabet).
> Im Deutschen ist es umgekehrt!

Angaben zur Art und Weise und Ortsangaben

S	V	O	(how?)	(where?)
She	worked		hard	at school.
She	has	lunch		at school.

> Angaben zur Art und Weise (*hard, quickly, well* etc.) und Ortsangaben (*in town, at home, at school* etc.) stehen nach dem Prädikat und Objekt.

LF 10 Bedingungssätze

If you **send** me a message, I'll come.
Wenn du mir eine Nachricht schickst, komme ich.

If it **rains** tomorrow, we **won't** play football.
Wenn es morgen regnet, spielen wir nicht Fußball.

Arsenal **will** win if they **shoot** two goals.
Arsenal wird gewinnen, wenn sie zwei Tore schießen.

Mit Bedingungssätzen sagst du, was unter bestimmten Bedingungen geschehen wird.

Sie bestehen aus zwei Teilen:
– einem Nebensatz mit *if* im *simple present*
– einem Hauptsatz mit *will*, *'ll* oder *won't*.

Der *if*-Satz kann vor oder nach dem Hauptsatz stehen.

If the food in the cafeteria doesn't get better, I'll take a sandwich from home.

If you **look** after your sister, I **can** go shopping.
Wenn du auf deine Schwester aufpasst, kann ich einkaufen gehen.

If you **go** shopping, **buy** some milk.
Wenn du einkaufen gehst, kaufe Milch.

Der Hauptsatz kann statt *will* auch *can* oder einen Imperativ (Befehl) enthalten.

If I'm quick, I can still arrive on time.

If plants **don't get** water, they **die**.
Wenn Pflanzen kein Wasser bekommen, gehen sie ein.

Bei allgemein gültigen Wahrheiten steht sowohl im *if*-Satz als auch im Hauptsatz das *simple present*. *If* bedeutet dann "immer wenn".

LF 11 Relativsätze

That's the guy *who* lives in our street.
Das ist der Typ, der in unserer Straße wohnt.

It's the app *which* we need.
Es ist die App, die wir brauchen.

Who
This is the man *who* works at the hotel. Are you the girl *who* won the first prize?

Which
The game *which* I bought yesterday is OK. The film *which* we saw was boring.

That
Sue is the girl *that* plays the drums. The mobile *that*'s on the table is mine.

Mit Relativsätzen kannst du zusätzliche Informationen über eine Person oder eine Sache geben. Sie werden durch die Relativpronomen *who, which* oder *that* eingeleitet.

Für Personen verwendest du *who*.

Für Dinge benutzt du *which*.

Das Relativpronomen *that* kann für Personen und Dinge stehen.

LF 12 Adverbien

Don't walk so *slowly*.
Geh nicht so langsam.

She's jumping angrily on her laptop.

clear – clearly	angry – angrily
nervous – nervously	happy – happily
quick – quickly	safe – safely
sad – sadly	full – fully
slow – slowly	realistic – realistically

Adverbien sagen, auf welche Weise etwas geschieht. Sie stehen meist nach dem Verb.

Verwechsle sie nicht mit Adjektiven. Adjektive beschreiben eine Person oder eine Sache genauer und stehen vor dem Nomen.

a careful driver ⟷ *(to) drive carefully*
a perfect dress ⟷ *it fits perfectly*

Die meisten Adverbien bildet man durch Anfügen von *-ly* an ein Adjektiv. Manchmal gibt es Unregelmäßigkeiten bei der Schreibung.

! Diese Ausnahmen musst du lernen:
Das Adverb zu *good* ist *well*: *She did well.*
Bei *hard* und *fast* sind Adjektiv und Adverb gleich: *He worked hard. She drives fast.*

LF 13 Die Vergleichsformen des Adjektivs

Mum is taller than dad. But I'm the tallest.

Mama ist größer als Papa. Aber ich bin der Größte.

This shop is more expensive than the market.

Dieses Geschäft ist teurer als der Markt.

The most expensive bike is not the best.

Das teuerste Fahrrad ist nicht das Beste.

Personen, Sachen und Tiere kann man vergleichen.

He's faster than me!

cheap	cheaper	cheapest
near	nearer	nearest
tall	taller	tallest

Bei einsilbigen Adjektiven und Adjektiven, die auf -y enden, hängst du -er bzw. -est an das Adjektiv.

big	bigger	the biggest
hot	hotter	the hottest
noisy	noisier	the noisiest
happy	happier	the happiest

Bei einigen Adjektiven musst du bei der Schreibung aufpassen.

famous	more famous	most famous
expensive	more expensive	most expensive
exciting	more exciting	most exciting
popular	more popular	most popular

Bei zweisilbigen Adjektiven, die nicht auf -y enden und dreisilbigen Adjektiven setzt du *more* bzw. *most* vor das Adjektiv.

Your eyes are worse than last year.

! Diese Ausnahmen musst du lernen:
good – better – best
gut – besser – am besten
bad – worse – worst
schlecht – schlechter – am schlechtesten
little – less – least
wenig – weniger – am wenigsten

Tom is as old as Luca

Tom ist so alt wie Luca.

I'm not as tall as my dad.

Ich bin nicht so groß wie mein Papa.

The red bike is as expensive as the green one.

Das rote Fahrrad ist so teuer wie das grüne.

Wenn du sagen willst, dass zwei Personen oder Dinge genau gleich alt, groß, teuer etc. sind, verwendest du *as ... as*.

LF 14 Mengenangaben

zählbar

nicht zählbar

Bei Mengenangaben im Englischen musst du oft unterscheiden, ob es sich um zählbare oder nicht zählbare Dinge handelt.

Zählbare Dinge kannst du in die Mehrzahl setzen: *one egg* → *two eggs*

Nicht zählbare Dinge haben keine Mehrzahl: *butter, cheese, money, tea, coffee, salt, pepper.*

Mit *lots of, much* oder *many* kannst du über größere Mengen sprechen.

In bejahten Sätzen verwendest du meistens *lots of* – bei zählbaren und nicht zählbaren Dingen.

lots of

We've got lots of eggs.
I don't like lots of salt on my chips.

She has lots of bags.

In verneinten Sätzen verwendest du
– *not many* bei zählbaren Dingen (nicht viele),

– *not much* bei nicht zählbaren Dingen (nicht viel).

not many

I don't have many pencils.
My dad doesn't watch many films.

not much

I don't eat much chocolate.
There isn't much sugar in my tea.

Bei kleinen Mengen verwendest du bei zählbaren Dingen
– *a few* (einige).

a few

There are only a few sausages left.
There are a few pencils on the table.

Bei nicht zählbaren Mengen sagst du
– *a little* (ein wenig).

a little

Can I have a little milk in my tea, please?
I take my coffee with a little sugar.

LF 15 *Some / no / any* und ihre Zusammensetzungen

some

Some of my friends live in America.

Einige meiner Freunde leben in Amerika.

There's somebody in the kitchen.

Da ist jemand in der Küche.

There's something in your eye.

Da ist etwas in deinem Auge.

Some bedeutet *einige* oder *etwas*.
Es gibt das Wort auch in Zusammensetzungen:

somebody / someone – jemand
something – etwas
somewhere – irgendwo

Du benutzt *some* und seine Zusammensetzungen **in bejahten Sätzen.**

no

I have no money.

Ich habe kein Geld.

Nobody was at home.

Es war niemand zu Hause.

I have nothing to say.

Ich habe nichts zu sagen.

No + Nomen *(no tea, no bread, no juice)*
verwendest du **in bejahten Sätzen** für *kein*.

Auch hier gibt es die Zusammensetzungen:

nobody – niemand
nothing – nichts
nowhere – nirgendwo

Nobody wants
to play with me.

any

There isn't any tea. Is there any juice?

Es ist kein Tee da. Gibt es Saft?

I don't have anything to wear
for the party.

Ich habe für die Party nichts anzuziehen.

Can you see mum anywhere?

Kannst du Mama irgendwo sehen?

In **verneinten Sätzen und Fragen**
verwendest du *any* und seine Zusammensetzungen:

not ... anybody – niemand
not ... anything – nichts
not ... anywhere – nirgendwo

anybody – jemand
anything – etwas
anywhere – irgendwo

LF 16 Personalpronomen

I like Jan. Jan likes me.

Ich mag Jan. Jan mag mich.

She's good at maths. Let's ask her.

Sie ist gut in Mathe. Fragen wir sie.

They're good songs. Listen to them.

Das sind gute Songs. Hör sie dir an.

Subjektform	Objektform
I	me
you	you
he/she/it	him/her/it
we	us
you	you
they	them

Personalpronomen ersetzen Nomen (z.B. *table* → *it*) oder Eigennamen (z.B. *Ben* → *he*).

Sie kommen in zwei Formen vor, je nachdem, ob sie Subjekt oder Objekt des Satzes sind.

Die Objektform steht nach Verben (z.B. *help, meet, see*) oder nach Präpositionen (z.B. *for, with, at*).

Das englische Pronomen *you* kann im Deutschen verschiedene Bedeutungen haben:

You are in my class, Ali. → du
Can *you* help me, boys? → ihr
Can *you* tell me the price, please? → Sie

LF 17 Possessivpronomen

This is my phone. It's mine.

Das ist mein Handy. Es ist meins.

I think it's her bike. It's hers.

Ich glaube, es ist ihr Fahrrad. Es ist ihres.

I've found this book. Is it yours?

Ich habe dieses Buch gefunden. Ist es deines?

mit Nomen	ohne Nomen
my game	mine
your game	yours
his/her/its game	his/hers/its
our game	ours
your game	yours
their game	theirs

Possessivpronomen zeigen an, wem etwas gehört.

Die Possessivpronomen *my, your, his, her, ...* werden vor einem Nomen gebraucht.

Die Possessivpronomen *mine, yours, his, hers, ...* stehen allein, ohne Nomen.

LF 18 Reflexivpronomen

It was my mistake, so I blame myself.

Es war mein Fehler, also gebe ich mir die Schuld.

He has cut himself.

Er hat sich geschnitten.

We can look after ourselves.

Wir können uns um uns selbst kümmern.

I wash myself.
You wash yourself.
He washes himself.
She washes herself.
It washes itself.
We wash ourselves.
You wash yourselves.
They wash themselves.

Reflexivpronomen enden auf *-self* oder *-selves*. Du sagst damit, dass jemand etwas selbst tut.

Vergleiche:
He washed the baby. Er wusch das Baby.
He washed himself. Er wusch sich selbst.

! Einige englische Verben stehen – anders als ihre deutschen Entsprechungen – ohne Reflexivpronomen, z.B.:

(to) change sich (ver-)ändern
(to) decide sich entscheiden
(to) feel sich fühlen
(to) get dressed sich anziehen
(to) hide sich verstecken
(to) meet sich treffen

He's enjoying himself.

Merke dir diese Ausdrücke:
Help yourself! Greif zu! Bediene dich.
Enjoy yourself! Viel Spaß!

Wordbank 1: Places and activities in Australia

I can see …

a desert

a waterfall

a sheep farm

rocks

the outback

a coral reef

a mountain

the sea

a track

a forest

People go …

climbing

camping

sailing

trampolining

fishing

scuba-diving

horse riding

swimming

hiking

snorkelling

skateboarding

surfing

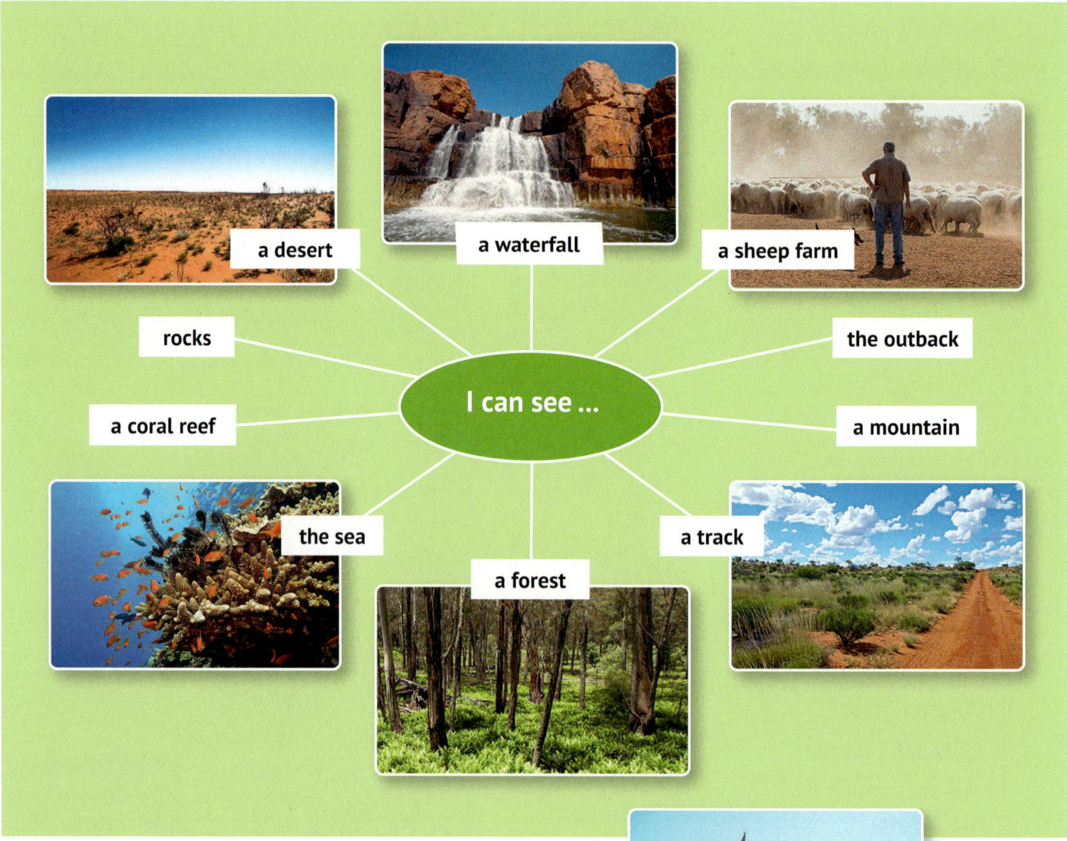

I have ...
a toothache.
a headache.
a stomach ache.
a cough.
a sore throat.
a cold.
the flu.
a temperature.
sunburn.
a rash.
an insect sting.

Ich habe ...
Zahnschmerzen.
Kopfschmerzen.
Magenschmerzen.
Husten.
Halsschmerzen.
Schnupfen.
die Grippe.
Fieber.
Sonnenbrand.
Hautausschlag.
einen Insektenstich.

I have hurt ...
my arm.
my ellbow.
my leg.
my knee.
my ankle.
my foot.
my shoulder.
my hand.

I habe mich ...
am Arm
am Ellenbogen
am Bein
am Knie
am Knöchel
am Fuß
an der Schulter
an der Hand
... verletzt.

General
I feel bad/weak.
I feel sick/dizzy.
I have to throw up.
My ... hurts.
I have a wound on my ...
I need a plaster.
I have sprained my ...
I have broken my ...
I am allergic to ...

Allgemeines
Ich fühle mich schlecht/schwach.
Mir ist schlecht/schwindelig.
Ich muss mich übergeben.
Mein/e ... tut weh.
Ich habe eine Wunde an ...
Ich brauche ein Pflaster.
Ich habe mir den/die ... verstaucht.
Ich habe mir den/die ... gebrochen.
Ich bin allergisch gegen ...

You should ...
rest.
stay in bed.
take painkillers.
take these tablets.
put a bandage on your ...
rub the cream on your skin.

Du solltest/Sie sollten ...
dich/sich ausruhen.
im Bett bleiben.
Schmerztabletten nehmen.
diese Tabletten nehmen.
dein(e)/ihr(e) ... bandagieren.
die Salbe einreiben.

Wordbank 3: Kinds of jobs

Management/Commerce
Verwaltung/Handel
administrative assistant
Verwaltungsangestellte/r
assistant tax inspector
Steuerfachangestellte/r
assistant bank manager
Bankkaufmann/-frau
sales representative
Vertriebsmitarbeiter/in
insurance sales representative
Versicherungskaufmann/-frau
legal assistant
Rechtsanwaltsfachangestellte/r
assistant logistics manager
Speditionskaufmann/-frau
**sales representative in wholesale
and foreign trade**
Kaufmann/-frau im Groß- und
   Außenhandel
office management assistant
Bürokaufmann/-frau
retail assistant manager
Kaufmann/-frau im Einzelhandel
sales assistant
Verkäufer/in
travel agent
Reiseverkehrskaufmann/-frau

Technology / **Technik**
automotive engineer
Fahrzeugtechnik-Ingenieur/in
chemical engineer
Chemieingenieur/in
design engineer
Konstrukteur/in
electrical engineer
Elektroingenieur/in
mechanical engineer
Maschinenbauingenieur/in
mechatronics technician
Mechatroniker/in
motor vehicle technician
Kfz-Mechaniker/in
telecom(munication)s engineer
Fernmeldeingenieur/in

Craft	**Handwerk**
baker	Bäcker/in
bricklayer	Maurer/in
carpenter	Zimmerer/Zimmerin
electrician	Elektriker/in
florist	Florist/in
joiner	Schreiner/in
mechanic	Mechaniker/in
metalworker	Schlosser/in
painter	Maler/in

Service	**Dienstleistung**
beautician	Kosmetiker/in
cashier	Kassierer/in
cook	Koch, Köchin
assistant hotel manager	Hotelkaufmann/-frau
lorry driver	LKW-Fahrer/in
postman/-woman	Briefträger/in
waiter/waitress	Kellner/in

IT and Media	**IT und Medien**
digital web analyst	Webanalyst/in
IT-technician	IT-Techniker/in
media designer	Mediendesigner/in
media technician	Medientechniker/in
programmer	Programmierer/in
software engineer	Software-Entwickler/in

Health care	**Gesundheit und Pflege**
animal keeper	Tierpfleger/in
dentist's assistant	Zahnarzthelfer/in
doctor's assistant	Arzthelfer/in
care worker	Altenpfleger/in
nursery teacher	Erzieher/in
midwife	Hebamme/Entbin-dungspfleger
nutritionist	Ernährungsberater/in
optical technician	Optiker/in
orthopaedic technician	Orthopädietechniker/in
paramedic	Sanitäter/in
physiotherapist	Physiotherapeut/in
nurse	Krankenpfleger/-schwester

Wordbank 4: Places of work

Unit 2 | p.39

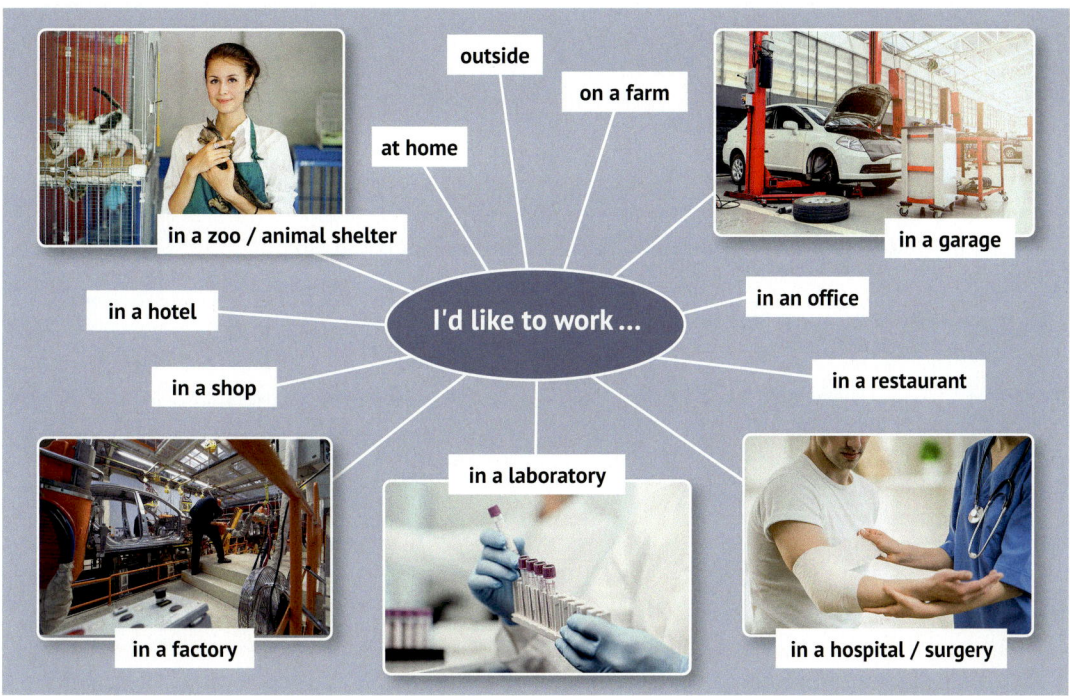

outside

on a farm

at home

in a zoo / animal shelter

in a garage

in a hotel

in an office

I'd like to work ...

in a shop

in a restaurant

in a laboratory

in a factory

in a hospital / surgery

Wordbank 5: Strengths and weaknesses

Unit 2 | p.40

Strengths

caring	warmherzig, liebevoll	**independent**	unabhängig
confident	selbstbewusst, selbstsicher	**motivated**	motiviert
		organized	organisiert, strukturiert
creative	kreativ	**patient**	geduldig
disciplined	diszipliniert	**practical**	geschickt
easy-going	gelassen	**polite**	höflich
energetic	aktiv	**punctual**	pünktlich
flexible	flexibel	**quiet**	ruhig
friendly	freundlich	**reliable**	verlässlich
hard-working	fleißig, tüchtig	**responsible**	verantwortungsbewusst
helpful	hilfsbereit	**sporty**	sportlich
honest	ehrlich, integer	**tidy**	ordentlich

Weaknesses

aggressive	aggressiv	**messy**	unordentlich
dishonest	unehrlich	**selfish**	egoistisch
disorganized	unstrukturiert	**shy**	schüchtern
impolite	unhöflich	**stubborn**	stur
impatient	ungeduldig	**undisciplined**	undiszipliniert
lazy	faul	**unfriendly**	unfreundlich

Wordbank 6: My mobile

Music and films

I have subscribed[1] to ...
I often listen to ...
I usually use ... to listen to music.
I save all my favourite songs to my library.
I usually watch / stream films together with my friends.
I don't often watch films on my mobile because the screen[2] is too small.

Apps

The app I use most often is ...
I use ... to look for information.
... is useful to find ...
... is fun / great / really useful / awesome / easy / ...

Problems

Mobiles are banned[3] at school / during meals / ...
Sometimes I forget to recharge the battery[4].
Sometimes there's no memory[5] left for new apps.
My parents always complain that I spend too much time on social media.
Sometimes I forget about time when I'm playing a game.
Sometimes I'm stressed when people want me to answer at once.
There are not enough hotspots in my town / village with free Wi-Fi.

Time

I usually spend ... every day on my mobile. It's very important in my life.

Games

At the moment I'm playing ...
I usually play alone / with friends / in an online community.
I love this game because it's fun / fast / exciting / awesome / a big challenge / ...

Social media

I need my mobile to stay in contact with my friends and family.
I get messages from / I post messages to my friends and family.
I arrange meetings.
I usually read / check what my friends are doing.
I have my own vlog.
I take / watch / send / post / share photos, videos, memes, ...
I have also subscribed to ...
I chat / follow / post / tweet / comment / reply to / tag / share / ...
I update my status every day / once a week / very rarely[6].

---

[1](to) **suscribe to** [səbˈskraɪb] *einen Account haben*   [2]**screen** [skriːn] *Bildschirm*   [3](to) **ban** [bæn] *verbieten*   [4](to) **recharge the battery** [riːˈtʃɑːdʒ ðə bætri] *den Akku aufladen*   [5]**memory** [ˈmeməri] *hier: Speicherplatz*   [6]**rarely** [ˈreəli] *selten*

It's made of ...
- wool
- leather
- fabric
- plastic
- metal
- wood
- silver
- gold

It's ...
- rectangular
- square
- round

Describing things

It has a ...
- pocket
- flap
- string
- sticker
- button
- zip

It's ...
- small
- big
- short
- long
- thick
- thin
- medium-sized

It's ...
- blue
- purple
- brown
- black
- white
- red
- pink
- orange
- yellow
- turquoise
- green

It's ...
- modern
- elegant
- old
- new
- vintage
- colourful
- patterned

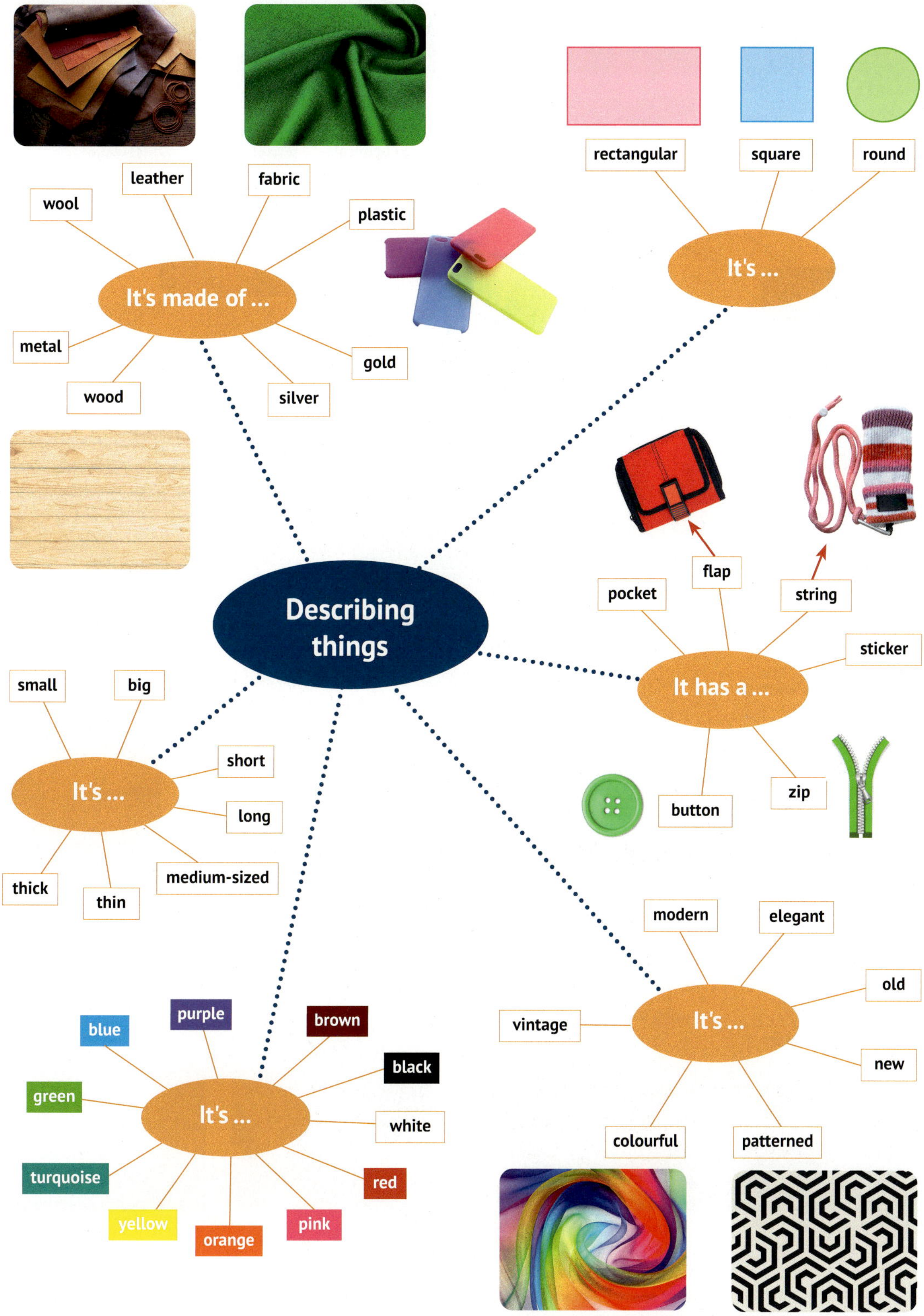

Wordbank 8: Pollution

Unit 4 | p.65

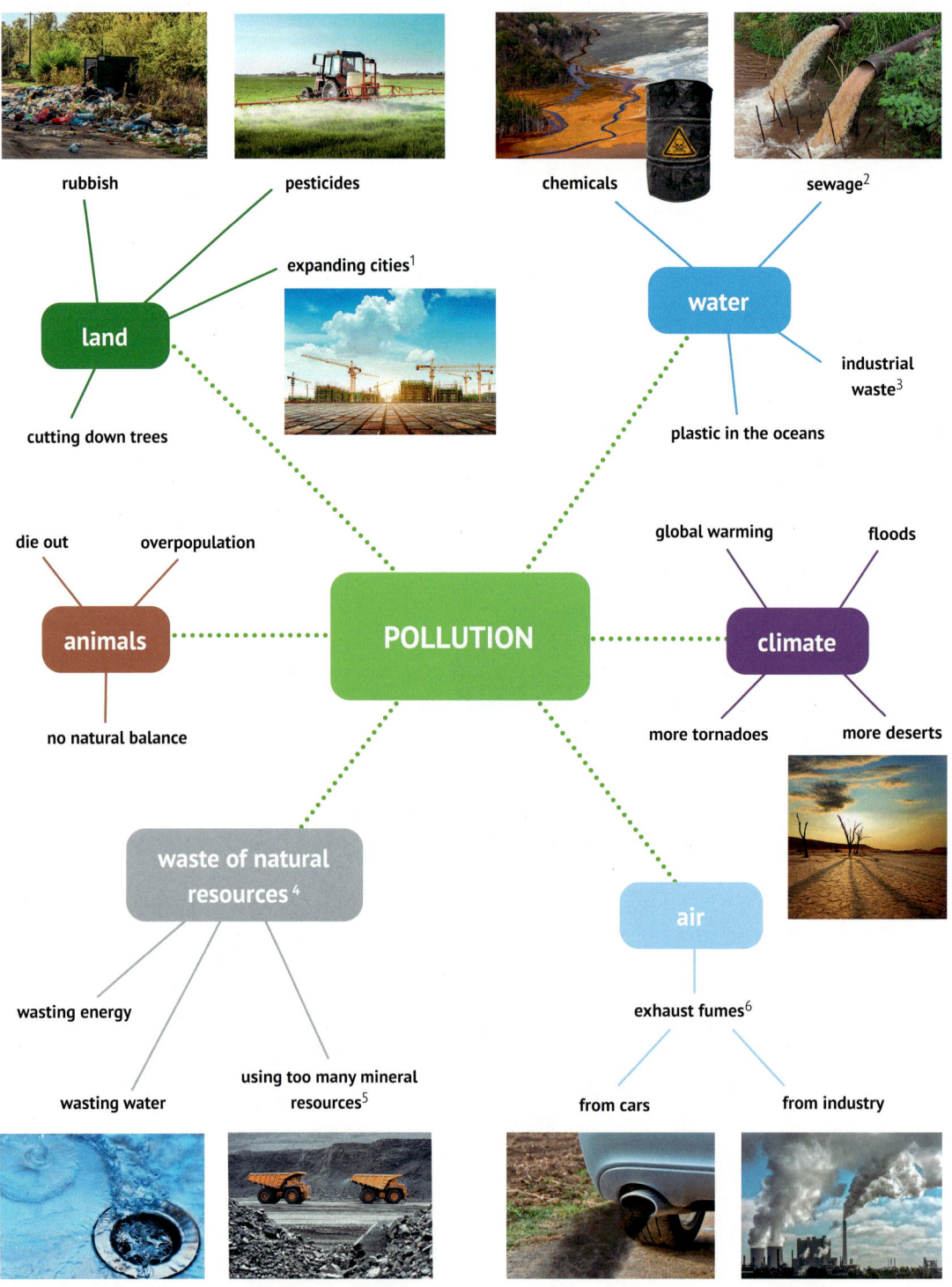

rubbish

pesticides

chemicals

sewage[2]

expanding cities[1]

land

industrial waste[3]

cutting down trees

plastic in the oceans

water

die out

overpopulation

global warming

floods

animals

POLLUTION

climate

no natural balance

more tornadoes

more deserts

waste of natural resources[4]

air

wasting energy

exhaust fumes[6]

wasting water

using too many mineral resources[5]

from cars

from industry

---

[1](to) **expand** [ɪkˈspænd] *sich ausbreiten*   [2] **sewage** [ˈsuːɪdʒ] *Abwasser*   [3] **industrial waste** [ɪnˈdʌstriəl weɪst] *Industrieabfall, Abwasser*
[4] **natural resources** [ˈnætʃrəl rɪˈsɔːsɪz] *natürliche Rohstoffe*   [5] **mineral resources** [ˈmɪnərəl rɪˈsɔːsɪz] *Bodenschätze*   [6] **exhaust fumes** [ɪgˈzɔːst fjumz] *Abgase*

Wordbank 9: Protecting the environment

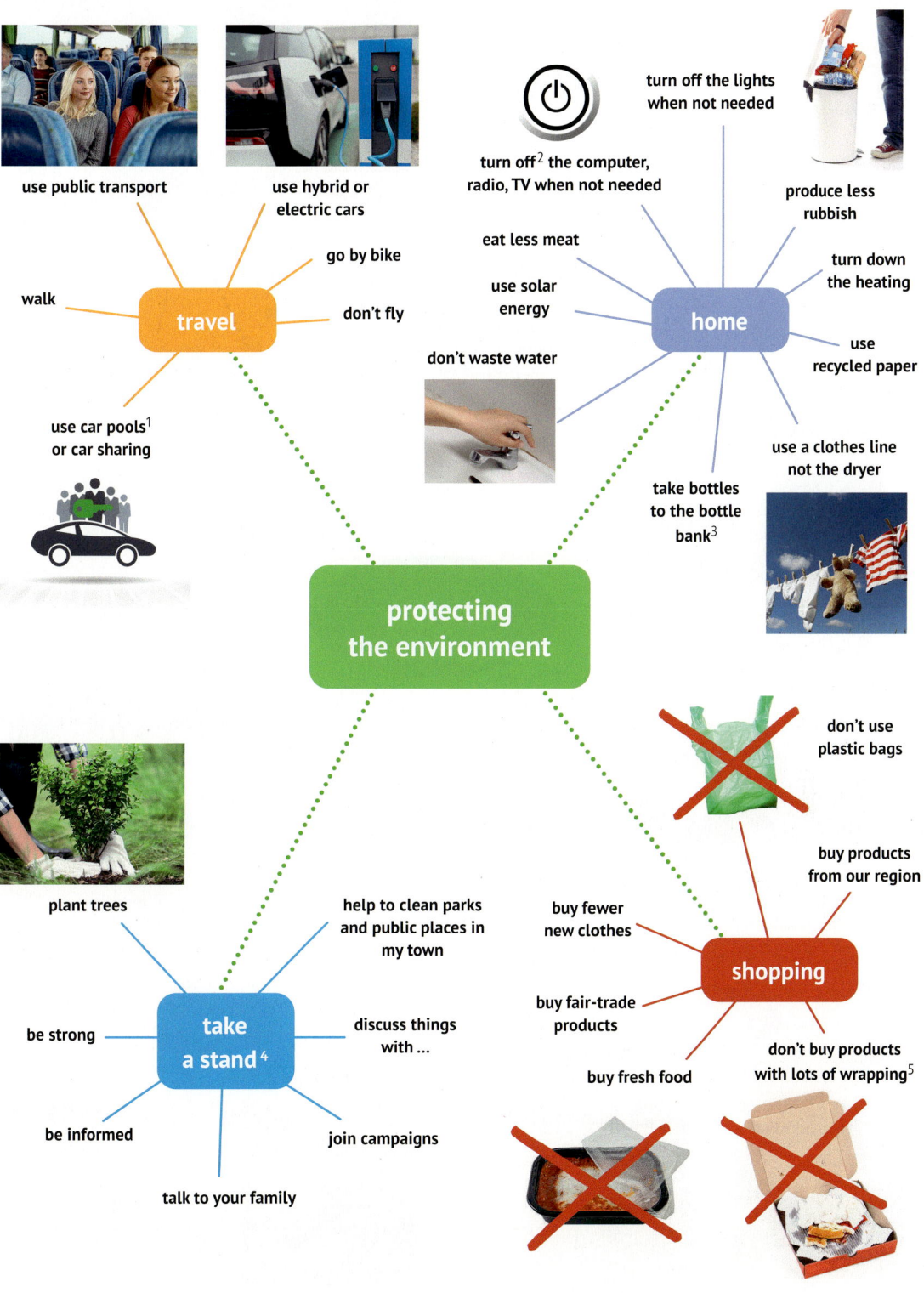

use public transport

use hybrid or electric cars

go by bike

walk

don't fly

travel

use car pools[1] or car sharing

turn off the lights when not needed

turn off[2] the computer, radio, TV when not needed

produce less rubbish

eat less meat

turn down the heating

use solar energy

home

use recycled paper

don't waste water

use a clothes line not the dryer

take bottles to the bottle bank[3]

protecting the environment

don't use plastic bags

buy products from our region

plant trees

help to clean parks and public places in my town

buy fewer new clothes

shopping

be strong

discuss things with ...

buy fair-trade products

don't buy products with lots of wrapping[5]

be informed

join campaigns

buy fresh food

take a stand[4]

talk to your family

---

[1] **car pool** [ˈkɑːpuːl] *Fahrgemeinschaft*   [2] (to) **turn off** [tɜːnˈɒf] *ausschalten*   [3] **bottle bank** [ˈbɒtlbæŋk] *(Alt-)Glascontainer*
[4] (to) **take a stand** [teɪk ə stænd] *sich engagieren, für etw. einsetzen*   [5] **wrapping** [ˈræpɪŋ] *Verpackung*

Wordbank 10: My day

Unit 4 | p.73

places

- on the bus / train
- at the youth centre
- in a fast-food restaurant
- in the country
- in the park
- at school
- in town
- at home
- at the swimming pool
- in my room
- at a friend's house
- on the football ground
- in the gym

times

- at breakfast
- in the morning
- at lunchtime
- during break
- after school
- at school
- in the afternoon
- at night
- in the evening
- at the weekend
- on weekdays

MO TU WE TH FR

My day

people

- classmates
- teacher
- family
- friend
- parents
- sister
- neighbour
- brother
- shop assistant
- bus driver
- coach

activities

- play ...
- meet
- message ...
- do ...
- go to ...
- have ...
- go by ...
- study ...
- work ...
- listen to ...
- take the ...
- post ...
- tweet ...
- chat with ...

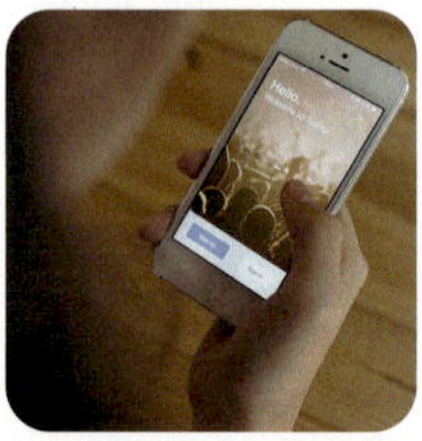

Das **Vocabulary** (Seiten 150–170) enthält alle neuen Wörter und Wendungen des Buches, die du **lernen** musst. Sie stehen in der Reihenfolge, in der sie im Buch zum ersten Mal vorkommen.

Hier siehst du, wie das **Vocabulary** aufgebaut ist:

Der **blaue Pfeil** heißt: Zu diesem Eintrag gibt es in der rechten Spalte einen blauen Kasten.

Die **blauen Kästen** solltest du dir immer besonders gut ansehen. Dort stehen wichtige Hinweise zu den neuen Wörtern.

Focus on language

p.69 **instead of** [ɪnˈsted əv]   anstatt, anstelle von

instead of – instead
- I'd like pasta **instead of** chips, plea…
  (= **anstelle von**)
- I don't like chips. Can I have pasta …
  (= **stattdessen**)

Diese Zahl gibt die **Seite** an, auf der die Wörter zum ersten Mal vorkommen: p.69 = Seite 69

sortieren   We always **sort** our rubbish. (sortieren) (to) **sort** sth. **out** = sich um etwas kümm… I'll help you to **sort out** this problem.

Die **Lautschrift** zeigt dir, wie ein Wort ausgesprochen wird. Eine Übersicht über die **Lautschriftzeichen** findest du auf Seite 193.

(to) **crash (into)** [kræʃ]   krachen; einen Unfall haben, zusammenstoßen (mit)   verb: (to) **crash** The car **crashed into** a wall. – noun: **crash** (Zusammenstoß, Unfall) Luckily nobody was hurt in the **crash**.

planet [ˈplænɪt]   Das **rote Ausrufezeichen** bedeutet: Vorsicht, hier macht man leicht Fehler!   (!) Betonung auf der **1.** Silbe: **pla**net [ˈplænɪt]

straw [strɔ:]   I always use a metal… It's better for the environment than pl…

Dies ist das „Gegenteil"-Zeichen. **illegal ◄► legal** bedeutet: „**illegal** ist das Gegenteil von **legal**".

alive [əˈlaɪv]   lebendig, am Leben   = living, not dead

illegal [ɪˈliːgl]   illegal, verboten   **illegal** [ɪˈliːgl] ◄► **legal** [ˈliːgl] (legal)

Skills training

p.71 **lorry** [ˈlɒri]   Lastwagen, LKW   a big **lorry**

(to) **knock** sb. **over/down** [nɒk]   jn. anfahren, jn. umfahren   verb: (to) **knock** (stoßen; schlagen; klopfen) – noun: **knock** (Stoß, Schlag; Klopfen)

(to) **bleed** [bliːd], **bled, bled** [bled]   bluten   verb: (to) **bleed, bled, bled** – noun: **blood** [blʌd] (Blut)

(to) **write down**   aufschreiben   Next Friday? On the 23rd? Let me **write down** the date.

(to) **skid** [skɪd]   schleudern; schlittern, (aus)rutschen   There was ice on the road, and the car **skidded**. It was very dangerous.

horse [hɔːs]   Pferd   a **horse**

Wir verwenden folgende **Abkürzungen**:

infml = *informal* (umgangssprachlich) • *p.* = *page* (Seite) • *sb.* = *somebody* (jemand) • *sth.* = *something* (etwas) • *AE* = *American English* • *BE* = *British English* • *pl* = *plural* (Mehrzahl) • *no pl* = *no plural* (es gibt das Wort nicht in der Mehrzahl) • jd. = jemand • jm. = jemandem • jn. = jemanden

Wenn du **nachschlagen** möchtest, was ein englisches Wort bedeutet oder wie man es ausspricht, dann solltest du das **Dictionary English – German** auf den Seiten 171–192 verwenden.

Do you speak English?

p.8	**useful (to** sb.**)** ['juːsfl]	nützlich (für jn.)	Here are some **useful** tips for your exam.
p.9	**first language** [fɜːst 'læŋgwɪdʒ]	Muttersprache	Mark's English is very good, but his **first language** is German.

Unit 1: G'day in Australia

p.10	**kangaroo** [kæŋgə'ruː]	Känguru	a **kangaroo**
p.11	**the outback** ['aʊtbæk]	*das Hinterland Australiens*	Australia's **outback** is far away from the coast and the towns.
	corner ['kɔːnə]	Ecke	There's a statue in each of the four **corners** of this square.
	except (for) [ɪk'sept]	außer, bis auf	In my family, everyone is tall **except (for)** me.
	coast [kəʊst]	Küste	**!** **on** the coast = **an** der Küste

Theme 1

p.12	**jellyfish** ['dʒelifɪʃ], *pl* **jellyfish**	Qualle	some **jellyfish** in the sea
	lifeguard ['laɪfgɑːd]	Rettungsschwimmer/in; Bademeister/in	The **lifeguards** at a beach watch people who are swimming in the sea and help them if they're in danger.
	risk [rɪsk]	Risiko	I wouldn't **take** that **risk**. (das Risiko eingehen) noun: **risk** – verb: (to) **risk** (riskieren, aufs Spiel setzen)
	sunburn ['sʌnbɜːn]	Sonnenbrand	When your skin is red and hurts after you've been in the sun for too long, you have **sunburn**.
	skin [skɪn]	Haut; Schale *(z.B. Banane)*	I need some face cream. My **skin** is too dry. There's a banana **skin** on the floor.
	sting [stɪŋ]	(Insekten-)Stich	I think this is a jellyfish **sting**.
	(to) **sting** [stɪŋ], **stung, stung** [stʌŋ]	stechen *(Insekt)*; brennen *(schmerzen)*	I think a jellyfish has **stung** you.
	shade [ʃeɪd]	Schatten *(vor der Sonne geschützt)*	It's cooler in the **shade** of the tree.
p.13	**litre** ['liːtə]	Liter	**!** *English:* 10 litre**s** *German:* 10 **Liter**

(to) **break down**	eine Panne haben, kaputt-gehen *(Auto)*	His car has **broken down**.
(to) **be lost**	sich verlaufen/verirrt haben	Excuse me, **I'm lost**. (Ich habe mich verlaufen/verirrt.) (to) **get lost** = sich verlaufen, sich verirren
torch [tɔːtʃ]	Taschenlampe	a **torch**
(to) **rely on** [rɪˈlaɪ ɒn]	sich verlassen auf	I can **rely on** my best friend: she's always there for me when I need her.
It might not work. [maɪt]	Es könnte nicht funktio-nieren. / Vielleicht funktioniert es nicht.	That **might** be true, but I'm not sure. You **might** hate school, but you learn useful things there.
sick [sɪk]	krank	! **1.** her **sick** mother = ihre kranke Mutter; **2.** I'm / I feel **sick**. = Mir ist schlecht/übel.
(to) **be thirsty** [ˈθɜːsti]	Durst haben	**I'm thirsty** ◄► **I'm hungry** I want to drink. ◄► I want to eat.
mouth [maʊθ]	Mund; *(Tier)* Schnauze	

Theme 2

p.14 **respect** [rɪˈspekt]	Respekt	noun: **respect** – verb: (to) **respect** (respektieren, achten)
painting [ˈpeɪntɪŋ]	Gemälde, *(gemaltes)* Bild	noun: **painting** – verb: (to) **paint**
(to) **hunt** [hʌnt]	jagen	verb: (to) **hunt** – noun: **hunt** (Jagd)
disease [dɪˈziːz]	Krankheit	! **disease** wird für ansteckende oder sehr ernsthafte Erkrankungen verwendet: She has a heart **disease**. Thousands of trees died from **disease**. • Das allgemeinere Wort für „Krankheit" ist **illness**: After a week of **illness**, she went back to school.
flu [fluː]	Grippe	I have a headache, a temperature and feel really bad. I **might** be getting the **flu**.
(to) **kill** [kɪl]	töten	Skin cancer is very dangerous – it can **kill** you. Use suncream!
prison [ˈprɪzn]	Gefängnis	(to) **put** sb. **in prison** = jn. ins Gefängnis sperren/stecken

racism ['reɪsɪzəm]	Rassismus	❗ Betonung auf der **1.** Silbe: **ra**cism ['reɪsɪzəm] / **ra**cist ['reɪsɪst] nouns: *(what people do/think)* **racism** / *(person)* **racist** (Rassist/in) – adjective: **racist** (rassistisch)
unemployment [ˌʌnɪm'plɔɪmənt]	Arbeitslosigkeit	**unemployment** ◄► **employment** [ɪm'plɔɪmənt] (Arbeit, Anstellung) noun: **unemployment** – adjective: **unemployed**
condition [kən'dɪʃn]	Bedingung; Zustand	Our house is thirty years old, but still in a very good **condition**. It's too cold and too noisy in this office. I can't work **in/under** these **conditions**. (bei/unter diesen Bedingungen)
harmony ['hɑ:məni]	Harmonie, Einklang	❗ Betonung auf der **1.** Silbe: **har**mony ['hɑ:məni]
nature ['neɪtʃə]	*(die)* Natur	noun: **nature** – adjective: **natural** ['nætʃrəl] (natürlich, Natur-)
p.15 **body** ['bɒdi]	Körper	**body painting** = Körperbemalung
step [step]	Schritt; Stufe	She's sitting on the **steps**.
Aboriginal [ˌæbə'rɪdʒənl]	aboriginal *(die Ureinwohner/innen Australiens betreffend)*; einheimisch, eingeboren	**Aboriginal** = 1. aboriginal (die Ureinwohner/innen Australiens betreffend: aboriginale Traditionen) 2. einheimisch, eingeboren **Aboriginal Australian** = australische/r Ureinwohner/in
What's more, ...	Darüber hinaus ..., Außerdem ...	There's too much sugar in this lemonade, and **what's more**, it's in a plastic bottle!
finally ['faɪnəli]	zum Schluss, schließlich	It was a long journey. I **finally** got home at 8.30.

Text

p.16 **character** ['kærəktə]	Figur, Person *(in Roman, Film usw.)*	❗ Betonung auf der **1.** Silbe: **char**acter ['kærəktə] Our cat is called Rocky – like the film **character**!
(to) swerve [swɜ:v]	*(das Auto/Steuer)* herumreißen, *(mit dem Auto)* ausweichen	Suddenly an animal ran out onto the road. I **swerved** and nearly hit a tree.
ponytail ['pəʊniteɪl]	Pferdeschwanz *(Frisur)*	She has her hair in a **ponytail**.
stranger ['streɪndʒə]	Fremde/r	Don't talk to **strangers**. (= to people you don't know)
dead [ded]	tot	My grandfather is **dead**. He died in 2012.
mirror ['mɪrə]	Spiegel	a car **mirror**

any	jegliche/r/s, jede/r/s beliebige	You can buy **any** of these bikes, they're all good. It wasn't just **any** car. = Es war kein beliebiges / nicht einfach irgendein Auto. **(at) any time** = zu jeder Zeit, jederzeit
engine ['endʒɪn]	Motor	This car has a special **engine**. It uses electricity.
examination [ɪgzæmɪ'neɪʃn] (*infml auch* **exam** [ɪg'zæm])	Prüfung	❗ (to) **take/do an exam** = eine Prüfung machen
p.17 **advice** [əd'vaɪs]	Rat; Ratschläge	❗ *German:* Er gab mir **einen Rat.** *English:* He gave me **some advice.**
desert ['dezət]	Wüste	❗ **desert** ['dezət] = Wüste **dessert** [dɪ'zɜːt] = Nachspeise
hitchhiker ['hɪtʃhaɪkə]	Anhalter/in, Tramper/in	a **hitchhiker**
fuel ['fjuːəl]	Treibstoff, Kraftstoff	Car engines which use **fuel** are bad for the environment.
(to) order ['ɔːdə]	bestellen	verb: (to) **order** – noun: **order** (Bestellung) (to) take an **order** = eine Bestellung annehmen, entgegennehmen
glamorous ['glæmərəs]	glamourös	= very beautiful; very exciting
fingernail ['fɪŋgəneɪl]	Fingernagel	red **fingernails**
(to) pull [pʊl]	ziehen	They're **pulling** hard.
hood [hʊd]	Kapuze	Put your **hood** up when it rains.
just	gerade (eben)	❗ **just** = **1.** einfach; nur, bloß; **2.** gerade (eben)
p.18 **owner** ['əʊnə]	Besitzer/in	Poppy couldn't drive, but he was the **owner** of a car. (= he had a car)
(to) follow ['fɒləʊ]	(be)folgen; verfolgen	Always **follow** the rules, please. (befolgen) Someone was **following** me on my way home. (folgen, verfolgen) the **following** day/week (am folgenden Tag / in der folgenden Woche)

Focus on language

p.19	(to) **shine** [ʃaɪn], **shone**, **shone** [ʃɒn]	scheinen *(Sonne)*; leuchten, strahlen, glänzen	Time to get out of bed! The sun is **shining**, and it's a beautiful day.
p.20	**seat** [siːt]	(Sitz-)Platz	Sit down. = Take a **seat**. (Nimm/Nehmen Sie Platz.)
p.21	**rock** [rɒk]	Fels(en)	❗ *German* Rock = **skirt** *English* **rock** = Fels(en)
p.22	(to) **fall in love** (**with** sb.)	sich verlieben (in jn.)	(to) **be in love** (**with** sb.) = verliebt sein (in jn.)
	(to) **turn** sb./sth. **into** sth.	jn./etwas in etwas verwandeln	In this old story Diana **turns** a man **into** an animal.
	(to) **equip** sb. **with** sth. [ɪˈkwɪp]	jn. mit etwas ausrüsten, ausstatten	When you go for a long walk, **equip** yourselves with food, water, a rain jacket … verb: (to) **equip** sb. **with** sth. – noun: **equipment**
	quality [ˈkwɒləti]	Qualität	More expensive clothes are often **better quality**. (… sind von besserer Qualität.) These shoes are **top quality**. (von bester Qualität)

Skills training

p.23	(to) **rest** [rest]	sich ausruhen; Pause machen, rasten	verb: (to) **rest** – noun: **rest** (Ruhe, Pause, Rast)
	painkiller [ˈpeɪnkɪlə]	Schmerzmittel	If your arm hurts too much, you can take these **painkillers**, but only four per day.
	bite [baɪt]	Biss; (Insekten-)Stich	noun: **bite** – verb (to) **bite**, **bit** [bɪt], **bitten** [ˈbɪtn] (beißen; stechen *(z.B. Insekten)*)
	insect [ˈɪnsekt]	Insekt	Betonung auf der **1.** Silbe: **in**sect [ˈɪnsekt] **Insects** are small. They have six legs and their bodies have three parts.
p.24	**profession** [prəˈfeʃn]	Beruf	I don't want just any stupid job. I want to train for a **profession** where I earn good money.
	government [ˈɡʌvənmənt]	Regierung	❗ Achte auf die Schreibweise: **government** Should the **government** tell people what to do? Or should people decide for themselves?
	(to) **steal** [stiːl], **stole** [stəʊl], **stolen** [ˈstəʊlən]	stehlen, rauben	I'm always careful. I didn't lose my phone. I'm sure someone **stole** it from me.
p.25	**learner** [ˈlɜːnə]	Lernende/r	**learner driver** = Fahrschüler/in, Fahrer/in mit einem Führerschein für Begleitetes Fahren **licence** = Genehmigung, Lizenz **learner licence** = Führerschein für Begleitetes Fahren
	plate [pleɪt]	(Metall-)Schild; Teller	**number plate** = Nummernschild, Autokennzeichen   plates
	speed [spiːd]	Geschwindigkeit	The car was driving along the street **at a speed** of 100 km/h – much too fast! (mit einer Geschwindigkeit von …)

speed limit [ˈspiːd lɪmɪt]	Höchstgeschwindigkeit, Geschwindigkeitsbegrenzung	This road has a 50 kph **speed limit**. = There's a **speed limit** of 50 kph on this road.
(to) drive: you have **driven** [ˈdrɪvn]	*(mit dem Auto)* fahren: du bist gefahren	I've never **driven** a muscle car. It must be exciting!
alcohol [ˈælkəhɒl]	Alkohol	Betonung auf der **1.** Silbe: <u>al</u>cohol [ˈælkəhɒl] Never drive when you've drunk **alcohol**.

Unit 2: *Kia ora* in New Zealand

p.26 **countryside** [ˈkʌntrisaɪd]	Land(schaft); Natur	The **countryside** in Scotland is beautiful.
up to	bis (zu)	This tree can get **up to** 35 metres high.

German „bis"		
zeitlich meist	**till** *or* **until**	I had to work **until** ten o'clock last night. We lived in Austria **till** I was six years old.
„bis jetzt"	**up to now**	**Up to now** everything has been OK.
„von ... bis ..."	**from ... to ...**	We're open **from** Monday **to** Friday **from** 9 **to** 5.
„bis zu" + Menge/Zahl	**up to**	There'll be **up to** 200 guests. You can earn **up to** £60,000 here.
räumlich meist	**up to**	Walk **up to** the school, then turn left.

Theme 1

p.28 **shot** [ʃɒt]	Aufnahme, Foto	noun: **shot** – verb: (to) **shoot**, **shot**, **shot** (fotografieren; *(Film)* drehen)
p.29 **volunteer** [vɒlənˈtɪə]	Freiwillige/r, Ehrenamtliche/r	noun: **volunteer** I work as a **volunteer** for a charity. – verb: (to) **volunteer** (freiwillig/ehrenamtlich arbeiten) I **volunteer** for a charity. – adjective: **voluntary** I'm a **voluntary** worker for a charity.
organic [ɔːˈgænɪk]	biologisch (angebaut), Bio-	**Organic** fruit and vegetables cost a bit more, but the way they're grown is better for the environment.
(to) **watch out for**	sich hüten vor, sich in Acht nehmen vor	**Watch out!** There's mud on the road. (Achtung! ...) **Watch out for** snakes. Their bites can be dangerous.
(to) **milk**	melken	verb: (to) **milk** – noun: **milk** He's **milking** a cow.
guide [gaɪd]	Reiseleiter/in, Fremdenführer/in; Ratgeber *(Buch, Website)*	**!** **guide** = **1.** Reiseleiter/in, Fremdenführer/in; **2.** Ratgeber *(Buch, Website)* noun: **guide** – verb: (to) **guide** (führen, leiten)

identity [aɪˈdentəti]	Identität	My first language is part of my **identity.**
local [ˈləʊkəl]	einheimisch, am/vom Ort	Do all your friends go to the **local** school? (Gehen ... hier im Ort zur Schule?)
(to) surprise [səˈpraɪz]	überraschen	verb: (to) **surprise** – noun: **surprise** Are you **surprised**? (überrascht) It's **surprising** that ... (es ist überraschend / es überrascht, dass ...) **Surprisingly**, he agreed. (überraschenderweise)
international [ɪntəˈnæʃnəl]	international	❗ Betonung auf der **2.** Silbe: **inter**national [ɪntəˈnæʃnəl] an **international** competition = a competition where people or teams from different countries take part **international** ◄► **national**

Theme 2

p.30	discrimination (against sb.) [dɪskrɪmɪˈneɪʃn]	Diskriminierung (eines Menschen)	❗ **discrimination against** women/black people = Diskriminierung **von** Frauen/Schwarzen noun: **discrimination (against)** – verb: (to) **discriminate against** sb. [dɪˈskrɪmɪneɪt] (jn. diskriminieren)
	thought [θɔːt]	Gedanke	verb: (to) **think, thought, thought** – noun: **thought**
	mental health [mentl ˈhelθ]	psychische/seelische Gesundheit	**mental** = geistig, psychisch, seelisch
	depression [dɪˈpreʃn]	Depression(en)	People who have **depression** feel very sad and aren't able to live a normal life.
p.31	(to) make sb.'s day	jm. den Tag verschönern, jm. eine Riesenfreude machen	What a nice surprise! This has really **made my day**!
	back	Rücken; Rückseite	❗ **back** = **1.** zurück; **2.** Rücken, Rückseite
	moment [ˈməʊmənt]	Moment	❗ Betonung auf der **1.** Silbe: **mo**ment [ˈməʊmənt] **at the moment** = im Moment **Just a moment.** = Einen Moment. / Moment mal.
	(to) apologize (to sb. for sth.) [əˈpɒlədʒaɪz]	sich (bei jm. für etwas) entschuldigen	= (to) say that you're sorry

Text

p.32	main [meɪn]	Haupt-, wichtigste(r, s)	the **main** thing/problem/point = the most important thing/problem/point **main road =** Hauptstraße
	strength [streŋθ]	Stärke, Kraft	One of my **strengths** is that I speak three languages.

weakness ['wiːknəs]	Schwäche	**strength** ◄► **weakness** **strong** ◄► **weak** [wiːk] (schwach)
(to) **get on (well) with** sb.	(gut) auskommen mit jm.	I **get on well** with Dave. = Dave and I **get on well**. (to) **get on (well)** = (gut) miteinander auskommen
(to) **fall out (with** sb.**)**	sich mit jm. zerstreiten	Joe and Bill don't get on well. They often **fall out with** each other.

each other [iːtʃ ˈʌðə]	einander,
	sich (gegenseitig)
		➡ **each other**
		• They **played** against each other.
		  Sie spielten gegeneinander.
		• They **talked** to each other.
		  Sie redeten miteinander.
		• Alex and Stan **like** each other.
		  Alex und Stan mögen sich.

(to) be/feel **ashamed (of)** [əˈʃeɪmd]	sich schämen (für)	I'm really **ashamed of** the stupid things I said. I'd like to apologize.
feeling ['fiːlɪŋ]	Gefühl	Do you know the **feeling** that you've seen a person before, but you don't remember when or where? noun: **feeling** – verb: (to) **feel, felt, felt**
folder ['fəʊldə]	Mappe, Ordner	**folders**
curious about sth. ['kjʊəriəs]	neugierig auf etwas	My little sister is **curious about** everything. She always asks questions.
(to) **thank** sb. (**for** sth.) [θæŋk]	jm. danken, sich bei jm. (für etwas) bedanken	I'd like to **thank** everybody for their help. (= say thank you to everybody …)
almost ['ɔːlməʊst]	fast, beinahe	= nearly When I left the train, I **almost** forgot my bag on the seat.
(to) **pick** sth. **off** sth.	etwas von etwas wegnehmen, herunternehmen; abzupfen	(to) **pick** sth. **up** = etwas aufheben (vom Boden)
p.33 **armchair** ['ɑːmtʃeə]	Sessel	an **armchair**
wage [weɪdʒ], oft auch: **wages** (pl)	Lohn, Gehalt	Many years ago my dad had a **wage** of £180 per week. Now his **wages** are much higher. **minimum wage** = Mindestlohn
(to) **notice** ['nəʊtɪs]	(be)merken	We all **noticed** that Jill looked very sad. I didn't **notice** him because I was talking to Sam.
thin [θɪn]	dünn, schlank	When you grow old, your hair gets **thinner**. As a boy he was very **thin**. He never ate much.

(to) **embarrass** sb. [ɪmˈbærəs]	jn. in Verlegenheit bringen	**embarrassed** = verlegen Mum, please don't **embarrass** me in front of my friends! It **embarrasses** me when this happens. = I'm **embarrassed** when this happens. (es ist <u>mir</u> peinlich …) It's **embarrassing** when this happens. (es ist peinlich …) It was so **embarrassing** … I was so **embarrassed** … when my phone rang in the concert hall.
p.34 **background** [ˈbækgraʊnd]	Herkunft	**people of different backgrounds** = Menschen unterschiedlicher Herkunft
serious [ˈsɪəriəs]	ernst(haft)	This is a **serious** problem. (ernst) **Seriously**, you're my best friend. (ernsthaft, im Ernst) (to) **take** sb./sth. **seriously** = jn./etwas ernst nehmen What he said was a joke. You can't **take** him **seriously**. (ernst nehmen)

Focus on language

p.35 **shed** [ʃed]	Schuppen; Stall	a **garden shed**
p.36 **choice** [tʃɔɪs]	(Aus-)Wahl	noun: **choice** – verb: (to) **choose** [tʃuːz], **chose** [tʃəʊz], **chosen** [ˈtʃəʊzn] ((aus)wählen)
review [rɪˈvjuː]	Rezension, Kritik	If you enjoyed your holiday on our campsite, then please write a **review** on our website.
in advance [ədˈvɑːns]	im Voraus	If you arrive at our hotel after 10 pm, please let us know **in advance**.
p.37 **cave** [keɪv]	Höhle	a **cave** with a lake
luge [luːʒ]	Rennrodeln	**luge** track = Rennrodelbahn
penguin [ˈpeŋgwɪn]	Pinguin	

	dolphin [ˈdɒlfɪn]	Delfin	
p.38	**large** [lɑːdʒ]	groß	**!** **big** und **large** sind oft austauschbar: a **big/large** family, a **big/large** house • **large** wird in der Regel aber nicht für Menschen verwendet. Menschen sind **big** (schwer, dick) oder **tall** (groß gewachsen).
	expert (on) [ˈekspɜːt]	Experte/Expertin (für)	**!** Betonung auf der **1.** Silbe: **expert** [ˈekspɜːt]
	effect (on) [ɪˈfekt]	(Aus-)Wirkung (auf), Einfluss (auf); Effekt	Eating less meat can have positive **effects on** the environment. **special effects** (pl) = Special Effects (in Filmen)
	whole [həʊl]	ganze(r, s)	Yesterday we played cards the **whole** evening. (= all evening) **on the whole** = im Großen und Ganzen
	(to) **lay** [leɪ], **laid, laid** [leɪd]	legen	**!** (to) **lie, lay, lain** = liegen – Our dog is not allowed to **lie** on the sofa. (to) **lay, laid, laid** = legen You can **lay** your jacket on the sofa.
	flash (of light) [flæʃ]	(Licht-)Blitz	**flash photos** = Fotos mit Blitz

Skills training

p.39	**nursing home** [ˈnɜːsɪŋ həʊm]	Pflegeheim	Mrs Cox is very old and can't live in her own house any more. She now lives in a **nursing home**.
	(working) hours (pl)	Arbeitszeit(en)	Cooks have long **working hours** – sometimes 14 hours a day. **opening hours** (pl) = Öffnungszeiten (to) **work long hours** = lange arbeiten, Überstunden machen
	handy [ˈhændi]	praktisch, nützlich	**!** *English:* **mobile phone** – *German:* Handy *English:* **handy** – *German:* praktisch, nützlich
	long-term [lɒŋ ˈtɜːm]	langfristig, Langzeit-	**long-term** ◄► **short-term** (kurzfristig, Kurzzeit-)
	security guard [sɪˈkjʊərəti gɑːd]	Sicherheitsbedienstete/r	**guard** = Wache, Wachposten; Garde
	colleague [ˈkɒliːg]	Kollege/Kollegin	**!** Betonung auf der **1.** Silbe: **coll**eague [ˈkɒliːg] **!** *English:* **college** – *German:* Fach(hoch)schule **!** *English:* **colleague** – *German:* Kollege/Kollegin
p.40	(to) **prepare (for)** [prɪˈpeə]	vorbereiten; sich vorbereiten (auf)	**well-prepared** = gut vorbereitet verb: (to) **prepare (for)** – noun: **preparation (for)** [prepəˈreɪʃn] (Vorbereitung (auf))
	(to) **react (to)** [riˈækt]	reagieren (auf)	verb: (to) **react (to)** – noun: **reaction (to)** [riˈækʃn] (Reaktion (auf))
	criticism [ˈkrɪtɪsɪzəm]	Kritik	noun: **criticism** [ˈkrɪtɪsɪzəm] – verb: (to) **criticize** [ˈkrɪtɪsaɪz] (kritisieren)
	punctual [ˈpʌŋktʃuəl]	pünktlich	= on time

project [ˈprɒdʒekt]	Projekt	❗ Betonung auf der **1.** Silbe: **pro**ject [ˈprɒdʒekt]
p.41 **structure** [ˈstrʌktʃə]	Struktur	❗ Betonung auf der **1.** Silbe: **struc**ture [ˈstrʌktʃə]
argument [ˈɑːgjumənt]	Argument	❗ Betonung auf der **1.** Silbe: **ar**gument [ˈɑːgjumənt] I'd like to think about my **arguments** before I talk to my boss about this.
On the one hand ... **On the other hand ...**	Einerseits ... Andererseits ...	**On the one hand** I really love fast cars. **On the other hand** bikes are much better for the environment.
above all	vor allem, in erster Linie	There are many good arguments for riding a bike, but **above all** it keeps me fit.

Irregular verbs

(to) **bite**	bit	bitten	*beißen; stechen (Insekt)*	(to) **shine**	shone	shone	*scheinen (Sonne); leuchten, strahlen*
(to) **choose**	chose	chosen	*(aus)wählen*	(to) **sit**	sat	sat	*sitzen; sich (hin)setzen*
(to) **drive**	drove	driven	*(Auto) fahren*	(to) **steal**	stole	stolen	*stehlen*
(to) **lay**	laid	laid	*legen*	(to) **sting**	stung	stung	*stechen (Insekt); brennen (schmerzen)*

▶ pp.200–201

Unit 3: *Sawubona* from South Africa

p.42 **widely spoken** [ˈwaɪdli]	weit verbreitet *(Sprache)*, viel gesprochen	English is **widely spoken** – *but*: it's a **widely-spoken** language
few [fjuː]	wenige	

(a) few (+ countable nouns)		**(a) little** (+ uncountable nouns)	
Only **few people** came to the party. *(= not many people)*	**wenige / nicht viele** Leute	He has very **little money**. *(= not much money)*	**wenig / nicht viel** Geld
I talked to **a few people there**. *(= some people)*	**einige / ein paar** Leute	She gave me **a little money**. *(= some money)*	**etwas / ein wenig** Geld
Fewer people had cars in 1960. *(= not so many people, not as many people as today)*	**weniger** Leute	Bikes cost **less money** than cars. *(= not as much as ...)*	**weniger** Geld

dramatic [drəˈmætɪk]	dramatisch; theatralisch	What people do can have **dramatic** effects on the environment.
rhino *(infml)* [ˈraɪnəʊ], *pl* **rhinos**	Nashorn	**Rhino** is short for **rhinoceros** (*pl* **rhinoceros** or **rhinoceroses**). [raɪˈnɒsərəs]
leopard [ˈlepəd]	Leopard	❗ Betonung auf der **1.** Silbe: **leo**pard [ˈlepəd]
lion [ˈlaɪən]	Löwe	
buffalo [ˈbʌfələʊ], *pl* **buffalo** or **buffaloes**	Büffel; Bison	

p.43	(to) **vote (on** sth.) [vəʊt]	wählen; abstimmen (über etwas)	verb: (to) **vote (on** sth.) – noun: **vote** (Abstimmung, Votum)
	system ['sɪstəm]	System	❗ Betonung auf der **1.** Silbe: **sys**tem ['sɪstəm]
	inequality [ɪnɪ'kwɒləti]	Ungleichheit	nouns: **equality** ◄► **inequality** adjectives: **equal** ◄► **unequal**
	soccer ['sɒkə]	Fußball	❗ In den USA ist mit **football** immer American football gemeint. Wenn man über **Fußball** spricht, verwendet man **soccer**.

Theme 1

p.44	(to) **discover** [dɪ'skʌvə]	entdecken	Many people came to this area when gold was **discovered** in the 1800s.
	shark [ʃɑːk]	Hai	a **shark**
p.45	**a must-do** *(infml)* [mʌst 'du]	ein Muss; etwas, was man unbedingt tun muss	❗ a **must** *(infml)* = ein Muss a **must-have** *(infml)* = etwas, was man unbedingt haben muss a **must-see** place *(infml)* = ein Ort, den man gesehen haben muss
	reply [rɪ'plaɪ]	Antwort	= answer; (to) answer noun: **reply** – verb: (to) **reply** (antworten)
	cell [sel]	Zelle	a prison **cell**

Theme 2

p.46	**issue** ['ɪʃuː]	Problem; (Streit-)Frage, Thema	= a problem; something that people have different opinions on Is racism an **issue** at the schools in this area?
	(to) **suffer (from)** ['sʌfə]	leiden (an), erleiden	I often **suffer from** headaches. (leiden an) He **suffered** a heart attack. (Er erlitt einen Herzinfarkt.)
	sanitary ['sænətri]	sanitär, hygienisch, Hygiene-	**sanitary product** = Hygieneprodukt
	(to) **study** ['stʌdi]	*studieren; lernen (z.B. für Prüfungen)*	He wants to **study** at the Edinburgh College of Art. I'll have to **study** a lot for our next maths test.
	(to) **influence** ['ɪnfluəns]	beeinflussen	verb: (to) **influence** – nouns: **influence** (Einfluss); *(person)* **influencer** (Influencer/in) The Beatles still **influence** many musicians today.

(to) **support** [sə'pɔːt]	unterstützen	= (to) **help** verb: **support** – My parents always **support** my dreams and plans. nouns: **support** (Unterstützung) – My parents are a great **support**.
crime [kraɪm]	Verbrechen; Kriminalität	**Crime** is a big problem in most cities. ❗ *German:* **Krimi** – *English:* **crime film**; *(Krimiserie)* **crime series**, **detective series** nouns: **crime**; *(person)* **criminal** ['krɪmɪnl] (Verbrecher/in) – adjective: **criminal** (kriminell)

Text

p.48	**minority** [maɪ'nɒrəti]	Minderheit	The boys in our class are in the **minority**. (= There are fewer boys than girls in our class.)
	majority [mə'dʒɒrəti]	Mehrheit, Mehrzahl	The girls in our class are in the **majority**. (= There are more girls than boys in our class.)
	university [juːnɪ'vɜːsəti]	Universität	❗ Betonung auf der **3.** Silbe: **university** [juːnɪ'vɜːsəti]
	lawyer ['lɔːjə]	(Rechts-)Anwalt/Anwältin	= someone who has studied **law** **law** [lɔː] = Gesetz; Jura *(Studium)*
	ambulance ['æmbjələns]	Krankenwagen	an **ambulance**
	sex [seks]	Sex; Geschlecht	What **sex** is your hamster, a "he" or a "she"? You're never too old to have **sex**.
	law firm ['lɔː fɜːm]	Anwaltskanzlei	**firm** = Firma
	peaceful ['piːsfl]	friedlich, friedfertig	adjective: **peaceful** – noun: **peace**
	act [ækt]	Tat, Handlung	noun: **act** – verb: (to) **act** = **1.** handeln, sich verhalten; so tun, als ob; **2.** *(Theater)* spielen; schauspielern; aufführen
	(to) **arrest** sb. [ə'rest]	jn. festnehmen, verhaften	verb: (to) **arrest** sb. – noun: **arrest** (Festnahme)
	for life	lebenslänglich; auf Lebenszeit	= as long as you live
	off	abseits von, entfernt von	**off the coast** = vor der Küste (im Meer)
p.49	**mat** [mæt]	Matte	a yoga **mat**
	bucket ['bʌkɪt]	Eimer	**buckets**
	(to) **be on**	an sein (eingeschaltet)	**on** ◄► **off** The light is still **on**. Please **turn** it **off**. (ausschalten) It's too dark when the lights are **off**. Please **turn** them **on**. (einschalten)

funeral [ˈfjuːnərəl]	Beerdigung, Begräbnis	Mr Miller died last week. The **funeral** will be tomorrow.
politics [ˈpɒlətɪks]	Politik	noun: **politics** – adjective: **political** **!** **politics** ist Singular, trotz des -s am Ende: **Politics is** very interesting for some people, and **it is** very boring for others.
warder [ˈwɔːdə]	Aufseher/in, Wärter/in *(im Gefängnis)*	Some of the **warders** treated the prisoners badly.
result [rɪˈzʌlt]	Ergebnis	**as a result** = folglich, demzufolge
campaign [kæmˈpeɪn]	Kampagne	I want to start a **campaign** against racism in our town.
wine [waɪn]	Wein	No **wine** for me, please. I never drink alcohol when I drive.
all the time	die ganze Zeit	**all your life** = dein ganzes Leben (lang)
secret [ˈsiːkrət]	geheim; Geheimnis	This is a **secret** message. (geheim) It's our **secret**. (Geheimnis) Don't tell anyone!
(to) **pass a law**	ein Gesetz verabschieden	Many countries have now **passed laws** against texting while you drive.
p.50 **role model** [ˈrəʊl mɒdl]	Vorbild	= a person you like very much, and you try to be like them

Focus on language

p.51 **defence** [dɪˈfens]	Verteidigung	**self-defence** = Selbstverteidigung noun: **defence** – verb: (to) **defend** [dɪˈfend] (verteidigen)
unfortunately [ʌnˈfɔːtʃənətli]	unglücklicherweise, leider	**unfortunately** ◄► **fortunately** [ˈfɔːtʃənətli] (zum Glück, glücklicherweise)
p.52 **royal** [ˈrɔɪəl]	königlich	the **royal** family = the family of the king or queen of a country
archbishop [ɑːtʃˈbɪʃəp]	Erzbischof/Erzbischöfin	An **archbishop** is a very important person of the church.
p.53 **robot** [ˈrəʊbɒt]	Roboter; *Südafrika:* (Verkehrs-)Ampel	Hello, **robot**!
p.54 **rich** [rɪtʃ]	reich	Would you like to be **rich** and famous?
by 1896	bis 1896	They should be here **by 8 pm**. (= not later than 8 pm)
mine [maɪn]	Bergwerk, Mine	People had to work in the gold **mines** under terrible conditions.

Skills training

| p.55 | **description** [dɪˈskrɪpʃn] | Beschreibung | noun: **description** – verb: (to) **describe** |

Nouns ending in -tion

With some verbs, you add the ending **-tion** to form the noun:

verb	noun	
(to) **describe**	descri**ption**	beschreiben/Beschreibung
(to) **introduce** sb. to sth.	introduc**tion**	jm. etwas vorstellen / Vorstellung
(to) **prepare**	prepara**tion**	vorbereiten/Vorbereitung
(to) **react**	reac**tion**	reagieren/Reaktion

(to) **carry** [ˈkæri]	tragen; befördern, transportieren	She was **carrying** a huge bag. This car can **carry** 5 people.
topic [ˈtɒpɪk]	Thema	The **topic** of my talk is "Road traffic and the environment".
(to) **imagine** sth. [ɪˈmædʒɪn]	sich etwas vorstellen	

verbs + -ing-form

I'll	**continue**	**learning** Chinese.	He	**likes/loves**	**dancing.**
Alex	**enjoys**	**making** things.	I	**remember**	**seeing** her in 1995.
I won't	**give up**	**collecting** old toys.	Jo	**started**	**volunteering** last year.
Can you	**imagine**	**being** a musician?	Please	**stop**	**making** so much noise!

p.56	**police station** [pəˈliːs steɪʃn]	Polizeiwache	Two men were arrested and taken to the **police station**.
	value [ˈvæljuː]	Wert	something **of value** = etwas von Wert, etwas Wertvolles
	insurance [ɪnˈʃʊərəns]	Versicherung	The storm broke our garden shed, but we have a good **insurance**. It'll pay for a new one.
	certificate [səˈtɪfɪkət]	Urkunde, Bescheinigung	**birth certificate** = Geburtsurkunde
	wallet [ˈwɒlɪt]	Brieftasche; Portemonnaie; Etui (Schutzhülle)	a **wallet**
	make [meɪk]	Marke; Fabrikat	I have a new phone. – Which **make** is it? (= which company made it?)
	credit card [ˈkredɪt kɑːd]	Kreditkarte	**credit card**
p.57	**booking** [ˈbʊkɪŋ]	Buchung, Reservierung	noun: **booking** I'd like to make a **booking** for next week. – verb: (to) **book** I'd like to **book** a room for next week.
	air conditioning [ˈeə kəndɪʃnɪŋ]	Klimaanlage	It's so hot in here! Let's turn on the **air conditioning**.
	reference [ˈrefərəns]	(Akten-)Zeichen, Referenznummer	**!** **reference** = 1. (Akten-)Zeichen, Referenznummer; 2. Referenz, Empfehlung; jd., der eine Referenz erteilt
	sauna [ˈsɔːnə]	Sauna	(to) **have/take a sauna** = in die Sauna gehen

Unit 4: *Namaste* from India

p.58	**solar** ['səʊlə]	Sonnen, Solar-	**solar energy** = Sonnenenergie, Solarenergie
	(to) **throw** [θrəʊ], **threw** [θruː], **thrown** [θrəʊn]	werfen	You **throw** the ball, and I'll try to catch it.
p.59	**engineer** [endʒɪˈnɪə]	Ingenieur/in; Techniker/in	I want to be an **engineer** and build cars that use solar energy.
	(to) **invent** [ɪnˈvent]	erfinden	verb: (to) **invent** – nouns: *(what you invent)* **invention** [ɪnˈvenʃn] (Erfindung); *(person)* **invent**<u>or</u> [ɪnˈventə] (Erfinder/in)
	underground [ˈʌndəɡraʊnd]	U-Bahn	Londoners call their **underground** the Tube.

Theme 1

p.61	**however** [haʊˈevə]	allerdings, jedoch	Sam wanted to stay up late. **However**, he fell asleep at 8 pm.
	BCE (= before the Common Era) [bɪfɔː ðə kɒmən ˈɪərə]	vor Christus (= vor der christlichen Zeitrechnung)	43 **BCE (before the Common Era)** = 43 <u>vor</u> Christus 43 **CE (Common Era)** = 43 <u>nach</u> Christus
	progress [ˈprəʊgres]	Fortschritt(e)	(to) **make progress** = Fortschritte erzielen/machen; vorankommen
	scientist [ˈsaɪəntɪst]	(Natur-)Wissenschaftler/in	I love science. I want to become a **scientist**. nouns: *(what you study)* **science**; *(person)* **scientist** – adjective: **scientific** [saɪənˈtɪfɪk] (wissenschaftlich)
	earth [ɜːθ]	Erde	the **earth**
	round [raʊnd]	rund	adjective: **round** A ball is **round**. – noun: **round** (Runde) Let's play a round of golf. – preposition: **round / around** (um ... (herum)) They sailed **(a)round** the world.
	zero [ˈzɪərəʊ], *pl* **zeros**	Null	One thousand is a one and three **zeros**: 1000.
	chess [tʃes]	Schach	
	extreme [ɪkˈstriːm]	extrem; Extrem	We had **extreme** temperatures. It was **extremely** hot. The weather went from one **extreme** to the other: first it was sunny and hot, then it was cold and rainy.
	poverty [ˈpɒvəti]	Armut	noun: **poverty** – adjective: **poor**
	hunger [ˈhʌŋgə]	Hunger	noun: **hunger** – adjective: **hungry**
	(to) **want** sb. **to do** sth.	wollen, dass jd. etwas tut	**!** *English:* I **want you to help** your sister. *German:* Ich **möchte, dass du** ... hilfst.

economy [ɪˈkɒnəmi]	(Volks-)Wirtschaft	noun: **economy** – adjective: **economic** [iːkəˈnɒmɪk] (wirtschaftlich, Wirtschafts-)
p.61 **tax** [tæks]	*(die)* Steuer	a salt **tax** = a **tax on** salt

Theme 2

p.62 **spacecraft** [ˈspeɪskrɑːft], *pl* **spacecraft**	Raumfahrzeug, Raumschiff	 a **spacecraft** on its way to the **moon**
moon [muːn]	Mond	
civilization [sɪvəlaɪˈzeɪʃn]	Zivilisation	In modern **civilization** everybody should have enough to eat and to drink.
probably [ˈprɒbəbli]	wahrscheinlich	Road traffic is too much stress for me, and it's bad for the environment. I'll **probably** sell my car.
democracy [dɪˈmɒkrəsi]	Demokratie	noun: **democracy** – adjective: **democratic** [deməˈkrætɪk] (demokratisch) **!** Betonung auf der **2.** Silbe: de**mo**cracy [dɪˈmɒkrəsi]
tasty [ˈteɪsti]	schmackhaft, lecker	adjective: **tasty** These burgers are very **tasty**. – noun: **taste** [teɪst] (Geschmack) – I like their **taste**. verb: (to) **taste** (schmecken; kosten, probieren) **Taste** these burgers! (kosten, probieren) They **taste** great. (schmecken)

Adjectives ending in -y

With some nouns, you add the ending **-y** to form the adjective:

noun	adjective	noun	adjective
hair *Haar(e)*	**hairy** *haarig*	**luck** *Glück*	*(to) be* **lucky** *Glück haben*
health *Gesundheit*	**healthy** *gesund*	**rain/wind** *Regen/Wind*	**rainy/windy** *regnerisch/windig*
hunger *Hunger*	**hungry** *hungrig*	**spice/taste** *Gewürz/Geschmack*	**spicy/tasty** *würzig/schmackhaft*

I wish I were …	Ich wünschte, ich wäre …	"Dear Sam, Scotland is so beautiful, I'm really enjoying my holiday. I just **wish you were** here!"
p.63 **misunderstanding** [mɪsʌndəˈstændɪŋ]	Missverständnis	noun: **misunderstanding** – verb: (to) **misunderstand** [mɪsʌndəˈstænd], **misunderstood**, **misunderstood** [mɪsʌndəˈstʊd] (missverstehen)

Theme 3

p.64 **drone** [drəʊn]	Drohne	a **drone**

by (10%)	um (10%)	The price for these articles has gone up **by** 10% since last year. Poverty is falling **by** 44 people per minute. (fällt um … pro Minute)
(to) **rise** [raɪz], **rose** [rəʊz], **risen** ['rɪzən]	(an)steigen; hochsteigen	Temperatures are **rising**. = It is getting warmer. Our workers' wages **rose by** 4,5% last year. (stiegen um …)
heatwave ['hiːtweɪv]	Hitzewelle	noun: **heat** (Hitze, Wärme) – verb: (to) **heat** (erwärmen, erhitzen) **wave** = Welle
level ['levl]	Grad, Stufe; Niveau, Ebene	Is the **level** of unemployment in your area very high? Our village is 600 metres above sea **level**. **sea level** = Meeresspiegel
drought [draʊt]	Dürre	**!** Aussprache: **drought** [draʊt] = a long time without rain
dirty ['dɜːti]	schmutzig, dreckig	adjective: **dirty** – noun: **dirt** [dɜːt] (Schmutz, Dreck)
pollution [pə'luːʃn]	(Umwelt-)Verschmutzung	noun: **pollution** – verb: (to) **pollute** [pə'luːt] *(die Umwelt)* verschmutzen
air [eə]	Luft	noun: **air** The **air** in here is bad. Open a window! – verb: (to) **air** ((aus)lüften) We should **air** this room.
electric [ɪ'lektrɪk]	elektrisch	adjective: **electric** – noun: **electricity**

Adjectives ending in -ic

With some nouns, you change the ending to **-ic** to form the adjectives:

noun	adjective	
democracy	**democratic**	*Demokratie / demokratisch*
economy	**economic**	*(Volks-)Wirtschaft / wirtschaftlich*
electricity	**electric**	*Elektrizität, Strom / elektrisch*
science	**scientific**	*Wissenschaft / wissenschaftlich*

p.65 **forest** ['fɒrɪst]	Wald	**!** **forest** = (großer) Wald **wood** = **1.** (kleiner) Wald; **2.** Holz
(to) **melt** [melt]	(ab)schmelzen; schmelzen lassen	The sun shone, and soon the ice **melted**. **Melt** the butter, then mix in the sugar.
kilo(gram) ['kiːləʊ]	Kilo(gramm)	We need two **kilos** of cherries for our pies.
(to) **charge** (a mobile phone) [tʃɑːdʒ]	(ein Mobiltelefon) aufladen	Do you **charge** your mobile every day?
(to) **turn** sth. **up**	etwas höher stellen *(weiter aufdrehen);* etwas lauter machen	I'm cold. Can we **turn up** the heating a bit?
(to) **turn** sth. **down**	etwas herunterregeln; etwas leiser stellen	Your music is too loud. Please **turn** it **down**.
heating ['hiːtɪŋ]	Heizung	nouns: *(system in a building)* **heating**; *(high temperatures)* **heat** (Hitze, Wärme) – verb: (to) **heat**

Text

p.66	**mission** [ˈmɪʃn]	Mission; Auftrag	❗ Betonung auf der **1.** Silbe: **mis**sion [ˈmɪʃn]
	module [ˈmɒdjuːl]	Modul; (Raum-)Kapsel	❗ Betonung auf der **1.** Silbe: **mo**dule [ˈmɒdjuːl]
	screen [skriːn]	Bildschirm; Leinwand *(Kino)*	a computer **screen**
	(back) then	damals	My grandma was born in 1952. Life was a lot slower **(back) then**, she says. ❗ **then** = **1.** dann, danach; **2.** damals
	success [səkˈses]	Erfolg	noun: **success** – adjective: **successful**
	communication [kəmjuːnɪˈkeɪʃn]	Kommunikation	nouns: **communication**; **communications** *(pl)* (Kommunikationstechnik; Kommunikationsnetz) – verb: (to) **communicate** [kəˈmjuːnɪkeɪt] (kommunizieren)
	satellite [ˈsætəlaɪt]	Satellit	❗ Betonung auf der **1.** Silbe: **sa**tellite [ˈsætəlaɪt]
	cart [kɑːt]	Karren; Wagen *(z.B. Einkaufswagen)*	an old **cart** made of wood
p.67	**nation** [ˈneɪʃn]	Nation	❗ Betonung auf der **1.** Silbe: **na**tion [ˈneɪʃn] noun: nation – adjective: national
	flood [flʌd]	Überschwemmung, Hochwasser; Flut	noun: **flood** There was a **flood** in our town. – verb: (to) **flood** (überfluten, überschwemmen) Many streets were **flooded**. (standen unter Wasser)
	blank [blæŋk]	leer *(Blatt, Zeile)*; schwarz *(Bildschirm)*; unbeschrieben *(Papier/Zettel)*	adjective: **blank** I kept my face **blank**. (= I didn't want to show any feelings) a **blank** page (= a page with nothing on it) – noun: **blank** (freie Stelle, Leerstelle *(in einem Text)*) mydog …? Oh dear, there's a **blank** missing!
	contact [ˈkɒntækt]	Kontakt	❗ Betonung auf der **1.** Silbe: **con**tact [ˈkɒntækt] noun: **contact** – verb: (to) **contact** (Kontakt aufnehmen mit/zu, sich in Verbindung setzen mit)
	astronaut [ˈæstrənɔːt]	Astronaut/in	❗ Betonung auf der **1.** Silbe: **as**tronaut [ˈæstrənɔːt]
p.68	**theory** [ˈθɪəri]	Theorie	**In theory** you can walk around the lake, but the ground is often too wet. (Theoretisch …)

Focus on language

p.69 **instead of** [ɪnˈsted əv]	anstatt, anstelle von	→ **instead of – instead** • I'd like pasta **instead of** chips, please. (= **anstelle von**) • I don't like chips. Can I have pasta **instead**? (= **stattdessen**)
(to) **sort** [sɔːt]	sortieren	We always **sort** our rubbish. (sortieren) (to) **sort** sth. **out** = sich um etwas kümmern I'll help you to **sort out** this problem.
p.70 (to) **crash (into)** [kræʃ]	krachen; einen Unfall haben, zusammenstoßen (mit)	verb: (to) **crash** The car **crashed into** a wall. – noun: **crash** (Zusammenstoß, Unfall) Luckily nobody was hurt in the **crash**.
planet [ˈplænɪt]	Planet	! Betonung auf der **1.** Silbe: **pla**net [ˈplænɪt]
straw [strɔː]	Strohhalm; Stroh	I always use a metal **straw**. It's better for the environment than plastic.
alive [əˈlaɪv]	lebendig, am Leben	= living, not dead
illegal [ɪˈliːgl]	illegal, verboten	**illegal** [ɪˈliːgl] ◄► **legal** [ˈliːgl] (legal)

Skills training

p.71 **lorry** [ˈlɒri]	Lastwagen, LKW	a big **lorry**
(to) **knock** sb. **over/down** [nɒk]	jn. anfahren, jn. umfahren	verb: (to) **knock** (stoßen; schlagen; klopfen) – noun: **knock** (Stoß, Schlag; Klopfen)
(to) **bleed** [bliːd], **bled, bled** [bled]	bluten	verb: (to) **bleed, bled, bled** – noun: **blood** [blʌd] (Blut)
(to) **write down**	aufschreiben	Next Friday? On the 23rd? Let me **write down** the date.
(to) **skid** [skɪd]	schleudern; schlittern, (aus)rutschen	There was ice on the road, and the car **skidded**. It was very dangerous.
horse [hɔːs]	Pferd	a **horse**
stairs (pl) [steəz]	Treppe; (Treppen-)Stufen	! *German:* **Die Treppe** dort **ist** gefährlich. *English:* **Those stairs are** dangerous.
p.72 (to) **push** [pʊʃ]	stoßen, schubsen; drücken	Do I have to **push** or pull this door to open it? verb: (to) **push** – noun: **push** (Stoß, Schubs)

track [træk]	(Bahn-)Gleis	❗ **track** = **1.** (Bahn-)Gleis; **2.** Pfad, (Feld-)Weg 
onto the track [ˈɒntu], [ˈɒntə]	auf das (Bahn-)Gleis	He's jumping **onto** a box. 
knee [niː]	Knie	❗ Aussprache – das „k" wird nicht gesprochen: **knee** [niː]
artificial [ɑːtɪˈfɪʃl]	künstlich, Kunst-	an **artificial leg** = eine Beinprothese
disabled [dɪsˈeɪbld]	(körper)behindert	adjective: **disabled** – noun: **disability** [dɪsəˈbɪləti] (Behinderung)
p.73 (to) **include** [ɪnˈkluːd]	(mit) einschließen	**including** = einschließlich, inklusive
(to) **shock** [ʃɒk]	schockieren	What **shocking** news! (schockierend) We were really **shocked**! (schockiert) verb: (to) **shock** – noun: **shock** (Schock, Schreck)

Verbs and nouns which look the same

act	1. handeln; so tun, als ob	2. Tat, Handlung	**knock**	1. stoßen; schlagen	2. Stoß, Schlag
air	1. (aus)lüften	2. Luft	**push**	1. stoßen, schubsen	2. Stoß, Schubs
arrest	1. festnehmen	2. Festnahme	**reply**	1. antworten	2. Antwort
contact	1. Kontakt aufnehmen mit/zu	2. Kontakt	**shock**	1. schockieren	2. Schock, Schreck
crash	1. einen Unfall haben, zusammenstoßen *(mit)*	2. Unfall, Zusammenstoß	**support**	1. unterstützen	2. Unterstützung
flood	1. überfluten, überschwemmen	2. Flut; Überschwemmung	**taste**	1. schmecken	2. Geschmack
influence	1. beeinflussen	2. Einfluss	**vote**	1. wählen; abstimmen	2. Abstimmung, Votum

Irregular verbs

(to) **bleed**	bled	bled	*bluten*	(to) **rise**	rose	risen	*(an)steigen; hochsteigen*
(to) **mis-understand**	mis-understood	mis-understood	*missverstehen*	(to) **throw**	threw	thrown	*werfen*
(to) **ride**	rode	ridden	*(Rad) fahren, reiten*	(to) **wear**	wore	worn	*tragen, anhaben (Kleidung)*

▶ *pp.200–201*

Im **Dictionary** werden folgende **Abkürzungen und Symbole** verwendet:

sb. = somebody   sth. = something   jn. = jemanden   jm. = jemandem

pl = plural (Mehrzahl)   *BE = British English*   *AE = American English*   *AustE = Australian English*

infml = informal (umgangssprachlich)

° Mit diesem Kringel sind Wörter markiert, die nicht zum Lernwortschatz gehören. Die Fundstellenangaben zeigen, in welchem Band ein Wort zum ersten Mal vorkommt: 5 = Highlight 5; 6 = Highlight 6; 7 = Highlight 7; 8 = Highlight 8. Beim vorliegenden Band mit genauer Unit- und Seitenangabe: 9: 1 (15) = Highlight 9, Unit 1, Seite 15.

A

a [ə] ein/e 5 **once a week** einmal pro Woche 6

able ['eɪbl] **be able to do sth.** etwas tun können, in der Lage sein etwas zu tun 8

Aboriginal [æbə'rɪdʒənl]:
1. einheimisch, eingeboren 9: 1 (15)
2. aboriginal *(die Ureinwohner/innen Australiens betreffend)* 9: 1 (15)

Aboriginal Australian [æbərɪdʒənl ɒ'streɪlɪən] australische/r Ureinwohner/in 9: 1 (15)

about [ə'baʊt]:
1. ungefähr 5
2. über 5
What about you? Und du? / Was ist mit dir? 5 **What's special about him?** Was ist das Besondere an ihm? 6
write about schreiben über 5

above [ə'bʌv] oben; über, oberhalb (von) 8

above all [əbʌv 'ɔːl] vor allem, in erster Linie 9: 2 (41)

abroad [ə'brɔːd] im/ins Ausland 8

°**abseiling** ['æbseɪlɪŋ] Abseilen

°**accent** ['æksent] Akzent

accident ['æksɪdənt] Unfall 7

°**according to** [ə'kɔːdɪŋ] laut, zufolge

across [ə'krɒs] hinüber, herüber 8
across the bridge über die Brücke 8

act [ækt]:
1. Theater spielen; schauspielern 6
2. aufführen, spielen 6
°**act out** vorspielen, aufführen

act [ækt]:
1. Tat, Handlung 9: 3 (48)
2. handeln, sich verhalten; so tun, als ob 9: 3 (48)

action ['ækʃn] Aktion, Tat, Handlung; Action *(spannende Filmhandlung)* 8

activity [æk'tɪvəti] Aktivität, Beschäftigung 6

actor ['æktə] Schauspieler/in 7

add [æd] *(infml) siehe* **advertisement**

°**adapted from** [ə'dæptɪd frɒm] basierend auf

°**add** [æd] hinzufügen, addieren

address [ə'dres] Adresse 5

adult ['ædʌlt] Erwachsene/r 6

advance [əd'vɑːns]: **in advance** im Voraus 9: 2 (36)

advantage [əd'vɑːntɪdʒ] Vorteil 8

adventure [əd'ventʃə] Abenteuer 6

advert ['ædvɜːt] *(infml) siehe* **advertisement**

advertisement [əd'vɜːtɪsmənt] *(infml auch* **ad, advert***)* Anzeige, Inserat; Werbespot 8

advice [əd'vaɪs] Rat; Ratschläge 9: 1 (17)

aerobics [eə'rəʊbɪks] Aerobic 6

after school [ɑːftə 'skuːl] nach der Schule 5

afternoon [ɑːftə'nuːn] Nachmittag 5
in the afternoon(s) nachmittags, am Nachmittag 5

again [ə'gen] wieder, noch einmal 5

against [ə'genst] gegen 7

age [eɪdʒ] Alter 7

aged [eɪdʒd]: **children aged 7** Kinder im Alter von 7 Jahren 7

ago [ə'gəʊ]: **two years ago** vor zwei Jahren 7

agree (with sb.) [ə'griː] (jm.) zustimmen 6

air [eə]:
1. (aus)lüften 9: 4 (64)
2. Luft 9: 4 (64)

air conditioning ['eə kəndɪʃnɪŋ] Klimaanlage 9: 3 (57)

airport ['eəpɔːt] Flughafen 6

album ['ælbəm] Album 8

alcohol ['ælkəhɒl] Alkohol 9: 1 (25)

alive [ə'laɪv] lebendig, am Leben 9: 4 (70)

all [ɔːl] alle(s) 5 **all day** den ganzen Tag (lang) 6 **all in all** alles in allem 9: 2 (41) **all over the world** überall auf der Welt, auf der ganzen Welt 8 **all the time** die ganze Zeit 9: 3 (49) **all your life** dein ganzes Leben (lang) 9: 3 (49) **above all** vor allem, in erster Linie 9: 2 (41) **not ... at all** überhaupt nicht ... 5

allergic (to) [ə'lɜːdʒɪk] allergisch (gegen) 7

allow [ə'laʊ]: **allow sb. to do sth.** jm. erlauben, etwas zu tun 9: 3 (50)

allowed [ə'laʊd]: **be allowed** erlaubt sein 7 **be allowed to do sth.** etwas tun dürfen 7

almost ['ɔːlməʊst] fast, beinahe 9: 2 (32)

alone [ə'ləʊn] allein(e) 6

along the street [ə'lɒŋ] die Straße entlang 6

already [ɔːl'redi] schon 7

also ['ɔːlsəʊ] auch 6

although [ɔːl'ðəʊ] obwohl 8

always ['ɔːlweɪz] immer 5

am [æm]: **I'm (= I am)** ich bin 5

am [eɪ 'em]: **11 am** 11 Uhr morgens/vormittags 5

°**amaze** [ə'meɪz] erstaunen, verblüffen

amazing [ə'meɪzɪŋ]:
1. erstaunlich 7
2. großartig 8

amazingly [ə'meɪzɪŋli] erstaunlicherweise 9: 3 (49)

ambulance ['æmbjələns] Krankenwagen 9: 3 (48)

an [ən] ein/e *(vor Vokalen)* 5

and [ænd], [ənd] und 5

angry ['æŋgri] wütend, ärgerlich 5

animal ['ænɪml] Tier 5

announcement [ə'naʊnsmənt] Durchsage, Ansage 7

another [ə'nʌðə] ein/e andere(r, s); noch ein/e 5

answer ['ɑːnsə]:
1. Antwort 5
2. antworten (auf), beantworten 5

any ['eni] jegliche/r/s, jede/r/s beliebige 9: 1 (16) **(at) any time** zu jeder Zeit, jederzeit 9: 1 (16) **Do you have any questions?** Hast du/Habt ihr (irgendwelche) Fragen? 6 **It wasn't just any car.** Es war kein beliebiges / nicht einfach irgendein Auto. 9: 1 (16) **not (...) any more** nicht mehr 8 **We don't have any pets.** Wir haben keine (Haus-)Tiere. 5

anybody ['enibɒdi]: **Does anybody speak ...?** Spricht (irgend)jemand ...? 7 **not ... anybody** niemand 7

anything ['eniθɪŋ]: **Anything else?** Sonst noch etwas? 5 **not (...) anything** nichts 6

apartheid [ə'pɑːtaɪt] Apartheid *(früheres System der Trennung zwischen Weißen und Schwarzen in Südafrika)* 9: 3 (43)

apologize (to sb. for sth.) [ə'pɒlədʒaɪz] sich (bei jm. für etwas) entschuldigen 9: 2 (31)

app [æp] App 9: 3 (55)

apple ['æpl] Apfel 5

apply (to sb. for sth.) [ə'plaɪ] sich (bei jm. um etwas) bewerben 8

apprenticeship [ə'prentɪʃɪp] Ausbildung, Lehre 8

April ['eɪprəl] April 5

archbishop [ɑːtʃ'bɪʃəp] Erzbischof/Erzbischöfin 9: 3 (52)

°**Arctic** ['ɑːktɪk] die Arktis; arktisch, Polar-

are [ɑː] bist, sind, seid 5 **They're £ 90.** Sie kosten 90 Pfund. 5

area ['eəriə] Bereich; Gebiet, Gegend 8

argument ['ɑːgjumənt] Argument 9: 2 (41)

arm [ɑːm] Arm 6

armchair ['ɑːmtʃeə] Sessel 9: 2 (33)

around [ə'raʊnd] umher- 5 **run around** umherrennen; herumlaufen 6 °**be around** da sein, vorhanden sein

arrange [ə'reɪndʒ] vereinbaren, ausmachen *(Termin)* 7

arrest [ə'rest]:
1. Festnahme 9: 3 (48)
2. arrest sb. jn. festnehmen, verhaften 9: 3 (48)

arrival [ə'raɪvl] Ankunft 8

arrive (at) [ə'raɪv] ankommen (in/an/bei) 5

art [ɑːt] Kunst 5 **work of art** Kunstwerk 7

article ['ɑːtɪkl] Artikel 7

artificial [ɑːtɪ'fɪʃl] künstlich, Kunst- 9: 4 (72)

artificial leg [ɑːtɪfɪʃl 'leg] Beinprothese 9: 4 (72)

artist ['ɑːtɪst] Künstler/in 7

as [æz], [əz] wie 5 **as a snack** als Snack 8 **as from … / as of …** ab …, von … an 8 **as in …** wie in … 5 **as often as** so oft wie 8

ashamed [ə'ʃeɪmd]: **be/feel ashamed (of)** sich schämen (für) 9: 2 (32)

ask [ɑːsk]:
1. fragen 5
ask a question eine Frage stellen 5
ask sb. about sth. sich bei jm. nach etwas erkundigen, jn. nach etwas fragen 6
2. ask for sth. um etwas bitten, nach etwas fragen 8

asleep [ə'sliːp]: **be asleep** schlafen 8 **fall asleep** einschlafen 8

°**aspect** ['æspekt] Aspekt

assistant [ə'sɪstənt]:
1. Helfer/in, Assistent/in 7
2. Verkäufer/in 7

astronaut ['æstrənɔːt] Astronaut/in 9: 4 (67)

at [æt], [ət] an, bei 5 **at a restaurant** in einem Restaurant 5 **at Eggbuckland** auf der Eggbuckland-Schule 5 **at Ellie's house** bei Ellie daheim, bei Ellie zu Hause 5 **at home** zu Hause 5 **at least** mindestens, wenigstens 6 **at MARTINS** bei MARTINS 5 **at night** nachts, in der Nacht 5 **at school** in der Schule 5 **at the cinema** im Kino 5 **at the top (of)** oben, am oberen Ende (von); an der Spitze (von) 6 **at this school** auf/an dieser Schule 5 **not … at all** überhaupt nicht … 5

ate [eɪt], [et] *siehe* **eat**

athlete ['æθliːt] (Leicht-)Athlet/in 8

athletics [æθ'letɪks] Leichtathletik 8

atmosphere ['ætməsfɪə] Atmosphäre 8

attach (to) [ə'tætʃ] anfügen; anhängen (an) *(Brief, E-Mail)* 8

attack [ə'tæk]:
1. Angriff, Attacke 8
2. angreifen, attackieren 8

August ['ɔːgəst] August 5

aunt [ɑːnt] Tante 6

autumn ['ɔːtəm] Herbst 8

available [ə'veɪləbl]: **be available** zur Verfügung stehen, Zeit haben 8

average ['ævərɪdʒ]:
1. Durchschnitt 8 **on average** im Durchschnitt, durchschnittlich 8
2. durchschnittlich 8

away [ə'weɪ] weg, fort 5

awesome ['ɔːsəm] *(AE, infml)* klasse, stark, großartig 8

B

baby ['beɪbi] Baby 5

babysitter ['beɪbisɪtə] Babysitter 5

back [bæk]:
1. zurück 5
2. Rücken; Rückseite 9: 2 (31)

background ['bækgraʊnd]:
1. Hintergrund 8
2. Herkunft 9: 2 (34)
people of different backgrounds Menschen unterschiedlicher Herkunft 9: 2 (34)

bacon ['beɪkən] Speck 7

bad [bæd] schlecht; schlimm 5

badminton ['bædmɪntən] Badminton, Federball 6

bag [bæg] Tasche 5

bagpipes *(pl)* ['bægpaɪps] Dudelsack 7

ball [bɔːl] Ball 5

banana [bə'nɑːnə] Banane 5

band [bænd] Band, Musikgruppe 5

bank [bæŋk] Bank *(Geldinstitut)* 6

banknote ['bæŋknəʊt] Geldschein, Banknote 9: 1 (13)

bar [bɑː] Bar 9: 3 (54)

°**bar chart** ['bɑː tʃɑːt] Balkendiagramm, Säulendiagramm 8

barbecue ['bɑːbɪkjuː] Grillfest, Grillparty 8

°**barrier** ['bæriə] Barriere, Hindernis

baseball ['beɪsbɔːl] Baseball 6

basketball ['bɑːskɪtbɔːl] Basketball 5

bathroom ['bɑːθruːm] Bad(ezimmer) 5

Bavaria [bə'veəriə] Bayern 6

Bavarian [bə'veəriən]:
1. Bayer/in 6
2. bayerisch 6

BCE (= before the Common Era) [biːfɔː ðə kɒmən 'ɪərə] vor Christus (= vor der christlichen Zeitrechnung) 9: 4 (60)

be [biː], **was/were, been** sein 5

beach ['biːtʃ] Strand 5 **on the beach** am Strand 5

bean [biːn] Bohne 8

bear [beə] Bär 5

beat [biːt] *(Musik)* Beat, Rhythmus 7

beautiful ['bjuːtɪfl] schön, wunderschön 7

beauty ['bjuːti] Schönheit 9: 4 (62)

became [bɪ'keɪm] *siehe* **become**

because [bɪ'kɒz] weil 5

become [bɪ'kʌm], **became, become** werden 7

bed [bed] Bett 5 **go to bed** ins Bett gehen, schlafen gehen 5

bed and breakfast (B&B) [bed ən 'brekfəst] Frühstückspension; Zimmer mit Frühstück 7

bedroom ['bedruːm] Schlafzimmer 5

been [biːn], [bɪn] *siehe* **be**

beer [bɪə] Bier 8

before [bɪ'fɔː]:
1. vor *(zeitlich)* 5
2. vorher; zuvor 7
3. before (you read) bevor (du liest) 5

began [bɪ'gæn] *siehe* **begin**

begin [bɪ'gɪn], **began, begun** anfangen, beginnen 7

beginner [bɪ'gɪnə] Anfänger/in 7

°**beginning** [bɪ'gɪnɪŋ] Anfang

begun [bɪ'gʌn] *siehe* **begin**

behind [bɪ'haɪnd] hinter 5

believe (in sth.) [bɪ'liːv] glauben (an etwas) 8

bell [bel] Glocke; Klingel 7

below [bɪ'ləʊ] unter(halb von); unten 7

best [best] beste(r, s); am besten 5 **All the best** Mit besten Grüßen, Alles Gute *(Briefschluss)* 7 **like sth. best** etwas am liebsten mögen 6

bet [bet], **bet, bet** wetten 8

better ['betə] besser 6 **do better** besser abschneiden 6 **like sth. better** etwas lieber mögen 6

between [bɪ'twiːn] zwischen 6

big [bɪg]:
1. groß 5
2. schwer, dick *(Person)* 8

bike [baɪk] Fahrrad 5 **ride a bike** Rad fahren 5

bikini [bɪ'kiːni] Bikini 7

°**billion** ['bɪliən] Milliarde

°**bindi** ['bɪndi] Bindi *(auf die Stirn aufgemalter Punkt oder aufgemalter Schmuck indischer Frauen)*

bird [bɜːd] Vogel 5

birth [bɜːθ] Geburt 7 **give birth (to)** hervorbringen; gebären, entbinden, zur Welt bringen 9: 4 (62)

birth certificate ['bɜːθ sətɪfɪkət] Geburtsurkunde 9: 3 (56)

birthday ['bɜːθdeɪ] Geburtstag 5 **Happy birthday!** Herzlichen Glückwunsch zum Geburtstag! 5 **It's her birthday.** Sie hat Geburtstag. 5 **When is your birthday?** Wann hast du Geburtstag? 7

biscuit ['bɪskɪt] Keks, Plätzchen 6

bit [bɪt] Teil, Stück(chen) 7 **a bit** ein bisschen 5

bit [bɪt] *siehe* **bite**

bite [baɪt]:
1. Biss; (Insekten-)Stich 9: 1 (23)
2. bite, bit, bitten beißen; stechen *(z.B. Insekten)* 9: 1 (23)

bitten ['bɪtn] *siehe* **bite**

black [blæk] schwarz 5

blank [blæŋk]:
1. leer *(Blatt, Zeile)*; schwarz *(Bildschirm)*; unbeschrieben *(Papier/Zettel)* 9: 4 (67)
2. freie Stelle, Leerstelle *(in einem Text)* 9: 4 (67)
bled [bled] *siehe* **bleed**
bleed [bliːd], **bled, bled** bluten 9: 4 (71)
blog [blɒg] Blog *(Internet-Tagebuch)* 6
blood [blʌd] Blut 9: 4 (71)
blue [bluː] blau 5
blues [bluːz] Blues *(Musikrichtung)* 7
boarding pass [ˈbɔːdɪŋ pɑːs] Bordkarte 8
boat [bəʊt] Boot; Schiff 5
body [ˈbɒdi] Körper 9: 1 (15)
body painting [ˈbɒdi peɪntɪŋ] Körperbemalung 9: 1 (15)
bodybuilder [ˈbɒdibɪldə] Bodybuilder/in 9: 1 (17)
°**bold** [bəʊld] fett (gedruckt)
bonfire [ˈbɒnfaɪə] *(Freuden-)*Feuer 6
bonus [ˈbəʊnəs] Bonus- 7
boo [buː] buhen 8
book [bʊk]:
1. Buch 5
2. buchen, reservieren 7
booking [ˈbʊkɪŋ] Buchung, Reservierung 9: 3 (57)
bookshop [ˈbʊkʃɒp] Buchladen 6
°**boomerang** [ˈbuːməræŋ] Bumerang 6
boot [buːt] Stiefel 5
bored [bɔːd] **be bored** Langeweile haben, gelangweilt sein 8
boring [ˈbɔːrɪŋ] langweilig 5
born [bɔːn] **they were born** sie wurden geboren 7
borrow [ˈbɒrəʊ] (aus)leihen, sich borgen 5
boss [bɒs] Boss, Chef/in 8
bossy [ˈbɒsi] herrisch 5
both [bəʊθ] beide 8
bottle [ˈbɒtl] Flasche 5
°**bottom** [ˈbɒtəm] unteres Ende, Unterteil **from the bottom** von unten
bought [bɔːt] *siehe* **buy**
bow [bəʊ] Schleife 7
bow tie [bəʊ ˈtaɪ] Fliege *(Krawatte)* 7
bowling [ˈbəʊlɪŋ]: **go bowling** Bowling spielen gehen 5
box [bɒks] Box, Kasten 5
boy [bɔɪ] Junge, Bub 5
boyfriend [ˈbɔɪfrend] (fester) Freund 6
°**bracket** [ˈbrækɪt] *(runde)* Klammer *(in Texten)*
brave [breɪv] mutig 7
bread [bred] Brot 6
break [breɪk] Pause 5
break [breɪk], **broke, broken** (zer)brechen 7 **break down** eine Panne haben, kaputtgehen *(Auto)* 9: 1 (13)
breakfast [ˈbrekfəst] Frühstück 5 **have breakfast** frühstücken 5
bridge [brɪdʒ] Brücke 6
brilliant [ˈbrɪljənt] genial 5
bring [brɪŋ], **brought, brought** bringen, mitbringen 5

brochure [ˈbrəʊʃə] Broschüre, Prospekt 5
broke [brəʊk] *siehe* **break**
broken [ˈbrəʊkən] *siehe* **break** **be broken** gebrochen; zerbrochen, kaputt sein 8
brother [ˈbrʌðə] Bruder 5
brought [brɔːt] *siehe* **bring**
brown [braʊn] braun 5
brunch [brʌntʃ] Brunch 8
bucket [ˈbʌkɪt] Eimer 9: 3 (49)
buffalo [ˈbʌfələʊ], *pl* **buffalo** *or* **buffaloes** Büffel; Bison 9: 3 (42)
build [bɪld], **built, built** (er)bauen 8
building [ˈbɪldɪŋ] Gebäude 7
built [bɪlt] *siehe* **build well built** gut gebaut 8
bungee jumping [ˈbʌndʒi dʒʌmpɪŋ] Bungee-Springen 9: 2 (26)
burger [ˈbɜːgə] Hamburger *(Frikadelle)* 6
burn [bɜːn] brennen; verbrennen 8
bus [bʌs] Bus 5
bus stop [ˈbʌs stɒp] Bushaltestelle 6
bush [bʊʃ] Busch, Strauch 7
business [ˈbɪznəs]:
1. Geschäft, Betrieb 7
start a business ein Geschäft aufmachen, einen Betrieb gründen/eröffnen 7
2. (= business studies) Wirtschaftslehre 7
business studies *(pl)* [ˈbɪznəs stʌdiz] Wirtschaftslehre 7
busy [ˈbɪzi]:
1. belebt; verkehrsreich 7
2. be busy beschäftigt sein, (viel) zu tun haben 6
but [bʌt] aber 5
butter [ˈbʌtə] Butter 6
buy [baɪ], **bought, bought** kaufen 5
by [baɪ]: **by (10%)** um (10%) 9: 4 (64) **by 1896** bis 1896 9: 3 (54) **by Berry** *(geschrieben)* von Berry 5 **by bus** mit dem Bus 5
Bye. [baɪ] Tschüs./Servus. 5

C

cafe [ˈkæfeɪ] Café 5
cafeteria [kæfəˈtɪəriə] Kantine *(mit Selbstbedienung)*, Cafeteria 8
cage [keɪdʒ] Käfig 5
cake [keɪk] Kuchen 5
calculator [ˈkælkjuleɪtə] Taschenrechner 5
calendar [ˈkælɪndə] Kalender 5
call [kɔːl]:
1. rufen; anrufen; nennen 7
2. *(kurz für:* **phone call**) (Telefon-)Anruf 6
called [kɔːld]: **be called** genannt erden, heißen 7
calm [kɑːm] ruhig, still; besonnen 8
came [keɪm] *siehe* **come**
camera [ˈkæmərə] Fotoapparat; Kamera 8
camp [kæmp]:
1. (Zelt-)Lager 8
°**2.** campen

campaign [kæmˈpeɪn] Kampagne 9: 3 (49)
camping [ˈkæmpɪŋ] Camping 5
campsite [ˈkæmpsaɪt] Campingplatz, Zeltplatz 5
can [kæn], [kən] können 5
can [kæn] Dose, Büchse 7
cancel [ˈkænsl] streichen, absagen, ausfallen lassen; *(Vorgang am Automaten)* abbrechen 8
cancer [ˈkænsə] Krebs *(Erkrankung)* 8
candidate [ˈkændɪdət] Bewerber/in, Kandidat/in 8
canoe [kəˈnuː]:
1. Kanu, Paddelboot 5
2. Kanu fahren, paddeln 8
canoeing [kəˈnuːɪŋ] Paddeln, Kanusport 8 **go canoeing** Kanu fahren gehen, paddeln gehen 8
can't (= cannot) [kɑːnt], [ˈkænɒt] nicht können 5
canteen [kænˈtiːn] (Schul-)Mensa, Kantine 5
canyoning [ˈkænjənɪŋ] Canyoning *(Begehen einer Schlucht als Sport, z.B. sich abseilen)* 9: 2 (26)
capital (city) [ˈkæpɪtl] Hauptstadt 7
car [kɑː] Auto 5
car number [ˈkɑː nʌmbə] Autokennzeichen 7
car park [ˈkɑː pɑːk] Parkplatz 7
°**carbon dioxide** [kɑːbən daɪˈɒksaɪd] Kohlendioxid
card [kɑːd] Karte 5
care [keə]: **care about sth.** etwas wichtig nehmen 8 **I care about you.** Du bist mir nicht egal. / Du liegst mir am Herzen. 8 **I don't care.** Es ist mir egal. 8 **take care** vorsichtig sein, aufpassen 8 **Take care.** Mach's gut! 8 **Who cares?** Wen interessiert das? / Was soll's? / Na und? 8
care worker [ˈkeə wɜːkə] Pflegekraft; Betreuer/in 8
careful [ˈkeəfl] vorsichtig; sorgfältig 6
carefully [ˈkeəfəli]: **listen carefully** ganz genau zuhören 6
Caribbean [kærɪˈbiːən] karibisch; Karibik 8
carnival [ˈkɑːnɪvl] Karneval 8
carrot [ˈkærət] Möhre, Karotte 6
carry [ˈkæri] tragen; befördern, transportieren 9: 3 (55)
cart [kɑːt] Karren, Wagen *(z.B. Einkaufswagen)* 9: 4 (66)
cartoon [kɑːˈtuːn] Zeichentrickfilm; Comic 6
cash [kæʃ] Bargeld 8
cashier [kæˈʃɪə] Kassierer/in 8
cashless [ˈkæʃləs] bargeldlos 9: 2 (38)
castle [ˈkɑːsl] Burg 7
cat [kæt] Katze 5
catch [kætʃ], **caught, caught**:
1. (ein)fangen 7
2. nehmen, erwischen *(Bus/Zug)* 7
catchy [ˈkætʃi] eingängig *(Lied, Slogan)* 8
category [ˈkætəgəri] Kategorie 7
caught [kɔːt] *siehe* **catch**

°cause sth. [kɔːz] etwas bewirken, verursachen

cave [keɪv] Höhle 9: 2 (37)

CCTV [siː siː tiː ˈviː] Überwachungssystem; Überwachungskamera(s) 7

CCTV camera [siː siː tiː ˈviː kæmərə] Überwachungskamera 7

CD [siːˈdiː] CD 5

CD player [siːˈdiː pleɪə] CD-Spieler 6

CE (= Common Era) [kɒmən ˈɪərə] nach Christus (= christliche Zeitrechnung) 9: 4 (60)

celebrate [ˈselɪbreɪt] feiern 6

°celebration [selɪˈbreɪʃn] Feier

cell [sel] Zelle 9: 3 (45)

cent [sent] Cent 8

central [ˈsentrəl] zentral 7 **Central London** London Stadtmitte 7

centre [ˈsentə] Zentrum, (Stadt-)Mitte 6

century [ˈsentʃəri] Jahrhundert 8

cereal [ˈsɪəriəl] Getreide; (Frühstücks-)Flocken 8

certificate [səˈtɪfɪkət] Urkunde, Bescheinigung 9: 3 (56) **birth certificate** Geburtsurkunde 9: 3 (56)

chair [tʃeə] Stuhl 5

challenge [ˈtʃælɪndʒ]:
1. Herausforderung 8
2. **challenge (sb. to sth.)** (jn. zu etwas) herausfordern 8

champion [ˈtʃæmpiən] Meister/in (Sport) 8

chance [tʃɑːns] Chance, Gelegenheit 8

change [tʃeɪndʒ]:
1. Wandel; Verwandlung 9: 4 (64)
2. (ver)ändern, sich (ver)ändern 6
3. **change (trains)** umsteigen (Zug) 7

changing room [ˈtʃeɪndʒɪŋ ruːm] Umkleide(kabine), Anprobe 7

character [ˈkærəktə] Figur, Person (in Roman, Film usw.) 9: 1 (16)

charge (a mobile phone) [tʃɑːdʒ] (ein Mobiltelefon) aufladen 9: 4 (65)

charity [ˈtʃærəti] wohltätige Organisation 6

charity shop [ˈtʃærəti ʃɒp] Geschäft, das gespendete Waren für wohltätige Zwecke verkauft 6

charts (pl) [tʃɑːts] Charts (Hitliste(n)) 8

chat [tʃæt]:
1. **chat (with)** plaudern (mit); „chatten" (mit) 5
2. Gespräch, Unterhaltung; Chat 6 **have a chat** sich unterhalten, reden 6

cheap [tʃiːp] billig, preiswert 6 **It's cheaper than that.** So viel kostet das nicht. 6

check [tʃek]:
1. (über)prüfen, kontrollieren 6
2. (Über-)Prüfung, Kontrolle 6

check in [tʃek ˈɪn] einchecken 8

check out [tʃek ˈaʊt] auschecken 8

°checklist [ˈtʃeklɪst] Checkliste 6

cheer [tʃɪə]:
1. Beifallsruf, Hurra(geschrei) 7
2. jubeln, (Sportler/innen) anfeuern 7

cheese [tʃiːz] Käse 5

cherry [ˈtʃeri] Kirsche 8

chess [tʃes] Schach 9: 4 (60)

chicken [ˈtʃɪkɪn] Huhn; (Brat-)Hähnchen 5

child [tʃaɪld], pl **children** Kind 5

children [ˈtʃɪldrən] Plural von **child**

chill [tʃɪl] (infml) relaxen, sich ausruhen 6

°chin [tʃɪn] Kinn 6

chips (pl) [tʃɪps] Pommes frites 5 **(potato) chips** (AE) (Kartoffel-)Chips 7

chocolate [ˈtʃɒklət] Schokolade; Praline 5 **hot chocolate** Kakao, heiße (Trink-)Schokolade 5

chocolate bar [ˈtʃɒklət bɑː] Schokoriegel 7

choice [tʃɔɪs] (Aus-)Wahl 9: 2 (36)

choose [tʃuːz], **chose, chosen** (aus)wählen 9: 2 (36)

chores [tʃɔːz]: **do chores** (Haus-)Arbeiten erledigen 6

chose [tʃəʊz] siehe **choose**

chosen [ˈtʃəʊzn] siehe **choose**

Christian [ˈkrɪstʃən]:
1. Christ/in 8
2. christlich 8

Christmas [ˈkrɪsməs] Weihnachten 7

Christmas Day [ˈkrɪsməs deɪ] 1. Weihnachtstag (25. 12.) 7

church [tʃɜːtʃ] Kirche 8

cinema [ˈsɪnəmə] Kino 5

°circle [ˈsɜːkl] Kreis 6

circus [ˈsɜːkəs] Zirkus 6

city [ˈsɪti] (Groß-)Stadt 5

civil rights (pl) [sɪvl ˈraɪts] Bürgerrechte 7

civilization [sɪvəlaɪˈzeɪʃn] Zivilisation 9: 4 (62)

clap [klæp] klatschen 8

class [klɑːs] (Schul-)Klasse 5 **in class** im Unterricht 5

class teacher [ˈklɑːs tiːtʃə] Klassenlehrer/in 5

classical [ˈklæsɪkl] klassisch 8

°classmate [ˈklɑːsmeɪt] Mitschüler/in 5

classroom [ˈklɑːsruːm] Klassenzimmer 5

clean [kliːn]:
1. sauber machen, putzen 5
2. sauber 7

clear [klɪə] deutlich, klar 6

clearly [ˈklɪəli]: **speak clearly** deutlich sprechen 6

clever [ˈklevə] schlau, klug 7

climate [ˈklaɪmət] Klima 8

climate change [ˈklaɪmət tʃeɪndʒ] Klimawandel 9: 4 (64)

climb [klaɪm] klettern (auf) 6

climbing [ˈklaɪmɪŋ] (das) Klettern (Sport) 6

clock [klɒk] Uhr 5

close [kləʊz] schließen, zumachen 7

closed [kləʊzd]: **be closed** geschlossen sein, zu sein 6

clothes (pl) [kləʊðz] Kleidung 5

cloud [klaʊd] Wolke 7

cloudy [ˈklaʊdi] wolkig, bewölkt 6

club [klʌb] Klub, Verein 5

coach [kəʊtʃ] Trainer/in 8

coast [kəʊst] Küste 9: 1 (11) **on the coast** an der Küste 9: 1 (11)

coat [kəʊt] Mantel; Jacke 7

code [kəʊd] Code 8

°coding [ˈkəʊdɪŋ] Codierung

coffee [ˈkɒfi] Kaffee 5

cold [kəʊld] kalt 5

colleague [ˈkɒliːg] Kollege/Kollegin 9: 2 (39)

collect [kəˈlekt] sammeln 6

college [ˈkɒlɪdʒ] Fach(hoch)schule 8

colonialist [kəˈləʊniəlɪst] Kolonialist/in 8

colonize [ˈkɒlənaɪz] kolonisieren 8

colony [ˈkɒləni] Kolonie 8

colour [ˈkʌlə] Farbe 5 **people of colour** nicht-weiße Menschen 8

colourful [ˈkʌləfl] farbenfroh, bunt 7

come [kʌm], **came, come**:
1. (mit)kommen 5
come (in) first Erste/r werden (z.B. Rennen) 7
come far es weit bringen, weit kommen 9: 4 (66)
come in hereinkommen 6
Come on! Na los! / Komm(t) (schon)! 5
2. **come true** wahr werden, Wirklichkeit werden 8

comedian [kəˈmiːdiən] Komiker/in 9: 1 (24)

comedy [ˈkɒmədi] Comedyshow; Komödie 6

comfort [ˈkʌmfət] Komfort, Bequemlichkeit 9: 1 (22)

comfortable [ˈkʌmftəbl] bequem, gemütlich 6

comic [ˈkɒmɪk] Comic(heft) 6

comment [ˈkɒment] Kommentar 7 **make a comment** einen Kommentar abgeben 7

°commercial [kəˈmɜːʃl] kommerziell (auf Gewinn ausgerichtet)

communicate [kəˈmjuːnɪkeɪt] kommunizieren 9: 4 (66)

communication [kəmjuːnɪˈkeɪʃn] Kommunikation 9: 4 (66)

communications (pl) [kəmjuːnɪˈkeɪʃnz] Kommunikationstechnik; Kommunikationsnetz 9: 4 (66)

company [ˈkʌmpəni] Gesellschaft, Firma 8

°compare [kəmˈpeə] vergleichen

competition [kɒmpəˈtɪʃn] Wettbewerb 7

complain (about/of) [kəmˈpleɪn] sich beschweren (über); jammern 7

°complete [kəmˈpliːt]:
1. vervollständigen
2. abschließen, beenden

computer [kəmˈpjuːtə] Computer 5

°computerized [kəmˈpjuːtəraɪzd] Computer-

concert [ˈkɒnsət] Konzert 5

condition [kənˈdɪʃn] Bedingung; Zustand 9: 1 (14) **in/under these conditions** bei/unter diesen Bedingungen 9: 1 (14)

confident [ˈkɒnfɪdənt] (selbst)sicher; zuversichtlich 8

contact ['kɒntækt]:
1. Kontakt 9: 4 (67)
2. **contact sb.** Kontakt aufnehmen mit/zu jm., sich in Verbindung setzen mit jm. 9: 4 (67)

container [kən'teɪnə] Behälter, Gefäß 8

continue [kən'tɪnjuː] fortfahren, weitermachen; (sich) fortsetzen, weitergehen 8 **continue to do sth.** etwas weiterhin tun 8

°**control** [kən'trəʊl] Kontrolle **lose control (of)** die Kontrolle verlieren (über)

°**conversation** [kɒnvə'seɪʃn] Gespräch

cook [kʊk]:
1. kochen 5
2. Koch, Köchin 8

cool [kuːl]:
1. cool 5
2. kühl 5

°**copy** ['kɒpi] kopieren, abschreiben

corner ['kɔːnə] Ecke 9: 1 (11)

correct [kə'rekt]:
1. korrekt 6
2. korrigieren, berichtigen 6

°**correction** [kə'rekʃn] Berichtigung, Korrektur

corridor ['kɒridɔː] Korridor 8

cost [kɒst], **cost, cost** kosten 5

cottage ['kɒtɪdʒ] Häuschen, Hütte 6

cotton ['kɒtn] Baumwolle 7

could [kʊd]:
1. **she could** sie konnte 6
2. **we could** wir könnten 5

country ['kʌntri] Land 5 **in the country** auf dem Land 5

countryside ['kʌntrisaɪd] Land(schaft); Natur 9: 2 (26)

°**couple** ['kʌpl] Paar

cousin ['kʌzn] Cousin/e 8

cover ['kʌvə]:
1. Hülle (DVD, CD); Einband, Umschlag (Buch) 7
°**2.** bedecken; abdecken, zudecken

cover letter ['kʌvə letə] Anschreiben, Begleitschreiben, Motivationsschreiben 8

cow [kaʊ] Kuh 5

crab [kræb] Krebs (Tier) 5

crash [kræʃ]:
1. Zusammenstoß, Unfall 9: 4 (70)
2. **crash (into)** krachen; einen Unfall haben, zusammenstoßen (mit) 9: 4 (70)

crazy ['kreɪzi] verrückt 7 **crazy about sth.** wild auf etwas, versessen auf etwas 7

cream [kriːm] Sahne 5

credit card ['kredɪt kɑːd] Kreditkarte 9: 3 (56)

crew [kruː] Mannschaft, Team; Clique 9: 1 (15)

cricket ['krɪkɪt] Kricket (Mannschaftssportart) 6

crime [kraɪm] Verbrechen; Kriminalität 9: 3 (46)

crime film ['kraɪm fɪlm] Krimi 9: 3 (46)

crime series ['kraɪm sɪəriːz], pl
crime series Krimiserie 6

criminal ['krɪmɪnl]:
1. Verbrecher/in 9: 3 (46)
2. kriminell 9: 3 (46)

crisps (pl) [krɪsps] (Kartoffel-)Chips 5

criticism ['krɪtɪsɪzəm] Kritik 9: 2 (40)

criticize ['krɪtɪsaɪz] kritisieren 9: 2 (40)

cross [krɒs]:
1. überqueren 6
2. Kreuz 6

crowd [kraʊd] (Menschen-)Menge 8

crowded ['kraʊdɪd] überfüllt, voll (von Menschen) 8

cry [kraɪ] weinen 6

cultural ['kʌltʃərəl] kulturell 8

culture ['kʌltʃə] Kultur 7

cup [kʌp]:
1. Tasse; Becher 8
a cup of tea eine Tasse Tee 8
2. Pokal (z.B. Sport) 9: 3 (46)
World Cup Weltmeisterschaft 9: 3 (43)

cupcake ['kʌpkeɪk] Cupcake (kleiner runder Kuchen) 7

curious about ['kjʊəriəs] neugierig auf 9: 2 (32)

curriculum vitae (= CV) [kərɪkjələm 'viːtaɪ] (BE) Lebenslauf 8

cushion ['kʊʃn] Kissen 5

customer ['kʌstəmə] Kunde, Kundin 7

cut [kʌt], **cut, cut**:
1. schneiden; (Rasen) mähen 6
cut sth. off etwas abschneiden; etwas amputieren 9: 4 (72)
2. reduzieren, senken; kürzen (finanzielle Mittel) 9: 4 (70)

cute [kjuːt] niedlich, süß 5

CV (= curriculum vitae) [siː 'viː] (BE) Lebenslauf 8

cycle ['saɪkl] Rad fahren 6

cycle track ['saɪkl træk] Radweg 7

cycling ['saɪklɪŋ] (das) Radfahren 5

cyclist ['saɪklɪst] Radfahrer/in 9: 4 (71)

D

dad [dæd] Papa, Vati 5

°**daily** ['deɪli] täglich

dance [dɑːns] tanzen 5

dancer ['dɑːnsə] Tänzer/in 7

dancing ['dɑːnsɪŋ] (das) Tanzen 5

danger ['deɪndʒə] Gefahr 8

dangerous ['deɪndʒərəs] gefährlich 5

dark [dɑːk] dunkel 7

date [deɪt] Datum 5

date of birth [deɪt əv 'bɜːθ] Geburtsdatum 7

daughter ['dɔːtə] Tochter 7

day [deɪ] Tag 5 **make sb.'s day** jm. den Tag verschönern, jm. eine Riesenfreude machen 9: 2 (31)

day out [deɪ 'aʊt], pl **days out** (Tages-)Ausflug 6

day pass [deɪ pɑːs] Tageskarte 8

daylight ['deɪlaɪt] Tageslicht 7

dead [ded] tot 9: 1 (16)

deal [diːl] Geschäft; Vereinbarung 6
It's a deal! Abgemacht! 6 **make a deal** ein Geschäft abschließen/vereinbaren 6

dear [dɪə]: **Dear ...** Liebe/r ... 5
Dear Sir/Madam Sehr geehrte Damen und Herren 7 **Oh dear.** Oje! 6

December [dɪ'sembə] Dezember 5

decide (to do sth.) [dɪ'saɪd] beschließen, (sich) entscheiden (etwas zu tun) 7

deep [diːp] tief 7

defence [dɪ'fens] Verteidigung 9: 3 (51)

defend [dɪ'fend] verteidigen 9: 3 (51)

degree [dɪ'griː] Grad 7

democracy [dɪ'mɒkrəsi] Demokratie 9: 4 (62)

democratic [demə'krætɪk] demokratisch 9: 4 (62)

depart [dɪ'pɑːt] abfahren, abreisen; abfliegen 8

department [dɪ'pɑːtmənt] Abteilung 7

department store [dɪ'pɑːtmənt stɔː] Kaufhaus 7

departure [dɪ'pɑːtʃə] Abfahrt, Abreise; Abflug 8

depend on [dɪ'pend ɒn] abhängen von 8 **It depends.** Es kommt drauf an. 8

depression [dɪ'preʃn] Depression(en) 9: 2 (30)

descendant [dɪ'sendənt] Nachfahre/Nachfahrin, Nachkomme 8

describe [dɪ'skraɪb] beschreiben 6

description [dɪ'skrɪpʃn] Beschreibung 9: 3 (55)

desert ['dezət] Wüste 9: 1 (17)

desk [desk] Schreibtisch 5

dessert [dɪ'zɜːt] Nachtisch, Dessert 8
for dessert zum Nachtisch/Dessert 8

destroy [dɪ'strɔɪ] zerstören, vernichten 8

°**detail** ['diːteɪl] Detail, Einzelheit

detective [dɪ'tektɪv] Detektiv/in 7

detective series [dɪ'tektɪv sɪəriːz], pl
detective series Krimiserie 9: 3 (46)

°**diagram** ['daɪəgræm] Diagramm

dialogue ['daɪəlɒg] Dialog 8

diary ['daɪəri] Tagebuch; Kalender 7
keep a diary Tagebuch führen 7

dictionary ['dɪkʃənri] Wörterbuch, (alphabetisches) Wörterverzeichnis 5

did [dɪd] siehe **do** He didn't do his homework. Er hat seine Hausaufgaben nicht gemacht. 5

°**didgeridoo** [dɪdʒəri'duː] Didgeridoo

die [daɪ] sterben 6 **die of** sterben an 9: 4 (60)

difference ['dɪfrəns] Unterschied 5
make a difference etwas bewirken, etwas ausmachen 5

different ['dɪfrənt] unterschiedlich, verschieden, anders 5

difficult ['dɪfɪkəlt] schwierig, schwer 5

diner ['daɪnə] (AE) Imbissstube, Lokal 6

dinner ['dɪnə] Abendessen 5 **have dinner** (zu) Abend essen 5

dinosaur ['daɪnəsɔː] Dinosaurier 7

direct [də'rekt] direkt 7

dirt [dɜːt] Schmutz, Dreck 9: 4 (64)

dirty ['dɜːti] schmutzig, dreckig
9: 4 (64)
disability [dɪsə'bɪləti] Behinderung
9: 4 (72)
disabled [dɪs'eɪbld] (körper)behindert
9: 4 (72)
disadvantage [dɪsəd'vɑːntɪdʒ]
Nachteil 8
disagree [dɪsə'griː] nicht zustimmen,
widersprechen 7
disappoint sb. [dɪsə'pɔɪnt] jn. ent-
täuschen 9: 4 (70)
disappointed (with sb./sth.)
[dɪsə'pɔɪntɪd] enttäuscht 6
disappointing [dɪsə'pɔɪntɪŋ] ent-
täuschend 9: 4 (70)
disaster [dɪ'zɑːstə] Katastrophe,
Unglück 7
discover [dɪ'skʌvə] entdecken
9: 3 (44)
discriminate against sb.
[dɪ'skrɪmɪneɪt] jn. diskriminie-
ren 9: 2 (30)
discrimination (against sb.)
[dɪskrɪmɪ'neɪʃn] Diskriminierung
(eines Menschen) 9: 2 (30)
°**discuss** [dɪ'skʌs] diskutieren
°**discussion** [dɪ'skʌʃn] Diskussion
disease [dɪ'ziːz] Krankheit 9: 1 (14)
dishwasher ['dɪʃwɒʃə] Geschirrspül-
maschine 6
°**dislike** [dɪs'laɪk] nicht mögen
distance ['dɪstəns] Distanz, Entfer-
nung 8 **in the distance** in der
Ferne 8
dive [daɪv] einen Kopfsprung
machen 5
diver ['daɪvə] Kunst-/Turmspringer/in
7
diving ['daɪvɪŋ] (das) Tauchen
(Sport) 6
DJ ['diː dʒeɪ] DJ (Discjockey) 7
do [duː], **did, done** machen, tun 5 **do
a trip** einen Ausflug machen 6 **do
sport** Sport treiben 5 **50p will do**
50 Pence reichen (auch) 6 **I do my
homework** ich mache (meine) Hausaufgaben 5
doctor ['dɒktə] Arzt/Ärztin,
Doktor/in 6
document ['dɒkjumənt] Dokument;
Text(datei) 8
dog [dɒg] Hund 5 **walk a dog** mit
einem Hund spazieren gehen 8
dog walker ['dɒg wɔːkə] Hunde-
ausführer/in 8
dog walking ['dɒg wɔːkɪŋ] Hunde
ausführen 8
dogs' home [dɒgz 'həʊm] Hundeheim 6
dollar ($) ['dɒlə] Dollar 7 **like a
million dollars** fantastisch 7
dolphin ['dɒlfɪn] Delfin 9: 2 (37)
done [dʌn] siehe **do**
donkey ['dɒŋki] Esel 5
donut ['dəʊnʌt] (AE) Donut (ring-
förmiges Hefegebäck) 8
door [dɔː] Tür 6
double ['dʌbl] doppelt, Doppel- 7

double room [dʌbl 'ruːm] Doppel-
zimmer 7
down the hill [daʊn] den Hügel
hinunter / runter 5
°**dozen** ['dʌzn], pl **dozen** Dutzend
drama ['drɑːmə] Schauspiel, dar-
stellende Kunst 5
dramatic [drə'mætɪk] dramatisch;
theatralisch 9: 3 (42)
drank [dræŋk] siehe **drink**
°**draw** [drɔː], **drew, drawn** zeichnen
°**drawn** [drɔːn] siehe **draw**
dream [driːm] Traum 6
dress [dres] Kleid 6
°**drew** [druː] siehe **draw**
drink [drɪŋk]:
  1. Getränk 5
  2. **drink, drank, drunk** trinken 5
drive [draɪv], **drove, driven** (mit dem
Auto) fahren 6
driven ['drɪvn] siehe **drive**
driver ['draɪvə] Fahrer/in 7
driving licence ['draɪvɪŋ laɪsns]
Führerschein 7
°**driving test** ['draɪvɪŋ test] Fahr-
prüfung, Führerscheinprüfung 7
drone [drəʊn] Drohne 9: 4 (64)
drought [draʊt] Dürre 9: 4 (64)
drove [drəʊv] siehe **drive**
drug [drʌg] Droge, Rauschgift;
Arzneimittel 7
drums (pl) [drʌmz] Schlagzeug;
Trommeln 5
drunk [drʌŋk] siehe **drink**
dry [draɪ]:
  1. trocken 8
  2. trocknen 9: 1 (13)
duck [dʌk] Ente 5
during ['djʊərɪŋ] während 8
DVD [diːviː'diː] DVD 5
°**dynamic** [daɪ'næmɪk] dynamisch

E

e-reader ['iː riːdə] E-Book-Reader 6
each [iːtʃ] jede(r, s) (einzelne) 7
  50 p each jeweils 50 Pence 7
each other [iːtʃ 'ʌðə] einander, sich
(gegenseitig) 9: 2 (32)
ear [ɪə] Ohr 6
early ['ɜːli] früh 5
earn [ɜːn] verdienen (Geld) 8
earth [ɜːθ] Erde 9: 4 (60)
earthquake ['ɜːθkweɪk] Erdbeben 7
east [iːst] Osten; östlich; Ost- 6
Easter ['iːstə] Ostern 8
eastern ['iːstən] östliche(r, s), Ost- 7
easy ['iːzi] einfach, leicht 6
eat [iːt], **ate, eaten** essen; fressen 5
eaten ['iːtn] siehe **eat**
economic [iːkə'nɒmɪk] wirtschaftlich,
Wirtschafts- 9: 4 (60)
economy [ɪ'kɒnəmi] (Volks-)Wirtschaft
9: 4 (60)
education [edʒu'keɪʃn] (Schul-)Bil-
dung 8
effect (on) [ɪ'fekt] (Aus-)Wirkung (auf),
Einfluss (auf); Effekt 9: 2 (38)
  special effects (pl) Special Effects
  (in Filmen) 9: 2 (38)
e.g. [iː 'dʒiː] z.B. (= zum Beispiel) 8

egg [eg] Ei 8
eight [eɪt] acht 5
°**election** [ɪ'lekʃn] Wahl (Abstimmung)
electric [ɪ'lektrɪk] elektrisch 9: 4 (64)
electrician [ɪlek'trɪʃn] Elektriker/in 8
electricity [ɪlek'trɪsəti] Strom,
Elektrizität 8 **run on electricity** mit
Strom fahren 8
electronic [ɪlek'trɒnɪk] elektronisch 7
elephant ['elɪfənt] Elefant 5
eleven [ɪ'levən] elf 5
else [els]: **Anything else?** Sonst noch
etwas? 5
email ['iːmeɪl] E-Mail 5
embarrass sb. [ɪm'bærəs] jn. in Verle-
genheit bringen 9: 2 (33)
embarrassed [ɪm'bærəst] verlegen
(Adj.) 9: 2 (33)
embarrassing [ɪm'bærəsɪŋ] peinlich 8
°**emergency services** [i'mɜːdʒənsi]
Notfall
employment [ɪm'plɔɪmənt] Arbeit,
Anstellung 9: 1 (14)
empty ['empti]:
  1. leer 6
  2. leeren 6
emu ['iːmjuː] Emu 9: 1 (17)
end [end]:
  1. Ende, Schluss 5
  at the end (of …) am Ende (von …)
  5 **in the end** schließlich, zum
  Schluss 5
  2. (be)enden 9: 4 (60)
ending ['endɪŋ] Ende (Text,
Geschichte); Endung 6 **happy
ending** Happy End 6
energy ['enədʒi] Energie 7
engine ['endʒɪn] Motor 9: 1 (16)
engineer [endʒɪ'nɪə] Ingenieur/in;
Techniker/in 9: 4 (59)
English-speaking ['ɪŋglɪʃ spiːkɪŋ]
englischsprachig 8
enjoy [ɪn'dʒɔɪ] genießen 6 **enjoy
yourself** Vergnügen/Spaß haben 8
enough [ɪ'nʌf] genug 6
entertainment park [entə'teɪnmənt
pɑːk] Erholungspark, Vergnügungspark 7
environment [ɪn'vaɪrənmənt]
Umwelt; Umfeld, Umgebung 8
environmental [ɪnvaɪrən'mentl]
Umwelt- 9: 4 (69)
equal ['iːkwəl] gleich(berechtigt)
9: 3 (43)
equality [ɪ'kwɒləti] Gleichheit
9: 3 (43)
equip sb. with sth. [ɪ'kwɪp] jn. mit
etwas ausrüsten, ausstatten 9: 1 (22)
equipment [ɪ'kwɪpmənt]
Ausrüstung, Ausstattung 7
especially [ɪ'speʃəli] insbesondere 7
etc. [et'setərə] (aus dem Lateinischen)
usw. (und so weiter) 6
euro (€) ['jʊərəʊ], pl **euros** Euro 8
even ['iːvn] sogar, selbst 7
evening ['iːvnɪŋ] Abend 5 **in the
evening(s)** abends, am Abend 5
event [ɪ'vent] Ereignis 8

ever ['evə] je(mals) 6 **Have you ever been ...?** Warst du schon mal ...? / Bist du schon mal ... gewesen? 6

every ['evri] jede(r, s) 5

everybody ['evribɒdi] jeder; alle 5

everyday ['evrideɪ] alltäglich, Alltags- 8

everyday life [evrideɪ 'laɪf] Alltag 8

everyone ['evriwʌn] jeder; alle 6

everything ['evriθɪŋ] alles 8

exam [ɪg'zæm] *siehe* **examination**

examination [ɪgzæmɪ'neɪʃn], *infml auch* **exam** Prüfung 9: 1 (16) **take/do an exam(ination)** eine Prüfung machen 9: 1 (16)

example [ɪg'zɑːmpl] Beispiel 5 **for example** zum Beispiel 5

except (for) [ɪk'sept] außer, bis auf 9: 1 (11)

°excite [ɪk'saɪt] aufregen, begeistern

excited [ɪk'saɪtɪd] aufgeregt, gespannt 5

exciting [ɪk'saɪtɪŋ] aufregend 5

Excuse me, ... [ɪks'kjuːz mi] Entschuldigung, ... 6

exercise ['eksəsaɪz] Übung, Aufgabe 5

exercise book ['eksəsaɪz bʊk] Schulheft, Übungsheft 5

exist [ɪg'zɪst] existieren 7

exotic [ɪg'zɒtɪk] exotisch 8

expect [ɪk'spekt] erwarten 7

expensive [ɪk'spensɪv] teuer 5

experience [ɪk'spɪəriəns]:
1. erfahren; erleben 8
2. Erfahrung; Erlebnis 8

expert (on) ['ekspɜːt] Experte/ Expertin (für) 9: 2 (38)

°explain sth. to sb. [ɪk'spleɪn] jm. etwas erklären

explore [ɪk'splɔː] erforschen, erkunden 8

extra ['ekstrə] zusätzliche(r, s), Extra-; Extra 8

extreme [ɪk'striːm]:
1. extrem 9: 4 (60)
2. Extrem 9: 4 (60)

eye [aɪ] Auge 6

F

face [feɪs]:
1. Gesicht 8
2. **face sb./sth.** vor etwas stehen *(Problem)*; jm./einer Sache ins Auge sehen, sich einer Sache stellen; jm./ einer Sache entgegentreten 8

°fact [fækt] Tatsache; Information **fun fact** witzige Tatsache, amüsanter Fakt

factory ['fæktri] Fabrik 6

fair [feə] Jahrmarkt; Messe 8

fall [fɔːl], **fell, fallen** fallen; hinfallen 5 **fall down** umfallen; hinfallen 8 **fall in love (with sb.)** sich verlieben (in jn.) 9: 1 (22) **fall off sth.** herunter- fallen von etwas *(Fahrrad, Pferd)* 5 **fall out (with sb.)** sich mit jm. zerstreiten 9: 2 (32)

fallen ['fɔːlən] *siehe* **fall**

false [fɔːls] falsch, unrichtig 6

°fame [feɪm] Ruhm

family ['fæməli], *pl* **families** Familie 5

family-friendly [fæməli 'frendli] familienfreundlich 7

family tree [fæməli 'triː] (Familien-) Stammbaum 8

famous (for) ['feɪməs] berühmt (für, wegen) 7

fan [fæn] Fan 5

fantastic [fæn'tæstɪk] fantastisch 6

fantasy ['fæntəsi] Fantasie; Fantasy *(Literatur-, Filmgattung)* 8

far [fɑː] weit 7

farm [fɑːm] Bauernhof 5

farmer ['fɑːmə] Bauer, Bäuerin; Landwirt/in 7

fashion ['fæʃn] Mode(trend) 7

fast [fɑːst] schnell 7

fat biking ['fæt baɪkɪŋ] Fatbike fahren 8

father ['fɑːðə] Vater 5

favourite ['feɪvərɪt]:
1. Liebling, Favorit/in 8
2. Lieblings- 5
favourite thing Lieblingssache 5

February ['februəri] Februar 5

fed [fed] *siehe* **feed feel fed up** genervt sein, sauer sein; die Nase voll haben 5

feed [fiːd], **fed, fed** füttern 5

feel [fiːl], **felt, felt** sich fühlen; fühlen 5

feeling ['fiːlɪŋ] Gefühl 9: 2 (32)

feet [fiːt] *Plural von* **foot**

fell [fel] *siehe* **fall**

felt [felt] *siehe* **feel**

ferry ['feri] Fähre 5

festival ['festɪvl] Fest 6

few [fjuː] wenige 9: 3 (42) **a few** ein paar, einige 5 **in the last few weeks** in den letzten paar Wochen 7

field [fiːld] Feld; Weide 5 **in the field** auf dem Feld/der Weide 5

fight [faɪt]:
1. Kampf; Schlägerei 8
have a fight (with sb.) sich streiten (mit jm.); sich prügeln (mit jm.) 8
2. **fight, fought, fought** kämpfen 8
fight back sich wehren 9: 4 (72)

fill [fɪl] füllen 6 **fill in** einsetzen; ausfüllen 7

film [fɪlm]:
1. Film 5
2. filmen 7

°film-maker ['fɪlm meɪkə] Filme- macher/in

film star ['fɪlm stɑː] Filmstar 7

final ['faɪnl] letzte(r, s), abschlie- ßend 7

finally ['faɪnəli] zum Schluss, schließ- lich 9: 1 (15)

find [faɪnd], **found, found** finden 5 **find out** herausfinden 6

fine [faɪn] gut, schön 5 **I'm fine.** Es geht mir gut. 5

fingernail ['fɪŋgəneɪl] Fingernagel 9: 1 (17)

finish ['fɪnɪʃ] beenden; enden 6

fire ['faɪə] Feuer 6

firefighter ['faɪəfaɪtə] Feuerwehr- mann, Feuerwehrfrau 5

firework ['faɪəwɜːk] Feuerwerks- körper 6 **fireworks** *(pl)* Feuerwerk 6

firm [fɜːm] Firma 9: 3 (48)

first [fɜːst]:
1. zuerst 5
2. **(= 1st)** erste, erster, erstes 5
at first zuerst, am Anfang 6

first aid [fɜːst 'eɪd] Erste Hilfe 6

first-aid kit [fɜːst 'eɪd kɪt] Erste-Hilfe- Set, Verbandkasten 6

first language [fɜːst 'læŋgwɪdʒ] Muttersprache 9: (9)

fish [fɪʃ], *pl* **fish** Fisch 5

fit [fɪt] fit 6

°fit [fɪt] passen (zu)

fitness ['fɪtnes] Fitness 6

five [faɪv] fünf 5 **Give me five!** *(Aufforderung zum Abklatschen, Geste der Freude/Begrüßung)* 6

fizzy (drink/water) ['fɪzi] (Getränk/ Wasser) mit Kohlensäure 6

flag [flæg] Fahne, Flagge 6

flash (of light) [flæʃ] (Licht-)Blitz 9: 2 (38)

flash photos *(pl)* ['flæʃ fəʊtəʊz] Fotos mit Blitz 9: 2 (38)

flat [flæt] Wohnung 5

flew [fluː] *siehe* **fly**

flight [flaɪt] Flug 8

flood [flʌd]:
1. Überschwemmung, Hochwasser; Flut 9: 4 (67)
2. überschwemmen, überfluten 9: 4 (67) **be flooded** unter Wasser stehen 9: 4 (67)

floor [flɔː] (Fuß-)Boden 8

flown [fləʊn] *siehe* **fly**

flu [fluː] Grippe 9: 1 (14)

°fluent ['fluːənt] flüssig, fließend *(Sprache)*

fly [flaɪ], **flew, flown** fliegen 8

°focus ['fəʊkəs] Schwerpunkt **focus on language** *(etwa)* Schwerpunkt: Sprache

foggy ['fɒgi] nebelig 6

folder ['fəʊldə] Mappe, Ordner 9: 2 (32)

follow ['fɒləʊ] (be)folgen; verfolgen 9: 1 (18) **the following day/week** am folgenden Tag / in der folgenden Woche 9: 1 (18)

food [fuːd] Essen, Lebensmittel; Futter 5

foot [fʊt], *pl* **feet** Fuß 8

football ['fʊtbɔːl] Fußball 5 **playing football** Fußballspielen 5

footballer ['fʊtbɔːlə] Fußball- spieler/in 7

for [fɔː], [fə] für 5 **for 100 metres** 100 Meter weit 6 **for once** aus- nahmsweise, dieses eine Mal 8 **for the last time** zum letzten Mal 7 **for three years** drei Jahre (lang); seit drei Jahren 8 **trains/the line for ...** Züge/die U-Bahn-Linie nach ... 7

forecast ['fɔːkɑːst] Vorhersage 6

foreground ['fɔːgraʊnd] Vorder- grund 8

forest [ˈfɒrɪst] Wald 9:4 (65)
forget (about) [fəˈget], **forgot,**
forgotten vergessen 7
forgot [fəˈgɒt] *siehe* **forget**
forgotten [fəˈgɒtn] *siehe* **forget**
fork [fɔːk] Gabel 8
form [fɔːm]:
  1. Formular 7
  2. Form 8
  3. (sich) formen, (sich) bilden 8
formal [ˈfɔːml] formell 7
formation [fɔːˈmeɪʃn]: **rock**
  formation Felsformation 9:1 (22)
fortunately [ˈfɔːtʃənətli] zum
  Glück, glücklicherweise 9:3 (51)
forum [ˈfɔːrəm] Forum 8
forward [ˈfɔːwəd]: **look forward**
  to doing sth. sich darauf freuen,
  etwas zu tun 8 **look forward**
  to sth. sich auf etwas freuen 8
fought [fɔːt] *siehe* **fight**
found [faʊnd] *siehe* **find**
four [fɔː] vier 5
fox [fɒks] Fuchs 7
free [friː]:
  1. frei 5
  Are you free at one o'clock?
  Hast du um ein Uhr Zeit? 5
  2. (for) free kostenlos 5
  3. free sb. jn. befreien 9:3 (49)
free time [friː ˈtaɪm] Freizeit 8
freestyle [ˈfriːstaɪl] Freestyle *(freier*
  Stil), im freien Stil ausgeführt 9:3 (43)
Freestyle football [friːstaɪl ˈfʊtbɔːl]
  Variante des Fußballs, die tänzerische
  und akrobatische Elemente be-
  inhaltet 9:3 (43)
French fries *(pl)* [frentʃ ˈfraɪz]
  (AE) Pommes frites 7
French-speaking [ˈfrentʃ spiːkɪŋ]
  französischsprachig 8
Friday [ˈfraɪdeɪ], [ˈfraɪdi] Freitag 5
friend [frend] Freund/in 5 **make**
  friends Freunde finden 6 **°a friend**
  of mine / of yours / of hers / ... ein/e
  Freund/in von mir / von dir / von
  ihr / ...
friendly [ˈfrendli] freundlich, nett 6
friendship [ˈfrendʃɪp] Freundschaft 8
fries *(pl)* [fraɪz]: **French fries** *(AE)*
  Pommes frites 7
frightened [ˈfraɪtnd]: **be frightened**
  Angst haben 8
from [frɒm]:
  1. aus 5
  from Plymouth aus Plymouth 5
  2. von 5 **from Monday to Friday**
  von Montag bis Freitag 5 **a text**
  from mum eine SMS von Mama 5
  as from ... ab ..., von ... an 8
front [frʌnt] Vorderseite, vorderer
  Teil 8 **in front of** vor 5
fruit [fruːt] Früchte, Obst; Frucht 5
fry [fraɪ] *(in der Pfanne)* braten,
  frittieren 8
fuel [ˈfjuːəl] Treibstoff, Kraftstoff
  9:1 (17)
full [fʊl] voll 7 **full (driving) licence**
  voll gültiger Führerschein 9:1 (25)
  full of ... voller ... 7

full-time [fʊl ˈtaɪm] Vollzeit- 8
full-time job [fʊl ˈtaɪm] Ganztagsjob,
  Vollzeitjob 8
fun [fʌn] Spaß 5 **... is fun.** ... macht
  Spaß. 5 **they're fun** es macht Spaß,
  mit ihnen zusammenzusein 5
°fun fact [ˈfʌn fækt] witzige Tatsache,
  amüsanter Fakt
funeral [ˈfjuːnərəl] Beerdigung,
  Begräbnis 9:3 (49)
funny [ˈfʌni] lustig; seltsam 5
future [ˈfjuːtʃə] Zukunft 6

G

gallery [ˈgæləri] Galerie 7
game [geɪm] Spiel 6
gang [gæŋ] Gang *(Bande)* 7
°gap [gæp] Lücke 6
garage [ˈgærɑːʒ] Garage 5
garage sale [ˈgærɑːʒ seɪl] Garagen-
  flohmarkt *(privater Flohmarkt)* 5
garden [ˈgɑːdn] Garten 5
gate [geɪt]:
  1. Tor 7
  2. Gate *(Flugsteig)* 8
gave [geɪv] *siehe* **give**
°G'day! [gəˈdeɪ] *(AustE, infml)* Hallo! /
  Guten Tag!
geek [giːk] *jemand, der sich sehr stark*
  für etwas begeistert (und manchmal
  von anderen deswegen belächelt
  wird) 7
geography [dʒiˈɒgrəfi] Geografie,
  Erdkunde 5
get [get], **got, got:**
  1. bekommen, kriegen 5
  get (to) kommen, gelangen (nach) 5
  get off a bus aussteigen aus einem
  Bus 5
  get on (well) with sb. (gut) auskom-
  men mit jm. 9:2 (32)
  get on a bus einsteigen in einen
  Bus 5
  get out herauskommen 5
  get sth. (sich) etwas holen, besor-
  gen 6
  get up aufstehen 5
  2. get wet nass werden 8
°geyser [ˈgiːzə] Geysir
ghost [gəʊst] Gespenst 7
ginger [ˈdʒɪndʒə]:
  1. Ingwer 5
  2. rotblond *(Haare)* 6
girl [gɜːl] Mädchen 5
girlfriend [ˈgɜːlfrend] *(feste)* Freundin
  6
give [gɪv], **gave, given** geben 5 **give a**
  talk einen Vortrag halten 6 **Give me**
  five! Gib mir fünf! *(Aufforderung zum*
  Abklatschen, Geste der Freude/Begrü-
  ßung) 6 **give sth. up** etwas aufgeben,
  aufhören mit etwas 7
given [ˈgɪvn] *siehe* **give**
glad [glæd]: **I'm glad.** Ich bin froh. 6
glamorous [ˈglæmərəs] glamourös
  9:1 (17)
glass [glɑːs] Glas 6
glasses *(pl)* [ˈglɑːsɪz] Brille 6
glove [glʌv] Handschuh 6

go [gəʊ], **went, gone:**
  1. gehen; fahren 5
  go away weggehen 5
  go on geschehen, vor sich gehen 8
  go on for (ten days) (zehn Tage lang)
  (an)dauern 8
  go out ausgehen; hinausgehen 6
  go up hochgehen; (an)steigen
  9:1 (13)
  go wrong schiefgehen; etwas falsch
  machen 8
  I'm going to help ich werde helfen 6
  2. go crazy verrückt werden 7
god [gɒd] Gott 8 **Oh my God!** Oh
  mein Gott! 8
gold [gəʊld] Gold 8
gone [gɒn] *siehe* **go be gone** weg
  sein 8
good [gʊd] gut 5 **Good morning.**
  Guten Morgen. 5 **Good night.** Gute
  Nacht. 5 **be good at sth.** etwas gut
  können, gut sein in etwas 6 **Have a**
  good day. Ich wünsche dir einen
  schönen Tag. / Schönen Tag noch. 5
Goodbye. [gʊdˈbaɪ] Auf Wiedersehen.
  5
got [gɒt] *siehe* **get**
government [ˈgʌvənmənt] Regierung
  9:1 (24)
GPS [dʒiː piː ˈes] GPS 7
grandad [ˈgrændæd] Opa 7
grandfather [ˈgrænfɑːðə] Großvater 5
grandma [ˈgrænmɑː] Oma 5
grandmother [ˈgrænmʌðə] Groß-
  mutter 5
grandpa [ˈgrænpɑː] Opa 5
grandparents *(pl)* [ˈgrænpeərənts]
  Großeltern 5
grass [grɑːs] Gras 6
great [greɪt] großartig, toll 5 **have a**
  great time viel Spaß haben 5
green [griːn] grün 5
°greenhouse gas [griːnhaʊs ˈgæs]
  Treibhausgas 8
grew [gruː] *siehe* **grow**
grey [greɪ] grau 7
grill [grɪl]:
  1. Grill 8
  2. grillen 8
ground [graʊnd] Erde *(Erdboden)* 6
group [gruːp] Gruppe 6
grow [grəʊ], **grew, grown** wachsen;
  (allmählich) werden 8
grown [grəʊn] *siehe* **grow**
°guarantee [gærənˈtiː] garantieren
guard [gɑːd] Wache, Wachposten;
  Garde 9:2 (39)
guess [ges]:
  1. Vermutung 8
  2. (er)raten 8
  Guess what! Stell dir / Stellt euch
  (mal) vor! 8
guest [gest] Gast 7
guide [gaɪd]:
  1. Reiseleiter/in, Fremdenführer/in;
  Ratgeber *(Buch, Website)* 9:2 (29)
  2. führen, leiten 9:2 (29)
guitar [gɪˈtɑː] Gitarre 5
°gun [gʌn] Schusswaffe, Pistole
guy [gaɪ] Typ, Kerl 8

guys *(pl)* [gaɪz] Leute *(Anrede)* 6
gym [dʒɪm] Turnhalle, Sporthalle; Fitnessstudio 8
gymnastics [dʒɪmˈnæstɪks] Turnen, Gymnastik 6

H

had [hæd], [həd] *siehe* **have**
hair [heə] Haar, Haare 6
hairdresser [ˈheədresə] Frisör/in 6
hairdryer [ˈheədraɪə] Föhn, Haartrockner 6
hairy [ˈheəri] behaart, haarig 6
half [hɑːf]:
 1. halbe(r, s), Halb- 7
 half price zum halben Preis 7
 2. *pl* **halves** Hälfte 7
half-brother [ˈhɑːf brʌðə] Halbbruder 9: 1 (18)
half-sister [ˈhɑːf sɪstə] Halbschwester 9: 1 (18)
hall [hɔːl] Halle; Saal 8 **school hall** Aula 8 **village hall** Gemeindesaal 9: 2 (31)
halves [hɑːvz] *Plural von* **half**
ham [hæm] *(gekochter)* Schinken 7
hamster [ˈhæmstə] Hamster 5
hand [hænd] Hand 6 **on the one hand** einerseits 9: 2 (41) **on the other hand** andererseits 9: 2 (41)
handy [ˈhændi] praktisch, nützlich 9: 2 (39)
hang-gliding [ˈhæŋ glaɪdɪŋ] Drachenfliegen 6
hang out [hæŋ ˈaʊt]**, hung, hung** rumhängen, abhängen 8
happen [ˈhæpən] geschehen, passieren 6
happy [ˈhæpi] glücklich, froh 5 **Happy birthday!** Herzlichen Glückwunsch zum Geburtstag! 5 **happy ending** Happy End 6 **be happy to do sth.** gerne etwas tun 7
harbour [ˈhɑːbə] Hafen 5
hard [hɑːd] schwer; schwierig; hart 5 **work hard** hart arbeiten 7
harmony [ˈhɑːməni] Harmonie, Einklang 9: 1 (14)
has [hæz], [həz] **he/she/it has** er/sie/ es hat 5
hash browns *(pl)* [hæʃ ˈbraʊnz] *Beilage aus Kartoffeln, ähnlich wie Rösti* 8
hashtag [ˈhæʃtæg] Hashtag 8
hat [hæt] Hut, Mütze 5
have [hæv]**, had, had** haben 5 **Have a good day.** Ich wünsche dir einen schönen Tag. / Schönen Tag noch. 5 **have to do sth.** etwas tun müssen 6
°hazard [ˈhæzəd] Gefahr
he [hiː] er 5 **he's (= he is)** er ist 5
head [hed] Kopf 8
head of state [hed əv ˈsteɪt] Staatsoberhaupt 8
headache [ˈhedeɪk]: **have a headache** Kopfschmerzen haben 6
°heading [ˈhedɪŋ] Überschrift
health [helθ] Gesundheit 6
healthy [ˈhelθi] gesund 6
hear [hɪə]**, heard, heard** hören 5
heard [hɜːd] *siehe* **hear**

heart [hɑːt] Herz 7
heat [hiːt]:
 1. erwärmen, erhitzen 9: 4 (64)
 2. Hitze, Wärme 9: 4 (64)
heating [ˈhiːtɪŋ] Heizung 9: 4 (65)
heatwave [ˈhiːtweɪv] Hitzewelle 9: 4 (64)
°height [haɪt] Höhe; Größe *(bei Menschen)*
held [held] *siehe* **hold**
helicopter [ˈhelɪkɒptə] Hubschrauber 8
hell [hel] Hölle 8 **Hell!** Verdammt! / Zum Teufel! 8 **nervous as hell** *(infml)* höllisch nervös, furchtbar nervös 8
Hello. [həˈləʊ] Hallo./Servus. 5
helmet [ˈhelmɪt] Helm 7
help [help]:
 1. helfen 5
 Help yourselves. Bedient euch! / Greift zu! 7
 2. Hilfe 5
helper [ˈhelpə] Helfer/in 6
°helpful [ˈhelpfl] hilfsbereit; hilfreich, nützlich
henna [ˈhenə] Henna 9: 4 (62)
her [hɜː]:
 1. her dad ihr Vater 5
 2. *(zu „she")* sie; ihr 5
 for her für sie 5 **with her** mit ihr 5
here [hɪə] hier; hierher 5
 Here you are. Bitte schön. / Hier, bitte. 5
°heritage [ˈherɪtɪdʒ] Erbe *(kulturhistorisch)*
hero [ˈhɪərəʊ]**,** *pl* **heroes** Held/in 8
hers [hɜːz] ihre/r, ihrs *(zu „she")* 7
herself [hɜːˈself] sie/sich selbst *(zu „she")* 7
Hi! [haɪ] Hallo. 5 **Say hi to your parents.** Grüß/t deine/eure Eltern. 9: 1 (21)
high [haɪ] hoch 7
high jump [ˈhaɪ dʒʌmp] Hochsprung 8
highway [ˈhaɪweɪ] *(AE)* Autobahn, Fernstraße (USA) 9: 1 (16)
°hike [haɪk] wandern
hiking [ˈhaɪkɪŋ] *(das)* Wandern 6
hill [hɪl] Hügel 5
hilly [ˈhɪli] hügelig 7
him [hɪm] ihn; ihm 5
himself [hɪmˈself] er/sich selbst 7
Hindi [ˈhɪndi] Hindi *(Amtssprache in Indien)* 9: 4 (58)
Hindu [ˈhɪnduː] Hindu 8
hip hop [hɪp hɒp] Hip-Hop 9: 3 (44)
hire [ˈhaɪə] mieten, leihen 7
his [hɪz]**: his bike** sein Fahrrad *(zu „he")* 5 **the bike is his** das Fahrrad ist seins *(zu „he")* 7
history [ˈhɪstri] Geschichte 5
hit [hɪt]**, hit, hit** schlagen; stoßen gegen/auf; treffen 8
hitchhiker [ˈhɪtʃhaɪkə] Anhalter/in, Tramper/in 9: 1 (17)
hobby [ˈhɒbi] Hobby 5
hockey [ˈhɒki] (Feld-)Hockey 7

hold [həʊld]**, held, held:**
 1. halten 8
 °2. besitzen, haben
holiday [ˈhɒlədeɪ] Urlaub 5
 holidays *(pl)* Ferien 5 **a week's / six weeks' holiday** eine Woche / sechs Wochen Urlaub 6
home [həʊm]:
 1. nach Hause 5
 I'm home ich bin zu Hause 5
 2. Heim, Zuhause 5 **at home** zu Hause 5
 dogs' home Hundeheim 6
 3. Startseite *(Internet)* 7
homeless [ˈhəʊmləs] obdachlos 8
homework [ˈhəʊmwɜːk] Hausaufgabe/n 5 **I do my homework** ich mache (meine) Hausaufgaben 5
honest [ˈɒnɪst] ehrlich 8
hood [hʊd] Kapuze 9: 1 (17)
hoodie [ˈhʊdi] Kapuzenpullover 5
hoover [ˈhuːvə] staubsaugen 6
hope [həʊp]:
 1. hoffen 5
 2. hope (for) Hoffnung (auf) 8
horn [hɔːn] Horn 9: 4 (70)
horror [ˈhɒrə] Horror 8
horse [hɔːs] Pferd 9: 4 (71)
hospital [ˈhɒspɪtl] Krankenhaus 5
hostel [ˈhɒstl] Hostel *(günstige Unterkunft für Reisende)* 8
°hostess [ˈhəʊstəs] Gastgeberin
hot [hɒt] heiß, warm 6
hot chocolate [hɒt ˈtʃɒklət] Kakao, heiße (Trink-)Schokolade 6
hot dog [ˈhɒt dɒg] Hot Dog 7
hotel [həʊˈtel] Hotel 7
hour [aʊə] Stunde 6 **(working) hours** *(pl)* Arbeitszeit(en) 9: 2 (39) **for hours and hours** stundenlang 6 **work long hours** lange arbeiten, Überstunden machen 9: 2 (39)
house [haʊs] Haus 5
houseboat [ˈhaʊsbəʊt] Hausboot 6
how [haʊ] wie 5 **How are you doing?** *(AE)* Wie geht's? / Wie geht es dir/ euch/Ihnen? 8 **How are you?** Wie geht's? / Wie geht es dir/euch? 5
however [haʊˈevə] allerdings, jedoch 9: 4 (60)
huge [hjuːdʒ] riesig, Riesen- 8
hundred [ˈhʌndrəd]**: a/one hundred** (ein)hundert 7
hung [hʌŋ] *siehe* **hang out**
hunger [ˈhʌŋgə] Hunger 9: 4 (60)
hungry [ˈhʌŋgri]**: Are you hungry?** Hast du / habt ihr Hunger? 5
hunt [hʌnt]:
 1. Jagd 9: 1 (14)
 2. jagen 9: 1 (14)
hunter [ˈhʌntə] Jäger/in 9: 1 (14)
hurricane [ˈhʌrɪkən] Hurrikan, Orkan 8
hurt [hɜːt]**, hurt, hurt** verletzen; wehtun 8

I

I [aɪ] ich 5 **I'm (= I am)** ich bin 5
ice [aɪs] Eis *(gefrorenes Wasser)* 9: 4 (65)

ice cream [aɪs ˈkriːm] (Speise-)Eis 5
ice hockey [ˈaɪs hɒki] Eishockey 7
ice skating [ˈaɪs skeɪtɪŋ] Schlittschuh-
laufen 6
**ICT (= information and communication
technology)** [aɪ siː ˈtiː] Informations-
und Kommunikationstechnologie 5
idea [aɪˈdɪə] Idee 5
identity [aɪˈdentəti] Identität 9: 2 (29)
idiot [ˈɪdiət] Idiot/in 7
if [ɪf]:
  1. wenn, falls 6
  2. ob 8
ill [ɪl] krank 6
illegal [ɪˈliːgl] illegal, verboten 9: 4 (70)
illness [ˈɪlnəs] Krankheit 8
imagine sth. [ɪˈmædʒɪn] sich etwas
vorstellen 9: 3 (55)
immigrant [ˈɪmɪɡrənt] Einwanderer,
Einwanderin 8
impolite [ɪmpəˈlaɪt] unhöflich 8
important [ɪmˈpɔːtənt] wichtig 5
°**improve** [ɪmˈpruːv] verbessern;
sich verbessern 6
in [ɪn]:
  1. herein, hinein 6
  2. in 5
  in English auf Englisch 5
  in four days' time in vier Tagen 8
  in my opinion meiner Meinung
  nach 8
  in the afternoon(s) nachmittags,
  am Nachmittag 5
  in the country auf dem Land 5
  in the evening(s) abends, am Abend
  5
  in the field auf dem Feld / der
  Weide 5
  in the morning(s) morgens, am
  Morgen 5
  in the photo auf dem Foto 5
  in the street auf der Straße 6
include [ɪnˈkluːd] (mit) einschließen
9: 4 (73)
including [ɪnˈkluːdɪŋ] einschließlich,
inklusive 9: 4 (73)
°**inclusion** [ɪnˈkluːʒn] Einbeziehung,
Einbindung, Inklusion
independence (from) [ɪndɪˈpendəns]
Unabhängigkeit (von) 7
Independence Day [ɪndɪˈpendəns deɪ]
Unabhängigkeitstag 7
independent (of/from) [ɪndɪˈpendənt]
unabhängig (von) 8
indigenous (to) [ɪnˈdɪdʒənəs]
einheimisch (in) 8
indigenous people [ɪndɪdʒənəs ˈpiːpl]
Einheimische, Ureinwohner/innen 8
industry [ˈɪndəstri] Industrie 8
inequality [ɪnɪˈkwɒləti] Ungleichheit
9: 3 (43)
influence [ˈɪnfluəns]:
  1. beeinflussen 9: 3 (46)
  2. Einfluss 9: 3 (46)
influencer [ˈɪnfluənsə]
Influencer/in 9: 3 (46)
informal [ɪnˈfɔːml] informell, locker 7
information (about) [ɪnfəˈmeɪʃn]
Information(en) (über) 6

**information and communication
technology (= ICT)**
[ɪnfəmeɪʃn ənd kəmjuːnɪkeɪʃn
tekˈnɒlədʒi] Informations- und
Kommunikationstechnologie 5
inhabitant [ɪnˈhæbɪtənt]
Einwohner/in, Bewohner/in 8
insect [ˈɪnsekt] Insekt 9: 1 (23)
inside [ɪnˈsaɪd] (nach) drinnen 6
instead [ɪnˈsted] stattdessen 9: 4 (69)
instead of [ɪnˈsted əv] anstatt,
anstelle von 9: 4 (69)
instruction [ɪnˈstrʌkʃn] Anweisung 8
instrument [ˈɪnstrəmənt] Instrument
5
insurance [ɪnˈʃʊərəns] Versicherung
9: 3 (56)
interest [ˈɪntrəst] Interesse 6
interested [ˈɪntrəstɪd]: **interested in
doing sth.** daran interessiert, etwas
zu tun 7 **be interested in** sich inter-
essieren für, interessiert sein an 6
interesting [ˈɪntrəstɪŋ] interessant 6
international [ɪntəˈnæʃnəl]
international 9: 2 (29)
internet [ˈɪntənet] Internet 6
°**interpret** [ɪnˈtɜːprɪt] interpretieren;
dolmetschen (gesprochenen Text
mündlich wiedergeben)
interview [ˈɪntəvjuː] Interview 5
  job interview Vorstellungsgespräch
  8
into [ˈɪntu], [ˈɪntə] in (... hinein) 6
introduce sb. to sb./sth. [ɪntrəˈdjuːs]
jm. jn./etwas vorstellen, jn. jn. mit jm./
etwas bekanntmachen 8
introduction [ɪntrəˈdʌkʃn]:
  1. Einleitung 7
  2. Vorstellung (Bekanntmachen) 8
invent [ɪnˈvent] erfinden 9: 4 (59)
invention [ɪnˈvenʃn] Erfindung
9: 4 (60)
inventor [ɪnˈventə] Erfinder/in
9: 4 (60)
invitation (to) [ɪnvɪˈteɪʃn] Einladung
(zu, nach) 5
invite [ɪnˈvaɪt] einladen 5
is [ɪz] (er/sie/es) ist 5 **It's £ 31.** Es
kostet 31 Pfund. 5
island [ˈaɪlənd] Insel 7
issue [ˈɪʃuː] Problem; (Streit-)Frage,
Thema 9: 3 (46)
it [ɪt] es, (bei Dingen und Tieren:) er,
sie 5 **it's (= it is)** es ist (Dinge/Tiere
auch: er ist, sie ist) 5
its [ɪts] sein/e; ihr/e (Dinge/Tiere) 7
itself [ɪtˈself] es/sich selbst 7

J

jacket [ˈdʒækɪt] Jacke, Jackett 5
jam [dʒæm] Marmelade 5
January [ˈdʒænjuəri] Januar 5
jazz [dʒæz] Jazz 8
jealous (of) [ˈdʒeləs] eifersüchtig
(auf); neidisch (auf) 6
jeans (pl) [dʒiːnz] Jeans 5
jellyfish [ˈdʒelifɪʃ], pl **jellyfish** Qualle
9: 1 (12)
jetboat [ˈdʒetbəʊt] Jetboot
(Wasserfahrzeug) 9: 2 (37)

job [dʒɒb] Job, Stelle 6
job interview [ˈdʒɒb ɪntəvjuː]
Vorstellungsgespräch 8
jogging [ˈdʒɒɡɪŋ] Jogging 6
join [dʒɔɪn] mitmachen (bei); (einem
Klub) beitreten 6 **join (sb.)** sich (jm.)
anschließen, sich dazugesellen (bei
jm.) 8 **join a school / a class** (neu)
auf eine Schule / in eine Klasse
gehen 9: 2 (32)
joke [dʒəʊk] Witz, Scherz 6
journey [ˈdʒɜːni] Reise 8 **Safe journey!** Gute Reise! 6
judo [ˈdʒuːdəʊ] Judo 6
juice [dʒuːs] Saft 5
July [dʒuˈlaɪ] Juli 5
jump [dʒʌmp]:
  1. springen 8
  2. Sprung 8
June [dʒuːn] Juni 5
junk food [ˈdʒʌŋk fuːd] Junkfood
(ungesundes Essen) 6
just [dʒʌst]:
  1. nur, bloß; einfach 7
  2. gerade (eben) 9: 1 (17)
  3. just like Berry genau wie Berry 6

K

kangaroo [kæŋɡəˈruː] Känguru
9: 1 (10)
kayak [ˈkaɪæk] Kajak (Sportpaddel-
boot) 8
kayaking [ˈkaɪækɪŋ] (das) Kajak-
fahren 8
keep [kiːp], **kept, kept** halten; be-
halten 7 **keep to sth.** sich an etwas
halten, etwas einhalten, bei etwas
bleiben 9: 1 (25)
kept [kept] siehe **keep**
kettle [ˈketl] Wasserkocher (elektrisch)
7
key [kiː] Schlüssel; Schlüssel- 8
key skills (pl) [ˈkiː skɪlz] Schlüssel-
qualifikationen, -kompetenzen 8
°**Kia ora!** [kiː ˈɔːrə] Hallo! (Begrüßung
der Maori, wörtlich etwa: Möge es dir
gut gehen!)
kick [kɪk] treten, schießen 7
kid [kɪd] Kind, Jugendliche/r 5
kill [kɪl] töten 9: 1 (14)
kilo(gram) [ˈkiːləʊ] Kilo(gramm)
9: 4 (65)
kilometre (km) [ˈkɪləmiːtə] Kilometer
6 **square kilometre(s) (= km²)**
Quadratkilometer 8
°**kilometres per hour (kph)**
[kɪləmiːtəz pər ˈaʊə] Kilometer pro
Stunde (km/h)
kilt [kɪlt] Kilt (Schottenrock) 7
kind [kaɪnd] freundlich, nett 6
kind (of) [kaɪnd] Art/Sorte (von) 6
king [kɪŋ] König 7
kiss [kɪs]:
  1. (sich) küssen 8
  2. Kuss 8
kitchen [ˈkɪtʃɪn] Küche 5
kitten [ˈkɪtn] Kätzchen, junge Katze 6
kiwi [ˈkiːwi] Kiwi (Vogel) 9: 2 (29)
kiwi fruit [ˈkiːwi fruːt], pl **kiwi fruit**
Kiwi(frucht) 9: 2 (29)

knee [niː] Knie 9: 4 (72)

knew [njuː] *siehe* **know**

knife [naɪf], *pl* **knives** Messer 7

knives [naɪvz] *Plural von* **knife**

knock [nɒk]:

1. Stoß, Schlag; Klopfen 9: 4 (71)

2. stoßen; schlagen; klopfen 9: 4 (71)

knock sb. over/down jn. anfahren, jn. umfahren 9: 4 (71)

know [nəʊ], **knew, known** wissen; kennen 5 **I don't know about ....** Bei ... bin ich mir nicht (so) sicher. 7

°**knowledge** [ˈnɒlɪdʒ] Wissen, Kenntnis(se)

known [nəʊn] *siehe* **know**

koala [kəʊˈɑːlə] Koala(bär) 9: 1 (11)

°**kph (kilometres per hour)** [keɪ piː ˈeɪtʃ] Kilometer pro Stunde (km/h)

L

°**L-plater** [ˈel pleɪtə] Fahrer/in mit L-Schild (L = Learner)

lady [ˈleɪdi] Dame 8

laid [leɪd] *siehe* **lay**

lain [leɪn] *siehe* **lie**

lake [leɪk] (Binnen-)See 6

lamp [læmp] Lampe 5

land [lænd]:

1. landen 7

2. Land 7

landing [ˈlændɪŋ] Landung *(Raumschiff, Flugzeug)* 9: 4 (66)

language [ˈlæŋgwɪdʒ] Sprache 7 **official language** Amtssprache 8

lantern [ˈlæntən] Laterne 6

laptop [ˈlæptɒp] Laptop 5

large [lɑːdʒ] groß 9: 2 (38)

lasagne [ləˈzænjə] Lasagne 6

last [lɑːst] letzte(r, s) 5 **last week** vorige/letzte Woche 6

late [leɪt] (zu) spät 5 **my bus is late** mein Bus hat Verspätung 5

later [ˈleɪtə] später 5

laugh [lɑːf] lachen 5 **laugh at** lachen über, sich lustig machen über 8

launch [lɔːntʃ] Start *(z.B. Rakete)*; Einführung *(z.B. eines Produktes)* 8

law [lɔː] Gesetz; Jura *(Studium)* 9: 3 (48)

law firm [ˈlɔː fɜːm] Anwaltskanzlei 9: 3 (48)

lawyer [ˈlɔːjə] (Rechts-)Anwalt/ Anwältin 9: 3 (48)

lay [leɪ] *siehe* **lie**

lay [leɪ], **laid, laid** legen 9: 2 (38)

layout [ˈleɪaʊt] Layout, Gestaltung 8

lazy [ˈleɪzi] faul 8

leader [ˈliːdə] Leiter/in, (An-)Führer/in 6

learn [lɜːn] lernen 6

learner [ˈlɜːnə] Lernende/r 9: 1 (25)

learner driver [lɜːnə ˈdraɪvə] Fahrschüler/in, Fahrer/in mit einem Führerschein für Begleitetes Fahren 9: 1 (25)

learner licence [ˈlɜːnə laɪsns] Führerschein für Begleitetes Fahren 9: 1 (25)

least [liːst] *(der/die/das)* wenigste, am wenigsten 7 **at least** mindestens, wenigstens 6

leave [liːv], **left, left:**

1. verlassen 6 **leave school** von der Schule abgehen 6

2. zurücklassen; abfahren 6

left [left] links; nach links 5 **on the left** links, auf der linken Seite 5

left [left] *siehe* **leave**

leg [leg] Bein 5

legal [ˈliːgl] legal 9: 4 (70)

legend [ˈledʒənd] Legende, Sage 8

lemonade [leməˈneɪd] Limonade 6

leopard [ˈlepəd] Leopard 9: 3 (42)

less [les] weniger 7

lesson [ˈlesn] (Unterrichts-)Stunde 5

let's (= let us) [lets] lass(t) uns 5 **Let's see.** Lass(t) uns (mal) sehen. 6

letter [ˈletə]:

1. Brief 5

2. Buchstabe 8

level [ˈlevl] Grad, Stufe; Niveau, Ebene 9: 4 (64) **at professional level** auf Profi-Ebene 9: 4 (64)

liberty [ˈlɪbəti] Freiheit 8

licence [ˈlaɪsns] Genehmigung, Lizenz 9: 1 (25) **driving licence** Führerschein 7 **full (driving) licence** voll gültiger Führerschein 9: 1 (25)

lie [laɪ], **lay, lain** liegen 8

life [laɪf], *pl* **lives** Leben 5 **for life** lebenslänglich; auf Lebenszeit 9: 3 (48)

lifeguard [ˈlaɪfgɑːd] Rettungsschwimmer/in; Bademeister/in 9: 1 (12)

lifestyle [ˈlaɪfstaɪl] Lebensstil 6

lift [lɪft]:

1. heben, hochheben; sich heben 8

2. Lift, Fahrstuhl 8

light [laɪt] Licht; Lampe 7

like [laɪk] mögen 5 **I'd (= I would) like** ich hätte gern, ich möchte (...) haben 5 **I'd (= I would) like to join** ich würde/möchte gern mitmachen 6

like [laɪk] wie 5 **like this** so, auf diese Art 7 **a hat like that** so(lch) eine Mütze 7 **an accident / accidents like this** so ein/ein solcher Unfall; solche Unfälle 7 **I don't feel like it.** Mir ist nicht danach. 6 **just like Berry** genau wie Berry 6 **What's it like?** Wie ist es (er, sie)? / Wie sieht es (er, sie) aus? 7

line [laɪn]:

1. Linie, Reihe 6

2. U-Bahn-Linie 7

lion [ˈlaɪən] Löwe 9: 3 (42)

liquid [ˈlɪkwɪd]:

1. Flüssigkeit 8

2. flüssig 8

list [lɪst] Liste 5

listen [ˈlɪsn]: **listen (to)** zuhören; *(sich etwas)* anhören 5 **listen for sth.** auf etwas horchen, *(beim Zuhören)* auf etwas achten 5

litre [ˈliːtə] Liter 9: 1 (13)

little [ˈlɪtl] wenig 7 **a little** ein wenig, ein bisschen 7

live [lɪv] leben, wohnen 5

live [laɪv] live 7

lives [laɪvz] *Plural von* **life**

living room [ˈlɪvɪŋ ruːm] Wohnzimmer 5

local [ˈləʊkəl] einheimisch, am/ vom Ort 9: 2 (29)

Londoner [ˈlʌndənə] Londoner/in 7

lonely [ˈləʊnli] einsam 6

long [lɒŋ] lang; lange 6

long-term [lɒŋ ˈtɜːm] langfristig, Langzeit- 9: 2 (39)

look [lʊk]:

1. aussehen 6

2. sehen, schauen 5 **Look, Adam.** Sieh mal, Adam. / Schau mal, Adam. 5 **look after** sich kümmern um; aufpassen auf 5 **look for** suchen 5 **look forward to doing sth.** sich darauf freuen , etwas zu tun 8 **look forward to sth.** sich auf etwas freuen 8

3. Blick 7

lorry [ˈlɒri] Lastwagen, LKW 9: 4 (71)

lose [luːz] **lost, lost** verlieren 6

lost [lɒst] *siehe* **lose** **be lost** sich verlaufen/verirrt haben 9: 1 (13) **get lost** sich verlaufen, sich verirren 9: 1 (13)

lot [lɒt] **a lot (of); lots (of)** viel(e) 5 **lots and lots of ...** unheimlich viel/e ... 7

loud [laʊd] laut 6

love [lʌv]:

1. lieben, sehr mögen 5 **I'd love to come. (= I would love to come.)** Ich komme sehr gern. / Ich würde sehr gern kommen. 5

2. Liebe 5 **be in love (with sb.)** verliebt sein (in jn.) 9: 1 (22) **fall in love (with sb.)** sich verlieben (in jn.) 9: 1 (22)

3. Liebling, Schatz 5

low [ləʊ] niedrig, tief 7

luck [lʌk] Glück *(glückliche Fügung)* 8 **Good luck.** Viel Glück! 8

luckily [ˈlʌkɪli] glücklicherweise 8

lucky [ˈlʌki] Glücks-, glücklich 8 **Lucky you!** Du Glückliche/r! 6 **you're lucky** du hast Glück 5

luge [luːʒ] Rennrodeln 9: 2 (37)

luge track [ˈluːʒ træk] Rennrodelbahn 9: 2 (37)

lunch [lʌntʃ] Mittagessen 5 **have lunch** (zu) Mittag essen 5

lunchtime [ˈlʌntʃtaɪm]: **at lunchtime** mittags, zur Mittagszeit 6

lyrics *(pl)* [ˈlɪrɪks] Liedtext 8

M

machine [məˈʃiːn] Maschine, Gerät, Automat 8

madam [ˈmædəm]: **Dear Sir/Madam** Sehr geehrte Damen und Herren 8

made [meɪd] *siehe* **make** **be made of** aus *(etwas)* (gemacht) sein, bestehen aus 8

magazine [mægəˈziːn] Zeitschrift, Magazin 6

main [meɪn] Haupt-, wichtigste(r, s) 9: 2 (32)

main road [meɪn 'rəʊd] Hauptstraße 9: 2 (32)

majority [mə'dʒɒrəti] Mehrheit, Mehrzahl 9: 3 (48)

make [meɪk]:
1. Marke; Fabrikat 9: 3 (56)
2. make, made, made machen, herstellen 5
make a deal ein Geschäft abschließen/vereinbaren 6
make friends Freunde finden 6
make money Geld verdienen 7
make sb. do sth. jn. dazu bringen, etwas zu tun 7
make sb./sth. sth. jn./etwas zu etwas machen 9: 4 (60)
make sb.'s day jm. den Tag verschönern, jm. eine Riesenfreude machen 9: 2 (31)
What makes a perfect weekend? Was macht ein perfektes Wochenende aus? 6
°make notes (sich) Notizen machen *(zur Vorbereitung)*

make-up ['meɪkʌp] Make-up 6

man [mæn], *pl* **men** Mann 5

man-made [mæn 'meɪd] künstlich, Kunst-; von Menschen verursacht/ hergestellt 9: 4 (60)

manager ['mænɪdʒə] Geschäftsführer/in, Manager/in 7

many ['meni] viele 5 **how many?** wie viele? 5

map [mæp] Landkarte, Stadtplan 5

March [mɑːtʃ] März 5

march [mɑːtʃ]:
1. Marsch 7
2. marschieren 7

market ['mɑːkɪt] Markt 5

marketing ['mɑːkɪtɪŋ] Marketing, Vermarktung 9: 3 (46)

married ['mærɪd] verheiratet 8

marry ['mæri] heiraten 8

mask [mɑːsk] Maske 6

mat [mæt] Matte 9: 3 (49)

match [mætʃ] Spiel *(z.B. Fußball)* 8

°match (with) ['mætʃ wɪð] zuordnen; (passend) zusammenfügen

maths [mæθs] Mathematik 5

matter ['mætə] von Bedeutung sein, wichtig sein 8 **It doesn't matter.** Es/Das ist egal. 8

°maximum (= max) ['mæksɪməm] Höchst-, maximal; Maximum

May [meɪ] Mai 5

May I …? [meɪ] Darf ich …? 8

maybe ['meɪbi] vielleicht 6

me [mi] mir; mich 5 **Me too.** Ich auch 5 **It's me.** Ich bin's. 5

meal [miːl] Mahlzeit, Essen 7 **hot meal** warme Mahlzeit 7

mean [miːn]:
1. gemein, fies 5
2. geizig 6

mean [miːn], **meant, meant** meinen, sagen wollen 7

°meaning ['miːnɪŋ] Bedeutung

meant [ment] *siehe* **mean**

meat [miːt] Fleisch 6

mechanic [mɪ'kænɪk] Mechaniker/in 8

medal ['medl] Medaille 8

media *(pl)* ['miːdiə] Medien 8

°mediate ['miːdieɪt] vermitteln, *(sprachlich)* inhaltlich wiedergeben

°mediation [miːdi'eɪʃn] Vermittlung, Sprachmittlung

meet [miːt], **met, met** kennenlernen; (sich) treffen 5 **meet (protests)** treffen auf, stoßen auf (Proteste) 9: 3 (49) **meet sb.** jn. abholen 6 **Nice to meet you.** Schön, dich/euch/Sie kennenzulernen. 6

meeting ['miːtɪŋ] Treffen; Zusammenkunft 7

mega ['megə] *(infml)* Riesen-, Mega- 9: 4 (58)

megawatt ['megəwɒt] Megawatt 9: 4 (58)

melody ['melədi] Melodie 8

melt [melt] (ab)schmelzen; schmelzen lassen 9: 4 (65)

member ['membə] Mitglied 8

men [men] *Plural von* **man**

mental ['mentl] geistig, psychisch, seelisch 9: 2 (30)

mental health [mentl 'helθ] psychische/seelische Gesundheit 9: 2 (30)

message ['mesɪdʒ]:
1. Nachricht, Mitteilung 5 **message in a bottle** Flaschenpost 5 **take a message** etwas ausrichten 7
2. Nachrichten schicken/austauschen 6

messy ['mesi] unordentlich 5

met [met] *siehe* **meet**

metal ['metl] Metall, Metall- 8

metre ['miːtə] Meter 6

mice [maɪs] *Plural von* **mouse**

middle ['mɪdl] Mitte 5

might [maɪt]: **It might not work.** Es könnte nicht funktionieren. / Vielleicht funktioniert es nicht. 9: 1 (13)

mile [maɪl] Meile *(ca. 1,6 km)* 6

milk [mɪlk]:
1. Milch 5
2. melken 9: 2 (29)

milkshake ['mɪlkʃeɪk] Milchshake 6

million ['mɪljən] Million 7 **like a million dollars** fantastisch 7

mind [maɪnd]: **I don't mind.** Es macht mir nichts aus. / Es ist mir egal. 8

mine [maɪn] meine/r; meins 7 **°a friend of mine** ein/e Freund/in von mir

mine [maɪn] Bergwerk, Mine 9: 3 (54)

mineral water ['mɪnərəl wɔːtə] Mineralwasser 6

minibar ['mɪnibɑː] Minibar 8

minimum ['mɪnɪməm] Minimum 8

minimum wage [mɪnɪməm 'weɪdʒ] Mindestlohn 9: 2 (33)

minority [maɪ'nɒrəti] Minderheit 9: 3 (48)

minute ['mɪnɪt] Minute 5

mirror ['mɪrə] Spiegel 9: 1 (16)

miss [mɪs] vermissen 5

missing ['mɪsɪŋ] vermisst 6 **be missing** fehlen 7 **the missing bags** die fehlenden Taschen 7

mission ['mɪʃn] Mission; Auftrag 9: 4 (66)

°mistake [mɪ'steɪk] Fehler

misunderstand [mɪsʌndə'stænd], **misunderstood, misunderstood** missverstehen 9: 4 (63)

misunderstanding [mɪsʌndə'stændɪŋ] Missverständnis 9: 4 (63)

misunderstood [mɪsʌndə'stʊd] *siehe* **misunderstand**

mix [mɪks]:
1. (ver)mischen 9: 2 (32)
2. Mix, Mischung 9: 2 (32)

mobile (phone) ['məʊbaɪl] Handy 5

modern ['mɒdn] modern 8

module ['mɒdjuːl] Modul; (Raum-) Kapsel 9: 4 (66)

mom [mɒm] *(AE)* Mutti, Mama 7

moment ['məʊmənt] Moment 9: 2 (31) **at the moment** im Moment 9: 2 (31) **Just a moment.** Einen Moment. / Moment mal. 9: 2 (31)

Monday ['mʌndeɪ], ['mʌndi] Montag 5

money ['mʌni] Geld 5 **make money** Geld verdienen 7

monitor ['mɒnɪtə] Monitor 7

monkey ['mʌŋki] Affe 5

monster ['mɒnstə] Monster 7

month [mʌnθ] Monat 5

mood [muːd] Stimmung, Laune 8

moon [muːn] Mond 9: 4 (62)

moped ['məʊped] Moped, Mofa 9: 4 (64)

more [mɔː] mehr, weitere 6 **more popular** beliebter, populärer 6 **not (…) any more** nicht mehr 8 **one more thing** noch ein/e Sache 6 **What's more, …** Darüber hinaus …, Außerdem … 9: 1 (15)

morning ['mɔːnɪŋ] Morgen 5 **Good morning.** Guten Morgen. 5 **in the morning(s)** morgens, am Morgen 5 **on Friday morning(s)** freitagmorgens, am Freitagmorgen 5

mosque [mɒsk] Moschee 8

most [məʊst]: **most famous** der/die/ das berühmteste, am berühmtesten 7 **most people** die meisten Leute 7

motel [məʊ'tel] Motel *(Hotel mit Zimmern und Garagen an einer Autostraße)* 9: 1 (16)

mother ['mʌðə] Mutter 5

motorbike ['məʊtəbaɪk] Motorrad 9: 4 (64)

mountain ['maʊntən] Berg 6

mouse [maʊs], *pl* **mice** Maus 6

mouth [maʊθ] Mund; *(Tier)* Schnauze 9: 1 (13)

move (to) [muːv] (um)ziehen (nach/in) 7

Mr Lee ['mɪstə] Herr Lee 5

Mrs Lee ['mɪsɪz] Frau Lee 5

Ms Lee [mɪz] Frau Lee 5

much [mʌtʃ] viel 5 **How much is / How much are …?** Was (Wie viel) kostet … / Was (Wie viel) kosten …?

5 **miss/like/love sb. so much** jn. so sehr vermissen/mögen/lieben 6
Thanks very much. Vielen Dank. 6
mud [mʌd] Matsch, Schlamm 6
multicultural [mʌltiˈkʌltʃərəl] multikulturell 8
mum [mʌm] Mama, Mutti 5
Munich [ˈmjuːnɪk] München 6
mural [ˈmjʊərəl] Wandgemälde 7
°**muscle car** [ˈmʌsl kɑː] Muscle-Car *(Serienmodell, nachgerüstet mit besonders starkem Motor)*
museum [mjuˈziːəm] Museum 7
music [ˈmjuːzɪk]:
1. Musik 5
2. Noten *(geschriebene Musik)* 8
be able to read music Noten lesen können 8
musical [ˈmjuːzɪkl] Musik-, musikalisch 9: 1 (14)
musician [mjuˈzɪʃn] Musiker/in 7
Muslim [ˈmʊzlɪm]:
1. Muslim/Muslima 8
2. muslimisch 8
must [mʌst]:
1. müssen 5
2. **a must** ein Muss 9: 3 (45)
a must-do *(infml)* ein Muss; etwas, was man unbedingt tun muss 9: 3 (45) **a must-have** etwas, was man unbedingt haben muss 9: 3 (45)
a must-see place ein Ort, den man gesehen haben muss 9: 3 (45)
mustn't do [ˈmʌsnt] nicht tun dürfen 6
my [maɪ] mein/e 5
myself [maɪˈself] ich/mich/mir selbst 7

N

°**Namaste.** [ˈnʌməsteɪ] *unter Hindus verbreitete Grußformel und Grußgeste*
name [neɪm] Name 5 **What's your name?** Wie heißt du? 5
narrow [ˈnærəʊ] eng, schmal 7
nation [ˈneɪʃn] Nation 9: 4 (67)
national [ˈnæʃnəl] national 6
national day [ˈnæʃnəl ˈdeɪ] Nationalfeiertag 7
national park [ˈnæʃnəl ˈpɑːk] Nationalpark *(staatliches Naturschutzgebiet)* 6
nationality [ˈnæʃəˈnæləti] Staatsangehörigkeit, Nationalität 7
natural [ˈnætʃrəl] natürlich, Natur- 9: 1 (14)
nature [ˈneɪtʃə] *(die)* Natur 9: 1 (14)
near [nɪə] in der Nähe von, nahe (bei) 6
nearly [ˈnɪəli] fast, beinahe 8
need [niːd] brauchen 5
negative [ˈnegətɪv] negativ 8 **negative about …** negativ in Bezug auf … 8
neighbour [ˈneɪbə] Nachbar/in 6
neighbourhood [ˈneɪbəhʊd] Nachbarschaft, Viertel, Gegend 6
nervous [ˈnɜːvəs] nervös, aufgeregt 5
never [ˈnevə] nie, niemals 5
new [njuː] neu 5

news [njuːz] Nachrichten; Neuigkeiten 5
newsletter [ˈnjuːzletə] Mitteilungsblatt, Informationsblatt 6
newspaper [ˈnjuːzpeɪpə] (Tages-)Zeitung 6
next [nekst]:
1. nächste(r, s) 5
the next day am nächsten Tag 6
2. als Nächstes 7
next to [ˈnekst tə] neben 5
nice [naɪs] nett, schön 5 **Nice to be together again.** Schön, wieder zusammen zu sein. 6 **Nice to meet you.** Schön, dich/euch/Sie kennenzulernen. 6
night [naɪt] Nacht 5 **at night** nachts, in der Nacht 5 **Good night.** Gute Nacht. 5
night-time [ˈnaɪt taɪm] nächtlich, Nacht- 8
nine [naɪn] neun 5
nineties [ˈnaɪntiz] **the 90s** die Neunzigerjahre 6
no [nəʊ]:
1. nein 5
2. kein/e 5
nobody [ˈnəʊbədi] niemand 6
noise [nɔɪz] Geräusch; Lärm 5
noisy [ˈnɔɪzi] laut, voller Lärm 5
non- [nɒn] Nicht-, nicht- 8
normal [ˈnɔːml] normal 6
north [nɔːθ] Norden; nördlich; Nord- 6
north-east [nɔːθˈiːst] Nordosten, nordöstlich 6
°**North Pacific Gyre** [nɔːθ pəsɪfɪk ˈdʒaɪə] Nordpazifischer Kreisel
north-west [nɔːθˈwest] Nordwesten, nordwestlich 6
northern [ˈnɔːðən] nördliche(r, s), Nord- 7
nose [nəʊz] Nase 8
not [nɒt] nicht; kein/e 5 **not … at all** überhaupt nicht … 5
°**note** [nəʊt]:
1. notieren; beachten
2. Notiz **make notes** (sich) Notizen machen *(zur Vorbereitung)*
take notes (sich) Notizen machen *(beim Lesen oder Zuhören)*
note [nəʊt] *(kurz für:* banknote*)* Geldschein, Banknote 9: 1 (13)
nothing [ˈnʌθɪŋ] nichts 6
notice [ˈnəʊtɪs] (be)merken 9: 2 (33)
November [nəʊˈvembə] November 5
now [naʊ]:
1. nun, jetzt 5
2. **Now, …** Also, … 9: 1 (13)
nowhere [ˈnəʊweə] nirgendwo(hin) 8
number [ˈnʌmbə] Zahl, Ziffer, Nummer; Anzahl 5 **car number** Autokennzeichen 7
number plate [ˈnʌmbə pleɪt] Nummernschild, Autokennzeichen 9: 1 (25)
nursing home [ˈnɜːsɪŋ həʊm] Pflegeheim 9: 2 (39)
nut [nʌt] Nuss 6

O

°**oath** [əʊθ] Eid **take an oath** einen Eid ablegen
°**oath of office** [əʊθ əv ˈɒfɪs] Amtseid
°**observe** [əbˈzɜːv] beachten, einhalten, beobachten
occasionally [əˈkeɪʒənəli] gelegentlich 7
ocean [ˈəʊʃn] Ozean 8
o'clock [əˈklɒk]: **at one o'clock** um 1 Uhr / um 13 Uhr 5
October [ɒkˈtəʊbə] Oktober 5
of [ɒv], [əv] von 5 **as of …** ab …, von … an 8 **die of** sterben an 9: 4 (60)
the last day of the holidays der letzte Tag der Ferien 5
of course [əv ˈkɔːs] natürlich, selbstverständlich 6
off [ɒf]:
1. von … herunter/hinunter 5
fall off sth. herunterfallen von etwas *(Fahrrad, Pferd)* 5
get off a bus aussteigen aus einem Bus 5
2. abseits von, entfernt von 9: 3 (48)
off the coast vor der Küste *(im Meer)* 9: 3 (48)
3. **be off** aus sein *(ausgeschaltet)* 9: 3 (49)
office [ˈɒfɪs] Büro 7
officer [ˈɒfɪsə] Beamter/Beamtin 8
police officer Polizeibeamter/-beamtin 7 **security officer** Sicherheitsbeauftragte/r 8
official [əˈfɪʃl]:
1. offiziell, amtlich 8
2. Beamter/Beamtin 8
official language [əfɪʃl ˈlæŋgwɪdʒ] Amtssprache 8
often [ˈɒfn], [ˈɒftən] oft 5
oh [əʊ] Null *(im gesprochenen Englisch)* 5
oil [ɔɪl] Öl 8
OK [əʊˈkeɪ]: **I'm OK.** Es geht mir gut. 5
old [əʊld] alt 5 **How old are you?** Wie alt bist du? 5
Olympic [əˈlɪmpɪk] olympisch 8 **the Olympic Games** *(pl)* die olympischen Spiele 8
omelette [ˈɒmlət] Omelett 8
on [ɒn]:
1. auf 5
on Friday morning(s) freitagmorgens, am Freitagmorgen 5
on his birthday an seinem Geburtstag 5
on Monday am Montag 5
on Mondays (immer) am Montag, montags 5
on page 18 auf Seite 18 5
on the bus im Bus 5
get on a bus einsteigen in einen Bus 5
work on sth. an etwas arbeiten 8
2. an *(eingeschaltet)* 9: 3 (49)
3. **be on** stattfinden, gezeigt werden *(Kino, Theater)* 7
once [wʌns] einmal; einst 6 **for once** ausnahmsweise, dieses eine Mal 8

one [wʌn] eins 5 **the most famous one** der/die/das Berühmteste 7

onion ['ʌnjən] Zwiebel 8

online [ɒn'laɪn] online, Online- 6

only ['əʊnli]:
1. nur, bloß; erst 5
2. **the only student** der einzige Schüler / die einzige Schülerin 5

onto the track ['ɒntu], ['ɒntə] auf das (Bahn-)Gleis 9: 4 (72)

open ['əʊpən]:
1. offen, geöffnet 5
2. öffnen, aufmachen 6
3. sich öffnen, aufgehen 7

opening hours (pl) ['əʊpənɪŋ aʊəz] Öffnungszeiten 9: 2 (39)

opening times (pl) ['əʊpənɪŋ taɪmz] Öffnungszeiten 8

opinion [ə'pɪnjən] Meinung 8 **in my opinion** meiner Meinung nach 8

opposite ['ɒpəzɪt] Gegenteil 7

°**option** ['ɒpʃn] Wahl(möglichkeit), Option

or [ɔː] oder 5

orange ['ɒrɪndʒ]:
1. orange(farben) 5
2. Orange 5

°**orbiter** [ɔːbɪtə] Orbiter (in eine Umlaufbahn gebrachter Raumflugkörper)

order ['ɔːdə]:
1. bestellen 9: 1 (17)
2. Bestellung 9: 1 (17)
take an order eine Bestellung annehmen, entgegennehmen 9: 1 (17)

organic [ɔː'gænɪk] biologisch (angebaut), Bio- 9: 2 (29)

organization [ɔːgənaɪ'zeɪʃn] Organisation 8

organize ['ɔːgənaɪz] organisieren 8

origin ['ɒrɪdʒɪn] Ursprung, Herkunft 8

original [ə'rɪdʒənl]:
1. Original 7
2. originell 7

other ['ʌðə] andere(r, s) 5

our ['aʊə], [ɑː] unser/e 5

ours [ɑːz], ['aʊəz] unsere/r, unseres 7

ourselves [aʊə'selvz] wir/uns selbst 7

out [aʊt] hinaus, heraus, raus 6 **be out** unterwegs sein 5 **go out** ausgehen; hinausgehen 6

out of ... ['aʊt əv] aus ... (heraus/hinaus) 6

out of this world [aʊt əv ðɪs 'wɜːld] (infml) fabelhaft 8

outback ['aʊtbæk] Hinterland Australiens 9: 1 (11)

outdoor ['aʊtdɔː] Outdoor-, Natursport- 8

outdoor activity ['aʊtdɔː] Aktivität für draußen / die draußen stattfindet 8

outside [aʊt'saɪd]:
1. draußen; nach draußen 5
2. außerhalb (von), vor 5

over ['əʊvə]:
1. vorbei 5
2. **over 18** über 18 7

over here [əʊvə 'hɪə] hier drüben; hier herüber 6

over there [əʊvə 'ðeə] da drüben; da hinüber 5

own [əʊn]: **its own team** seine eigene Mannschaft 7

owner ['əʊnə] Besitzer/in 9: 1 (18)

P

p [piː]: **50p** 50 Pence 5

pack [pæk] packen, einpacken 6

page (= p.) [peɪdʒ] (Buch-, Heft-) Seite 5

paid [peɪd] siehe **pay**

°**pain** [peɪn] Schmerz

painkiller ['peɪnkɪlə] Schmerzmittel 9: 1 (23)

paint [peɪnt] malen 8

painting ['peɪntɪŋ] Gemälde, (gemaltes) Bild 9: 1 (14)

pair [peə] Paar 6

palace ['pæləs] Palast 7

palm (tree) [pɑːm] Palme 8

panda ['pændə] Panda 7

panic ['pænɪk] Panik bekommen 6 **Don't panic.** Keine Panik. / Immer mit der Ruhe. 6

paper ['peɪpə]:
1. Zeitung 6
do a paper round Zeitungen austragen 6
°**2.** Papier
°**piece of paper** Stück Papier, Zettel

parade [pə'reɪd] Parade, Umzug 7

paragliding ['pærəglaɪdɪŋ] Gleitschirmfliegen 9: 3 (44)

°**paragraph** ['pærəgrɑːf] (Text-) Abschnitt

°**parallel** ['pærəlel] parallel, Parallel-

parents (pl) ['peərənts] Eltern 5

park [pɑːk] Park 5

park (a car) [pɑːk] parken 6

parliament ['pɑːləmənt] Parlament 7

part [pɑːt] Teil 6 **take part (in)** teilnehmen (an), mitmachen (bei) 7

part-time [pɑːt 'taɪm] Teilzeit- 8

part-time job [pɑːt 'taɪm] Teilzeitjob, Halbtagsjob 8

partner ['pɑːtnə] Partner/in 5

partner work ['pɑːtnə wɜːk] Partnerarbeit 5

party ['pɑːti] Party 5 **have a party** eine Party feiern 5

pass [pɑːs]:
1. vorbeifahren (an), vorbeigehen (an) 8
2. **pass a law** ein Gesetz verabschieden 9: 3 (49)

pass [pɑːs] Ausweis, Karte (Dokument) 8 **boarding pass** Bordkarte 8 **day pass** Tageskarte 8

passenger ['pæsɪndʒə] Passagier/in, Fahrgast 8

passenger seat ['pæsɪndʒə siːt] Beifahrersitz 9: 1 (25)

passport ['pɑːspɔːt] (Reise-)Pass 8

past the shop [pɑːst] am Geschäft vorbei 6

pasta ['pæstə] Pasta; Nudeln 8

pasty ['pæsti] Pastete (mit Fleisch- oder Gemüsefüllung) 6

°**patient** ['peɪʃnt] Patient/in

°**pause** [pɔːz] Pause

pay [peɪ]:
1. Bezahlung, Lohn 9: 2 (39)
2. **pay, paid, paid** (be)zahlen 8

PE (= physical education) [piː 'iː] (Schul-)Sport 5

peace [piːs] Frieden 8

peaceful ['piːsfl] friedlich, friedfertig 9: 3 (48)

pen [pen] Kugelschreiber, Stift; Füller 5

pence [pens] Plural von **penny**

pencil ['pensl] Bleistift 5

pencil case ['pensl keɪs] Federmäppchen 5

pencil sharpener ['pensl ʃɑːpnə] Bleistiftanspitzer 5

penfriend ['penfrend] Brieffreund/in 6

penguin ['peŋgwɪn] Pinguin 9: 2 (37)

penny ['peni], pl **pence** Penny (kleinste britische Münze) 6

people (pl) ['piːpl] Leute, Menschen 5

people of colour (pl) [piːpl əv 'kʌlə] nicht-weiße Menschen 5

pepper ['pepə] Pfeffer 6

per (person) [pɜː] pro (Person) 7

°**perception** [pə'sepʃn] Wahrnehmung

perfect ['pɜːfɪkt] perfekt 6

performance [pə'fɔːməns] Vorstellung, Aufführung 7

perhaps [pə'hæps] vielleicht 6

°**period** ['pɪəriəd] Zeit(raum)

person ['pɜːsn] Person 7

personal ['pɜːsənl] persönlich 8

personal statement [pɜːsənl 'steɪtmənt] persönliche Beschreibung, Selbstbeschreibung 8

pet [pet] Haustier 5

pet shop ['pet ʃɒp] Zoogeschäft, Tierhandlung 5

°**phase** [feɪz] Phase

phone [fəʊn]:
1. anrufen 5
2. Telefon 5

phone call ['fəʊn kɔːl] (Telefon-) Anruf 6

phone number ['fəʊn nʌmbə] Telefonnummer 5

photo ['fəʊtəʊ] Foto 5 **in the photo** auf dem Foto 5 **take a photo** ein Foto machen 6

phrase [freɪz] Ausdruck, (Rede-)Wendung 5

physical education (= PE) [fɪzɪkl edʒu'keɪʃn] (Schul-)Sport 5

piano [pi'ænəʊ] Klavier 5

pick [pɪk] (aus)wählen, aussuchen 5 **pick sth. off sth.** etwas von etwas wegnehmen, herunternehmen; abzupfen 9: 2 (32) **pick up** aufheben (vom Boden) 9: 2 (32)

picnic ['pɪknɪk] Picknick 5 **have a picnic** ein Picknick machen 5

picture ['pɪktʃə] Bild 5

°**picture-based interview** [pɪktʃə beɪst 'ɪntəvjuː] Interview anhand von / auf der Basis von Bildern

pie [paɪ] Obsttörtchen; Pastete 8

piece (of ...) [piːs] Stück 8 **°piece of paper** Stück Papier, Zettel

pig [pɪg] Schwein 5

pineapple ['paɪnæpl] Ananas 8

pink [pɪŋk] rosa 5

pirate ['paɪrət] Pirat/in 8

pitta (bread) ['piːtə] Pitta(brot) 8

pity ['pɪti]: **That's a pity.** Das ist schade. 5

pizza ['piːtsə] Pizza 7

place [pleɪs] Ort, Platz, Stelle 5 **take place** stattfinden 8

place of birth [pleɪs əv 'bɜːθ] Geburtsort 7

°placemat ['pleɪsmæt] Platzdeckchen

plan [plæn]:
1. Plan 5
2. planen 5

plane [pleɪn] Flugzeug 7

planet ['plænɪt] Planet 9: 4 (70)

plant [plɑːnt]:
1. Pflanze 8
2. pflanzen 8

plastic ['plæstɪk] Plastik, Kunststoff 6

plastic bag [plæstɪk 'bæg] Plastiktüte 6

plate [pleɪt] (Metall-)Schild; Teller 9: 1 (25)

platform ['plætfɔːm] Bahnsteig 6

play [pleɪ]:
1. spielen 5
playing football Fußballspielen 5
2. Theaterstück 6

player ['pleɪə] Spieler/in 6

please [pliːz] bitte 5

pm [piː 'em]: **6 pm** 6 Uhr abends, 18 Uhr 5

pocket ['pɒkɪt] Tasche *(an Kleidungsstücken)* 6

pocket money ['pɒkɪt mʌni] Taschengeld 6

poem ['pəʊɪm] Gedicht 6

point (at/to) [pɔɪnt] zeigen, deuten (auf) 7

police *(pl)* [pə'liːs] Polizei 7

police officer [pə'liːs ɒfɪsə] Polizeibeamter/-beamtin 7

police station [pə'liːs steɪʃn] Polizeiwache 9: 3 (56)

polite [pə'laɪt] höflich 8

political [pə'lɪtɪkl] politisch 8

politics ['pɒlətɪks] Politik 9: 3 (49)

pollute [pə'luːt] *(die Umwelt)* verschmutzen 9: 4 (64)

pollution [pə'luːʃn] (Umwelt-)Verschmutzung 9: 4 (64)

pony ['pəʊni] Pony 5

ponytail ['pəʊniteɪl] Pferdeschwanz 8

pool [puːl] Pfütze, Lache 9: 2 (38)

poor [pʊə] arm **poor Mrs Trent** (die) arme Mrs Trent 6 **Poor you!** Du Arme/r! 6

°pop [pɒp] *(infml)* Papa, Vati

popular ['pɒpjələ] beliebt, populär 6

population [pɒpju'leɪʃn] Bevölkerung, Einwohner(zahl) 8

pork [pɔːk] Schweinefleisch 8

positive ['pɒzətɪv] positiv 8 **positive about ...** positiv in Bezug auf ... 8

possible ['pɒsəbl] möglich 8

post [pəʊst]:
1. Post *(Teil eines Blogs)* 5
2. posten *(im Internet veröffentlichen)* 8

post office ['pəʊst ɒfɪs] Post(amt) 6

postcard ['pəʊstkɑːd] Postkarte 6

posted by ['pəʊstɪd baɪ] gepostet von *(im Internet veröffentlicht)* 5

poster ['pəʊstə] Poster 5

potato [pə'teɪtəʊ], *pl* **potatoes** Kartoffel 6

potato chips *(pl)* [pə'teɪtəʊ tʃɪps] *(AE)* Kartoffelchips 7

pound (£) [paʊnd] Pfund *(britische Währung)* 5

poverty ['pɒvəti] Armut 9: 4 (60)

°practical ['præktɪkl] praktisch 8

practice ['præktɪs] Übung(en); Training 8

practise ['præktɪs] üben 8

prefer sth. to sth. [prɪ'fɜː] etwas lieber mögen als etwas, etwas einer Sache vorziehen 6

preparation (for) [prepə'reɪʃn] Vorbereitung (auf) 9: 2 (40)

prepare (for) [prɪ'peə] vorbereiten; sich vorbereiten (auf) 9: 2 (40) **well-prepared** gut vorbereitet 9: 2 (40)

present ['preznt] Geschenk 5

president ['prezɪdənt] Präsident/in 7

press [pres] drücken 5

price [praɪs] (Kauf-)Preis 5 **half price** zum halben Preis 7

°pride [praɪd] Stolz

primary school ['praɪməri skuːl] Grundschule 8

°prime minister [praɪm 'mɪnɪstə] Premierminister/in 6

prince [prɪns] Prinz 5

principal ['prɪnsəpl] Schulleiter/in 5

prison ['prɪzn] Gefängnis 9: 1 (14) **put sb. in prison** jn. ins Gefängnis sperren/stecken 9: 1 (14)

prisoner ['prɪznə] Gefangene/r, Häftling 9: 3 (49)

prize [praɪz] Preis *(Gewinn)* 5

probably ['prɒbəbli] wahrscheinlich 9: 4 (62)

problem ['prɒbləm] Problem 5

produce [prə'djuːs] produzieren 8

product ['prɒdʌkt] Produkt 7

°production [prə'dʌkʃn] Produktion

profession [prə'feʃn] Beruf 9: 1 (24)

profit ['prɒfɪt] Gewinn, Profit 7

program ['prəʊgræm]:
1. (Computer-)Programm 8
2. programmieren 8

programme ['prəʊgræm] (Fernseh-)Sendung 5

programmer ['prəʊgræmə] Programmierer/in 8

progress ['prəʊgres] Fortschritt(e) 9: 4 (60) **make progress** Fortschritte erzielen/machen, vorankommen 9: 4 (60)

project ['prɒdʒekt] Projekt 9: 2 (40)

°protect (from/against) [prə'tekt] (be)schützen (vor)

protest [prə'test] protestieren 7

protest ['prəʊtest] Protest(demonstration) 7

proud (of) [praʊd] stolz (auf) 5

°provisional [prə'vɪʒənl] vorläufig

°provisional licence [prəvɪʒənl 'laɪsns] vorläufige Fahrerlaubnis

pub [pʌb] Kneipe 7

public holiday [pʌblɪk 'hɒlədeɪ] (gesetzlicher) Feiertag 7

public transport [pʌblɪk 'trænspɔːt] öffentlicher Personenverkehr 8

pull [pʊl] ziehen 9: 1 (17)

pullover ['pʊləʊvə] Pullover 5

punctual ['pʌŋktʃuəl] pünktlich 9: 2 (40)

push [pʊʃ]:
1. Stoß, Schubs 9: 4 (72)
2. stoßen, schubsen; drücken 9: 4 (72)

put [pʊt], **put, put** *(etwas wohin)* tun, legen, stellen 6 **put in** einsetzen 6 **put sth. on** etwas anziehen *(Kleidung)*; etwas aufsetzen *(Hut, Brille)* 6 **put sth. up** etwas anbringen, aufhängen 7 **He puts it with the other things.** Er legt sie zu den anderen Dingen. 6

puzzled ['pʌzld] verwirrt, verwundert 7

pyramid ['pɪrəmɪd] Pyramide 7

Q

°qualification [kwɒlɪfɪ'keɪʃn] Qualifikation; (Schul-)Abschluss

quality ['kwɒləti] Qualität 9: 1 (22) **be better quality** von besserer Qualität sein 9: 1 (22) **top quality** von bester Qualität 9: 1 (22)

quarter ['kwɔːtə] Viertel 7

queen [kwiːn] Königin 7

question (to sb.) ['kwestʃən] Frage (an jn.) 5 **ask a question** eine Frage stellen 5

questionnaire [kwestʃə'neə] Fragebogen 7

quick [kwɪk] schnell 5

quiet ['kwaɪət] ruhig, still, leise 7

quite [kwaɪt] ziemlich 8

quiz [kwɪz] Quiz 5

R

R & B (= rhythm and blues) [ɑːr ən 'biː] **Rhythm & Blues** *(Musikrichtung)* 9: 3 (44)

rabbit ['ræbɪt] Kaninchen 5

race [reɪs]:
1. (Wett-)Rennen 8
2. um die Wette laufen, Rennen fahren 8

racism ['reɪsɪzəm] Rassismus 9: 1 (14)

racist ['reɪsɪst]:
1. rassistisch 9: 1 (14)
2. Rassist/in 9: 1 (14)

radio station ['reɪdiəʊ steɪʃn] Radiosender 9: 1 (14)

raft [rɑːft] Floß 8

rafting ['rɑːftɪŋ] Rafting *(Schlauchbootfahren auf Flüssen)* 9: 2 (26)

rain [reɪn]:
1. Regen 6
2. regnen 6
rain jacket [ˈreɪn dʒækɪt] Regenjacke
6
rain trousers *(pl)* [ˈreɪn traʊzəz]
Regenhose 6
rainy [ˈreɪni] regnerisch 6
ran [ræn] *siehe* **run**
rang [ræŋ] *siehe* **ring**
ranger [ˈreɪndʒə] *Aufseher/in in einem
Nationalpark* 6
rap [ræp]:
1. Rap 5
2. rappen 5
rapper [ˈræpə] Rapper/in 5
rat [ræt] Ratte 5
react (to) [riˈækt] reagieren (auf)
9: 2 (40)
reaction (to) [riˈækʃn] Reaktion
(auf) 9: 2 (40)
read [red] *siehe* **read**
read [riːd], **read, read** lesen 5
reader [ˈriːdə] Leser/in 7
reading [ˈriːdɪŋ] *(das)* Lesen 5
ready [ˈredi] bereit, fertig 8
real [rɪəl] echt, wirklich 5
°**realistic** [riːəˈlɪstɪk] realistisch
reality [riˈæliti] Realität, Wirklichkeit 6
really nice [ˈrɪəli] wirklich nett 5
reason [ˈriːzn] Grund, Begründung 8
for this reason aus diesem Grund 8
rebuild [riːˈbɪld], **rebuilt, rebuilt**
wiederaufbauen 8
rebuilt [riːˈbɪlt] *siehe* **rebuild**
reception [rɪˈsepʃn] Empfang *(auch
beim Telefon)*; Rezeption 7 **in
reception** an der Rezeption 7
receptionist [rɪˈsepʃənɪst] Empfangs-
mitarbeiter/in 7
recipe [ˈresəpi] *(Koch-)*Rezept 8
record [ˈrekɔːd] Schallplatte 8
red [red] rot 5
°**reef** [riːf] Riff
reference [ˈrefrəns]:
1. Referenz, Empfehlung; jd., der
eine Referenz erteilt 8
2. *(Akten-)*Zeichen, Referenznummer
9: 3 (57)
refugee [refjuˈdʒiː] Flüchtling 8
reggae [ˈregeɪ] Reggae*(musik)* 9: 3 (44)
relax [rɪˈlæks] sich entspannen 7
reliable [rɪˈlaɪəbl] zuverlässig,
verlässlich 8
religion [rɪˈlɪdʒən] Religion 8
religious [rɪˈlɪdʒəs] religiös 8
rely on [rɪˈlaɪ ɒn] sich verlassen auf
9: 1 (13)
remember [rɪˈmembə]:
1. sich erinnern an 5
2. daran denken, nicht vergessen 5
remote control [rɪməʊt
kənˈtrəʊl] Fernbedienung 8
repair [rɪˈpeə]:
1. Reparatur 8
2. reparieren 8
repeat [rɪˈpiːt] wiederholen 7

reply [rɪˈplaɪ]:
1. Antwort 9: 3 (45)
2. antworten 9: 3 (45)
report [rɪˈpɔːt]:
1. Bericht 7
weather report Wetterbericht 7
2. report (from) berichten (von/
aus) 7
°**report back (to sb.)** (jm.)
Bericht erstatten
reporter [rɪˈpɔːtə] Reporter/in 7
°**represent** [reprɪˈzent] repräsentieren,
vertreten
respect [rɪˈspekt]:
1. Respekt 9: 1 (14)
2. respektieren, achten 9: 1 (14)
rest [rest]:
1. Ruhe; Pause, Rast 9: 1 (23)
2. sich ausruhen; Pause machen,
rasten 9: 1 (23)
restaurant [ˈrestrɒnt] Restaurant 5
result [rɪˈzʌlt] Ergebnis 9: 3 (49)
as a result folglich, demzufolge
9: 3 (49)
retell [riːˈtel], **retold, retold** nacher-
zählen, noch einmal erzählen 8
rethink [riːˈθɪŋk], **rethought, rethought** nochmals überdenken,
umdenken 8
rethought [riːˈθɔːt] *siehe* **rethink**
retold [riːˈtəʊld] *siehe* **retell**
return (ticket) [rɪˈtɜːn] Rückfahr-
karte 7
reuse [riːˈjuːz] wiederverwenden 8
review [rɪˈvjuː] Rezension, Kritik
9: 2 (36)
revolt [rɪˈvəʊlt] Aufstand, Revolte 8
reward [rɪˈwɔːd] Belohnung 6
rewrite [riːˈraɪt], **rewrote, rewritten**
neu schreiben, umschreiben 8
rewritten [riːˈrɪtn] *siehe* **rewrite**
rewrote [riːˈrəʊt] *siehe* **rewrite**
rhino [ˈraɪnəʊ] *(infml)*, *pl* **rhinos**
Nashorn 9: 3 (42)
rhinoceros [raɪˈnɒsərəs], *pl* **rhinoceros**
or **rhinoceroses** Rhinozeros,
Nashorn 9: 3 (42)
rhythm and blues (R & B) [rɪðəm ən
ˈbluːz] Rhythm & Blues *(Musikrichtung)* 9: 3 (44)
rich [rɪtʃ] reich 9: 3 (54)
°**rickshaw** [ˈrɪkʃɔː] Rikscha
ridden [ˈrɪdn] *siehe* **ride**
ride [raɪd] Ritt; Fahrt; Fahrgeschäft
(auf Volksfest, in Vergnügungspark) 8
ride [raɪd], **rode, ridden:**
1. reiten 5
ride a pony auf einem Pony / ein
Pony reiten 5
2. fahren 5
ride a bike Rad fahren 5
right [raɪt] rechts; nach rechts 5
on the right rechts, auf der rechten
Seite 5
right [raɪt] richtig 5 **that's right**
das stimmt, das ist richtig 5
rights *(pl)* [raɪts] Rechte 7 **civil
rights** Bürgerrechte 7
ring [rɪŋ], **rang, rung** läuten,
klingeln 6

ringtone [ˈrɪŋtəʊn] Klingelton
(Handy) 7
rise [raɪz], **rose, risen** sich erheben;
(an)steigen 9: 4 (64)
risen [ˈrɪzən] *siehe* **rise**
risk [rɪsk]:
1. riskieren, aufs Spiel setzen
9: 1 (12)
2. Risiko 9: 1 (12)
take a risk ein Risiko eingehen
9: 1 (12)
river [ˈrɪvə] Fluss 6
road [rəʊd] Straße *(Landstraße zwischen Orten / Straße in Orten)* 5
robot [ˈrəʊbɒt] Roboter; *Südafrika:*
*(Verkehrs-)*Ampel 9: 3 (53)
rock [rɒk] Fels(en) 9: 1 (21)
rock (music) [ˈrɒk mjuːzɪk]
Rock(musik) 6
rock and roll [rɒk ənd ˈrəʊl] Rock and
Roll *(Musikrichtung)* 7
rock formation [ˈrɒk fɔːmeɪʃn] Felsformation 9: 1 (22)
rocket [ˈrɒkɪt] Rakete 8
rode [rəʊd] *siehe* **ride**
°**role** [rəʊl] Rolle *(Theater, Rollenspiel)*
role model [ˈrəʊl mɒdl] Vorbild
9: 3 (50)
°**roll as one** [rəʊl əz ˈwʌn] gemeinsam
vorankommen
°**roo** [ruː] *(infml)* Känguru
roof [ruːf] Dach 7
room [ruːm] Raum, Zimmer 5
root [ruːt] Wurzel 8
rose [rəʊz] *siehe* **rise**
round [raʊnd]:
1. rund 9: 4 (60)
2. Runde 9: 4 (60)
3. round ... um (... herum); in ...
umher 9: 4 (60)
routine [ruːˈtiːn] Routine 8
royal [ˈrɔɪəl] königlich 9: 3 (52)
rubber [ˈrʌbə] Radiergummi 5
rubbish [ˈrʌbɪʃ]:
1. Müll, Abfall 5
2. Unsinn, dummes Zeug 7
rubbish bin [ˈrʌbɪʃ bɪn] Mülleimer 6
rucksack [ˈrʌksæk] Rucksack 6
rugby [ˈrʌgbi] Rugby *(Ballsportart)* 6
ruin [ˈruːɪn]:
1. Ruine 7
in ruins in Trümmern 8
2. ruinieren, verderben 8
rule [ruːl] Regel, Vorschrift 6
ruler [ˈruːlə] Lineal 5
run [rʌn], **ran, run** rennen 6 **run into
sb./sth.** in jn./etwas hineinfahren
9: 4 (71) **run sb./sth. over** jn./etwas
überfahren 9: 4 (72)
°**rung** [rʌŋ] *siehe* **ring**
runner [ˈrʌnə] Läufer/in 7
°**rupee** [ruːˈpiː] Rupie *(Währung in
Indien)*

S

sad [sæd] traurig 6
safari [səˈfɑːri] Safari 9: 3 (44)
safe [seɪf] sicher *(gefahrlos)*; in
Sicherheit 6
said [sed] *siehe* **say**

salad ['sæləd] Salat *(als Gericht oder Beilage)* 5

sale [seɪl] Verkauf; Schlussverkauf 5

sales assistant ['seɪlz əsɪstənt] Verkäufer/in 7

salt [sɔːlt] Salz 7

same [seɪm]: **the same (as)** dasselbe / das gleiche (wie); gleich 6

sandwich ['sænwɪtʃ] Sandwich 5

sang [sæŋ] *siehe* **sing**

sanitary ['sænətri] sanitär, hygienisch, Hygiene- 9: 3 (46)

sanitary product ['sænətri prɒdʌkt] Hygieneprodukt 9: 3 (46)

sat [sæt] *siehe* **sit**

satellite ['sætəlaɪt] Satellit 9: 4 (66)

Saturday ['sætədeɪ], ['sætədi] Samstag 5

sauna ['sɔːnə] Sauna 9: 3 (57) **have/take a sauna** in die Sauna gehen 9: 3 (57)

sausage ['sɒsɪdʒ] Wurst, Würstchen 5

save [seɪv] retten 7

saw [sɔː] *siehe* **see**

°Sawubona. [saʊˈbɒʊnə] Hallo! / Guten Tag! *(aus Zulu; wörtlich:* I/We see you.*)*

say [seɪ], **said, said** sagen 5 **Say hi to your parents.** Grüß/t deine/eure Eltern. 9: 1 (21) **say sorry** sich entschuldigen 8

°scan a text (for) [skæn] einen Text absuchen / überfliegen (nach) 6

scared [skeəd]: **be scared (of)** Angst haben (vor) 6

scary ['skeəri] unheimlich, gruselig 6

scene [siːn] Szene 5

school [skuːl] Schule 5

school hall [skuːl 'hɔːl] Aula 8

sci-fi ['saɪ faɪ] *siehe* **science fiction**

science ['saɪəns] Naturwissenschaft 5

science fiction [saɪəns 'fɪkʃn] *(infml auch* **sci-fi***)* Sciencefiction 8

scientific [saɪən'tɪfɪk] wissenschaftlich 9: 4 (60)

scientist ['saɪəntɪst] (Natur-)Wissenschaftler/in 9: 4 (60)

scone [skɒn] *Milchbrötchen, leicht süß, oft mit Rosinen* 5

score [skɔː]: **1.** Spiel-/Punktestand; Punkt *(Spiel/Sport)* 7 **2.** einen Punkt / ein Tor erzielen 7

scream [skriːm] schreien 5

screen [skriːn] Bildschirm; Leinwand *(Kino)* 9: 4 (66)

sea [siː] Meer 5

sea level ['siː levl] Meeresspiegel 9: 4 (64)

seaside ['siːsaɪd]: **at the seaside** am Meer 6

season ['siːzn] Jahreszeit; Saison 8

seat [siːt] (Sitz-)Platz 9: 1 (20) **Take a seat.** Nimm / Nehmen Sie Platz. 9: 1 (20)

second ['sekənd]: **1.** zweite(r, s) 5 **°2.** Sekunde

second-hand shop [sekənd 'hænd ʃɒp] Second-Hand-Laden 6

°secondary school ['sekəndri skuːl] weiterführende Schule

secret ['siːkrət]: **1.** Geheimnis 9: 3 (49) **2.** geheim 9: 3 (49)

°section ['sekʃn] Abschnitt

security [sɪ'kjʊərəti] Sicherheit 7

security guard [sɪ'kjʊərəti gɑːd] Sicherheitsbedienstete/r 9: 2 (39)

security officer [sɪ'kjʊərəti ɒfɪsə] Sicherheitsbeauftragte/r 8

see [siː], **saw, seen** sehen 5 **See you.** Bis dann. / Tschüs. 5 **You see, …** Weißt du, … / … nämlich … 8

seen [siːn] *siehe* **see**

self [self] Selbst 9: 1 (22)

self-defence [self dɪ'fens] Selbstverteidigung 9: 3 (51)

sell [sel], **sold, sold** verkaufen 7

send (to) [send], **sent, sent** schicken, senden (an) 5

sent [sent] *siehe* **send**

sentence ['sentəns] Satz 6

September [sep'tembə] September 5

series ['sɪəriːz], *pl* **series** Serie; (Sende-)Reihe, Staffel 5

serious ['sɪəriəs] ernst(haft) 9: 2 (34)

seriously ['sɪəriəsli] im Ernst 9: 2 (34) **take sb./sth. seriously** jn./etwas ernst nehmen 9: 2 (34)

serve [sɜːv] servieren *(Essen, Getränke)*; bedienen *(Kundschaft)* 8

service ['sɜːvɪs] Service; Dienst 8 **(train) service** (Zug-)Verbindung 8

seven ['sevn] sieben 5

sex [seks] Sex; Geschlecht 9: 3 (48)

sexism ['seksɪzəm] Sexismus 8

shade [ʃeɪd] Schatten *(vor der Sonne geschützt)* 9: 1 (12)

Shall we …? [ʃæl], [ʃəl] Sollen wir …? 7

shampoo [ʃæm'puː] Shampoo 9: 4 (62)

share [ʃeə] teilen; austauschen 6

shark [ʃɑːk] Hai 9: 3 (44)

sharpener ['ʃɑːpnə] Anspitzer 5

she [ʃiː] sie *(weibliche Person)* 5 **she's (= she is)** sie ist 5

shed [ʃed] Schuppen; Stall 9: 2 (35)

sheep [ʃiːp], *pl* **sheep** Schaf 5

shelter ['ʃeltə] Schutzraum, Unterstand; (Obdachlosen-)Unterkunft 8

shine [ʃaɪn], **shone, shone** scheinen *(Sonne)*; leuchten, strahlen, glänzen 9: 1 (19)

ship [ʃɪp] Schiff 5

shirt [ʃɜːt] Hemd 5

shock [ʃɒk]: **1.** Schock, Schreck 9: 4 (73) **2.** schockieren 9: 4 (73)

shocked [ʃɒkt] schockiert 9: 4 (73)

shocking ['ʃɒkɪŋ] schockierend 9: 4 (73)

shoe [ʃuː] Schuh 5

shone [ʃɒn] *siehe* **shine**

shoot [ʃuːt], **shot, shot**: **1.** (er)schießen 8 **shoot at sb.** auf jn. schießen 8 **2.** fotografieren; *(Film)* drehen 9: 2 (28)

shop [ʃɒp]: **1.** Geschäft, Laden 5 **be at the shops** Einkäufe erledigen 5 **2. shop for sth.** etwas kaufen (gehen) 5

shopping ['ʃɒpɪŋ]: **go shopping** einkaufen gehen 5

shopping centre ['ʃɒpɪŋ sentə] Einkaufszentrum 7

shopping list ['ʃɒpɪŋ lɪst] Einkaufsliste 6

short [ʃɔːt] kurz; klein *(Person)* 6

short-term [ʃɔːt 'tɜːm] kurzfristig, Kurzzeit- 9: 2 (39)

shorts *(pl)* [ʃɔːts] *(eine)* kurze Hose 9: 1 (12)

shot [ʃɒt]: **1.** *siehe* **shoot 2.** Aufnahme, Foto 9: 2 (28)

should [ʃʊd]: **you should** du solltest 6

shoulder ['ʃəʊldə] Schulter 5

shout [ʃaʊt] rufen 5 **shout at sb.** jn. anschreien 9: 2 (34)

show [ʃəʊ]: **1.** Show, Vorführung, Aufführung 5 **2. show, showed, shown** zeigen 6

shower ['ʃaʊə] Dusche; Schauer 7

shown [ʃəʊn] *siehe* **show**

Shut up! [ʃʌt 'ʌp] Halt den Mund! 5

°shy [ʃaɪ] scheu, schüchtern

sick [sɪk] krank 9: 1 (13) **I'm/I feel sick.** Mir ist schlecht/übel. 9: 1 (13)

side [saɪd] Seite 6

sight [saɪt] Sehenswürdigkeit 8

sightseeing ['saɪtsiːɪŋ] Besichtigungen *(von Sehenswürdigkeiten)* 8

sign [saɪn]: **1.** Schild; Zeichen 5 **2.** unterschreiben 8

signal ['sɪgnəl] Signal 7

signature ['sɪgnətʃə] Unterschrift 7

silly ['sɪli] albern, dumm, blöd 5

silver ['sɪlvə] Silber 8

since [sɪns] seit 8

since then [sɪns 'ðen] seitdem 9: 4 (70)

sincerely [sɪn'sɪəli] **Yours sincerely** Mit freundlichen Grüßen *(Briefschluss)* 7

sing [sɪŋ], **sang, sung** singen 5

singer ['sɪŋə] Sänger/in 5

single ['sɪŋgl]: **1.** einzeln, Einzel- 7 **2. single (ticket)** einfache Fahrkarte *(nur Hinfahrt)* 7

single room [sɪŋgl 'ruːm] Einzelzimmer 7

sir [sɜː]: **1.** *Anrede für einen Lehrer* 8 **2. Dear Sir/Madam** Sehr geehrte Damen und Herren 7

sister ['sɪstə] Schwester 5

sit [sɪt], **sat, sat** sitzen; sich (hin)setzen 5 **sit down** sich (hin)setzen 9: 2 (32)

°site [saɪt] Stelle, Platz, Stätte

°situation [sɪtʃu'eɪʃn] Situation

six [sɪks] sechs 5

size [saɪz] Größe 7 **What size do you take?** Welche Größe hast du? 7

skate park ['skeɪt pɑːk] Skatepark 7
skateboard ['skeɪtbɔːd]:
  1. Skateboard 6
  2. Skateboard fahren 6
skateboarding ['skeɪtbɔːdɪŋ] *(das)* Skateboardfahren 5
skating ['skeɪtɪŋ]: **go skating** (Inline-) Skaten gehen 6
skid [skɪd] schleudern; schlittern, (aus)rutschen 9: 4 (71)
skiing ['skiːɪŋ] *(das)* Skilaufen *(Sport)* 6
skill [skɪl] Fähigkeit, Fertigkeit 7
skim a text [skɪm] einen Text überfliegen *(um den Inhalt grob zu erfassen)* 7
skin [skɪn] Haut; Schale *(z.B. Banane)* 9: 1 (12)
skirt [skɜːt] Rock 6
skive [skaɪv] *(infml)* schwänzen *(Schule)* 6
sky [skaɪ] Himmel 7 **in the sky** am Himmel 7
skyscraper ['skaɪskreɪpə] Wolkenkratzer 8
slave [sleɪv] Sklave, Sklavin 8
sled [sled] *(AE)* Schlitten 8
sleep [sliːp]:
  1. Schlaf 7
  2. **sleep, slept, slept** schlafen 5
sleeping bag ['sliːpɪŋ bæg] Schlafsack 6
sleepover ['sliːpəʊvə] Übernachtungsparty 5
sleepy ['sliːpi] verschlafen, müde 7
slept [slept] *siehe* **sleep**
°slither ['slɪðə] gleiten, rutschen, schlittern
slow [sləʊ] langsam 6
small [smɔːl] klein 5
smart [smɑːt] schick, smart; schlau, clever 7
smartphone ['smɑːtfəʊn] Smartphone 9: 4 (58)
smell [smel]:
  1. Geruch; Gestank 8
  2. riechen; schlecht riechen 8
smile [smaɪl]:
  1. lächeln 6
  smile at sb. jn. anlächeln 6
  2. *(ein/das)* Lächeln 6
smoothie ['smuːði] Smoothie *(Getränk aus Fruchtpüree)* 7
smuggler ['smʌglə] Schmuggler/in 5
snack [snæk] Snack, kleine Mahlzeit 5
snake [sneɪk] Schlange 5
snorkelling ['snɔːkəlɪŋ] Schnorcheln 8
snow [snəʊ]:
  1. Schnee 8
  2. schneien 8
so [səʊ]:
  1. so 5
  so cute so niedlich 5
  2. also 5
  3. **so (that)** sodass 7
  4. **I think so.** Ich glaube/denke ja. 7
  I don't think so. Das glaube/denke ich nicht. 7

soap [səʊp] Seife; *(infml auch:)* Seifenoper 6
soccer ['sɒkə] Fußball 9: 3 (43)
social ['səʊʃl] sozial 8
social media *(pl)* ['səʊʃl 'miːdiə] soziale Medien 8 **on social media** in den sozialen Medien 8
sock [sɒk] Socke 7
sofa ['səʊfə] Sofa 5
solar ['səʊlə] Sonnen, Solar- 9: 4 (58)
solar energy [səʊlə 'enədʒi] Sonnenenergie, Solarenergie 9: 4 (58)
sold [səʊld] *siehe* **sell**
°solution [sə'luːʃn] Lösung *(eines Problems)*
some [sʌm], [səm] einige, ein paar; etwas 5
somebody ['sʌmbədi] jemand 6
someone ['sʌmwʌn] jemand 6
something ['sʌmθɪŋ] etwas 5
sometimes ['sʌmtaɪmz] manchmal 5
son [sʌn] Sohn 7
song [sɒŋ] Lied 5
soon [suːn] bald 5
sore [sɔː] schmerzhaft 6 **a sore throat** Halsschmerzen 6 **Her leg was sore.** Ihr Bein tat weh. 6
sorry ['sɒri]: **Sorry. / I'm sorry.** Tut mir leid. / Entschuldigung. 5 **be/feel sorry for sb.** Mitleid mit jm. haben 6 **say sorry** sich entschuldigen 8
sort [sɔːt] sortieren 9: 4 (69)
  sort sth. out sich um etwas kümmern 9: 4 (69)
sort (of) [sɔːt] Art, Sorte (von) 7 **What sort of ...?** Welche Art/Sorte (von) ...? 7
sound [saʊnd]:
  1. Geräusch; Klang; Laut 5
  2. klingen, sich anhören 5
  Sounds fun. Hört sich gut an. / Klingt, als ob es Spaß macht. 5
soup [suːp] Suppe 5
south [saʊθ] Süden; südlich; Süd- 6
south-east [saʊθ'iːst] Südosten, südöstlich 6
south-west [saʊθ'west] Südwesten, südwestlich 6
southern ['sʌðən] südliche(r, s), Süd- 7
space [speɪs]:
  1. Platz, Raum 6
  2. Weltraum 8
spacecraft ['speɪskrɑːft], *pl* **spacecraft** Raumfahrzeug, Raumschiff 9: 4 (62)
speak, spoke, spoken [spiːk]: **speak (to)** sprechen (mit) 5 **speaking to friends** mit Freunden/Freundinnen sprechen 5 **Who's speaking?** Wer spricht (da)? *(am Telefon)* 7
°speaker ['spiːkə] Sprecher/in
special ['speʃl] besondere(r, s) 5
special effects *(pl)* [speʃl ɪ'fekts] Special Effects *(in Filmen)* 9: 2 (38)
°speech bubble ['spiːtʃ bʌbl] Sprechblase
speed [spiːd] Geschwindigkeit 9: 1 (25) **at a speed of ...** mit einer Geschwindigkeit von ... 9: 1 (25)

speed limit ['spiːd lɪmɪt] Höchstgeschwindigkeit, Geschwindigkeitsbegrenzung 9: 1 (25)
spell [spel] buchstabieren 5
spend money/time (on) [spend], **spent, spent** Geld ausgeben (für); Zeit verbringen (mit) 8
spent [spent] *siehe* **spend**
spice [spaɪs] Gewürz 8
spicy ['spaɪsi] würzig; pikant 9: 4 (63)
spoke [spəʊk] *siehe* **speak**
spoken ['spəʊkən] *siehe* **speak**
spoon [spuːn] Löffel 5
sport [spɔːt] Sport; Sportart 5
  do sport Sport treiben 5
sports hall ['spɔːts hɔːl] Sporthalle 6
sports shop ['spɔːts ʃɒp] Sportgeschäft 5
sportsperson ['spɔːtspɜːsn], *pl* **sportspeople** Sportler/in 6
sporty ['spɔːti] sportlich 6
spot [spɒt] Tupfen *(Leopard)*; Pickel 6
spray-paint ['spreɪ peɪnt] mit Farbe/Lack besprühen 8
spring [sprɪŋ] Frühling 8
sprinter ['sprɪntə] Kurzstreckenläufer/in 8
square [skweə]:
  1. Platz *(in der Stadt)* 8
  2. **square kilometre(s) (= km²)** Quadratkilometer 8
stadium ['steɪdiəm] Stadion 6
°staff [stɑːf] Personal, Belegschaft
°stage [steɪdʒ] Stadium, Phase, Abschnitt, Etappe
stairs *(pl)* [steəz] Treppe; (Treppen-) Stufen 9: 4 (71)
stand [stænd], **stood, stood** stehen 6
  stand up aufstehen 6
star [stɑː]:
  1. Star 7
  2. Stern 7
start [stɑːt]:
  1. anfangen 5
  2. Anfang, Start 7
state [steɪt] (Bundes-)Staat 7
  head of state Staatsoberhaupt 8
statement ['steɪtmənt] Aussage(satz) 7
station ['steɪʃn] Bahnhof 6
statue ['stætʃuː] Statue 8
stay [steɪ] bleiben 5
steak [steɪk] Steak 6
steal [stiːl], **stole, stolen** stehlen, rauben 9: 1 (24)
steel drum [stiːl 'drʌm] Steeldrum *(Musikinstrument)* 8
step [step] Schritt; Stufe 9: 1 (15)
stepbrother ['stepbrʌðə] Stiefbruder 5
stepdad ['stepdæd] Stiefvater 5
stepfather ['stepfɑːðə] Stiefvater 5
stepmother ['stepmʌðə] Stiefmutter 5
stepmum ['stepmʌm] Stiefmutter 5
stepsister ['stepsɪstə] Stiefschwester 5
still [stɪl] (immer) noch; trotzdem 6

sting [stɪŋ]:
1. (Insekten-)Stich 9: 1 (12)
2. **sting, stung, stung** stechen *(Insekt)*; brennen 9: 1 (12)
stole [stəʊl] *siehe* **steal**
stolen [ˈstəʊlən] *siehe* **steal**
stone [stəʊn] Stein 6
stood [stʊd] *siehe* **stand**
stoop [stuːp] *(AE)* kleine Terrasse vor der Tür 8
stop [stɒp]:
1. anhalten; stehen bleiben; aufhören (mit) 5
2. **(bus) stop** (Bus-)Haltestelle 6
store [stɔː] Geschäft 8
storm [stɔːm] Sturm; Gewitter 8
story [ˈstɔːri] Geschichte 5
straight [streɪt] direkt, gleich; gerade; *(Haare)* glatt 8 **Go straight on.** Geh geradeaus (weiter). 6
stranger [ˈstreɪndʒə] Fremde/r 9: 1 (16)
straw [strɔː] Strohhalm; Stroh 9: 4 (70)
streaming service [ˈstriːmɪŋ sɜːvɪs] Streamingdienst 9: 4 (65)
street [striːt] Straße *(in Ortschaften)* 5
street surfing [ˈstriːt sɜːfɪŋ] Waveboarden 6
strength [streŋθ] Stärke, Kraft 9: 2 (32)
stress [stres] Stress 9: 2 (40)
strict [strɪkt] streng, strikt 6
°**strong** [strɒŋ] stark
structure [ˈstrʌktʃə] Struktur 9: 2 (41)
°**stud** [stʌd] (Ohr-/Nasen-)Stecker
student [ˈstjuːdnt] Schüler/in; Student/in 5
studio [ˈstjuːdiəʊ] Studio 7
study [ˈstʌdi] studieren; lernen *(z.B. für Prüfungen)* 9: 3 (46)
stuff [stʌf] *(infml)* Zeug, Kram 6
stung [stʌŋ] *siehe* **sting**
stupid [ˈstjuːpɪd] dumm, blöd; albern 5
style [staɪl] Stil; Art 8
°**Subtropical Convergence Zone** [sʌbtrɒpɪkl kənˈvɜːdʒəns zəʊn] Subtropische Konvergenzzone
subway [ˈsʌbweɪ] *(AE)* U-Bahn 8
success [səkˈses] Erfolg 9: 4 (66)
successful [səkˈsesfl] erfolgreich 7
sudden [ˈsʌdn] plötzliche(r, s) 8
suddenly [ˈsʌdənli] plötzlich 7
suffer (from) [ˈsʌfə] leiden (an), erleiden 9: 3 (46)
sugar [ˈʃʊgə] Zucker 7
sugary [ˈʃʊgəri] süß(lich), zuckerhaltig 6
suitable (for) [ˈsuːtəbl] geeignet, passend (für) 8
summary [ˈsʌməri] Zusammenfassung 8
summer [ˈsʌmə] Sommer 5
sun [sʌn] Sonne 7
sunburn [ˈsʌnbɜːn] Sonnenbrand 9: 1 (12)
suncream [ˈsʌnkriːm] Sonnencreme 5
Sunday [ˈsʌndeɪ], [ˈsʌndi] Sonntag 5
°**sung** [sʌŋ] *siehe* **sing**
sunglasses *(pl)* [ˈsʌnglɑːsɪz] Sonnenbrille 5

sunny [ˈsʌni] sonnig 6
supermarket [ˈsuːpəmɑːkɪt] Supermarkt 6
superstar [ˈsuːpəstɑː] Superstar 8
support [səˈpɔːt]:
1. unterstützen 9: 3 (46)
2. Unterstützung 9: 3 (46)
suppose [səˈpəʊz] glauben, denken 8 **..., I suppose.** ..., glaube ich. /..., denke ich. 8
sure [ʃʊə] sicher 5
surfing [ˈsɜːfɪŋ] Surfing; *(das)* Surfen 9: 1 (21)
surprise [səˈpraɪz]:
1. Überraschung 5
2. überraschen 9: 2 (29)
surprised [səˈpraɪzd] überrascht 6
surprising [səˈpraɪzɪŋ] überraschend 9: 2 (29)
surprisingly [səˈpraɪzɪŋli] überraschenderweise 9: 2 (29)
survival [səˈvaɪvl] Überleben 8
°**swag** [swæg] *(AustE, infml)* Bettrolle *(Gepäckrolle, die man auf der Schulter trägt)*
swam [swæm] *siehe* **swim**
°**swap** [swɒp] tauschen
sweet [swiːt] süß 8
sweets *(pl)* [swiːts] Bonbons, Süßigkeiten 5
swerve [swɜːv] *(das Auto/Steuer)* herumreißen, *(mit dem Auto)* ausweichen 9: 1 (16)
swim [swɪm], **swam, swum** schwimmen 5
swimming [ˈswɪmɪŋ] *(das)* Schwimmen 5 **go swimming** schwimmen gehen 5
swimming pool [ˈswɪmɪŋ puːl] Schwimmbad 5
swimming trunks *(pl)* [ˈswɪmɪŋ trʌŋks] Badehose 5
swimsuit [ˈswɪmsuːt] Badeanzug 5
°**swum** [swʌm] *siehe* **swim**
symbol (of) [ˈsɪmbl] Symbol (für) 8
system [ˈsɪstəm] System 9: 3 (43)

T

T-shirt [ˈtiːʃɜːt] T-Shirt 5
table [ˈteɪbl]:
1. Tisch 5
°2. Tabelle
table tennis [ˈteɪbl tenɪs] Tischtennis 6
tae kwon do [taɪ kwɒn ˈdəʊ] Taekwondo 6
tail [teɪl] Schwanz 6
take [teɪk], **took, taken**:
1. bringen 6
2. nehmen, mitnehmen 5
take a message etwas ausrichten 7
take a photo ein Foto machen 6
take care vorsichtig sein, aufpassen 8 **take off** abheben, starten *(Flugzeug)* 8
take part (in) teilnehmen (an), mitmachen (bei) 7
take place stattfinden 8
°**take an oath** einen Eid ablegen

°**take notes** (sich) Notizen machen *(beim Lesen oder Zuhören)*
take-off [ˈteɪk ɒf] Start *(Flugzeug)* 8
taken [ˈteɪkən] *siehe* **take**
°**talent** [ˈtælənt] Talent
talk [tɔːk]:
1. **talk (to)** sprechen (mit) 5
2. Vortrag, Rede; Gespräch 6
give a talk einen Vortrag halten 6
talk show [ˈtɔːk ʃəʊ] Talkshow 6
talker [ˈtɔːkə] Redner/in 7
tall [tɔːl] groß *(Person)*; hoch *(Gebäude)* 5
taste [teɪst]:
1. schmecken; kosten, probieren 9: 4 (62)
2. Geschmack 9: 4 (62)
tasty [ˈteɪsti] schmackhaft, lecker 9: 4 (62)
tattoo [təˈtuː] Tattoo, Tätowierung 9: 2 (29)
taught [tɔːt] *siehe* **teach**
tax [tæks] *(die)* Steuer 9: 4 (61)
taxi [ˈtæksi] Taxi 7
tea [tiː] Tee 5
teach [tiːtʃ], **taught, taught** unterrichten, lehren 7
teacher [ˈtiːtʃə] Lehrer/in 5
team [tiːm] Team, Mannschaft 6
team player [tiːm ˈpleɪə] Teamplayer/in 9: 2 (40)
technology [tekˈnɒlədʒi] Technik, Technologie 6
teen [tiːn] *(infml)* Teenager 6
teenage life [ˈtiːneɪdʒ] *(etwa:)* das Leben der Teenager 6
teenager [ˈtiːneɪdʒə] Teenager 5
tell [tel], **told, told** erzählen, sagen 5
tell sb. the way jm. den Weg beschreiben 6
temperature [ˈtemprətʃə] Temperatur; Fieber 6 **I have a temperature.** Ich habe Fieber. 6
ten [ten] zehn 5
tennis [ˈtenɪs] Tennis 6
tent [tent] Zelt 5
terrible [ˈterəbl] schrecklich 5
test [test]:
1. Test; Klassenarbeit; Prüfung 6
2. Versuch *(z.B. Labor)*; Untersuchung 9: 4 (66)
text [tekst] Text 7
text (message) [ˈtekst mesɪdʒ]:
1. SMS 5
2. **text sb.** jm. eine SMS schicken 5
than [ðən] **older than me** älter als ich 6 **It's cheaper than that.** So viel kostet das nicht. 6
thank sb. (for sth.) [θæŋk] jm. danken, sich bei jm. (für etwas) bedanken 9: 2 (32)
thank you [ˈθæŋk juː] danke (schön) 5
°**thankful** [ˈθæŋkfl] dankbar
thanks [θæŋks] danke 5
that [ðæt]:
1. das (da) 5
That's £ 5. Das macht 5 Pfund. 5
that's why deswegen 6

Is that Mr Taylor? Ist da Herr Taylor? *(am Telefon)* 7
2. dass 5 **she thinks that ...** sie denkt, dass ... 5
so that sodass 5
3. der, die, das *(Relativpronomen)* 7 **words that you know ...** Wörter, die du kennst ... 7
the [ðə] der, die, das 5
theatre [ˈθɪətə] Theater 6
their [ðeə] ihr/e *(Plural)* 5
theirs [ðeəz] ihre/r, ihrs *(zu „they")* 7
them [ðem], [ðəm] sie, ihnen *(Plural)* 5
°theme [θiːm] Thema 5
theme park [ˈθiːm pɑːk] Themenpark *(Freizeitpark mit Attraktionen zu einem bestimmten Thema)* 8
themselves [ðəmˈselvz] sie/sich selbst (Plural) 7
then [ðen]:
1. dann 5
2. (back) then damals 9: 4 (66)
since then seitdem 9: 4 (70)
°theoretical [θɪəˈretɪkl] theoretisch 5
theory [ˈθɪəri] Theorie 9: 4 (68)
in theory theoretisch 9: 4 (68)
there [ðeə] da, dort; dahin, dorthin 5
there are ... es sind ... / es gibt ... 5
there's es ist ... / es gibt ... 5
these kids [ðiːz] diese Kinder (hier) 6
they [ðeɪ] sie *(Plural)* 5 **they're (= they are)** sie sind 5
thin [θɪn] dünn, schlank 9: 2 (33)
thing [θɪŋ] Ding, Sache 5
think [θɪŋk], **thought, thought** denken, meinen, glauben 5 **think of/ about** halten von, denken über 6
What do you think? Was meinst du? / Was denkst du? 5
third [θɜːd]:
1. dritte(r, s) 5
2. one third ein Drittel 7
thirsty [ˈθɜːsti]: **be thirsty** Durst haben 9: 1 (13)
this [ðɪs] diese(r, s) 5 **This is Rob Blake.** Hier spricht Rob Blake. *(am Telefon)* 7 **This is ...** Dies ist ... / Das ist ... 5 **this morning/afternoon/evening** heute Morgen/Nachmittag/Abend 6
those CDs [ðəʊz] die CDs dort, jene CDs 6
though [ðəʊ] obwohl 8
thought [θɔːt]:
1. *siehe* **think**
2. Gedanke 9: 2 (30)
thousand [ˈθaʊznd] tausend 7
three [θriː] drei 5 **3-D** 3-D 7
threw [θruː] *siehe* **throw**
throat [θrəʊt] Hals 6 **a sore throat** Halsschmerzen 6
through [θruː] durch 5
throw [θrəʊ], **threw, thrown** werfen 9: 4 (58)
thrown [θrəʊn] *siehe* **throw**
Thursday [ˈθɜːzdeɪ], [ˈθɜːzdi] Donnerstag 5
°tick [tɪk] Häkchen 5

ticket [ˈtɪkɪt] Eintrittskarte, Fahrkarte 5
tidy [ˈtaɪdi]:
1. aufräumen 6
2. ordentlich 6
tie [taɪ] Krawatte 5
tiger [ˈtaɪgə] Tiger 5
till [tɪl] bis *(zeitlich)* 8
time [taɪm]:
1. Zeit; Uhrzeit 5
have a great time viel Spaß haben 5
in four days' time in vier Tagen 8
in time rechtzeitig 8
on time pünktlich 6
What's the time? Wie spät ist es? 5
2. Mal 6 **next time** nächstes Mal 6
timetable [ˈtaɪmteɪbl] Stundenplan 5
tip [tɪp] Tipp 8
tired [ˈtaɪəd] müde 5
title [ˈtaɪtl] Titel, Überschrift 7
to [tu], [tə]:
1. zu, nach, in 5
to the country aufs Land 5
go to bed ins Bett gehen, schlafen gehen 5
go to dad's flat in Papas Wohnung gehen 5
Have you ever been to London? Warst du schon mal in London? 6
talk to sprechen mit 5
2. bis 5 **from Monday to Friday** von Montag bis Freitag 5
3. (um) zu 5 **time to go home** Zeit, nach Hause zu gehen 5
toast [təʊst] Toast(brot) 6
today [təˈdeɪ] heute 5
together [təˈgeðə] zusammen 5
toilet [ˈtɔɪlət] Toilette 5
told [təʊld] *siehe* **tell**
tomato [təˈmɑːtəʊ], *pl* **tomatoes** Tomate 7
tomorrow [təˈmɒrəʊ] morgen 5
°tonne [tʌn] Tonne *(= 1.000 kg)*
too [tuː]:
1. auch 5
Me too. Ich auch. 5
2. too small zu klein 5
took [tʊk] *siehe* **take**
top [tɒp]:
1. Spitze, oberes Ende 6
top of the charts *(infml)* Nummer eins / Platz eins der Charts 8
at the top (of) oben, am oberen Ende (von); an der Spitze (von) 6
2. Top *(ärmelloses Oberteil)* 7
topic [ˈtɒpɪk] Thema 9: 3 (55)
°topic-based talk [tɒpɪk beɪst ˈtɔːk] themenbezogener Vortrag
torch [tɔːtʃ] Taschenlampe 9: 1 (13)
°total [ˈtəʊtl] Gesamt-; total
tour [tʊə]:
1. Tour; Rundfahrt 7
2. tour (of) Rundgang (durch) 5
a tour of the school ein Rundgang durch die Schule 5
tourist [ˈtʊərɪst] Tourist/in 6
towards [təˈwɔːdz] nach, auf ... zu, in Richtung (von) 8
towel [ˈtaʊəl] Handtuch 5
tower [ˈtaʊə] Turm 7

town [taʊn] Stadt 5 **in town** in der Stadt 5
township [ˈtaʊnʃɪp] Township *(überwiegend von Schwarzen bewohnte Siedlung in Südafrika)* 8
toy [tɔɪ] Spielzeug 6
track [træk]:
1. Pfad, (Feld-)Weg 6 **°stay on track** auf dem richtigen Weg bleiben
2. (Bahn-)Gleis 9: 4 (72)
tradition [trəˈdɪʃn] Tradition 8
traditional [trəˈdɪʃənl] traditionell 8
traffic [ˈtræfɪk] (Straßen-)Verkehr 8
traffic lights *(pl)* [ˈtræfɪk laɪts] Verkehrsampel 6
°trail [treɪl] Weg, Pfad, Route 5
train [treɪn] Zug, Eisenbahn 6
train [treɪn] trainieren *(z.B. im Sport)* 8 **train (as ... / to become ...)** eine Ausbildung machen (zu/als), ausgebildet werden (zu/als) 8 **train sb.** jn. trainieren, ausbilden 8
train station [ˈtreɪn steɪʃn] Bahnhof 6
trainers *(pl)* [ˈtreɪnəz] Sportschuhe 5
°tram [træm] Straßenbahn, Tram 5
°translate [trænsˈleɪt] übersetzen 5
transport [ˈtrænspɔːt] Verkehrsmittel; Transport(wesen) 7
travel [ˈtrævl]:
1. reisen; fahren, sich fortbewegen 7
2. *(das)* Reisen 9: 2 (29)
traveller [ˈtrævələ] Reisende/r 9: 3 (45)
treat [triːt] behandeln 8
tree [triː] Baum 5
trick [trɪk] Trick, Kunststück 7
trip [trɪp] Fahrt, Ausflug 5 **do a trip** einen Ausflug machen 6 **go on a trip** einen Ausflug machen 5
trouble [ˈtrʌbl] Ärger, Schwierigkeit(en) 5
trousers *(pl)* [ˈtraʊzəz] Hose 5
truck [trʌk] Lastwagen, Lkw 9: 1 (17)
true [truː] wahr 6 **come true** wahr werden, Wirklichkeit werden 8
try [traɪ] versuchen, (aus)probieren 6 **try sth. on** etwas anprobieren *(Kleidung)* 7
°tuatara [tuːəˈtɑːrə] Brückenechse 5
Tube [tjuːb] U-Bahn *(London)* 7
Tuesday [ˈtjuːzdeɪ], [ˈtjuːzdi] Dienstag 5
°tuk-tuk [ˈtʊk tʊk] Tuk Tuk *(Autorikschal)*
turn [tɜːn] sich umdrehen 8 **turn around** sich umdrehen 8 **turn off** (sich) ausschalten 9: 3 (49)
turn on (sich) einschalten 9: 3 (49)
turn right/left (nach) rechts/links abbiegen 6 **turn sb./sth. into sth.** jn./etwas in etwas verwandeln 9: 1 (22)
turn sth. down etwas herunterregeln; etwas leiser stellen 9: 4 (65) **turn sth. up** etwas höher stellen *(weiter aufdrehen)*; etwas lauter machen 9: 4 (65)
TV [tiːˈviː] Fernseher 5
twelve [twelv] zwölf 5
twice [twaɪs] zweimal 6
twin room [twɪn ˈruːm] Zweibettzimmer 7

twins *(pl)* [twɪnz] Zwillinge 7

two [tuː] zwei 5

typical (of) ['tɪpɪkl] typisch (für) 8

U

ugly ['ʌgli] hässlich 6

uncle ['ʌŋkl] Onkel 8

uncool [ʌn'kuːl] uncool 6

under ['ʌndə] unter 5

underground ['ʌndəgraʊnd] U-Bahn 9: 4 (59)

°underline [ʌndə'laɪn] unterstreichen

understand [ʌndə'stænd], **understood, understood** verstehen 6

understood [ʌndə'stʊd] *siehe* **understand**

underwater [ʌndə'wɔːtə] unter Wasser, Unterwasser- 8

unemployed [ʌnɪm'plɔɪd] arbeitslos 7

unemployment [ʌnɪm'plɔɪmənt] Arbeitslosigkeit 9: 1 (14)

unequal [ʌn'iːkwəl] ungleich 9: 3 (43)

unfair [ʌn'feə] unfair 8

unfit [ʌn'fɪt] nicht fit 7

unfortunately [ʌn'fɔːtʃənətli] unglücklicherweise, leider 9: 3 (51)

unfriendly [ʌn'frendli] unfreundlich 6

unhappy [ʌn'hæpi] unglücklich 5

unhealthy [ʌn'helθi] ungesund 6

uniform ['juːnɪfɔːm] (Schul-)Uniform 5

uninteresting [ʌn'ɪntrəstɪŋ] uninteressant 6

unit ['juːnɪt] Unit *(Lerneinheit)* 5

university [juːnɪ'vɜːsəti] Universität 9: 3 (48)

unlucky [ʌn'lʌki]: **be unlucky** Pech haben 9: 2 (35)

unpopular [ʌn'pɒpjələ] unbeliebt 6

unreal [ʌn'rɪəl] unwirklich 6

unsure [ʌn'ʃʊə] unsicher 6

untidy [ʌn'taɪdi] unordentlich, unaufgeräumt 7

until [ən'tɪl] bis *(zeitlich)* 6 **not (...) until I'm 13** erst, wenn ich 13 bin 6

up [ʌp] hinauf, hoch 5

up to ['ʌp tə] bis (zu) 9: 2 (26)

up to now [ʌp tə 'naʊ] bis jetzt 9: 2 (26)

upstairs [ʌp'steəz] oben; nach oben 5

us [ʌs], [əs] uns 5

USB port [juː es 'biː pɔːt] USB-Port *(USB-Schnittstelle)* 9: 4 (59)

use [juːz] benutzen 5

useful (to sb.) ['juːsfl] nützlich (für jn.) 9: (8)

user ['juːzə] (Be-)Nutzer/in 9: 2 (31) **wheelchair user** Rollstuhlfahrer/in 9: 2 (31)

usually ['juːʒʊəli] meistens, normalerweise 5

V

value ['væljuː] Wert 9: 3 (56) **something of value** etwas von Wert, etwas Wertvolles 9: 3 (56)

van [væn] Transporter, Lieferwagen 7

vegan ['viːgən] vegan; Veganer/in 8

vegetables *(pl)* ['vedʒtəblz] Gemüse 5

vegetarian [vedʒə'teərɪən] (*infml auch* **veggie**) vegetarisch; Vegetarier/in 6

veggie ['vedʒi] *(infml) siehe* **vegetarian**

°verse [vɜːs] Vers, Strophe *(Lied)*

°version ['vɜːʃn] Version

very ['veri] sehr 5 **Thanks very much.** Vielen Dank. 6

video ['vɪdiəʊ] Video 6

video chat ['vɪdiəʊ tʃæt] Videochat 6

video clip ['vɪdiəʊ klɪp] Videoclip 8

view [vjuː]:
1. anschauen 8
2. **view (of)** (Aus-)Sicht, (Aus-)Blick (auf, über) 8

viewer ['vjuːə] Zuschauer/in 9: 3 (46)

viewing area ['vjuːɪŋ eəriə] Aussichtsbereich *(von wo aus man etwas betrachten kann)* 8

village ['vɪlɪdʒ] Dorf 5

village hall ['vɪlɪdʒ hɔːl] Gemeindesaal 9: 2 (31)

violence ['vaɪələns] Gewalt; Gewalttätigkeit 7

violent ['vaɪələnt] gewalttätig 7

°vision ['vɪʒn] Vision

visit ['vɪzɪt]:
1. besuchen 6
2. Besuch 7

visitor ['vɪzɪtə] Besucher/in, Gast 5

vlog [vlɒg] Vlog *(Video-Blog)* 9: 3 (46)

voice [vɔɪs] Stimme 7

°volcano [vɒl'keɪnəʊ], *pl* **volcanos** *or* **volcanoes** Vulkan

volleyball ['vɒlibɔːl] Volleyball 6

voluntary ['vɒləntri] freiwillig, ehrenamtlich 8

volunteer [vɒlən'tɪə]:
1. Freiwillige/r, Ehrenamtliche/r 9: 2 (29)
2. freiwillig/ehrenamtlich arbeiten *(unbezahlt)* 9: 2 (29)

vote [vəʊt]:
1. Abstimmung, Votum 9: 3 (43)
2. **vote (on sth.)** wählen; abstimmen (über etwas) 9: 3 (43)
vote for stimmen für 6

W

wage [weɪdʒ], *oft auch:* **wages** *(pl)* Lohn, Gehalt 9: 2 (33)

wait (for) [weɪt] warten (auf) 6 **Wait for this.** *(infml)* Stell dir nur vor! / Du wirst es kaum glauben! 6

waiter ['weɪtə] Kellner 7

waitress ['weɪtrəs] Kellnerin 7

wake [weɪk], **woke, woken** wecken 5

walk [wɔːk] (zu Fuß) gehen, wandern 5 **walk a dog** mit einem Hund spazieren gehen 8 **walk around** umhergehen (in) 5

walker ['wɔːkə] Wanderer/Wanderin, Fußgänger/in 7

wall [wɔːl] Wand; Mauer 6

wallet ['wɒlɪt] Brieftasche; Portemonnaie; Etui *(Schutzhülle)* 9: 3 (56)

want [wɒnt] wollen 5 **want sb. to do sth.** wollen, dass jd. etwas tut 9: 4 (60) **want to do** tun/machen wollen 5

warder ['wɔːdə] Aufseher/in, Wärter/in *(im Gefängnis)* 9: 3 (49)

wardrobe ['wɔːdrəʊb] Kleiderschrank 5

warm [wɔːm] warm 6

warn sb. (about/against/of sth.) [wɔːn] jn. warnen (vor etwas) 9: 4 (67)

was [wɒz], [wəz] *siehe* **be**

wash [wɒʃ] waschen 6

wash up [wɒʃ 'ʌp] abwaschen 5

waste [weɪst] Verschwendung 7

watch [wɒtʃ] *(sich etwas)* anschauen; beobachten 5 **watch out for** sich hüten vor, sich in Acht nehmen vor 9: 2 (29) **Watch out!** Achtung! 9: 2 (29) **watching TV** Fernsehen 5

water ['wɔːtə] Wasser 5

waterfall ['wɔːtəfɔːl] Wasserfall 9: 1 (11)

wave [weɪv] Welle 9: 4 (64)

way [weɪ]:
1. Weg 6
ask sb. the way jn. nach dem Weg fragen 6
one way eine Strecke (= ohne Rückfahrt) 7
tell sb. the way jm. den Weg beschreiben 6
2. Art (und Weise) 8
do it my way es so machen, wie ich es will 8
that way so, auf jene Art 8
this way so, auf diese Art 8
You can't always have things your way. Es kann nicht immer nach deiner Nase gehen. 8

we [wiː] wir 5 **we're (= we are)** wir sind 5

weak [wiːk] schwach 9: 2 (32)

weakness ['wiːknəs] Schwäche 9: 2 (32)

wear [weə], **wore, worn** tragen, anhaben *(Kleidung)* 6

weather ['weðə] Wetter 6

weather forecast ['fɔːkɑːst] Wettervorhersage 6

weather report ['weðə rɪpɔːt] Wetterbericht 7

°web [web] Netz(werk)

webcode ['webkəʊd] Webcode 6

website ['websaɪt] Website 7

wedding ['wedɪŋ] Hochzeit 8

wedding dress ['wedɪŋ dres] Hochzeitskleid 8

Wednesday ['wenzdeɪ], ['wenzdi] Mittwoch 5

week [wiːk] Woche 5

weekend [wiːk'end] Wochenende 5 **at the weekend** am Wochenende 5

welcome ['welkəm]:
1. **welcome sb. (to)** jn. begrüßen (in), jn. willkommen heißen (in) 7
Welcome to Plymouth. Willkommen in Plymouth! 5
2. **You're welcome.** Bitte, gern geschehen. / Nichts zu danken. 5

well [wel] gut *(Adverb)* 6 **Well, ...** Nun, ... / Also, ... 5 **Well done.** Gut gemacht! 5 **do well** es gut machen; gut abschneiden, erfolgreich sein 7

she can't walk well sie kann nicht gut gehen/laufen 6 **She isn't feeling well.** Es geht ihr nicht gut. 6
well paid [wel 'peɪd] gut bezahlt 8
well-prepared [wel prɪ'peəd] gut vorbereitet 9: 2 (40)
went [went] *siehe* **go**
were [wɜː], [wə] *siehe* **be** **I wish I were …** Ich wünschte, ich wäre … 9: 4 (62)
west [west] Westen; westlich; West- 6
western [westən] westliche(r, s), West- 7
wet [wet] nass 5
whale [weɪl] Wal 8
whale watching [weɪl wɒtʃɪŋ] Walbeobachtung 8
whale-watching trip [weɪl wɒtʃɪŋ trɪp] Walbeobachtungstour 8
what [wɒt]:
1. was 5
What about you? Und du? / Was ist mit dir? 5
What do you call …? Wie nennt man …? 8
What do you think? Was meinst du? / Was denkst du? 5
What's the time? Wie spät ist es? 5
What's more, … Darüber hinaus …, Außerdem … 9: 1 (15)
What's your name? Wie heißt du? 5
2. welche(r, s) 5
wheelchair [wiːltʃeə] Rollstuhl 5
wheelchair user [wiːltʃeə juːzə] Rollstuhlfahrer/in 9: 2 (31)
when [wen]:
1. wann 5
When is your birthday? Wann hast du Geburtstag? 5
2. wenn 5
3. als 5
where [weə] wo(hin) 5
which [wɪtʃ]:
1. welche(r, s) 6 **Which club?** Welcher Klub? 6
2. der, die, das; die *(Relativpronomen)* 7
while [waɪl] während 8
whisper [wɪspə]:
1. flüstern 8
2. *(ein/das)* Flüstern 8
whistle [wɪsl] (Triller-)Pfeife 6
white [waɪt] weiß 5
who [huː]:
1. wer 5
Who are you? Wer bist du? / Wer seid ihr? 5
2. wem; wen 5
3. der, die *(Relativpronomen, Person)* 7
somebody who can help jemand, der helfen kann 7
whole [həʊl] ganze(r, s) 9: 2 (38)
on the whole im Großen und Ganzen 9: 2 (38)
why [waɪ] warum 5 **that's why** deswegen 6
Wi-Fi [waɪ faɪ] WLAN, kabellose Datenübertragung 7
wide [waɪd] breit, weit 8

widely spoken [waɪdli 'spəʊkən] weit verbreitet *(Sprache)*, viel gesprochen 9: 3 (42)
wife [waɪf], *pl* **wives** (Ehe-)Frau 8
wild [waɪld] wild; wild lebend 5
wildlife [waɪldlaɪf] Tiere *(in freier Wildbahn)*, Tierwelt 8
will [wɪl]: **I'll (= I will) find him.** Ich werde ihn finden. 6 **50p will do** 50 Pence reichen (auch) 6
win [wɪn], **won, won** gewinnen 6
wind [wɪnd] Wind 6
window [wɪndəʊ] Fenster 6
windy [wɪndi] windig 6
wine [waɪn] Wein 9: 3 (49)
winner [wɪnə] Gewinner/in 5
winter [wɪntə] Winter 6
wish [wɪʃ]:
1. Wunsch 5
Best wishes Viele Grüße, … *(Briefschluss)* 5
2. wünschen 9: 4 (62)
I wish I were … Ich wünschte, ich wäre … 9: 4 (62)
with [wɪð] mit 5 **with Ellie** bei Ellie 5 **He puts it with the other things.** Er legt sie zu den anderen Dingen. 6
without [wɪ'ðaʊt] ohne 6
wives [waɪvz] *Plural von* **wife**
°**woke** [wəʊk] *siehe* **wake**
°**woken** [wəʊkən] *siehe* **wake**
woman [wʊmən], *pl* **women** Frau 5
women [wɪmɪn] *Plural von* **woman**
won [wʌn] *siehe* **win**
won't [wəʊnt]: **it won't rain** es wird nicht regnen 6
wood [wʊd]:
1. Holz 7
2. Wald 7
word [wɜːd] Wort 5 **words (of a song)** (Song-)Text 7
°**wordbank** [wɜːdbæŋk] Sammlung von Wörtern zu einem Thema 7
°**wordweb** [wɜːdweb] Wortnetz 7
wore [wɔː] *siehe* **wear**
work [wɜːk]:
1. Arbeit 5
at work bei der Arbeit, am Arbeitsplatz 5
2. arbeiten; funktionieren 5
work on sth. an etwas arbeiten 8
work experience [wɜːk ɪkspɪərɪəns] Arbeitserfahrung(en) 8
work of art [wɜːk əv 'ɑːt] Kunstwerk 7
worker [wɜːkə] Arbeiter/in; Arbeitskraft 7
working hours *(pl)* [wɜːkɪŋ aʊəz] Arbeitszeit(en) 9: 2 (39)
world [wɜːld] Welt 7 **in the world** auf der Welt 7 **out of this world** *(infml)* fabelhaft 8
World Cup [wɜːld 'kʌp] Weltmeisterschaft 9: 3 (43)
worldwide [wɜːldwaɪd] weltweit 8
worn [wɔːn] *siehe* **wear**
worried [wʌrid]: **be worried (about)** beunruhigt sein, besorgt sein (wegen) 8

worry [wʌri]:
1. **worry (about)** sich Sorgen machen (wegen, um) 6
2. **No worries.** *(infml)* Kein Problem. 7
worse [wɜːs] schlechter, schlimmer 6
worst [wɜːst] der/die/das schlechteste, schlimmste; am schlechtesten, am schlimmsten 6
would [wʊd]: **I'd (= I would) like** ich hätte gern, ich möchte (…) haben 5 **I'd (= I would) love to come.** Ich komme sehr gern. / Ich würde sehr gern kommen. 5 **I'd (= I would) like to join** ich würde/möchte gern mitmachen 6
write [raɪt], **wrote, written** schreiben 5 **write down** aufschreiben 9: 4 (71) **write to sb.** an jn. schreiben 5
writer [raɪtə] Autor/in, Verfasser/in 7
written [rɪtn] *siehe* **write**
wrong [rɒŋ] falsch 5 **go wrong** schiefgehen; etwas falsch machen 8 **that's wrong** das stimmt nicht, das ist falsch 5 **What's wrong with …?** Was stimmt nicht mit …? 6
wrote [rəʊt] *siehe* **write**

X

X-ray [eksreɪ] Röntgen(strahlen) 7

Y

yeah [jeə] *(infml)* ja 6
year [jɪə] Jahr(gang) 5
yell (at sb.) [jel] (jn. an)schreien 8
yellow [jeləʊ] gelb 5
yes [jes] ja 5
yesterday [jestədeɪ] gestern 5
yet [jet]: **not … yet** noch nicht 7
yoga [jəʊgə] Yoga 9: 4 (62)
yogurt [jɒgət] Joghurt 6
you [juː]:
1. du; ihr; Sie 5
you're (= you are) du bist, ihr seid, Sie sind 5
2. dich; dir; euch; Sie; Ihnen 5
young [jʌŋ] jung 6
your [jɔː] dein/e, euer/eure 5
yours [jɔːz] deine/r; deins; eure/r, eures 7
yourself [jə'self] du/dir/dich selbst 7
yourselves [jɔː'selvz] ihr/euch selbst; Sie/sich selbst 7
youth [juːθ] Jugend 8
youth camp [juːθ kæmp] Jugendlager 8
°**Yuck!** [jʌk] Igitt!
yum! [jʌm] lecker! 6

Z

zebra [zebrə] Zebra 7
zero [zɪərəʊ], *pl* **zeros** Null 9: 4 (60)
zone [zəʊn] Zone 7
zoo [zuː] Zoo 5

English sounds

[iː]	green, he, tea
[ɑː]	ask, class, car, park
[ɔː]	or, ball, four, morning
[uː]	ruler, blue, too, two, you
[ɜː]	early, her, girl, work, T-shirt
[ɪ]	in, big, expensive
[e]	yes, bed, again, breakfast
[æ]	animal, Africa, black, cat
[ʌ]	mum, bus, colour
[ɒ]	song, on, dog, what
[ʊ]	book, good, pullover
[ə]	again, today, a sister
[i]	happy, monkey
[u]	you, to
[eɪ]	name, eight, play, great
[aɪ]	I, time, right, my
[ɔɪ]	boy, toilet, noise
[əʊ]	old, no, road, yellow
[aʊ]	now, house
[eə]	where, chair, bear
[ɪə]	here, dear
[ʊə]	your
[b]	bike, table, crab
[p]	pen, stupid, shop
[d]	day, idea, good
[t]	ten, letter, at
[g]	go, again, bag
[k]	kitchen, car, black
[m]	man, remember, mum
[n]	no, one, ten
[ŋ]	wrong, England, thanks
[l]	like, old, small
[r]	ruler, friend, sorry
[w]	we, where, one
[j]	yes, you, uniform
[f]	family, after, laugh
[v]	very, seven, have
[s]	six, poster, yes
[z]	zoo, quiz, his, music, please
[ʃ]	she, brochure, English
[ʒ]	garage
[tʃ]	child, teacher, watch
[dʒ]	German, orange
[θ]	thing, three, bathroom, month
[ð]	the, brother, with
[h]	house, who, behind

The English alphabet

a	[eɪ]	o	[əʊ]
b	[biː]	p	[piː]
c	[siː]	q	[kjuː]
d	[diː]	r	[ɑː]
e	[iː]	s	[es]
f	[ef]	t	[tiː]
g	[dʒiː]	u	[juː]
h	[eɪtʃ]	v	[viː]
i	[aɪ]	w	['dʌbljuː]
j	[dʒeɪ]	x	[eks]
k	[keɪ]	y	[waɪ]
l	[el]	z	[zed]
m	[em]		
n	[en]		

Country/Continent	Adjective	Person	People
Afghanistan [æf'gɑnɪstən] *Afghanistan*	**Afghan** ['æfgæn]	an Afghan	the Afghans
Africa ['æfrɪkə] *Afrika*	**African** ['æfrɪkən]	an African	the Africans
America [ə'merɪkə] *Amerika*	**American** [ə'merɪkən]	an American	the Americans
Asia ['eɪʃə, 'eɪʒə] *Asien*	**Asian** ['eɪʃn, 'eɪʒn]	an Asian	the Asians
Australia [ɒ'streɪliə] *Australien*	**Australian** [ɒ'streɪliən]	an Australian	the Australians
Austria ['ɒstriə] *Österreich*	**Austrian** ['ɒstriən]	an Austrian	the Austrians
Bangladesh [bæŋglə'deʃ]	**Bangladeshi** [bæŋglə'deʃi]	a Bangladeshi	the Bangladeshis
Botswana [bɒt'swɑːnə]	**Botswanan** [bɒt'swɑːnən]	a Botswanan	the Botswanans
Brazil [brə'zɪl] *Brasilien*	**Brazilian** [brə'zɪliən]	a Brazilian	the Brazilians
Bulgaria [bʌl'geəriə] *Bulgarien*	**Bulgarian** [bʌl'geəriən]	a Bulgarian	the Bulgarians
Canada ['kænədə] *Kanada*	**Canadian** [kə'neɪdiən]	a Canadian	the Canadians
China ['tʃaɪnə] *China*	**Chinese** [tʃaɪ'niːz]	a Chinese	the Chinese
Croatia [krəʊ'eɪʃə] *Kroatien*	**Croatian** [krəʊ'eɪʃn]	a Croatian	the Croatians
the Czech Republic [tʃek rɪ'pʌblɪk] *Tschechien, die Tschechische Republik*	**Czech** [tʃek]	a Czech	the Czechs
Denmark ['denmɑːk] *Dänemark*	**Danish** ['deɪnɪʃ]	a Dane [deɪn]	the Danes
Egypt ['iːdʒɪpt] *Ägypten*	**Egyptian** [i'dʒɪpʃn]	an Egyptian	the Egyptians
England ['ɪŋglənd] *England*	**English** ['ɪŋglɪʃ]	an Englishman/-woman	the English
Europe ['jʊərəp] *Europa*	**European** [ˌjʊərə'piːən]	a European	the Europeans
Finland ['fɪnlənd] *Finnland*	**Finnish** ['fɪnɪʃ]	a Finn [fɪn]	the Finns
France [frɑːns] *Frankreich*	**French** [frentʃ]	a Frenchman/-woman	the French
Germany ['dʒɜːməni] *Deutschland*	**German** ['dʒɜːmən]	a German	the Germans
Grenada [grɪ'neɪdə] *Grenada*	**Grenadian** [grə'neɪdiən]	a Grenadian	the Grenadians
(Great) Britain ['brɪtn] *Großbritannien*	**British** ['brɪtɪʃ]	a Briton ['brɪtn]	the British
Greece [griːs] *Griechenland*	**Greek** [griːk]	a Greek	the Greeks
India ['ɪndiə] *Indien*	**Indian** ['ɪndiən]	an Indian	the Indians
Iran [ɪ'rɑːn] *Iran*	**Iranian** [ɪ'reɪniən]	an Iranian	the Iranians
Iraq [ɪ'rɑːk] *Irak*	**Iraqi** [ɪ'rɑːki]	an Iraqi	the Iraqis
Ireland ['aɪələnd] *Irland*	**Irish** ['aɪrɪʃ]	an Irishman/-woman	the Irish
Italy ['ɪtəli] *Italien*	**Italian** [ɪ'tæliən]	an Italian	the Italians
Japan [dʒɜ'pæn] *Japan*	**Japanese** [ˌdʒæpə'niːz]	a Japanese	the Japanese
Latin America [lætɪn ə'merɪkə] *Lateinamerika*	**Latin American** [lætɪn ə'merɪkən]	a Latin American	the Latin Americans
Nepal [nə'pɔːl]	**Nepalese** [nepə'liːz]	a Nepalese	the Nepalese
the Netherlands ['neðələndz] *die Niederlande, Holland*	**Dutch** [dʌtʃ]	a Dutchman/-woman	the Dutch
New Zealand [njuː 'ziːlənd] *Neuseeland*	**New Zealand**	a New Zealander	the New Zealanders
Norway ['nɔːweɪ] *Norwegen*	**Norwegian** [nɔː'wiːdʒən]	a Norwegian	the Norwegians
Pakistan [pækɪ'stæn] *Pakistan*	**Pakistani** [pækɪ'stæni]	a Pakistani	the Pakistanis
the Philippines ['fɪlɪpiːnz] *die Philippinen*	**Filipina** [fɪlɪ'piːnə] **Filipino** [fɪlɪ'piːnəʊ]	a Filipina/Filipino	the Filipinas/ Filipinos
Poland ['pəʊlənd] *Polen*	**Polish** ['pəʊlɪʃ]	a Pole [pəʊl]	the Poles
Romania [ru'meɪniə] *Rumänien*	**Romanian** [ru'meɪniən]	a Romanian	the Romanians
Russia ['rʌʃə] *Russland*	**Russian** ['rʌʃn]	a Russian	the Russians

Country/Continent	Adjective	Person	People
Scotland ['skɒtlənd] *Schottland*	**Scottish** ['skɒtɪʃ]	a **Scotsman/-woman**	the **Scots**
Serbia ['sɜːbiə] *Serbien*	**Serbian** ['sɜːbiən]	a **Serb** [sɜːb]	the **Serbs**
Slovakia [sləˈvækiə] *die Slowakei*	**Slovak** ['sləʊvæk]	a **Slovakian** [sləˈvækiən]	the **Slovakians**
Slovenia [sləˈviːniə] *Slowenien*	**Slovene** ['sləʊviːn]	a **Slovenian** [sləˈviːniən]	the **Slovenians**
Spain [speɪn] *Spanien*	**Spanish** ['spænɪʃ]	a **Spaniard** ['spæniəd]	the **Spaniards**
Sweden ['swiːdn] *Schweden*	**Swedish** ['swiːdɪʃ]	a **Swede** [swiːd]	the **Swedes**
Syria ['sɪriə] *Syrien*	**Syrian** ['sɪriən]	a **Syrian**	the **Syrians**
Turkey ['tɜːki] *die Türkei*	**Turkish** ['tɜːkɪʃ]	a **Turk** [tɜːk]	the **Turks**
the United Kingdom (the UK) [junaɪtɪd 'kɪŋdəm, juːˈkeɪ] *das Vereinigte Königreich (Großbritannien und Nordirland)*	**British** ['brɪtɪʃ]	a **Briton** ['brɪtn]	the **British**
the United States of America (the USA) [də junaɪtɪd steɪts əv əˈmerɪkə, juː es 'eɪ] *die Vereinigten Staaten von Amerika*	**American** [əˈmerɪkən]	an **American**	the **Americans**
Venezuela [venəˈzweɪlə] *Venezuela*	**Venezuelan** [venəˈzweɪlən]	a **Venezuelan**	the **Venezuelans**
Vietnam [viːetˈnɑːm]	**Vietnamese** [viːetnəˈmiːz]	a **Vietnamese**	the **Vietnamese**
Zimbabwe [zɪmˈbɑːbwi] *Zimbabwe*	**Zimbabwean** [zɪmˈbɑːbwiən]	a **Zimbabwean**	the **Zimbabweans**

First names (Vornamen)

Aarav [ˈɑːrəv]
Adem [əˈdem]
Aditi [ɑːdɪˈti]
Aisha [aɪˈiːʃə]
Alina [əˈliːnə]
Alison [ˈælɪsn]
Amar [əˈmɑː]
Amy [ˈeɪmi]
Anh [ɑːn]
Anna [ˈænə]
Ari [ˈɑːri]
Arunima [ɑːruˈniːmə]
Bandile [bænˈdiːlə]
Baz [bæz]
Bella [ˈbelə]
Ben [ben]
Brian [ˈbraɪən]
Dan [dæn]
Daniel [ˈdænjəl]
Danny [ˈdæni]
David [ˈdeɪvɪd]
Demi [ˈdemi]
Demi-Leigh [demi ˈli]
Desmond [ˈdezmənd]
Diya [ˈdiːjʌ]
Don [dɒn]
Enzokuhle [enzəˈkuːlə]
Erin [ˈerɪn]
Faiza [ˈfaɪzʌ]
Farida [fəˈriːdə]
Fatima [ˈfætɪmə]
Fluffy [ˈflʌfi]
Geeta [ˈgiːtʌ]
Gunnedoo [gʌnəˈduː]
Harper [ˈhɑːpə]
Harry [ˈhæri]
Hashim [həˈʃiːm]
Hugh [hjuː]
Hunter [ˈhʌntə]
Huong [hwɒŋ]
Imran [ˈɪmræn]
Jack [dʒæk]
James [dʒeɪmz]
Jimmy [ˈdʒɪmi]
Kagiso [ˈkʌxɪsəʊ]
Kahurangi [kʌhʊˈrʌŋgi]
Kara [ˈkɑːrə]
Karan [ˈkɑːrən]
Katie [ˈkeɪti]
Khoa [kwɑː]
Laura [ˈlɔːrə]
Lee [liː]
Leo [ˈliːəʊ]
Lerato [ləˈrɑːtəʊ]
Lizzy [ˈlɪzi]
Luisa [luˈiːz]
Lulama [lʊˈlɑːmə]

Mahatma [məˈhʌtmə]
Manaia [məˈnaɪə]
Mandeep [mænˈdiːp]
Mara [ˈmɑːrə]
Marama [məˈrɑːmə]
Meehni [ˈmiːni]
Meghan [ˈmegən]
Mike [maɪk]
Muthaya [mʊtʌˈjɑː]
Nelson [ˈnelsn]
Olivia [əˈlɪvɪə]
Omar [ˈəʊmɑː]
Pamir [pəˈmɪə]
Phillip [ˈfɪlɪp]
Poppy [ˈpɒpi]
Priya [ˈpriːjʌ]
Ritu [ˈriːtu]
Rob [rɒb]
Rolihlahla [rəʊˈhɪlələ]
Sai [saɪ]
Sam [sæm]
Sameena [səˈmiːnə]
Sarah [ˈseərə]
Satish [sʌˈtiːʃ]
Simona [sɪˈməʊnə]
Steve [stiːv]
Tai [taɪ]
Tarek [ˈtærɪk]
Theo [ˈθiːəʊ]
Timothy [ˈtɪməθi]
Vihaan [vɪˈhɑːn]
Vikram [ˈvɪkrʌm]
Vulu [ˈvuːlu]
Walid [wəˈliːd]
Wei [weɪ]
Wimlah [ˈwɪmlʌ]

Family names / Surnames (Familiennamen)

Amla [ˈʌmlə]
Attenborough [ˈætənbərə]
Berners-Lee [bɜːnəz ˈli]
de Klerk [də ˈkleək]
Dhawan [dʌˈwʌn]
Do [dəʊ]
Gandhi [ˈgændi], [ˈgɑːndi]
Gwynne [gwɪn]
Karidhal [ˈkʌrɪdʌl]
Khan [kɑːn]
Knox [nɒks]
Mandela [mænˈdelə]
Markle [ˈmɑːkl]
Nel-Peters [nel ˈpiːtəz]
Sinha [ˈsɪnʌ]
Tutu [ˈtuːtu]
Vanitha [vəˈniːtə]

Place names (Ortsnamen)

Adelaide [ˈædəleɪd]
Akaroa [ɑːkʌˈrəʊə]
Alice Springs [ælɪs ˈsprɪŋz]
Antarctica [ænˈtɑːktɪkə]
Aotearoa [aʊteɪəˈrəʊə]
Auckland [ˈɔːklənd]
Bangalore [bæŋgəˈlɔː]
Bengaluru [ˈbeŋgəlʊru]
Boulders Beach [bəʊldəz ˈbiːtʃ]
Brain [braɪn]
Burdekin [ˈbɜːdəkɪn]
California [kæləˈfɔːniə]
Canberra [ˈkænbərə]
Cape Town [ˈkeɪp taʊn]
CERN [sɜːn]
Chennai [ˈtʃenaɪ], [tʃeˈnaɪ]
Colombo [kəˈlʌmbəʊ]
Coober Pedy [kuːbə ˈpiːdi]
Darling [ˈdɑːlɪŋ]
Drakensberg Mountains
    [drɑːkənsbɜːg ˈmaʊntənz]
Dubai [duːˈbaɪ]
Durban [ˈdɜːbən]
Fiordland [fiˈɔːdlənd]
Geneva [dʒəˈniːvə]
Great Barrier Reef [greɪt bæriə ˈriːf]
Hanmer Spring [hæmə ˈsprɪŋ]
Hermanus [ˈhɜːmənəs]
Himalayas [hɪməˈleɪəz]
Invercargill [ɪnvəˈkɑːgɪl]
Johannesburg [dʒəʊˈhænəzbɜːg]
Kawarau [kəˈwɑːru]
Kaziranga National Park
    [kæzɪræŋgə næʃnəl ˈpɑːk]
Kruger National Park
    [kruːgə næʃnəl ˈpɑːk]
Las Vegas [læs ˈveɪgəs]
London [ˈlʌndən]
Lucknow [ˈlʌknaʊ]
Malleshwaram [mʌˈleɪʃwʌrʌm]
Manly Beach [mænli ˈbiːtʃ]
Mars [mɑːz]
Mecca Masjid [mekə ˈmæsdʒɪd]
Mesopotamia [mesəpəˈteɪmiə]
Mount Cook [maʊnt ˈkʊk]
Mount Everest [maʊnt ˈevərɪst]
Mumbai [mʊmˈbaɪ]
New Delhi [njuː ˈdeli]
Oamaru [ˈɒməru]
Orewa [əˈriːwə]
Pietermaritzburg
    [piːtəˈmærɪtsbɜːg]
Pretoria [prɪˈtɔːriə]
Queenstown [ˈkwiːnztaʊn]
Robben Island [rɒbən ˈaɪlənd]
Sharpeville [ˈʃɑːpvɪl]
Soweto [səˈwetəʊ]

Sriharikota [srɪhærɪˈkəʊtə]
Susannah Place [suˈzænə pleɪs]
Sydney [ˈsɪdni]
Taj Mahal [tɑːdʒ məˈhɑːl]
Te Anau [tiˈ ɑːnəʊ]
Tzaneen [tsəˈniːn]
Uluru [ʊˈluəru], [uːləˈru]
Vancouver [vænˈkuːvə]
Waikato River [waɪˈkætəʊ rɪvə]
Wai-O-Tapu [ˈwaɪtʌpu]
Wales [weɪlz]
Wellington [ˈwelɪŋtən]
Weta Workshop Studio
  [wetə ˈwɜːkʃɒp stuːdiəʊ]
Whangarei [wɒŋəˈreɪ]
Windsor [ˈwɪnzə]
Yulara [jʊˈlɑːrə]

Other names (Andere Namen)

African National Congress
  [æfrɪkən næʃnəl ˈkɒŋgres]
Afrikaans [æfrɪˈkɑːns]
Brothablack [brʌðəˈblæk]
Buddhism [ˈbʊdɪzəm]
Chandrayaan [tʃʌnˈdraɪən]
Hinduism [ˈhɪnduːɪzəm]
Holden Monaro
  [həʊldən məˈnɑːrəʊ]
Holi [ˈhəʊli]
Lord of the Rings
  [lɔːd əv ðə ˈrɪŋz]
Māori [ˈmaʊri]
Miss Universe [mɪs ˈjuːnɪvɜːs]
Pohuto [pəʊˈhuːtu], [pəˈhuːtu]
Sikh [siːk]
Star Wars [ˈstɑː wɔːz]
Typhoon [taɪˈfuːn]
Unesco [juˈneskəʊ]
vuvuzela [vuːvuːˈzeɪlə]
Xhosa [ˈkɔːsə]
Zulu [ˈzuːlu]

adjective	[ˈædʒɪktɪv]	Adjektiv (Eigenschaftswort)	*good, red, new, boring, …*
adverb of manner	[ædvɜːb əv ˈmænə]	Adverb der Art und Weise	*work quickly, run fast, speak English well*
adverb of place	[ædvɜːb əv ˈpleɪs]	Adverb des Ortes	*here and there and everywhere*
adverb of time	[ædvɜːb əv ˈtaɪm]	Adverb der Zeit	*today and tomorrow*
comparative	[kəmˈpærətɪv]	Komparativ	*cheaper, more expensive*
comparison	[kəmˈpærɪsn]	Vergleich, Steigerung	*old – older – oldest*
chunk	[tʃʌŋk]	zusammenhängende Wortgruppe	*Would you like to …?*
countable	[ˈkaʊntəbl]	zählbar	*boy, girl, class, …*
form	[fɔːm]	Form	*forms of "(to) be": am, is, are, was, …*
going to-future	[ˈgəʊɪŋ tʊ fjuːtʃə]	Futur mit *going to*	*I'm going to travel to York.*
grammar	[ˈgræmə]	Grammatik	
if-clause	[ˈɪf klɔːz]	Nebensatz mit *if*	*If it rains, …*
conditional sentence	[kənˈdɪʃənl sentəns]	Bedingungssatz	*If it rains, we'll stay at home.*
irregular verb	[ɪregjələ ˈvɜːb]	unregelmäßiges Verb	*go – went – gone*
linking word	[ˈlɪŋkɪŋ wɜːd]	Bindewort (Konjunktion)	*and, because, but, so*
negative	[ˈnegətɪv]	negativ, verneint	*I don't know …*
noun	[naʊn]	Nomen, Hauptwort	*boy, mother, time, crab, …*
numbers	[ˈnʌmbəz]	Zahlen	*one, two, three, …*
object	[ˈɒbdʒɪkt]	Objekt, Satzergänzung	*Berry loves **animals**.*
past progressive	[pɑːst prəˈgresɪv]	Verlaufsform der Vergangenheit	*I was reading.*
plural	[ˈplʊərəl]	Plural, Mehrzahl	*apples, lessons, colours, …*
positive	[ˈpɒzətɪv]	positiv, bejaht	*I know …*
possessive pronoun	[pəzesɪv ˈprəʊnaʊn]	Possessivpronomen	*my, your, his/her …*
preposition	[prepəˈzɪʃn]	Präposition	*in, on, at, next to, under, …*
present perfect	[preznt ˈpɜːfɪkt]	Perfekt	*I have been here before.*
present progressive	[preznt prəˈgresɪv]	Verlaufsform der Gegenwart	*They**'re having** lunch.*
pronoun	[ˈprəʊnaʊn]	Pronomen, Fürwort	*I, you, he, it, …*
question word	[ˈkwestʃən wɜːd]	Fragewort	*what?, when?, where?, how?, …*
regular verb	[regjələ ˈvɜːb]	regelmäßiges Verb	*help – helped – helped*
relative clause	[ˈrelətɪv klɔːz]	Relativsatz	*I know a man who is 101 years old.*
sentence	[ˈsentəns]	Satz	*It's not new.*
short answer	[ʃɔːt ˈɑːnsə]	Kurzantwort	*Yes, I do. / No, I'm not.*
simple past	[sɪmpl ˈpɑːst]	einfache Vergangenheit	*Yesterday we **went** to school.*

simple present	[sɪmpl ˈpreznt]	einfache Gegenwart	*I always **go** to school by bike.*
singular	[ˈsɪŋgjələ]	Singular, Einzahl	*an apple, a lesson, a colour, …*
statement	[ˈsteɪtmənt]	Aussage(satz)	*That's sad. / I can't sing.*
subject	[ˈsʌbdʒɪkt]	Subjekt, Satzgegenstand	***Berry** loves animals.*
superlative	[suˈpɜːlətɪv]	Superlativ	*cheapest, most expensive*
tense	[tens]	Zeit(form), Tempus	*present tense, past tense*
time phrase	[ˈtaɪm freɪz]	Zeitangabe, Zeitbestimmung	*today, last week, …*
uncountable	[ʌnˈkaʊntəbl]	unzählbar	*sugar, weather, water, …*
verb	[vɜːb]	Verb, Prädikat	*go, see, have, …*
will-future	[ˈwɪl fjuːtʃə]	Futur mit *will*	*It will/won't rain.*
word order	[ˈwɜːd ɔːdə]	Wortstellung	*subject – verb – object (S-V-O)*

IRREGULAR VERBS (unregelmäßige Verben)

infinitive	simple past	past participle	
(to) **be**	*he/she/it* **was** *you/we/you/they* **were**	**been**	sein
(to) **become**	**became**	**become**	werden
(to) **bet**	**bet**	**bet**	wetten
(to) **begin**	**began**	**begun**	beginnen, anfangen
(to) **bite**	**bit**	**bitten**	beißen; stechen *(z.B. Insekten)*
(to) **bleed**	**bled**	**bled**	bluten
(to) **break**	**broke**	**broken**	(zer)brechen; kaputtgehen/-machen
(to) **bring**	**brought**	**brought**	bringen, mitbringen
(to) **build**	**built**	**built**	(er)bauen
(to) **buy**	**bought**	**bought**	kaufen
(to) **catch**	**caught**	**caught**	(ein)fangen; erwischen
(to) **choose**	**chose**	**chosen**	(aus)wählen
(to) **come**	**came**	**come**	(mit)kommen
(to) **cost**	**cost**	**cost**	kosten
(to) **cut**	**cut**	**cut**	schneiden; *(Rasen)* mähen
(to) **do**	**did**	**done** [ʌ]	machen, tun
(to) **draw**	**drew**	**drawn**	zeichnen
(to) **drink**	**drank**	**drunk**	trinken
(to) **drive**	**drove**	**driven**	fahren *(mit dem Auto)*
(to) **eat**	**ate** [et, eɪt]	**eaten**	essen; fressen
(to) **fall**	**fell**	**fallen**	fallen; hinfallen
(to) **feed**	**fed**	**fed**	füttern
(to) **feel**	**felt**	**felt**	sich fühlen; fühlen
(to) **fight**	**fought**	**fought**	kämpfen
(to) **find**	**found**	**found**	finden
(to) **fly**	**flew**	**flown**	fliegen
(to) **forget**	**forgot**	**forgotten**	vergessen
(to) **get**	**got**	**got**	bekommen, kriegen
(to) **give**	**gave**	**given**	geben
(to) **go**	**went**	**gone** [ɒ]	gehen; fahren
(to) **grow**	**grew**	**grown**	wachsen; werden
(to) **hang out**	**hung**	**hung**	rumhängen; abhängen
(to) **have**	**had**	**had**	haben
(to) **hear** [ɪə]	**heard** [ɜː]	**heard** [ɜː]	hören
(to) **hit**	**hit**	**hit**	schlagen; stoßen; treffen
(to) **hold**	**held**	**held**	halten
(to) **keep**	**kept**	**kept**	behalten
(to) **know** [nəʊ]	**knew** [njuː]	**known** [nəʊn]	wissen; kennen
(to) **lay**	**laid**	**laid**	legen
(to) **leave**	**left**	**left**	verlassen; zurücklassen; abfahren
(to) **lose**	**lost**	**lost**	verlieren

infinitive	simple past	past participle	
(to) **lie**	**lay**	**lain**	liegen
(to) **make**	**made**	**made**	machen, herstellen
(to) **mean**	**meant**	**meant**	bedeuten; meinen, sagen wollen
(to) **meet**	**met**	**met**	kennenlernen; (sich) treffen; abholen
(to) **misunderstand**	**misunderstood**	**misunderstood**	missverstehen
(to) **pay**	**paid**	**paid**	(be)zahlen
(to) **put**	**put**	**put**	stellen, legen, *(etwas wohin)* tun
(to) **read** [iː]	**read** [e]	**read** [e]	lesen
(to) **ride** [aɪ]	**rode**	**ridden** [ɪ]	reiten; (Rad) fahren
(to) **ring**	**rang**	**rung**	läuten, klingeln
(to) **rise**	**rose**	**risen**	(an)steigen; hochsteigen
(to) **run**	**ran**	**run**	rennen
(to) **say** [eɪ]	**said** [e]	**said** [e]	sagen
(to) **see**	**saw**	**seen**	sehen
(to) **sell**	**sold**	**sold**	verkaufen
(to) **send**	**sent**	**sent**	schicken, senden (an)
(to) **shine**	**shone**	**shone**	scheinen *(Sonne)*; leuchten, strahlen, glänzen
(to) **shoot**	**shot**	**shot**	(er)schießen; *(Film)* drehen; fotografieren
(to) **sit**	**sat**	**sat**	sitzen; sich (hin)setzen
(to) **steal**	**stole**	**stolen**	stehlen, rauben
(to) **sting**	**stung**	**stung**	stechen *(Insekt)*; brennen *(schmerzen)*
(to) **throw**	**threw**	**thrown**	werfen
(to) **teach**	**taught**	**taught**	unterrichten; lehren
(to) **tell**	**told**	**told**	erzählen, sagen
(to) **think**	**thought**	**thought**	denken, meinen, glauben
(to) **take**	**took**	**taken**	(mit)nehmen; bringen
(to) **understand**	**understood**	**understood**	verstehen
(to) **wake**	**woke**	**woken**	wecken
(to) **wear** [eə]	**wore** [ɔː]	**worn** [ɔː]	tragen, anhaben *(Kleidung)*
(to) **win**	**won**	**won**	gewinnen
(to) **write** [aɪ]	**wrote**	**written** [ɪ]	schreiben

Cardinal numbers

0	**oh, zero, nil** [əʊ, 'zɪərəʊ, nɪl]
1	**one** [wʌn]
2	**two** [tuː]
3	**three** [θriː]
4	**four** [fɔː]
5	**five** [faɪv]
6	**six** [sɪks]
7	**seven** ['sevn]
8	**eight** [eɪt]
9	**nine** [naɪn]
10	**ten** [ten]
11	**eleven** [ɪ'levn]
12	**twelve** [twelv]
13	**thirteen** [θɜː'tiːn]
14	**fourteen** [fɔː'tiːn]
15	**fifteen** [fɪf'tiːn]
16	**sixteen** [sɪks'tiːn]
17	**seventeen** [sevn'tiːn]
18	**eighteen** [eɪ'tiːn]
19	**nineteen** [naɪn'tiːn]
20	**twenty** ['twenti]
21	**twenty-one** [twenti'wʌn]
22	**twenty-two** [twenti'tuː]
23	**twenty-three** [twenti'θriː]
...	
30	**thirty** ['θɜːti]
40	**forty** ['fɔːti]
50	**fifty** ['fɪfti]
60	**sixty** ['sɪksti]
70	**seventy** ['sevnti]
80	**eighty** ['eɪti]
90	**ninety** ['naɪnti]
100	**a/one hundred** [ə/wʌn 'hʌndrəd]
101	**one hundred and one**
...	
400	**four hundred**
...	
1,000	**one thousand**
1,001	**one thousand and one**
...	
5,169	**five thousand one hundred and sixty-nine**
...	
100,000	**one hundred thousand**
1,000,000	**one million**
2,600,000	**two million six hundred thousand**

Ordinal numbers

1st	**first** [fɜːst]
2nd	**second** ['sekənd]
3rd	**third** [θɜːd]
4th	**fourth** [fɔːθ]
5th	**fifth** [fɪfθ]
6th	**sixth** [sɪksθ]
7th	**seventh** ['sevnθ]
8th	**eighth** [eɪtθ]
9th	**ninth** [naɪnθ]
10th	**tenth** [tenθ]
11th	**eleventh** [ɪ'levnθ]
12th	**twelfth** [twelfθ]
13th	**thirteenth** [θɜː'tiːnθ]
14th	**fourteenth** [fɔː'tiːnθ]
15th	**fifteenth** [fɪf'tiːnθ]
16th	**sixteenth** [sɪks'tiːnθ]
17th	**seventeenth** [sevn'tiːnθ]
18th	**eighteenth** [eɪ'tiːnθ]
19th	**nineteenth** [naɪn'tiːnθ]
20th	**twentieth** ['twentiəθ]
21st	**twenty-first** [twenti'fɜːst]
22nd	**twenty-second** [twenti'sekənd]
23rd	**twenty-third** [twenti'θɜːd]
...	
30th	**thirtieth** ['θɜːtiəθ]
40th	**fortieth** ['fɔːtiəθ]
50th	**fiftieth** ['fɪftiəθ]
60th	**sixtieth** ['sɪkstiəθ]
70th	**seventieth** ['sevntiəθ]
80th	**eightieth** ['eɪtiəθ]
90th	**ninetieth** ['naɪntiəθ]
100th	**hundredth** ['hʌndrədθ]
101th	**one hundred and first**
...	
400th	**four hundredth**
...	
1,000th	**one thousandth**
1,001st	**one thousand and first**
...	
5,169th	**five thousand one hundred and sixty-ninth**
...	
100,000th	**one hundred thousandth**
1,000,000th	**one millionth**
2,600,000th	**two million six hundred thousandth**

Titelbild

Shutterstock.com/**Bernd Leitner Fotodesign**

Illustrationen

Carlos Borrell Eiköter (Karten: **U II**/vordere Umschlagseite innen, **U III**/hintere Umschlagseite innen, S.8, 9, 110); **Michael Fleischmann** (S.53, 153 ob. u. 2. v. ob.); **Jeongsook Lee (**S.149); **David Norman** (S.15 body painting u. dance steps, 16, 17, 18, 32, 33, 34, 35, 39, 68, 72, 90, 94 un.); **Dorina Tessmann** (S.12, 13, 19 un. li. u. re., 23, 36, 57, 63, 71, 74, 75, 94 ob., 104, 105, 111, 121, 141)

Fotos

S.4 Mi. li.: Shutterstock.com/Kjuuurs, Mi. re.: Shutterstock.com/Mr Aesthetics, un. li.: Shutterstock.com/Pi-Lens, un. re.: Shutterstock.com/Edu_Cate; **S.6** ob. li.: Shutterstock.com/lkpro, ob. re.: Shutterstock.com/GREEN STUDIO, Mi. li.: Shutterstock.com/Rawpixel.com, Mi. re.: Shutterstock.com/Vectorfair.com; **S.8** Enzokuhle: Shutterstock.com/Ollyy; **S.9** Aarav: mauritius images/alamy stock photo/Photosindia, Olivia: mauritius images/Cultura, Marama: Shutterstock.com/Molly NZ; **S.10** Känguru: Shutterstock.com/Tribalium, Bild A: interfoto e.k./David Wall, Bild B: interfoto e.k./David Wall, Bild C: Shutterstock.com/mjtim photography, Bild D: mauritius images/Bluegreen Pictures/Roberto Rinaldi, Bild E: Shutterstock.com/Radoslav Cajkovic; **S.11** Bild F Hintergrund: Shutterstock.com/Totajla, Bild F Schild: Shutterstock.com/max blain, Bild G: Shutterstock.com/Steve Allen; **S.12** Bild A: Shutterstock.com/WorldStock, Bild B: Shutterstock.com/Robyn Mackenzie, Bild C: mauritius images/alamy stock photo/Amanda Shackleton, Bild D: Shutterstock.com/Sam72; **S.13** Royal Flying Doctor Service of Australia; **S.14** ob.: mauritius images/alamy stock photo/Doug Steley B, un.: Shutterstock.com/MarTata; **S.15** ob. re.: The Burdekin Crew/Smugglers of Light Foundation/Desert Pea Media, Didgeridoo: Shutterstock.com/olgankort, Flagge: stock.adobe.com/oxygen64, Jasmin: Cornelsen/Yvonne Thron – ThronDesign; **S.16** ob. re.: mauritius images/alamy stock photo/martin berry, Australien: Shutterstock.com/alison1414; **S.19** Huong: Shutterstock.com/Dragon Images, Huong Icon: Cornelsen/Yvonne Thron – ThronDesign; Brücke: Shutterstock.com/Serega-SibTravel; **S.20** Shutterstock.com/Alberto Loyo; **S.21** ob.: mauritius images/Loop Images, un.: Shutterstock.com/chinasong; **S.22** Shutterstock.com/ian woolcock; **S.24** imago images/AAP; **S.25:** Shutterstock.com/TonyNg; **S.26** Bild A: Shutterstock.com/Alizada Studios, Bild B: akg-images/Heritage-Images/The Print Collector, Kiwi: Shutterstock.com/Koshevnyk; **S.27** Bild E: Shutterstock.com/Darth_Vector, Bild F: Shutterstock.com/Mats Schroeter, Bild G: Shutterstock.com/Dmitry Pichugin, un. re.: Run Rabbit/Robin Paterson/New Zealand/2018/Interfilm Berlin Management GmbH; **S.28** Bild A: Shutterstock.com/Nate Hovee, Bild B: mauritius images/

alamy stock photo/Molly Marshall, Bild C: Shutterstock.com/SasinTipchai, Bild D: Shutterstock.com/wavebreakmedia, Bild E: Shutterstock.com/Jiri Prochazka, Bild F: Shutterstock.com/matiascausa; **S.29** stock.adobe.com/Cozyta, Tattoo: Shutterstock.com/Monoka, stock.adobe.com/; **S.30** Shutterstock.com/grejak; **S.37** Bild 1: Shutterstock.com/LittlePerfectStock, Bild 2: Shutterstock.com/Emanuel Metzenthin, Bild 3: Shutterstock.com/Dmitry Naumov, Bild 4: Shutterstock.com/PedkoAnton, Bild 5: Shutterstock.com/Daboost, Bild 6: Shutterstock.com/Matej Halouska; **S.38** ob.: Shutter-stock.com/pikselstock, Mi.: Shutterstock.com/Evgeny Gorodetsky, un.: Shutterstock.com/John Yunker; **S.40** Cornelsen/Rockfinch/Claire Cunningham; **S.42** ob. li.: Shutterstock.com/Grobler du Preez, ob. re.: Shutterstock.com/GuilhermeMesquita, Wasserbüffel: Shutterstock.com/Nicci Auchincloss, Nashorn: Shutterstock.com/Pierre-Yves Babelon, Leopard: Shutterstock.com/Dave Pusey, Löwe: Shutterstock.com/Michael Potter11, Elefant: Shutterstock.com/EcoPrint, un. re.: mauritius images/Florian Kopp; **S.43** akg-images/Africa Media Online/Guy Tillim; **S.44** ob. li.: Shutterstock.com/Matej Kastelic, ob. re.: mauritius images/Bluegreen Pictures, un. li.: Shutterstock.com/DisobeyArt, un. re.: Shutterstock.com/Aleksandr Stezhkin; **S.46** ob.: Shutterstock.com/Daniel M Ernst, 2. v. ob.: Shutterstock.com/John Warner, 2. v. un.: Shutterstock.com/Sielemann, un.: Shutterstock.com/blvdone; **S.48** Bild A: Bridgeman Images/Spaarnestad Photo, Bild B: akg-images/Africa Media Online/Eric Miller, Bild C: mauritius images/United Archives/TopFoto, Bild D: Bridgeman Images/Jason Edwards/National Geographic Image Collection; **S.49** li.: bpk/The Trustees of the British Museum, re. ob.: dpa Picture-Alliance/AP Photo, re. un.: dpa Picture-Alliance/AP Images; **S.51** ob.: imago images/Starface, un.: imago images/ZUMA Press; **S.52** ob.: imago images/PA Images, un.: Shutterstock.com/javi_indy; **S.54** ob.: Shutterstock.com/Everett Historical, un.: mauritius images/alamy stock photo/ARTHUR WEST; **S.55** imago images/Design Pics; **S.56** Shutterstock.com/Lineicons freebird; **S.58** ob.: Shutterstock.com/pjhpix, Mi.: Shutterstock.com/Rawpixel.com, un. li.: Shutterstock.com/Swansiri, un. re.: Shutterstock.com/Kristin F. Ruhs, Hintergrund: Shutterstock.com/Vandathai; **S.59** Bild A: Shutterstock.com/Sanga Park, Bild B: Shutterstock.com/RuthChoi, Bild C: Shutterstock.com/Sevenpixels; **S.60** Bild 2: Shutterstock.com/Sergey Mironov, Bild 3: Shutterstock.com/saisnaps, Bild 4: interfoto e.k./TopFoto, Bild 5: Shutterstock.com/Novikov Aleksey; **S.61** ob.: mauritius images/alamy stock photo/Dinodia Photos, un.: akg-images/World History Archive; **S.62** li. ob.: Shutterstock.com/AJP, li. un.: Shutterstock.com/mimagephotography, re. ob.: stock.adobe.com/icsnaps, re. Mi.: Shutterstock.com/Ashwin, re. un.: Shutterstock.com/Tukaram.Karve; **S.63** Bild A ob.: Shutterstock.com/Nasa/Dima Zel, Bild B ob.: Shutterstock.com/Ricardo Reitmeyer, Bild C: Shutterstock.com/2020 Photography,

Bild D: Shutterstock.com/monticello; **S. 64** ob.: Shutterstock.com/Intellistudies, Mi.: Shutterstock.com/pernsanitfoto, un.: mauritius images/alamy stock photo/paul kennedy; **S. 65** Bild A: Shutterstock.com/Bernhard Staehli, Bild B: Shutterstock.com/VanderWolf Images, Bild C: Shutterstock.com/Petrov Stanislav, Bild D: Shutterstock.com/bibiphoto, Bild E: Shutterstock.com/Rich Carey, Bild F: Shutterstock.com/Snowshill; S. 66: imago images/Xinhua; **S. 67** ob.: Shutterstock.com/Nasa/Raymond Cassel, un.: dpa Picture-Alliance/REUTERS/Stringer; **S. 70** Shutterstock.com/neelsky; **S. 72** dpa Picture-Alliance/AP/Bikram Rai; **S. 73** Amar/PILGRIM FILMS PRODUCTION/Interfilm Berlin Management GmbH; **S. 80** Shutterstock.com/chinasong; **S. 83** li.: Shutterstock.com/Ricky Edwards, re.: Shutterstock.com/Paul Stringer; **S. 85** Bild 1: Shutterstock.com/yanik88, Bild 2: Shutterstock.com/G-Stock Studio, Bild 3: Shutterstock.com/Serhii Bobyk, Bild 4: Shutterstock.com/Monkey Business Images, Bild 5: Shutterstock.com/Prostock-studio, Bild 6: Shutterstock.com/Diego Cervo, un.: Shutterstock.com/wavebreakmedia; **S. 89** stock.adobe.com/creedline; **S. 90** Tim Berners-Lee (Sir Timothy John Berners-Lee): World Wide Web inventor and director of the WWW Consortium. July 11, 1994/Bridgeman Images/© CERN/Novapix; **S. 96** Shutterstock.com/wavebreakmedia; **S. 97** ob.: dpa Picture-Alliance/REUTERS, un.: mauritius images/alamy stock photo/Allstar Picture Library; **S. 98** li.: Shutterstock.com/Peter Waters, re.: Shutterstock.com/RugliG; **S. 99** ob.: Shutterstock.com/Istimages, un.: Shutterstock.com/Stanislav Fosenbauer; **S. 100** sciencephotolibrary/Nasa/Jessica Wilson; **S. 102** Mi.: Shutterstock.com/Kionerst; u.: Shutterstock.com/Kubko; **S. 106** Shutterstock.com/CRS PHOTO; **S. 108** Icon Population, Klima u. Hintergrund: stock.adobe.com/a7880ss, Icon Sports: Shutterstock.com/graphixmania, Icon Feuer: Shutterstock.com/Victor Z, Icon Big Cities: Shutterstock.com/anthonycz; **S. 109** ob. re.: Shutterstock.com/John Crux, un. li.: Shutterstock.com/Yatra, un. Mi.: Shutterstock.com/Neale Cousland, un. re.: Shutterstock.com/Ken Griffiths; **S. 110** ob. li.: Shutterstock.com/Rich Carey, ob. re.: dpa Picture-Alliance/AP Photo/Peter Dejong, un. re.: Shutterstock.com/Gilda Villarreal; **S. 111** re: dpa Picture-Alliance/AP Photo/The Ocean Cleanup; **S. 112** ob.: stock.adobe.com/Andrey Popov, Mi.: Shutterstock.com/wacpan, un.: stock.adobe.com/Syda Productions; **S. 115** ob.: stock.adobe.com/Bernd Leitner, Mi.: Shutterstock.com/Antonio Guillem, un.: Cornelsen/Yvonne Thron – ThronDesign; **S. 118** Shutterstock.com/Ron Leishman; **S. 122:** Shutterstock.com/BlueRingMedia; **S. 123** Shutterstock.com/Jose Luis Carrascosa; **S. 124** mauritius images/Image Source; **S. 125** ob.: Shutterstock.com/Henryk Sadura, Mi.: Shutterstock.com/bbernard, un.: Shutterstock.com/Karen Kaspar; **S. 126–135** Shutterstock.com/Ron Leishman; **S. 136** ob. li. u. re.: Shutterstock.com/tillydesign, un. re.: Shutterstock.com/Ron Leishman; **S. 137–139** Shutterstock.com/Ron Leishman; **S. 140** desert: Shutterstock.com/Edward Haylan, waterfall: Shutterstock.com/Janelle Lugge, sheep farm: Shutterstock.com/John Carnemolla, track: Shutterstock.com/Konrad Mostert, forest: Shutterstock.com/Andreas Altenburger, sea: Shutterstock.com/Pete Niesen, trampolining: Shutterstock.com/Pete Pahham, sailing: stock.adobe.com/birdiegal, scuba-diving: Shutterstock.com/JonMilnes, snorkeling: Shutterstock.com/Vibrant Image Studio, surfing: Shutterstock.com/Arek Rainczuk, skateboarding: mauritius images/Johnér; **S. 143** ob. li.: Shutterstock.com/Mila Supinskaya Glashchenko, ob. re.: Shutterstock.com/Memory Stockphoto, un. li.: Shutterstock.com/TRMK, un. Mi.: Shutterstock.com/RossHelen, un. re.: Shutterstock.com/VGstockstudio; **S. 144** Shutterstock.com/vasabii; **S. 145** leather: Shutterstock.com/optimarc, fabric: Shutterstock.com/Tatyana Mi, plastic: Shutterstock.com/RomanJuve, wood: Shutterstock.com/Stone background, flap: Shutterstock.com/InspiringMoments, string: Shutterstock.com/Olga Popova, zip: Shutterstock.com/M.Stasy, button: Shutterstock.com/koosen, colourful: Shutterstock.com/severija, patterned: Shutterstock.com/Curly Pat; **S. 146** rubbish: stock.adobe.com/Oleg Zhukov, pesticides: stock.adobe.com/Dusan Kostic, chemicals: Shutterstock.com/Victor Rotaru, Chemikalientonne: Shutterstock.com/cromic, sewage: Shutterstock.com/keantian, cities: Shutterstock.com/gyn9037, deserts: Shutterstock.com/Galyna Andrushko, wasting water: stock.adobe.com/studioDG, mineral resources: Shutterstock.com/abutyrin, cars: Shutterstock.com/Juergen Faelchle, industry: stock.adobe.com/Ralf Geithe; **S. 147** public transport: stock.adobe.com/Syda Productions, electric cars: stock.adobe.com/kasto, less rubbish: stock.adobe.com/shootingankauf, car sharing: stock.adobe.com/blue_island, waste water: Shutterstock.com/wattana, clothes line: Shutterstock.com/Gemenacom, plant trees: stock.adobe.com/Africa Studio, plastic bags: Shutterstock.com/Chones, fresh food: Shutterstock.com/mikeledray, wrapping: stock.adobe.com/siraphol; **S. 148** gym: Shutterstock.com/MyImages – Micha, weekdays: Shutterstock.com/scheresteinpapier, classmates: Shutterstock.com/Monkey Business Images, meet: Shutterstock.com/Tyler Olson, coach: stock.adobe.com/Monkey Business, post/tweet: Shutterstock.com/10 FACE; **S. 149** ob.: Shutterstock.com/Nerthuz; Mi.: Shutterstock.com/Mor65; **S. 150** ob.: Shutterstock.com/Anan Kaewkhammul, Mi.: Shutterstock.com/saraporn, un.: Shutterstock.com/T. Kimmeskamp; **S. 151** ob.: Shutterstock.com/Goncharov_Artem, 2. v. ob.: Shutterstock.com/ghrzuzudu, 2. v. un.: Shutterstock.com/stopabox, un.: Shutterstock.com/Hanaha; **S. 152** ob. li.: Shutterstock.com/oksmit, ob. re.: Shutterstock.com/StockHouse, 2. v. un.: Shutterstock.com/Eladora, un.: Shutterstock.com/vectorpouch; **S. 153** fingernails: Shutterstock.com/Viktoriia_P, pulling hard: Shutterstock.com/Peshkova, un.: Shutterstock.com/Eugene Partyzan; **S. 154** li.: Shutterstock.com/Krasovski

Dmitri, re.: Shutterstock.com/Bashutskyy; **S. 155** Shutter-
stock.com/Hennadii H; **S. 156** ob.: Shutterstock.com/
Demja, un.: Shutterstock.com/Albina Glisic; **S. 157** ob. li.
u. re.: Shutterstock.com/nito, un.: Shutterstock.com/
Room27; **S. 158** ob.: Shutterstock.com/tektur, 2. v. ob.:
Shutterstock.com/TayHamPhotography, 2. v. un. li.:
Shutterstock.com/Inc, 2. v. un.re.: Shutterstock.com/
aurielaki, un.: Shutterstock.com/Alexey Seafarer; **S. 159**
Shutterstock.com/Pannochka; **S. 160** Shutterstock.com/
ylq; **S. 161** ob.: Shutterstock.com/Kletr, un.: Shutterstock.
com/karenfoleyphotography; **S. 162** ob.: Shutterstock.
com/Digital Storm, Mi.: Shutterstock.com/Gearstd, un.:
Shutterstock.com/Photo Melon; **S. 163** Shutterstock.com/
Lecter; **S. 164** Shutterstock.com/SD illustrations; **S. 165**
ob.: Shutterstock.com/ixpert, un.: Shutterstock.com/idey-
web; **S. 166** ob.: Shutterstock.com/Nasa/Nostalgia for
Infinity, un.: Shutterstock.com/Slavoljub Pantelic; **S. 168**
ob.: Shutterstock.com/Sergiy1975, Mi.: Shutterstock.com/
thanatphoto; un.: Shutterstock.com/80's Child; **S. 169** ob.:
Shutterstock.com/topimages, Mi.: Shutterstock.com/
Nerthuz, un.: Shutterstock.com/Mor65_Mauro Piccardi;
S. 170 ob.: Shutterstock.com/Gerald Bernard, un.:
Shutterstock.com/Snap2Art

Texte

S.16/17 Swerve, adapted from Phillip Gwynne, Penguin
Books Australia; 2009
S.79 *Eyes Wide Open* by The Burdekin Crew, cooperation
between Smugglers of Light Foundation and Desert Pea
Media; 2012

General

Answer the questions (using information from the text).	
Cross out the wrong word.	
Fill in the missing words/details/information/sentences.	
Short answers are possible.	
There is only one possible answer.	
There is an example at the beginning.	
There is one mistake in each sentence.	
Tick the correct box.	
Write the letters in the box / on the lines below.	
Write short answers.	
Write the letter in the correct box.	
Write the letters on the lines below.	
You can use any letter more than once.	
You do not need all the letters.	

Allgemein

Beantworte die Fragen (und verwende dabei Informationen aus dem Text).	
Streiche das falsche Wort durch.	
Füge die fehlenden Wörter/Details/Informationen/Sätze ein.	
Kurze Antworten sind möglich.	
Es gibt nur eine mögliche Antwort.	
Am Anfang gibt es ein Beispiel.	
In jedem Satz gibt es einen Fehler.	
Hake das richtige Kästchen ab.	
Schreibe die Buchstaben ins Kästchen / auf die Linien unten.	
Schreibe kurze Antworten.	
Schreibe den Buchstaben in das richtige Kästchen.	
Schreibe die Buchstaben auf die Linien unten.	
Du kannst jeden Buchstaben mehr als einmal verwenden.	
Du brauchst nicht alle Buchstaben.	

Listening

There are four parts to the test.	
You'll hear each part twice.	
At the end of each part you'll have some time to complete the tasks.	

Hörverstehen

Es gibt vier Teile im Test.	
Du wirst jeden Teil zweimal hören.	
Am Ende jedes Teils wirst du etwas Zeit haben, um die Aufgaben zu lösen.	

Use of English

Change the words to make them fit the sentence.	
Choose the correct word from the box.	
Complete each sentence with one suitable word.	
Complete the text with words from the box.	
Do not change the text.	
Fill each gap with one suitable word.	
Fill in the gaps using the words in brackets.	
Find the six mistakes in the text and write the correct word on the numbered line.	
There is one word for each gap.	
Write the word that matches the definition.	
You don't need all of the statements.	

Gebrauch des Englischen

Verändere die Wörter, sodass sie in den Satz passen.	
Wähle das korrekte Wort aus dem Kasten.	
Vervollständige jeden Satz mit einem passenden Wort.	
Vervollständige den Text mit Wörtern aus dem Kasten.	
Verändere den Text nicht.	
Füge in jede Lücke ein passendes Wort ein.	
Fülle die Lücken aus und verwende dabei die Wörter in Klammern.	
Finde die sechs Fehler im Text und schreibe das richtige Wort auf die nummerierte Linie.	
Es gibt ein Wort für jede Lücke.	
Schreibe das Wort, das der Definition entspricht.	
Du brauchst nicht alle Aussagen.	

Reading | Leseverstehen

Reading	Leseverstehen
Answer the questions using information from the text.	Beantworte die Fragen und verwende dabei die Informationen aus dem Text.
Choose the right title (A–G) for each paragraph of the text.	Wähle den richtigen Titel (A–G) für jeden Absatz des Textes.
Decide in which paragraph (A–F) you find the answer to each question (1–5).	Entscheide, in welchem Absatz (A–F) du die Antwort auf jede Frage (1–5) findest.
Five of the statements are true. Choose the statements according to the information given in the text.	Fünf der Aussagen sind wahr. Wähle die Aussagen entsprechend der Informationen im Text.
Match the titles (1–8) to the paragraphs (A–E). Write the correct number in the boxes below. Use each number only once. There are three extra titles.	Ordne die Titel (1–8) den Absätzen (A–E) zu. Schreibe die richtige Zahl in die Kästchen unten. Verwende jede Zahl nur einmal. Es gibt drei zusätzliche Titel.
One title is already matched. There is one extra title.	Ein Titel ist bereits zugewiesen. Es gibt einen Titel zu viel.
Read the parts 1–5 and match them with one of the parts A–H.	Lies die Teile 1–5 und ordne sie einem der Teile A–H zu.
The following words have different meanings. Which of the meanings below is the one used in the text? Tick the correct meaning.	Die folgenden Wörter haben unterschiedliche Bedeutungen. Welche der Bedeutungen unten ist diejenige, die im Text verwendet wird? Mache ein Häkchen bei der richtigen Bedeutung.
Write down the complete sentence from the text.	Schreibe den ganzen Satz aus dem Text auf.

Speaking | Sprechen

Speaking	Sprechen
I'm going to give you a picture.	Ich werde dir ein Bild geben.
You have 30 seconds to look at the picture.	Du hast 30 Sekunden, um das Bild zu betrachten.
Then we'll talk about the picture.	Dann werden wir über das Bild sprechen.
Describe where the people are.	Beschreibe, wo die Menschen sind.
Describe the clothes.	Beschreibe die Kleidung.
Describe the landscape / the building / the animals.	Beschreibe die Landschaft / das Gebäude / die Tiere.
What can you see in the background?	Was kannst du im Hintergrund sehen?
What are the people doing?	Was tun die Menschen?
What's the weather like?	Wie ist das Wetter?
How do you think the people are feeling?	Wie glaubst du fühlen sich die Menschen gerade?
Why could this be …?	Warum könnte das … sein?
Would you like to …?	Würdest du gern …?
Explain why you think …	Erkläre, warum du glaubst …
Could you say that again, please?	Könntest du das bitte wiederholen?

Du und dein Lehrer / deine Lehrerin

Guten Morgen, Herr / Frau … _____

Guten Tag, Herr / Frau … _____

Entschuldigung, dass ich zu spät komme. _____

Kann ich bitte das Fenster öffnen / zumachen? _____

Kann ich bitte zur Toilette gehen? _____

Auf Wiedersehen! / Bis morgen. _____

You and your teacher

Good morning, Mr / Mrs … (bis 12 Uhr)

Good afternoon, Mr / Mrs… (ab 12 Uhr)

Sorry, I'm late.

Can I open / close the window, please?

Can I go to the toilet, please?

Goodbye. / See you tomorrow.

Hausaufgaben und Übungen

Es tut mir leid, ich habe mein Schulheft nicht dabei. _____

Ich verstehe die Übung nicht. _____

Ich kann Nummer 4 nicht lösen. _____

Entschuldigung, ich bin noch nicht fertig. _____

Ich habe … Ist das auch richtig? _____

Es tut mir leid, das weiß ich nicht. _____

Was haben wir (als Hausaufgabe) auf? _____

Entschuldigung, ich habe meine Hausaufgaben vergessen. _____

Homework and exercises

Sorry, I have no exercise book.

I don't understand this exercise.

I can't do number 4.

Sorry, I haven't finished.

I have … Is that right too?

Sorry, I don't know.

What's for homework?

Sorry, I've forgotten to do my homework.

Du brauchst Hilfe

Können Sie mir bitte helfen? _____

Auf welcher Seite sind wir / steht das? _____

Was heißt … auf Englisch / Deutsch? _____

Können Sie das bitte an die Tafel schreiben? _____

Kann ich das auf Deutsch sagen? _____

Können Sie / Kannst du bitte lauter sprechen? _____

Können Sie das bitte noch einmal sagen / abspielen? _____

You need help

Can you help me, please?

What page is it, please?

What's … in English / German?

Can you write it on the board, please?

Can I say it in German?

Can you speak louder, please?

Can you say / play that again, please?

Partnerarbeit

Kann ich mit Julian arbeiten? _____

Wer ist dran? / Du bist / Ich bin dran. _____

Was machen wir zuerst? _____

Lass uns ein … machen / zeichnen. _____

Lass uns die Geschichte / den Dialog spielen. _____

Work with a partner

Can I work with Julian?

Whose turn is it? / It's your / my turn.

What are we going to do first?

Let's make / draw a …

Let's act the story / dialogue.

Was dein Lehrer / deine Lehrerin sagt

Schlagt bitte Seite 8 auf. _____

Schreibt die Sätze ab und vervollständigt sie. _____

Korrigiert die Fehler. _____

Füllt die Tabelle aus. _____

Hört zu und macht euch Notizen. _____

Hört bitte zu. / Ruhe bitte. _____

Ordnet den Sätzen die richtigen Fotos zu. _____

Wählt die richtige Antwort. _____

Arbeitet in verschiedenen Rollen. _____

Tauscht die Rollen. _____

Seid ihr fertig? _____

Macht bitte Übung … als Hausaufgabe. _____

Das ist alles für heute. Ihr könnt gehen. _____

What your teacher says

Open your books at page 8, please.

Copy and complete the sentences.

Correct the mistakes.

Fill in the table.

Listen and take notes.

Listen, please. / Quiet, please.

Match the sentences with the right photos.

Pick the correct answer.

Take roles.

Swap roles.

Have you finished?

Do exercise … for homework, please.

That's all for today. You can go.

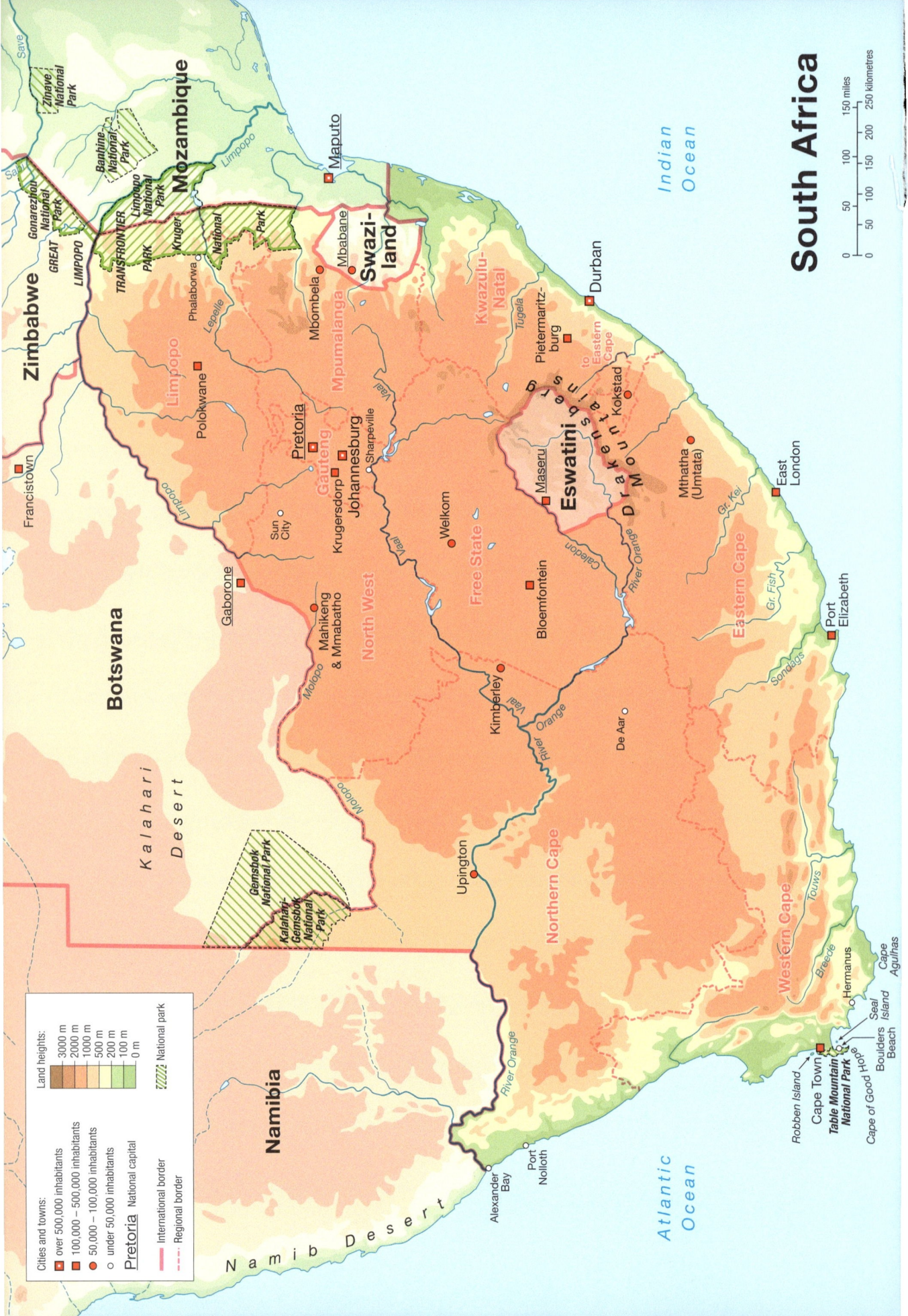

South Africa

Zinave National Park

Banhine National Park

Save

Mozambique

Limpopo

☐ Maputo

Gonarezhou National Park

GREAT

Zimbabwe

LIMPOPO

TRANSFRONTIER

Limpopo National Park

Kruger National Park

PARK

Phalaborwa

Lepelle

Mbabane ☐

Swazi-land

□ Francistown

Limpopo

Limpopo

Mbombela ●

Mpumalanga

Kwazulu-Natal

Tugela

Durban ☐

☐ Polokwane

Pretoria ☐

Gauteng

Krugersdorp

Johannesburg

Sharpeville

Vaal

Pietermaritz-burg

to **Eastern Cape**

Kokstad ●

Eswatini

☐ Maseru

Drakensberg

Mthatha (Umtata) ●

East London ☐

Botswana

Sun City ○

Welkom ●

Free State

Caledon

River Orange

Namibia

Gaborone ☐

Mahikeng & Mmabatho ●

North West

Bloemfontein ☐

Gr. Kei

Limpopo

Molopo

Kimberley ●

Vaal

River Orange

De Aar ○

Eastern Cape

Gr. Fish

Port Elizabeth ☐

Kalahari Desert

Molopo

Upington ●

Northern Cape

Sondags

Gemsbok National Park

Kalahari-Gemsbok National Park

River Orange

Touws

Western Cape

Breede

Cape Agulhas

Hermanus

Seal Island

Namibia

River Orange

Robben Island

Cape Town ☐

Table Mountain National Park

Boulders Beach

Cape of Good Hope

Alexander Bay

Port Nolloth ○

Namib Desert

Indian Ocean

Atlantic Ocean

Atlantic Ocean

0 50 100 150 miles

0 50 100 150 200 250 kilometres

Land heights:
- 3000 m
- 2000 m
- 1000 m
- 500 m
- 200 m
- 100 m
- 0 m

▨ National park

Cities and towns:
- ☐ over 500,000 inhabitants
- ■ 100,000 – 500,000 inhabitants
- ● 50,000 – 100,000 inhabitants
- ○ under 50,000 inhabitants

Pretoria National capital

— International border

--- Regional border